DOM IOAO III REY
DE PORTVGAL

Created and Directed by Hans Höfer

INSIGHT GUIDES

PORTUGAL

Edited by Alison Friesinger Hill
Update Editor: Marion Kaplan
Photography by Tony Arruza

Editorial Director: Brian Bell

HOUGHTON MIFFLIN COMPANY

APA PUBLICATIONS

ABOUT THIS BOOK

Höfer

Portugal has been changing so quickly in the 1990s, transforming itself from being one of Europe's most backward economies into one of the most buoyant, that a guidebook has to run just to keep up. Apa Publications accepted this challenge, thoroughly revamping its much-praised *Insight Guide: Portugal* for this edition. The text has been completely revised and expanded, and many new photographs have been added.

This is one book in the 190-title award-winning *Insight Guides* series, created in 1970 by Hans Höfer, founder of Apa Publications and still the company's driving force. Each book encourages readers to celebrate the essence of a place rather than try to tailor it to their expectations and is edited in the belief that, without insight into a people's character and culture, travel can narrow the mind rather than broaden it.

Insight Guide: Portugal is carefully structured: the first section covers the country's history and culture in a series of magazine-style essays. The main Places section provides a comprehensive run-down on the things worth seeing and doing, with a little bit of gossip thrown in for good measure. Finally, a fact-packed listings section contains all the information you'll need on travel, hotels, shops, restaurants and opening times. Complementing the text, remarkable photography sets out to communicate directly and provocatively life as it is lived by the locals.

A.F. Hill

T. Hill

With a history as rich as any in Europe, and with an abundance of hidden corners where little seems to have changed over the centuries, Portugal is an ideal subject for this kind of perceptive and explorative travel writing. At the outer edge of Europe but bound in by membership of the European Union, isolated by Spain on two sides and by the Atlantic round the rest, Portugal has an integrity which gives the nation a potent allure.

At one stage Portugal had an empire many times the size of the home nation, and that empire's riches flooded up the Tagus river. Today, it is a welcoming and rewarding land, often for very simple reasons. "I am very happy here, because I love oranges, and talk bad Latin to the monks," wrote Lord Byron. Modern visitors are more likely to seek out golf and beaches, fresh sardines and well-matured port, but they are still apt to echo the judgment of another famous visitor, H. G. Wells, who declared: "Wet or fine, the air of Portugal has a natural happiness in it, and the people of the country should be as happy and prosperous as any people in the world."

Howe

In creating this new edition, **Andrew Eames**, Insight Guides' London-based executive editor, had a strong foundation on which to build. The original book has been imaginatively put together by **Alison Friesinger Hill**, a Harvard graduate who had worked for a wide variety of publications, including the *New York Times Book Review*.

Her talents had been paired with the expertise of **Tony Arruza**, a Cuban photographer based in Florida who has since produced memorable images for many *Insight Guides*.

To bring the book up-to-date, Eames enlisted the support of **Marion Kaplan** in Lisbon. She is the author of *The Portuguese*, a perceptive account of this people on the edge of Europe, and she also wrote *Insight*

Brammer

Wise

Pocket Guide: Lisbon. Her first visit to Lisbon was soon after the 1974 "Young Captains" bloodless revolution that overthrew Salazarist authoritarianism, and she has been based there since 1980. Besides completely revising the Travel Tips information section and updating all other chapters, Kaplan wrote a new chapter on the Azores for which she also contributed the photographs.

The chapters tracing Portugal's dramatic and complex history were written by **Thomas Hill**, a Harvard graduate in History and Literature. **Peter Wise**, an Englishman resident in Portugal and married to a Portuguese, wrote the chapter about Portugal's trees and its coastal communities. Wise, also an expert on Portuguese politics, has written for the AP wire service and many newspapers.

Wine and food are vital subjects for most visitors: the former was covered by **Scott Carney**, a New York wine expert, and the latter by **Jean Anderson**, an acknowledged expert and author of *The Food of Portugal*.

Anderson

F or the section on Lisbon and its surroundings, and on the most important wine provinces, the editor turned to **Marvine Howe**, a widely experienced journalist who was based in Lisbon for many years before joining the staff of the *New York Times*.

Sharon Behn, who contributed the chapters on the Algarve and on manor house (*pousada*) accommodation is also well-travelled. Born in Peru, she has lived in the US, England, Brazil and Portugal. She wrote for a wide variety of international newspapers before becoming a stringer for the UPI wire service in Lisbon.

English-born **Deborah Brammer**, who wrote about the Alentejo, also now lives in Lisbon, where she is married to a Portuguese.

Jeremy Boultbee, who put together the sections on the remote areas of Portugal, Trás-os-Montes and the Beiras, was born in Canada, although he now lives in Sintra. Besides being a writer, he is also an accomplished canoeist, ceramicist and actor.

Arruza

Jenny Wittner wrote the sections on Coimbra and its surrounding areas, as well as compiling the original Travel Tips. As an undergraduate at Harvard, she worked on an American travel series and later moved to Lisbon to teach English.

The chapter on Portuguese art and architecture was written by **Ruth Rosengarten**, an artist herself, and a resident of Lisbon. Born in Israel, Rosengarten received her BA in Johannesburg and her MA in London.

Also contributing to the original edition were **Katherine Barrett Swett**, editor of *Insight Guide: Italy*, with her chapter on travellers' accounts of Portugal, and **Antonio Dos Santos**, a Portuguese academic who wrote the chapter on saints and shrines.

Among the contributors new to this edition were a member of the Symington port family, **Martin Symington**, a freelance writer in London who put together an expert chapter on Portuguese boats, and **Nigel Tisdall**, a travel writer and regular *Insight Guide* contributor who wrote the chapter on Madeira.

The new photographs for this edition are primarily the work of **Bill Wassman**, a New York-based photographer and lover of the Iberian peninsula. The book was proofread and indexed by **John Goulding**.

CONTENTS

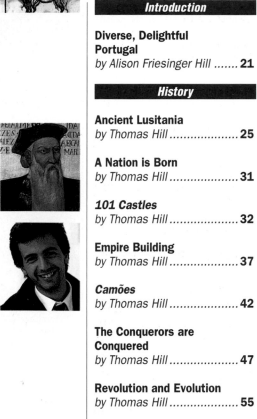

Preceding pages: ancient royal coat of arms; Swan Ceiling, Royal Palace, Sintra; countryside near Villa Viçosa; coastline at Sagres, Europe's most southwesterly point.

CONTENTS

TRAVEL TIPS

DIVERSE, DELIGHTFUL PORTUGAL

Portugal is a land on the edge, "where land ends and sea begins" as the 16th-century epic poet Luís Vaz de Camões put it. At the western periphery of Europe, it is also caught between traditional living – fishing and farming – and the technology that has made the world smaller, more integrated, more complex.

It is a cosy country, measuring 88,684 sq. km (34,216 sq. miles), with a stunning diversity of lovely landscapes: long white beaches and pretty coves, ranges of rolling hills and mountains – the central Serra da Estrela (mountains of the stars) being the highest at 1,993 metres (6,539 ft), numerous rivers and, in the southern central area, the Alentejo's broad plain which is patched with cork oaks and olive plantations.

Crowning Portugal's natural beauty for much of the year are blue skies and a glowing light in an agreeable climate of hot summers and chilly but never frozen winters. A temperate country, in mood as in weather, its people (numbering just over 10 million) are for the most part gentle, courteous, hospitable to visitors, fatalistic and immensely tolerant.

The traveller is welcome in every corner, from the discos and *boîtes* in Lisbon, open for dancing until 4am, to the most obscure village in Trás-os-Montes, with its simple ways of baking, spinning and farming. Sample whatever is to your taste, perhaps a little of everything.

This guide will start you off with a thorough lesson in Portugal's long and fascinating history, followed by a brief introduction to its people, insofar as it is possible to sum up any nation of individuals. Next, the book's features will familiarise you with Portugal's foods and wines, its wonderful *pousada* inns and manor house accommodation, and with its glorious art and architecture. Finally, the Places section will take you on a tour of the entire country. It's a trip well worth making.

1147

1227

1497

1762

1385

Portugal is something of an anomaly on the map of Western Europe. It is separated from Spain, a neighbour five times as large, not so much by natural frontiers but rather by the dictates of historical destiny. Geographically almost every region of Portugal corresponds closely to a region across the border. The northern Minho district is similar to Spanish Galicia; the southern Algarve and Alentejo districts bear a resemblance to Andalusia. The Tagus and Douro rivers and the mountains of the Beiras extend from Spain. In fact, the natural division of the Iberian peninsula would divide not east from west, but north from south, the Atlantic culture and climate from that of the Mediterranean.

Yet Portugal, with borders established by the 13th century, is one of the oldest nations in Europe. It has discovered and lost an empire, lost and regained its cherished autonomy and, since the 1974 revolution that ended decades of dictatorship, has formed new ties with old possessions.

A rich prehistoric culture has left its archaeological traces throughout Portugal. There is evidence of the earliest stages of human evolution and a large number of megalithic sites. The variety and quantity of these finds have led many scholars to a theory that cultural diffusion came primarily from overseas. Opponents of this notion point out that most of the megalithic sites are far from the coastline. They think the population grew via natural land routes of settlement which, not surprisingly, correspond to the paths invaders have taken throughout Portugal's history: across the Minho river from the north and over the Alentejo flatlands from the south.

In any case, by the 2nd millennium BC, the social organisation was composed of scattered *castros*, garrisoned hilltop villages that suggest warfare between tribes. The people subsisted on goat-herding and primitive agriculture, and clad themselves in woollen cloaks. Some of their constructions are still standing, for example, at the Citânia de Briteiros near Guimarães.

Preceding pages: the evolution of Portugal's flag. **Left**, Roman milestones in north Portugal.

In the south, tribes came under the influence of 9th-century Phoenician and 6th-century Greek trade settlements, both on the coast and inland, where metals were mined. Interestingly, it is only at this late point that there is evidence of a significant fishing economy among the indigenous people. Perhaps before then the rough-hewn and storm-beaten Atlantic coast was too intimidating for their small boats. During the 5th century BC, the Carthaginians wrested control of the Iberian peninsula from these earlier traders, but lost it to the Roman Empire in the Second Punic War.

Wars of conquests: The Romans called the peninsula Hispania Ulterior. Here, as elsewhere in the empire, they combined their economic exploitation with cultural upheaval. They were not traders, after all, but conquerors, who set about the business of founding cities, building roads, and reorganising territories. They also implemented governmental and judicial systems.

The locals resisted. The largest and most intransigent group were the Lusitani, who lived north of the Tagus, and after whom the region was called Lusitania. Bitter guerrilla fighting was intermittent for two centuries. The most renowned rebel was a shepherd named Viriathus. He led uprisings until he was assassinated in 139 BC by three treacherous comrades who had been bribed by the Romans. It was during these wars of conquest that Roman troops are said to have refused to cross the Lima river, believing it to be the Lethe, the mythological river of forgetfulness. Their commander, the story goes, had to cross the river alone, then call each soldier by name to prove that the dip had not affected his memory.

Beginning in 60 BC, Julius Caesar governed the province from the capital established at Olisipo (Lisbon). Cities were established and colonised at Évora, Beja, Santarém, and elsewhere. Roads linked the north and south. Before the decline and fall, the Romans had infused the area with their language, legal systems, currency, agriculture and, eventually, with Christianity. The organisation of *latifundia* was particularly significant as it brought large-scale farming to the area for the first time. The centres and routes the Romans chose have waned in importance, but today many are still geographic focal points – most notably Lisbon.

With the conversion of the late Roman emperors, the tenets and organisations of Christianity spread throughout the fading empire. Bishoprics were established in a number of cities, Braga and Évora among them. As the church expanded it usurped the administrative power that had been developed by the empire.

Heretical Christian doctrines held sway in Portugal during the 3rd and 4th centuries. In the early 5th century various groups of barbarians occupied the land. The Alani and

457, the Suevi kingdom survived, led by Masdra. In 465, Masdra's son Remismund converted to Arianism, probably to appease the Visigoths. By 550, the growing power of the Catholic Church led to a new round of conversions led by St Martin of Dume. The remnants of the Suevi were politically extinguished in 585.

Invaders from the south: Visigoth rule, an elective monarchy that soon bred internal dissent, was not seriously challenged until the Moors, who had arrived on the southern coast in 711, began their expansion northward. The south of Portugal was now a part of Moslem Spain, loosely organised under the Cordoba caliph. To the Moors, this coun-

Vandals each settled for a short time, but by 419 the Suevi were in sole, if not steady, possession of Galicia, and from there they conquered Lusitania and most of the Iberian peninsula. The Suevi apparently assimilated easily with the existing Hispano-Roman population. The tide turned on them with the arrival of the Visigoths. For the next 50 years, military conquest meant religious conversion. In 448, Rechiarius, king of a diminished Suevi empire, converted to Catholicism, perhaps hoping to elicit aid from Rome in battling against the Visigoths who were Christian but clung to the heretical Arianism. When Rechiarius was killed in

try was *Al-Gharb*, (the West), from which was derived the modern name of Algarve. The Moors soon ruled all of Portugal, and Christianity was forced north of the Minho where it lay gathering strength for the *Reconquista*.

For centuries, the Moors ruled tolerantly, living in relative tranquillity with Jews and Christians. But in 868 the first significant efforts by Portugal to break from Spain began. A revolt was staged by a rich landowner nicknamed "The Galician" because he was a native of Spain whose family had converted to Islam. After three failed rebellions, he succeeded in founding a semi-independent state, in 885. His son took over after his death, but showed less fortitude, losing it all back to the caliph by 930.

Over the next decade, the overarching authority of the caliph decayed, and small kingdoms, *taifas*, took over. The decentralisation naturally led to internal dissent, partly caused by the rise of a religious sect called Sufi. Sufism was a subversive and heretical brand of mysticism that grew popular in reaction to the rationalism of Islam. Its significance was two-fold: just as it allowed Christian forces to push the frontier lines down from the north, it also allowed radical Moslem military groups like the Almoravids and the Almohads to rise to power quickly.

The first serious blows for a Christian return were struck in the mid-8th century by marauders from Asturias-León (northern Spain). All of northern Portugal became a battleground. Slowly towns fell before the Christian armies: Oporto in 868, Coimbra in 878, and by 955 the king of León, Ordona III, engineered a raid on Lisbon. Most of the victories below the Douro, however, amounted to nothing more than raids, as the territory was seldom held for more than a season or two.

The split with Spain: Portugal's independence from Spain has been attributed to various causes, including the indigenous megalithic cultures whose borders were accepted

The Almoravids, who had built an empire in Africa, came north. After helping the Islamic rulers to force the Christians back, they decided to take over, to unify the *taifas* under them. By 1095 the Almoravids had succeeded, installing an austere military system and harsh government. As if that weren't enough, they were soon followed by the still more fanatical Almohads. The simmering *Reconquista* took on the aspect of a Holy War for both Christians and Moslems.

Left, Roman temple in Évora, possibly dedicated to the goddess Diana. **Above**, remnants of a Visigothic pillar in Serpa.

by Rome and the resistance that the Suevi offered to the Visigoth hordes. However, it was during the Christian reconquest of Iberia that Portugal first truly asserted its independent stance and its leaders their sense of national destiny. Late in the 9th century, the area between the Lima and Douro rivers became a territory named Portucale. The area was variously divided under the unstable feudal states. Stability came when the province was held by one family for a century beginning in 950. It was still under the supreme control of the Kingdom of León, but unlike León's other provinces, the power and autonomy of Portucale were on the rise.

Self-proclaimed emperor: Fernando I of León was the great consolidating force of northern Spain during the 11th century. As part of his policy of centralising authority, he tried to dismantle Portugal, dividing it into different provinces under separate governors. When Fernando's successor Alfonso VI took the title of emperor, he ruled over the kingdoms of León, Castile, Galicia and Portugal. "Emperor" was a pronounced exaggeration, given the unstable ties of vassalage between the various players of the period, but it was an important claim if only because an emperor rules over kings. Yet it may have been the lure of the title "king" that inspired Afonso Henriques to battle, deal and connive for the autonomy of his particular *terra*, Portugal.

Afonso Henriques was the son of Henri of Burgundy and his wife Teresa. Henri was among a number of French knights who had arrived in the late 11th century to fight the infidels. They were mostly second and third sons, who, in the feudal system, were left with no real inheritance. If they wanted land and riches, they usually had to travel abroad to win them. Henri's cousin Raymond, like Henri a fourth son, also came south. After proving his heroism in battle, Raymond married Alfonso VI's daughter Urraca, and was granted the territories of Galicia and Coimbra. With Henri's marriage to Teresa, who was Alfonso's favourite, though illegitimate daughter, he was given the territory of Portugal. With the death of Raymond and Alfonso VI, Urraca inherited that crown, but her second marriage, to another Alfonso, this one known as Alfonso I of Aragon, also set off a complex round of civil wars.

During this period, Henri made significant strides toward the autonomy of the state of Portugal. The most important of these was the support he offered to the archbishops of Braga in a dispute with those of Toledo.

In 1126 Urraca died and her son, Alfonso Raimundez, became the Emperor Alfonso VII. Henri had died and Teresa ruled Portugal as regent for her son, Afonso Henriques. Without wasting much time in mourning, she took a Galician count, Fernão Peres, as a lover, displeasing some of the nobility and her son. Continuing Henri's policies, Teresa schemed successfully to maintain Portugal's independence, but in 1127 she submitted to Alfonso VII's dominion after her army was defeated. In 1128 the 18-year-old Afonso Henriques led his first rebellion, ending his mother's rule at the battle of São Mamede, near their castle in Guimarães.

A king is crowned: Over the next decade, Afonso Henriques vied with his emperor cousin for ultimate control of Portugal. After a brilliant military conquest over the Moors in the Battle of Ourique in 1139, he began to refer to himself as king. In 1143, the Treaty of Zamora was signed between them wherein Alfonso VII gave Afonso Henriques the title of King of Portugal in exchange for the usual feudal ties of military aid and loyalty.

Yet Afonso Henriques sought to fix the title more firmly by seeking recognition from Rome. Pope Lucius II refused, keeping

to a policy of supporting Iberian union in the hope of stemming the tide of Islam. It was only in 1179 that Pope Alexander III, in exchange for a yearly tribute and various other privileges, finally granted recognition of the Portuguese kingdom. By that late date, papal acceptance served only to formalise an entity that was not only well-established but growing. Afonso Henriques had enlisted the aid of crusaders and beaten back the Moors, adding his conquests to the emerging nation. Santarém and Lisbon were both taken in 1147; the first by surprise attack, the second in a siege that was supported by French, English, Flemish and German crusaders who were passing through Portugal on their way to the Holy Land. The inestimable assistance of these 164 ships of men was entirely fortuitous; it very nearly fell through when Afonso Henriques pronounced that he expected them to fight only for Christianity and not for earthly rewards. The English and Germans walked out; the king quickly rescinded, offering loot and land grants.

The western crusade: The bishop also added his aid in recruiting foreign crusaders, providing theological assurance that the enemies were the same as would be found in the Holy Land. However, Afonso Henriques's confessor questioned the diversion of troops from the crusade, and legend has it that on the

was the founding of military-religious organisations like the Knights Templar and the Hospitallers. These groups were rewarded with land grants in exchange for chasing out the Moors, and grew wealthy and powerful.

In 1170 Afonso Henriques fought his last battle, at Badajoz. The powerful Almohads had enlisted the aid of Fernando II of León, who felt that the Portuguese were recapturing not only the Moorish land, but land that was by right a part of León. The most renowned of Afonso Henriques's military cohorts was Geraldo Geraldes, a local adventurer dubbed *O Sem Pavor* (the Fearless) for his brilliant raids into Moslem territory. This national hero had won a string of epic

way to Santarém – with crusaders in tow – the king was besieged by guilt and anxiety because of the Moorish stronghold's reputation of impregnability. To soothe his torment, he vowed that he would build an abbey at Alcobaça in the Virgin's honour if the battle was successful. The battle was won: the abbey still stands.

Convincing crusaders that one batch of infidels was as good as another was crucial to the *Reconquista*. A result of crusade-status

victories. But, at Badajoz, the combination of Moorish and Leónese forces was too much for Geraldes and his king. The aging Afonso Henriques broke his leg and was captured. His release came only after he had surrendered castles and territories to enemy parties. His retreat allowed the Moors to entrench along the battle zone.

The founding king of Portugal's days of victory were over, with the *Reconquista* still a century away. Yet, with Henriques' monarchy, a country was born. Whether it was an act of political will or not, the independence and individuality of the Portuguese nation was forever determined.

Left, Afonso Henriques, first king of Portugal. Above, 18th-century engraving of Afonso rallying his troops at the conquest of Lisbon in 1147.

For a century after the death of Afonso Henriques in 1285, the first order of business was the slow riddance of the remaining, and still feisty, Moors. The *Reconquista*, now as good as sanctioned by the church with various papal bulls and indulgences as a "western crusade," was still very much under way.

The Knights Templar had arrived in Portugal with the crusaders stopping on their way to Palestine in 1128. They were soon followed by other military-religious orders: Hospitallers, Calatrava, and Santiago. These groups clung to the religious justification for their war-mongering and for their massive accumulation of land and loot. Still, the western crusade remained an awkward idea. Unlike Palestine, where the dividing line between Christians and infidels was clearly drawn, the south of Iberia had intermingled Moslem, Christian, and Jewish peoples in economic, cultural, and even political spheres. In 1197, papal indulgences were even promised in a war against Alfonso IX of León, a Christian, though at that time an ally of the Moslems.

The frontier war proceeded steadily, if somewhat slowly. The first kings of the Burgundian line after Afonso Henriques continued to press the borders southward. Under Sancho II, the eastern Algarve and Alentejo were incorporated into the burgeoning nation. Under Afonso III, the western Algarve and Faro had fallen by 1249. By about 1260 he had also moved the capital south from Coimbra to Lisbon. These boundaries – much like today's – were finally recognised by Castile in the Treaty of Alcañices in 1297.

The *Reconquista* brought Portugal fundamental social transformation. Having reclaimed the lands of the south, they now needed to populate them. To do this, the Burgundian kings needed to balance their centralised, essentially military power with popular support. The need for popular and financial support forced kings to consult with *cortes*, local assemblies of nobles, clergy, and, somewhat later, mercantile classes. At the *cortes* of Leiria (1254), Afonso

III conceded the right of municipal representation in taxation and other economic issues. For the most part, the *cortes* were gathered whenever the king needed to raise money. When later monarchs used trade and their own military orders to reap great and independent profits, the *cortes* fell into disuse.

Another result of the *Reconquista*, with the expansion of properties and the need for labourers who were willing to resettle, was an increase in social mobility among the lower classes. Distinctions fell away among the various levels of serfs as farm workers became a scarcer and so a more valuable commodity. Another, more general effect was the beginning of amalgamation of the divergent cultures of north and south. The south was still marked by refinement and urbanity; it was a culture of tolerance. In contrast, the northern culture had a rough arrogance, the attitude of invaders. Differences remain even now.

The church rode the *Reconquista* to riches. The various orders were granted vast areas of land by the kings in return for their military aid. The church and clergy were also free of taxation, and were granted the right to collect their own "tenths" from the population. Their power was such that it soon threatened the monarchy. Afonso II was the first ruler of Portugal to defy the church in attempting to curb its voracious acquisition of property. His efforts generally failed, as did those of his successor, Sancho II, who was finally excommunicated and dethroned in 1245 for his insistence on royal prerogatives.

It was the reign of Dinis, who was known as both the farmer king and the poet king, that truly cemented Portuguese independence, and the power of the monarchy. After briefly joining Aragon in war against Castile, Dinis ushered in a long period of peace and progress. He encouraged learning and literature, establishing the first university in 1288, initially in Lisbon then transferred to Coimbra. Portuguese, having distinguished itself from its Latin roots and from Castilian (which would become Spanish), established itself as the language of the troubadour culture, and the official language of law and state.

The troubadour culture – poetry and music

Left, King Dinis, founder of the University of Coimbra, in a 17th-century screen made in China.

101 CASTLES

I t is said that there are 101 castles in Portugal. In fact there are more, many of them built or rebuilt between the 12th and 14th centuries. King Dinis (1279–1325) began constructing or expanding more than 50 fortresses during his reign. His labours can be seen throughout Portugal, but he concentrated his efforts along the eastern boundary. He strengthened the towns of Guarda, Penedo, Penamacor, Castelo Mendo, Pinhel and others, attempting to secure the area from the threat of Castile. He was rewarded: the Treaty of Alcañices, signed in 1297, gave Portugal the Ribacoa.

Dinis provided the money for the castles, and even the exact measurements of the walls and towers. Those initiated by him were of a particularly fine construction, with decorations and designs not found on other buildings. Some of the towers were slender and elegant; many balconies elaborate, with detailed machicolations. Dinis often gave a certain character or grandness to the structures, as in the 15 towers he had built at Numão, or the delightful Torre do Galo, "Rooster Tower," at Freixo de Espada à Cinta, with its unusual and beautiful seven faces.

Dinis also organised the first national maritime organisation, hiring skilled Genoese sailors for the task. In 1308 he signed the original pact of friendship with England that has been reconfirmed and expanded many times since. The "farmer king" also reformed the national agriculture, establishing forest plantations and other programmes that soon allowed the export of grain, olive oil, wine and other foodstuffs. Portugal also profited from illicit trade with Islamic countries, acting as intermediary between them and the northern countries. These coastal developments finally began to shift the population centre of the nation from north to south.

Many castles – built by Dinis and others – were on the sites of earlier forts: Moorish, Visigothic, Roman, or earlier. It is interesting to note developments in warfare as they are reflected in physical features of Portugal's castles. Long verandas of wood, for example, were in early days attached to the castles' walls. Later these were covered with animal hides so they could not be burned easily by flaming arrows, but were abandoned at the end of the 13th century. By then, the carved stone balconies were used for the same purpose, with machicolations which allowed defenders to repel attackers as they attempted to scale the castle wall.

But the most significant change came with the advent of gunpowder and artillery. The heavy cannons required thicker walls to be built, and these walls were sloped to resist the more powerful projectiles. Another reason for the thicker walls was so that the ramparts, running along the tops of the walls, could be wider. Earlier, only men and their bows stood here. Now the castles' heavy artillery was perched on top. Arrow slits, a common feature in castles, were rounded to accommodate the new artillery, then abandoned as impractical.

All Portugal's castles, many still sound or in semi-ruin, are dramatically sited. Among them: Almeida, east of Guarda; Almourol, perhaps the most romantic of all, set on its own tiny island in the Tagus river and surrounded by myths; and, of course, Guimarães, birthplace of Portugal's first king, Afonso Henriques. Guimarães is one of Portugal's oldest castles, having been built in the 10th century, and restored many times since. Early in the 19th century the castle was used as a debtors' prison.

Most castles are open to visitors; some have been converted to hotels, and some stand, ignored, in empty fields. Solid though their construction may have been, be careful when visiting the latter; it wouldn't do to end your visit under a piece of falling masonry. ∎

spread by peripatetic minstrels – was greatly influential. Drawing upon the French tradition and Moorish influences, the Portuguese troubadours created a unique native literature. These song-poems of love and satire were often written by nobles, among them Dinis the "poet king", of course, and Sancho I as well. Other forms of literary expression lagged far behind poetry.

Dinis's rule also brought political progress. Landmark agreements were made to seal peace with Castile (the Treaty of Alcañices, 1297) and the clergy (the Concordat of 1289). The latter agreement was a major victory for royal jurisdiction in matters of property. During his reign, Dinis fortified the frontier

trade into fairs also, not coincidentally, allowed for a more systematic taxation.

The only section of the economy to lag during this period was industrial production. In this case Dinis, and later kings, were counterproductive in their resistance to the idea of corporations. Craftsmen tended to work on their own, and thus confined themselves to local markets and limited quantities. Some goldsmithing, shipbuilding, and pottery was done in commercial quantities.

Perhaps most significant of all of Dinis's accomplishments was the way in which he managed the disbanding of the Knights Templar in 1312. The order was under fire throughout Europe; their demise was immi-

with the construction of some 50 castles.

By now a monetary economy was well established, not only for international trade, but internally. Agricultural production was more and more geared toward markets, though self-sufficient farming did not disappear. Dinis encouraged the expansion of the economic system with fairs, large chartered trading centres that encouraged internal trade. Dinis was responsible for chartering 48 of these fairs, more than all the other Portuguese kings combined. The concentration of

Left, the island castle at Almourol. **Above**, the Convent of Christ in Tomar.

nent. Dinis's triumph was to retain their great wealth within the country and to prevent the church from taking it over. In 1317 he founded the Order of Our Lord Jesus Christ, which was granted all the former possessions of the Knights Templar, but under royal, not papal control.

Economic crises: Afonso IV succeeded Dinis. His administration was less sure, and hostilities with Castile waxed and waned. More significantly, his reign was burdened with the Black Death. The first bout devastated the country, particularly the urban centres, in 1348–49. Throughout the next century the pestilence would return again and again, causing both depopulation and despondency. Concurrently, various demographic and economic crises were beginning to undermine the nation. The attraction of the urban centres left the interior underpopulated, causing inflation in food prices. The kings tried to regulate the movements of the population but their methods were ineffectual. The economic stagnation, whose dreary influence extended to literature, religion, and every element of daily life, would not truly end until the coming of the maritime empire.

Politics of this period were motivated largely by fear of Castilian domination. In fact, continual intermarriage between the two royal families did keep the possibility of

Inês was banished in 1340, but upon the death of the princess Constanza in 1345, she returned to her lover. She lived in Coimbra with her children, perhaps secretly married to Pedro. The threat of a Castilian heir was intolerable to Afonso, who finally sanctioned her brutal assassination in 1355.

After being rebuffed in a brief civil war, Pedro, later known as "the Cruel" for his half-mad administration of justice and government, waited patiently for his revenge. He assumed the throne upon his father's death in 1357 and quickly tracked down his lover's assassins. They were brought before the king, who ordered their hearts to be torn out. In 1361, more than five years after her

unification open. But the Portuguese were committed to maintaining total independence, and this, coupled with general social unrest, caused turbulence for Pedro I and his son Fernando, and finally brought down the House of Burgundy.

Love story: Betrothed to a Spanish princess, Pedro I instead fell madly in love with her alluring lady-in-waiting, Inês de Castro. It was not long before their dalliance became an open affair, much to the displeasure of his father, Afonso IV, and powerful members of the court. Inês was from a powerful Castilian family, and according to some, was manipulating Pedro for political ends.

burial, Pedro ordered Inês to be exhumed, dressed in royal robes and crown, and placed next to him on the throne. Each member of the court was then forced to pay homage by kissing the dead queen's decomposed hand.

Aside from its immediate political consequences, this gruesome tale also later proved to be inspirational. Adapted by writers such as Camões (in *Os Lusíadas*) and António Ferreira (in *Castro*), the story became a central legend for the Portuguese literary imagination. Today, the tombs of Inês de Castro and Pedro I can be seen in the Santa Maria Monastery in Alcobaça.

Despite the instability of the monarch himself, the reign of Pedro I was marked by peaceful coexistence with Castile. Social and political growth developed as the country recovered from the convulsions of the plague. However, the increasing power of the nobles, the clergy and the emergent bourgeoisie, all represented in the *cortes*, would break loose in active social discontent during the reign of his son, Fernando I.

Fernando tried to unite Portugal and Castile under his rule, engaging the country in a series of unpopular and unsuccessful wars with its neighbour. France and England joined the turmoil, using the Iberian peninsula as a theatre of the Hundred Years' War. In 1373, Enrique II of Castile attacked Lisbon, burning and pillaging the city and forcing Fernando to pledge his alliance. To add to the confusion, the "Great Schism" divided the Catholic Church under opposing Popes from 1378 onwards, and Fernando alternated his loyalties frequently. The wars had ravaged the whole country, leaving the populace both tired and angry.

Fernando had further alienated his subjects with his unpopular marriage to Leonor Teles, who was perceived to represent the landed gentry. Riots broke out at the marriage and again in 1383 when Fernando died, leaving his widow (with her lover, the Galician count, João Fernandez Andeiro) to rule as Queen Mother.

Andeiro was assassinated within weeks by João, illegitimate son of Pedro I and Master of Avis, one of the national military-religious orders. In the ensuing civil war for the throne, Leonor had the support of most of the nobles and clergy, while João relied upon the support of the middle class. He depended upon the deepening resentment the people now felt toward Castile – Leonor had fled to Juan I of Castile after Andeiro's death – and rode this growing wave to victory. The final military conflict was the Battle of Aljubarrota, a decisive victory for João's troops, despite being outnumbered, and thanks in part to a squadron of English archers.

A number of stories and legends surround this battle. The "Holy Constable" Nuno Alvares Pereira was captain of João's small army. As he valiantly led his charges in the battle, Nuno was agonisingly thirsty, with no

water to be had anywhere on the plain. He swore that no traveller would ever go thirsty here again, and since 1385 a small pitcher of water has been daily placed in a niche of the Aljubarrota chapel of São Jorge.

João, too, made a vow. Seeing that his army was vastly outnumbered, he swore to build a great church in the Virgin Mary's honour if he won. As the Castilian army turned tail and fled, João hurled his lance into the air to choose the place for the construction that would be the great Monastery of Batalha. If the story is true, João had a very strong arm, because the battlefield is some 16 km (10 miles) from the monastery.

The subsequent rule of João I, founder of

the House of Avis, represented a new political beginning. The disputes with Castile continued, but they were winding down. The unsteady Anglo-Portuguese alliance was cemented by the Treaty of Windsor in 1386, a document which has been cited as recently as World War II, when Britain invoked it to gain fuelling stations in the Azores.

João I brought stability, but the change of order was not a social revolution. New political representation was established by the mercantile class, but in time it was clear that only the names had changed among the landed aristocracy who still held real power. The new dynasty was much like the old.

Left, Pedro I's tomb in the monastery in Alcobaça. Right, portal to the unfinished chapels at Batalha.

João I ruled from 1385 to 1433, fending off the demands of a resurgent nobility by installing his legitimate sons Duarte, Pedro, Henry, Fernão, and João in powerful positions as the leaders of military-religious orders. Henry the Navigator, for example, headed the wealthy Order of Christ. It was under João I that Portugal first began to look across the seas for solutions to internal economic and political problems. Trade and exploration would serve both to occupy the nobility and to boost commerce.

João's successor, King Duarte, initially continued with overseas expansion, but drew back after a disastrous failed attack on Tangiers. In 1438, Duarte died, setting off a brief civil war to determine who would be regent to his young son Afonso V.

Two of Afonso's uncles were particularly trusted advisers, and stand as symbols of the ambitions Afonso held throughout his reign: Henry the Navigator, leader of conquest, and another Afonso, the Duke of Bragança and leader of the newly strengthened nobility. Each was granted a large share of independent power. For himself, King Afonso remained above the fray of administration. He did not rule ineptly, but he was a chivalric leader in an era where politics had been sullied by the growing power of mercantilists and low nobility. He concerned himself largely with martial glory, which he found crusading in North Africa. In 1471 he took Tangiers. Another of his accomplishments was the minting of the first *cruzado*, the gold coin that became a symbol of the wealth flowing in from the voyages.

In 1475 there was civil discord in Castile because of a dispute over the crown. Afonso decided to marry Juana, one of the claimants, and thus unite Portugal and Castile under his monarchy. He invaded in support of her claims, occupied León, but failed to hold his ground. He tried to enlist the aid of King Louis XI of France in support of his claims to the Castilian throne, travelling to France to make a personal plea. He arrived in the midst of Louis XI's tumultuous rivalry with the Duke of Burgundy and proved to be a hapless diplomat, quickly alienating both sides. Frustrated, he abdicated his throne to go on a pilgrimage to the Holy Land, but even this quixotic voyage was thwarted. Louis prevented the Portuguese monarch from embarking, and the despondent Afonso was deported to his homeland. His son, the future João II, stepped down from the throne, letting Afonso resume his nominal position, though thenceforth the rule was shared.

Under these kings, the overseas expansion began in earnest. It began, but no one prepared or knew how to prepare for the empire that was to come. The policy that existed was a strange mix of crusading ideals, romantic curiosity, and profit motive. Charting the world was a secondary matter to João II – less important, for example, than spices and the search for the odd figure who was known as Prester John.

A mythical priest and king, Prester John was supposed to have been the leader of a vast and powerful Christian empire located somewhere in the African interior. His legend was elaborated with tales of a kingdom

Left, detail of a Japanese screen (*circa* 1593) commemorating the arrival of Portuguese traders. **Right**, a statue of Infante Dom Henrique in Lagos.

t was an earthly paradise peopled with a bizarre menagerie of chimeras and mythical characters. Strange as it seems, this tale had an enormous influence on early exploration of Africa. In fact in 1455, after the Portuguese had established their dominance all along the northern coast, a papal bull granted them the sole right to discovery and conquest of all of Africa except those parts ruled by Prester John. It was only later, by the early 16th century, that Portugal's explorers began to realise that spice and gold were more accessible goals, and the voyages in and around Ethiopia were replaced with more profitable itineraries.

Another goal of seafarers was the still-tually did find its way into the coffers of Lisbon, but it also proved to be a debilitating obsession, diverting attention from surer if less spectacular sources of profit. These lesser goals were nevertheless an impetus for exploration from the start. Fishing ships had circled further and further out in search of richer waters. Moroccan grain, sugar, dyestuffs, and slaves were all prized. These were eventually joined by the spices and rare woods of India and the Orient.

Preliminary to any exploration, of course, the technical aspects of navigation had to be mastered and improved. Navigators, familiar with the Pole star, dead reckoning and the compass, began to establish their position

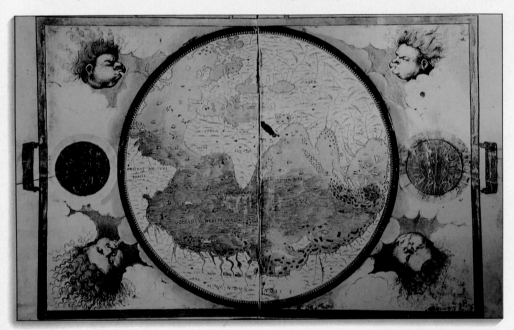

popular slaughter of the infidel. Attacking Moslems wherever they could be found gave the voyages all the benefits of a crusade: the effort was legitimised, and the church lent its financial resources along with spiritual support in the form of indulgences and martyrdoms. The sanctions of Rome, like the bull of 1455, would become an important factor when maritime competition intensified.

Economic and social needs undoubtedly lay at the base of the voyages. Certainly there was a shortage of gold all over Europe. Without it, coinage was severely debased and the growth of commerce was retarded. Gold from Africa, America, and India even-with the quadrant, the astrolabe adapted for sea use, and a simple cross-staff from which they calculated latitude. Celestial tables and so-called *portolano* charts, basic maps, became ever more detailed. Ships, too, radically changed – neatest of all the nimble caravel, derived from the heftier cargo-carrying *caravela* of the Douro river. Prince Henry, who was born in Oporto, would have known it well.

Henry the Navigator (as the prince became known) is often credited with leading the discoveries, masterminding them while surrounded by expert astronomers and shipbuilders at his school of navigation in Sagres.

The truth is more complex. His financial sponsorship and enthusiasm made him a profound influence, but discovering the world – and the Portuguese were the first Europeans in two-thirds of it – was beyond the scope of any one man.

With many hands at the tillers, the enterprise was not well-coordinated. The main goal was to press the crusade forward and eventually to reconquer Jerusalem. Maps were accurate enough to suggest that there were islands in the unknown Sea of Darkness, and land beyond it, but it needed courage and determination to sail into oceans that legend had filled with fearsome monsters.

Prince Henry's main goal was primarily

Henry give the discoveries his full attention – with fiscal profit firmly in mind.

Epic voyages: It is easy to see why popular history might accord undue credit to an individual like Henry. The Age of Discovery was a time for heroes and adventurers, and also a time for the rebirth of knightly ideals. Fearless mariners sailed off into unknown realms. Their voyages were imbued with noble intentions: the greater glory of the church, the service of knowledge, and the benefit of their nation.

Popular history also makes unverifiable claims that Portuguese mariners were the first Europeans in America. Among venturesome explorers who sailed from the Azores

the taming of the North African coast, which meant the banishment of the Moors. He never travelled further than Morocco himself (his brother, Pedro, was a true wanderer – in Europe – sending Henry every relevant map and book he found). The chronicles portray Henry devoting most of his time to squeezing profits out of his various tithes, monopolies and privilege revenues. Only later in life, with increasing reports of wondrous and far-off places to inspire him, did

Left, the four winds blow hard and steady for the Portuguese Discoverers in this unusual 1519 map. **Above**, Cabral lands in Brazil.

were members of the Corte Real family who explored the north American coast in the 1470s. One of them, Miguel, may have been marooned there.

Perhaps the first indisputable hero of the discoveries was Gil Eanes. Madeira and the Azores, along with the north of Africa, had been charted. The islands had begun to be colonised. The fabulous tales of the edge of the world and the various horrors of the south seas were soon connected with the stormy promontory of Cape Bojador, on the west coast of Africa. It became the boundary. Finally, in 1434, Gil Eanes, a pilot commissioned by Henry the Navigator, broke the barrier. He found more coast and safe water behind. He returned to Portugal triumphant, bringing wild plants plucked from the land beyond. The next year he led voyages further down Africa's coast, and the way was open for the many who followed. They searched primarily for the legendary *Rio do Ouro* (River of Gold). Eventually some of that precious ore was found.

In 1482, Portuguese ships explored the mouth of the Congo river. In 1487, Bartolomeu Dias rounded the Cape of Good Hope. In 1494, papal intervention in the growing competition between Spain and Portugal resulted in the famous Treaty of Tordesillas, which divided the newly dis-

DOM VASCO DA GAMA
1469 - 1524

DESCOBRIDOR E ALMIRANTE DO MAR DA INDIA
E CONDE DA VIDIGUEIRA
VICE-REI DA INDIA

"...AQUELE ILUSTRE GAMA
QUE PARA SI DE ENEAS TOMA A FAMA."
CAMÕES, LUS, I-12

covered as well as the still unknown lands between the two countries. This treaty granted Portugal the lands east of a line of demarcation 592 km (370 miles) west of the Azores. This put Brazil within Portugal's sphere. In 1497–99, Vasco da Gama sailed to Calicut in India and back, immediately throwing Portugal into competition with Moslem and Venetian spice traders. In 1500, Pedro Álveres Cabral discovered Brazil. In 1519–22, Ferdinand Magellan, or Fernão de Magalhães, a Portuguese in the service of Spain, led the first voyage to circumnavigate the globe, though he died before the journey was completed.

The expeditions opened the seaways, but there were battles to be fought to establish trading posts in Africa and the Indies. Arabs, protecting their own trade interests, fought the Portuguese wherever they could. The Portuguese, of course, were still intent on eradicating such infidels from the face of the earth. So although Portugal had no intentions of land conquest, by simply striving to establish and maintain a monopoly of the high seas, they were constantly at war.

Colonies: The great leader of these campaigns was Governor Afonso de Albuquerque, a brilliant strategist and, in essence, the founding father of the empire in Asia. His victories allowed garrisoned ports and fortresses to be built in key locations. Goa, in India, conquered in 1510, became the centre for all operations. Malacca fell in 1511 and served as the East Indies hub, while Ormuz came under Portuguese control in 1515, proving the ideal seat from which to dominate the Persian Gulf. Later, in 1557, Macau was established on a kind of permanent lease with China, extending Portugal's reach to the Far East.

Albuquerque administered these new holdings with a basic policy of colonisation rather than exploitation. All the major cities, Goa in particular, were converted by architecture and government into European towns. Interracial marriages were encouraged and Catholic missions established.

The growth of Goa was extraordinary. By 1540 there were 10,000 European-descended households and the town was the seat of a bishopric. However, these few altered cities and the battles of the Indies were in marked contrast to the general policy of peaceful coexistence that Portugal adopted wherever it could. In Africa, Brazil, and the various islands and archipelagos, they tried to set up trade stations without interfering with local customs or politics.

It is, however, the exceptions that proved the most interesting: in the Congo, for example, where a number of missions were sent. The people of the kingdom there were quite taken with their European visitors, though they could provide little of interest to the traders. The Portuguese had begun by overestimating the political and cultural sophistication of these people, and once the Congolese were exposed to certain Western practices, they embraced them. They took to

Christianity, and imitated the manners and fashions of the Portuguese. Their first Christian monarch dropped the unwieldy "Nzinga a Nkuwu" and renamed himself João I. His son took the name Afonso, and from that point into the 17th century the land was ruled by a succession of native Henriques, Pedros, and Franciscos.

The Congo, though it did provide both ivory and slaves, was not of central economic importance. The Portuguese ships were too busy reaping bounty elsewhere to pay much attention to cultural matters: spices were carried from the Indies, gold was found in the Sudan and other parts of Africa, sugar and wine were brought from Madeira, sugar

the later Dutch empire, organisation and central authority were more important than mere size. Furthermore, the early expeditions required little manpower. It was only later, when they found themselves trying to enforce the worldwide trade monopoly, that the smallness of Portugal's population began to tell. It has been suggested that a crucial deficiency was Portugal's lack of a middle class – quashed by royal and noble dominance of commerce – a group that might have provided qualified and educated planners, pilots and administrators.

In explaining the empire's failure, some have pointed to widespread corruption or to the foreign control of profits garnered from

and dyestuffs came from Brazil.

The wealth reaped overseas made for a stable economy, but it did not make Portugal rich. Individuals and the monarchy – taking its royal fifth of all trade revenues – became rich, but even they eventually found it difficult to build or hold their fortunes.

At its beginning, the "empire" demanded little from its diminutive fatherland. Like other small trading centres in Italy and like

Left, Vasco da Gama stands tall in Sines, the town where he was born. **Right**, Afonso de Albuquerque in a portrait (*circa* 1509) by an unknown artist.

Portuguese expeditions. How great an effect they had is arguable. Certainly the religious efforts that went hand in hand with Portuguese voyages did not make the wheels of commerce spin any more freely. Whether fighting Moslems with whom they had once peacefully coexisted, or trying to force Christianity down the throats of local populations, the Portuguese lost time and focus from the business of business. Whatever the causes, potential benefits of the burgeoning overseas trade were not being reaped. Deflation in Europe stifled trade. Domestic agricultural production, hampered by a lack of manpower, lagged, occasionally causing serious

CAMÕES

Luís Vaz de Camões (1524–80), Portugal's greatest poet, never reaped fame or riches during his own lifetime. He was born poor, and he died poor, but the life that he led – of passion and adventure – enthrals the Portuguese almost as much as the epic, eloquent phrases in his works that many Portuguese can quote at length even today.

After attending the University at Coimbra, the young poet's prospects were good. However, many twists of fate lay ahead. An affair with one of the queen's ladies-in-waiting caused his banishment to North Africa, where he lost an eye in

military service. Returning to Lisbon, Camões was involved in a skirmish that wounded a magistrate. He ended up in prison and then was banished again, in 1553, this time to the colony of Goa in India.

It was 1570 before he returned to Lisbon. Having written poetry and plays for many years with some success, he published *Os Lusíadas* in 1572. The poem's worth was recognised immediately, and as a reward Camões received a small royal pension. His final illness, however, was spent in a public hospital. When he died, he was buried in a common grave.

The title *Os Lusíadas* means the sons of Lusus, the mythical founder of Portugal: poetically,

then, it means "the Portuguese". Echoing classical models, the poem chronicled the voyages of Vasco da Gama, before a panorama of strangely mixed Christian and pagan images.

Os Lusíadas has been hailed throughout Europe (Lope de Vega and Montesquieu were early admirers), sometimes to the detriment of the rest of Portugal's other extensive and dynamic literature. Under Salazar, *Os Lusíadas* became an icon of Portuguese nationalism. Speeches and propaganda were peppered with quotes drawn from the great book, providing a mythos for imperialism, without reflection upon the differences between the 16th and 20th centuries.

The 18th-century verse translation done by W. J. Mickle, which is quoted below, though tinged with the lyrical romanticism of that era, captures the proud spirit of the poem from the opening lines:

Arms and the heroes, who from Lisbon's shore, / Thro' seas where sail was never spread before, / Beyond where Ceylon lifts her spicy breast, / And waves her woods above the watery waste, / With prowess more than human forc'd their way / To the fair kingdoms of the rising day.

In the second canto the treacherous Moslems – "faithless race" – prepare to attack:

On shore the truthless monarch arms his bands, / And for the fleet's approach impatient stands: / That soon as anchor'd in the port they rode / Brave Gama's decks might reek with Lusian blood: / Thus weening to revenge Mozambique's fate, / And give full surfeit to the Moorish hate...

In the world of the Portuguese discoverers, the enemy forces take their strength from the netherworld:

As when the whirlwinds, sudden bursting, bear / Th' autumnal leaves high floating through the air; / So rose the legions of th' infernal state, / Dark Fraud, base Art, fierce Rage, and burning Hate: / Wing'd by the Furies to the Indian strand / They bend; the Demon leads the dreadful band, / And in the bosoms of the raging Moors / All their collected living strength he pours.

At Vasco da Gama's request, the chronicler aboard the ship retells Portugal's history, and, in this section, recounts the "glad assistance" brought by the crusaders who helped take Lisbon from the Moors. *Their vows were holy, and the cause the same, / To blot from Europe's shores the Moorish name. / In Sancho's cause the gallant navy joins, / And royal Sylves to their force resigns. / Thus sent by heaven a foreign naval band / Gave Lisboa's ramparts to the Sire's command.* ∎

shortages of meat and grain. Even the Crown was in debt, as the cost of the trading empire rose higher than its revenues. It was, of course, many years before these flaws and inabilities truly sank the empire. Trade continued for several centuries, although it steadily deteriorated.

At home: Before the slide began, the lucrative age of empire did bring sufficient peace and prosperity for Portugal to sustain truly great eras of artistic and humanist achievement. João II had taken over from the flighty Afonso V in 1481. Revitalising the throne, he managed to take up where Henry the Navigator, who died in 1460, had left off. João turned away from the nobility, minimising their rights and calling upon the *cortes* for support. A conspiracy soon gathered against the king, but he learned of the central traitors soon enough to strike back. In 1484, the Duke of Bragança was briefly tried and beheaded. When other members of the nobility fled the country, their titles and holdings reverted to the Crown.

The Duke of Viseu, who was both cousin and brother-in-law, unwisely mounted a second plot, and was stabbed by the king himself. Another group fled the country, and João II was in full command.

The prestige and authority that these fierce, Machiavellian tactics had given to the monarchy would stand undiminished for centuries. However, João's successor, Manuel I, had to steer a course between the ferocity of his predecessor and the idealistic nobility of Afonso V. This was accomplished with diplomatic and farsighted administration. The estates of the noble families were largely restored, though this did not restore their political power. Judicial and tax reforms worked to bring authority to government on both the national and local levels. The postal system was instituted. Public services like hospitals were centralised. And essentially, Manuel lifted the power of the monarchy above both the nobles and the *cortes*, launching the first era of enlightened absolutism.

Importance of education: Manuel also fostered contacts with the Renaissance humanism then spreading throughout Europe. There were many trade, religious and cultural contacts with Italy, in particular, and young

Portuguese men began to seek education abroad, at the universities in France or Spain. Manuel actually tried to buy Paris's renowned Saint Barbara College. Though he failed, it became a centre for Portuguese students. By 1487 a printing press had been established in Lisbon. Portugal entered the 16th century with a rush of new cultural currents.

New colleges and educational reforms were basic elements of the next century's progress. Teaching methods were modernised and the curriculum expanded. The students were drawn from a larger pool, including aristocrats and wealthy bourgeois in addition to young members from the religious orders.

These changes were not without crises.

The University of Lisbon had a cultural and political influence that threatened the Crown. It was difficult to impinge on its traditional autonomy, but Manuel, as part of his process of centralisation, tried to force change through economic and legal pressure.

Finding great resistance, he turned to the idea of founding a new university elsewhere, without success. João III continued these efforts, later giving control of national education to the Jesuits and quashing the University of Lisbon. It was a victory for the monarchy. There would be no university in Lisbon again until 1911.

Nonetheless, the century inspired a broad-

Left, bust of Camões. **Right**, baroque decor in the library at the University of Coimbra.

ranging intellectual vigour. Some of the works produced were directly attributable to the expeditions. Travel books, of both scientific and cultural themes, were a rich vein of literature.

Tomé Pires wrote *Suma Oriental* (1550), which described his voyages in the East. Many of these wandering writers were Jesuit missionaries, whose concerns with converting the natives led them to make careful sociological and ethnological observations. The most renowned traveller, the Marco Polo of Portugal, was Fernão Mendes Pinto, whose *Peregrinação* (*Pilgrimage*) brought imagination and lively style to the form. Among the historians of this period were

Fernão Lopes, who wrote a history of João I's reign, and João de Barros, who chronicled the conquests in Asia.

The courtly verses typical of King Dinis's reign were still very popular, but the strong influence of the Italian Renaissance broadened the themes of poetry. Out of the troubadour tradition, but going far beyond it, was Gil Vicente, the founder of the Portuguese theatre, who wrote scores of satirical and comic one-act plays. Vicente began life as a goldsmith, and in *Farsa dos Almocreves* he writes himself into a farce about an impoverished nobleman. When the goldsmith asks, eloquently, for long overdue payment, the

nobleman equally eloquently procrastinates:

> How most cunningly inlaid
> And enamelled is each word!
> I rejoice not to have paid
> For the sake of having heard
> Phrases with such skill arrayed.

In the second half of the 16th century, a new group of writers emerged, including António Ferreira, Diogo Bernardes, and, the most renowned of all, Luís de Camões. *Os Lusíadas,* Camões's masterpiece, is an epic national poem celebrating the discoveries that was first published in 1572. It is a classic of world literature.

However, these great writers aside, Portugal's main contributions to the intellectual ferment of the Renaissance were in science, particularly in navigation, astronomy, mathematics, and geography. The contribution was not the mere accumulation of facts from foreign places. New methods amounted to a kind of scepticism, a science based on experience. Having disproved a dozen theories of the shape, limits, and contours of the earth, the Portuguese felt free to question the other dogmas of antiquity.

Yet even as new writers and new sciences were coming to the fore, a Counter-Reformation (though there had been no real Reformation, the Portuguese Catholics having an essential antipathy to the simplifying and icon-destroying Germanic philosophies) was casting a pall of religious conformism over learning and creativity. In addition, the political threat to Portuguese autonomy – the future union with Spain was already an undercurrent – hung over all these achievements. In fact, Camões, Vicente and many of the others wrote as much as half their works in Castilian, the rest in their native Portuguese.

Portuguese Inquisition: João III ruled from 1521–57. He continued Manuel's expansion of the trade empire and royal authority. Perhaps his most significant act was the establishment of the Inquisition in Portugal. The Inquisition was intended to be a tool of the monarchy, and for a time it was. Eventually, however, it took on a direction and authority of its own. The Papacy knew that there was no real need for it, no menaces to the unity of faith in Portugal, so resisted its introduction. But João III used every diplomatic intrigue at his disposal and finally won approval for a greatly limited version in 1536. In 1547 those restrictions were lifted.

With this turn of events the rule of João III turned, too – away from the humanist influences of Europe and toward religious fanaticism. The bureaucracy of the Inquisition expanded quickly, its main target being the converted Jews known as New Christians. The victimised group was persecuted as much for their role as middle-class merchants as for religious deviation. The power of the Inquisition grew quickly, with the inquisitor-generals taking orders from Rome. They had the right of excommunication and, utilising the spectacular *autos-da-fé*, soon had an influence far beyond their legal authority.

The influence of the Inquisition, with its rigid orthodoxy, vengeful judiciary, and general intolerance, was equally deadening to both culture and commerce. Many of the bourgeois leaders of trade were targets. Later, the Inquisition would virtually govern Portugal, usurping the authority of the monarchy during the union with Spain.

The accession of King Sebastião in 1568, when he was 14 years old, only exacerbated these excesses. His regency, from 1557–68, was a period of stability, though marked by signs of trouble to come. The Inquisition grew. The *Casa da India*, the national trade corporation, went into bankruptcy in 1560.

An unstable and idealistic king, with a dangerous streak of chivalry like Afonso V, Sebastião took upon himself the crusade against the Moors of North Africa. A lack of funds prevented him from undertaking the task for many years. In the meantime he surrounded himself with cohorts no older and no more sensible than himself, dismissing the warnings of older, more prudent statesmen. Finally sensing that the time was right, he spent every *cruzado* he could raise on mercenaries and outfitting his troops. He set sail for Morocco in 1578. Sebastião was no better a military leader than administrator, madly dismissing stratagem and planning as cowardice. He refused, for example, to consider the possibility of retreat – and therefore had no plan for it. Outnumbered and outmanoeuvred at the Battle of Alcacer-Quiber, his army of 18,000 men was destroyed. Some 8,000, including Sebastião and most of Portugal's young nobility, were slaughtered. Only 100 or so escaped. With this debilitating disaster, the way was open for Spain to step in. From 1578 to 1580, Cardinal Henrique was king, occupied primarily with raising the ruinous ransoms for the captured soldiers of Alcacer-Quiber. In 1580, Philip II of Spain invaded and within a year was installed as Philip I of Portugal.

Left, João III by Cristovão Lopes. **Above**, an *auto-da-fé* (execution of heretics) procession.

THE CONQUERORS ARE CONQUERED

Throughout their rule over Portugal, the Spanish Habsburg kings faced many challenges to their authority. Not the least of their problems was that King Sebastião kept rising from the grave. After the massacre at Alcacer-Quiber, a devastating blow to national pride, there arose a popular belief that the lost Portuguese king would rise again. Consequently, a number of false Sebastiãos tried and failed to reclaim the throne.

At the root of the continuation of the Iberian Union was the support provided by merchants and traders. The Dutch and other countries were strongly challenging Portuguese shipping, slicing into vital profits. It was supposed by the bourgeoisie that by combining Spanish and Portuguese interests, the maritime empire could be reclaimed. The "alliance" with Spain would also open up inland trade. At any rate, there were few options: Portugal's treasury was empty.

Politically, the union was accomplished by Philip II of Spain. After Alcacer-Quiber, a number of candidates had aspirations to the Portuguese throne. Though his genealogical claim to the throne was more tenuous than his competitors', Philip II was a far more viable ruler than any of them. He was the grandson of Manuel I. The majority of the populace was opposed to the Spanish king, but the relatively impoverished nobles, clergy, and upper bourgeoisie saw that Philip could provide fiscal and military stability. Ironically, the most powerful group to resist the union were the *Spanish* ruling classes, who saw the danger of untrammelled Portuguese trading within their traditional markets.

Part of Philip's appeal was that he promised to maintain Portugal's autonomy: no Spanish representation in Portuguese legislative and judicial bodies; no change in official language; the overseas empire would still be ruled by Portugal; no grants of Portuguese assets to non-Portuguese; and so forth. Philip took up residence in Lisbon. In 1581 he summoned the *cortes* to declare him king with the title Philip I.

After the years of mismanaged govern-

ment, the efficient bureaucracy of the union provided relief. However, with the succession of Philip II (III of Spain), the Spanish began to press their powers too far. Lacking Philip I's diplomatic savvy, they bungled relations between the two countries, and tried to correct their mistakes through force. Resistance grew. Philip III managed to succeed to the throne in 1619, but the union continued to erode. Spain was weakened by its involvement in the Thirty Years' War with France. Portuguese troops were forced into battle and taxes increased.

The 60 years of union with Spain did nothing to protect Portugal's empire. Between 1620 and 1640, Ormuz, Baia, São Jorge da Mina and many more trade centres fell. In 1630 the Dutch established themselves in Brazil; in 1638 they took Ceylon. There were still ports and territories controlled by the Portuguese traders, but the "monopoly of the seas" was an era quickly fading from memory. What's more, to a country once intent upon ridding the earth of the last vestige of the infidels, it was devastating to surrender their missions to the Dutch, purveyors of the heretical Protestantism.

For the Portuguese, each of the three Philips

Left, a 19th-century political cartoon satirising Napoleon. **Right**, one of the movers and shakers of the Restoration, Antão de Almada.

who reigned over them was worse than the last. Philip II did not even deign to visit the country for years after his coronation. Philip III systematically breached all the guarantees put in place by his grandfather. The incipient revolution was aided by secret diplomatic agents sent by the French, who were still embroiled with Spain in the Thirty Years' War.

The Bragança regime: On 1 December 1640, a coup in Lisbon reflected the growing revolutionary fervour. The palace was attacked and the reigning Spanish governor, the Duchess of Mantua, was deposed and arrested while her strongman, Miguel de Vasconcelos, was fatally defenestrated. The Duke of

Bragança, though he had been reluctant to lead the revolt, was declared King João IV. So was ushered in Portugal's final royal period, as the House of Bragança would hold power until the 20th century.

Most of João IV's 16-year reign was occupied in hapless efforts to form diplomatic ties in Europe. France, England, Holland, and the Pope all refused to confirm Portuguese independence. Only Spain's preoccupation with other battles, some heroic Portuguese military stands along the frontier, and a well-organised national administration managed to hold the restored independence.

When he ascended the throne in 1656,

Afonso VI was still a minor, although his youth was the least of his problems. Later, married off to a French princess, he associated with base criminal elements and, worst of all, proved to be impotent, a fact elicited from the public inquiry that was necessary to annul his marriage. He was eventually usurped by his brother, who ruled as Pedro II.

War with Spain waxed and waned from 1640 until 1655. It was 1668 before the Spanish officially recognised Portugal's independence. In 1654 a treaty of friendship and cooperation was signed with England, a useful link, but also the first step down a primrose path that guaranteed Portugal's economic subservience to Britain for centuries to come. In 1661 a treaty was also signed with Holland, and the alliance with England was sealed by the marriage of Princess Catarina to Charles II. Included in her dowry gifts to England were Tangiers and Bombay. These moves sparked a new round of battles with Spain. In 1665 a decisive Portuguese victory at Montes Claros ended the fighting.

Pedro II became prince-regent to his brother in 1668, was officially crowned king in 1683 and ruled until 1706. His long reign, though stable, was deeply marked by an unrelenting economic depression. The spice trade was almost entirely out of Portuguese hands, while trade in sugar and slaves went through periods of competition and crisis when Portugal could ill afford such instability. On the mainland, olive trees and grape vineyards offered good profits, but they were largely controlled by British interests. Grain shortages were common throughout the era.

Two of Pedro's finance ministers, the Count of Ericeira and the Marquês of Fronteira, helped plan numerous factories. Glass, textile, iron, tiles and pottery industries were all supported by the state in an effort to balance national trade deficits.

The mercantilist approach made some headway, but what finally dispelled the economic gloom was the discovery of gold in Brazil. With a constant stream pouring in, Portugal could once again rely on the exports of wine, olive oil and sugar. The infant industries sputtered and halted. The Count of Ericeira committed suicide, while Fronteira renounced his previous economic philosophy.

Even before gold, Brazil offered a number of valuable commodities: sugar, cotton, tobacco, and some spices and dyestuffs as well. The husbandry of cattle started slowly, but by the end of the 17th century was providing lucrative exports of meat and leather.

The Jesuit missionaries were extremely influential in Brazil, as both explorers and settlers. Among other things they held the brazilwood monopoly for over two decades (1625–49). More importantly, they were successful in winning over the native populace to Christianity, and in large part preventing their enslavement. But the abundant colonial economy naturally had much need for native labour, and the Jesuits were pressured to step aside, though they had the clear support of Rome in the form of a papal bull (1639) that threatened excommunication for the trading of natives.

In 1706, João V succeeded Pedro II, and began to spend the Brazilian gold with a vengeance. Taking his cue from other monarchs, particularly the French court of Louis XIV, he quickly earned the nickname "the Magnanimous". Palaces, churches and monasteries were erected, and support was granted to the arts and to education. Along with this extravagance came a moral profligacy. Convents around Lisbon were converted from religious houses into aristocratic brothels, while the inhabitants were still nuns, more or less. Among the royal constructions were palaces to house João's numerous bastard sons, born of various nuns.

When João died in 1750 his son José succeeded him, but proved to be more interested in opera than in matters of state. The full power of the crown was entrusted to a diplomat, Sebastião José de Carvalho e Melo, who eventually earned the title by which he is better known, Marquês de Pombal.

Enlightened absolutism, as typified by the ministry of Pombal, represented both a beginning and an end. The enlightenment ideal of rationalism meant a leap toward modernity, while the concomitant republican ideal of social equality meant that royal absolutism was on its last legs.

Pombal's insistence on exercising royal prerogative sounded a death knell for the political power of nobles and clergy alike, and, quite unintentionally, allowed the bour-

geoisie to take over administrative and economic control. His was an oppressive, dictatorial rule, though he was careful never to claim any personal power.

The great earthquake: In 1755, on All Saints' Day – just as Mass was beginning – Lisbon was destroyed by a massive earthquake. Estimates vary, but at least 5,000 people were killed in the initial impact, many while attending morning services. Many more died later. Fallen church candles quickly ignited the wreckage around them. Survivors rushed toward the safety of the Tagus, only to be met by a massive tidal wave.

In the weeks afterwards infected wounds, epidemics and famine increased the death

toll, which may have been as high as 40,000. The Jesuits tried to fix the blame for this divine retribution upon Pombal's wayward and "atheistic" policies. He weathered both their criticism and their plot to assassinate him. The Jesuits' power throughout Europe was dissolving, and in 1759 they were officially disbanded and exiled from Portugal.

The catastrophe that shook the country's faith allowed Pombal's policies of secularisation and rational government to take firm hold. He took absolute control, and with the order to "close the ports, bury the dead, feed the living", began reconstruction. José granted his minister emergency powers

Left, Pedro II, a more potent leader than his brother Afonso VI. **Right**, scene in Lisbon harbour during the earthquake of 1755.

(which were not rescinded for some 20 years) and Pombal used them to rebuild Lisbon according to an eminently neoclassical plan, both neatly geometric and functionally sound. The social and legal distinction between old and "new Christians" (Jews) was abolished. Pombal's economic reforms helped Portugal remain stable when Brazilian gold production waned around 1760. And he managed to rebuild Lisbon without depleting the state treasury.

As Pombal's sponsor-king José neared the end of his reign, the Marquês plotted to force the crown-princess Maria to renounce her rights so that her son José, a disciple of Pombal, could continue the policy of despot-

Both Maria's political and personal health were badly shaken by news of the French Revolution in 1789. In 1798, long after her behaviour had become an embarrassment, she was declared insane. Her son João, an awkward and nervous man, took over the crown as regent, officially becoming king after Maria died in 1816.

The Portuguese monarchy and nobility feared that the French Revolution, and to a lesser extent, that of America, might be contagious. They were particularly wary about the possibility of democratic insurgency in Brazil. Though gold exports from that country were on the decline, they were quickly being supplanted by beef, cotton and to-

ism. The efforts failed and Maria, a pious but somewhat unbalanced woman with no sympathy for Pombal's oppressive rule, took over in 1777. She immediately tried the former minister for various crimes against the state and of course found him guilty, confining him to his estate rather than prison, out of deference to his age.

Though she revived religious elements of a government and culture that had been increasingly secular, she allowed most of Pombal's very necessary economic and administrative reforms to stay in place. Her reign was conservative with steady, if slow, economic progress.

bacco. In 1793, Portugal sent troops to fight revolutionary France, further aligning itself with Britain and against French-controlled Spain. In 1801, Spain invaded in the War of the Oranges. Portugal ceded various political concessions, and lost forever the town of Olivença.

In 1807, Napoleon delivered an ultimatum to Portugal, in which he demanded that Portugal declare war on Britain, and, specifically, that it close its ports to British shipping. But Portugal could not possibly turn on its long-term allies. Napoleon was defied. While the royal family speedily sailed to Brazil for safety, the French General Junot marched into Lisbon. Initially, the Portuguese government offered no resistance.

In July 1808, Britain came galloping to the rescue under the leadership of the master military tactician, Sir Arthur Wellesley, who was later dubbed the Duke of Wellington. The Peninsular War, sometimes called the War of National Liberation, lasted two years, expelling the French, but devastating the country. Three waves of attacks were halted by Portuguese victories at Roliça, Vimeiro, Buçaco, and the famous Lines at Torres Vedras. The wars left the country in rocky shape. Portugal's capital was now located across the ocean in Rio de Janeiro and the nation's general weakness fostered Brazil's

the revolution that would break out in 1820.

The British military occupation, under the leadership of Marshal William Beresford, though necessary and sometimes appreciated, further undermined Portuguese self-determination. British control had been growing throughout the 18th century. The Treaty of Methuen (1703) established their dominance of the wine industry and generally served to stifle industrialisation in Portugal. Various treaties continued this relationship, and in 1810, Portugal was forced to cede to Britain the right to trade directly with Brazil, eliminating its rôle as middleman. In this and in other ways Portugal was taking on all the aspects of a British protectorate with Mar-

claims for autonomy. In 1815 Brazil was declared a kingdom on an equal footing with Portugal.

The French (and English) had sacked many national treasures in Portugal, stealing paintings, sculptures, jewellery, books. The regency in Lisbon showed no intelligence in their rule, governing with uncoordinated despotism, ignoring the burgeoning democratic groundswell. The monarchy's blindness to contemporary political ideas fostered

While Carlotta Joaquina led the debaucheries at Queluz (left), the citizens (above) rallied in the streets for the Liberal Revolution of 1820.

shal William Beresford wielding virtually dictatorial control.

Revolution: The roots of the liberal revolution of 1820 lay in the French influences picked up by various military and secret societies, especially a Masonic lodge called Sinédrio. One of the primary events that coalesced the movement involved a plot by one of these clandestine groups against British rule. A dozen conspirators were accused of plotting to assassinate Marshal Beresford in 1817. All of them were summarily tried and executed. Naturally, this brutal reprisal heated Portuguese resentment and fostered support for the Liberal movement. The tyranny of the British-dominated regime could no longer be denied.

In 1820, the Spanish Liberal movement won control of their government, providing further inspiration, as well as political support, for Portuguese Liberal forces. The moment arrived for Portugal when Beresford left the country to go to Brazil on a diplomatic mission to discuss the growing problem. His absence was the spark, and the Portuguese military revolted. The uprising began in Oporto, and eventually forced João VI to return from Brazil where he had been trying to ignore the turmoil at home. By the time he arrived, the new constitutional ideology was firmly in place. A constitution was

princess Carlotta Joaquina, who had made herself an epitome of the "old regime". She tried her best to make a Versailles of her palace at Queluz, surrounding herself with absolutists and engaging in outrageous royal decadence, begetting numerous children by various lovers. Her flamboyant leadership of the absolutist cause made her popular. However, the failure of her conspiracy to dethrone her husband in favour of her son, after which Miguel was banished to Brazil, marked the end of her influence.

The politics of the next 50 years were endlessly complex. In 1826 João VI died, leaving Pedro, his eldest son, who was still in Brazil, as heir to the throne. After failing to

adopted in 1822. The document was ahead of its time, with broad guarantees of individual liberties and no special prerogatives for nobles or clergy. It lasted only two years, but did succeed in legally ending the Inquisition.

Greedy for power: Portugal's profoundly conservative streak made the revolution a simple split between republicans and absolutists. New charters and new efforts to restore full-bodied monarchy kept the country unsettled throughout the first half of the 19th century. In 1824, for example, João VI resisted a conspiracy of royalist extremists led by his own wife Carlotta and his son Miguel. João's queen was the notorious Spanish

unite the two kingdoms through political manoeuvres, Pedro chose to stay in Brazil, abdicating the Portuguese throne to his seven-year-old daughter, who became Maria II. Pedro's plan was that the girl would marry her uncle, the exiled Miguel, who would rule as her regent under a moderate constitution.

Miguel had other ideas. Upon his return he abolished the constitution and invoked a counter-revolutionary *cortes* to name him king. There was considerable popular sup-

Above, King Carlos and his heir, Luis Filipe, now honoured in death, were assassinated by revolutionaries in 1910.

port for these moves, but still enough sympathy for constitutional ideas that Pedro could return and eventually defeat his brother in what were known as the Miguelist Wars. Pedro had abdicated his Brazilian empire so that he could defend his appointment of Maria II.

Pedro died in 1834 and his daughter, now 15, finally took the throne as Maria II. She reigned until 1853, during which time the first political parties developed. The liberals, victorious over absolutism, divided into conservatives and progressives. The *Septembrists*, given their name for their revolutionary victory in September of 1836, came into power first. They initially restored the constitution of 1822, but then adopted a more moderate one. They were opposed by *Chartists* who took their stand, and name, from the conservative charter of 1826.

In 1839, as the Septembrists were suffering from internal disagreements, the Chartists came to the fore. Supported by the Queen, they were led by Costa Cabral and took power in 1839. Costa Cabral's government was authoritarian, and, though it provided stability, became more and more corrupt and autocratic. In 1846 a popular uprising named after the woman who sparked it, Maria da Fonte, demanded his downfall. Maria II tried to replace him with the equally conservative Duke of Saldanha, a grandson of Pombal, and the country stood at the edge of civil war. English and Spanish intervention prevented mass violence, but resulted in Costa Cabral being returned to power. In 1851, without a war, Costa Cabral was ousted for good and Saldanha took his place.

The early period of Saldanha's rule was a period of transformation out of which came the political divisions that would exist throughout the century. Saldanha introduced a compromise to the constitutional debate that allowed his new party, *Regeneração*, to encompass both the old Chartists and the moderate progressives. The amendments to the constitution allowed for direct elections and an expanded electorate. Those who were still more radical, a small group at first, would become known as the *Históricos* and then *Progressistas*.

In 1853 Maria II died in childbirth. Her husband, the German Duke Ferdinand of Saxe-Coburg-Gotha, ruled as the regent until their son Pedro V, came of age in 1855.

Pedro, a young but wise ruler, died in 1861 and was succeeded by his brother, Luís I. The constitutional monarchs judged best tend to be those who most avoid politics, and the change from the meddling Maria to the literary Luís was a clear victory for the republican government. Among his other accomplishments, King Luís translated Shakespeare into Portuguese.

The reign of Luís lasted until 1889 and was a period of relative peace. Conservatives and liberals alternated in controlling the legislature. Portugal's external affairs were more or less dictated by England, their protector under the Congress of Vienna's partitioning of smaller countries under major powers. Portugal was, however, tenacious in holding on to many of its colonial claims and territories in Africa. The high expense of maintaining those colonies was a burden to the rickety national economy, but it would stand them in good stead when the holdings finally did pay off during the 20th century.

In the meantime, Portugal's finances at home were a muddle. The havoc wrought by the Peninsular and Miguelist wars, on top of the loss of Brazil, was insurmountable. In 1889, Carlos I became king, setting African expansion as his primary goal, but his efforts were unsuccessful. In 1892, Portugal declared bankruptcy.

Carlos, still dreaming of restoring the empire, could do little to defuse the growing anti-monarchical sentiment. Socialism and trade unionism were growing influences. The legislative *cortes* had degenerated into a powerless assembly full of obstructive and self-promoting debate. Corruption and inefficiency were rampant.

In 1906, struggling to maintain some form of control, Carlos appointed João Franco as Prime Minister, endowing him with dictatorial powers. He quickly dissolved the useless legislature. In 1908 unknown parties, either members of a republican secret society or isolated anti-monarchical fanatics, assassinated Carlos as well as his son Luís Filipe, heir to the throne. In the assault upon the royal carriage, Manuel, the king's second son, was wounded but survived. In the next two years Manuel II tried to save the monarchy, offering various concessions, but the assassination had served to fortify the republican movement. The long-decrepit House of Bragança finally crumbled into dust.

great grandfather became a young man and left Portugal for the U.S. (pre-Ellis island) (1908 or farmer?) an urbanite (Lisbon learned) or a fisherman

REVOLUTION AND EVOLUTION

The paths of Portuguese cultural development in the 19th century followed many of the same byways as the country's politics. The influence of the rest of Europe was both heavily felt and intermittently resisted. The slow turning from conservative romanticism to modern rationalism was experienced as a series of shocks.

Arts and literature were greatly influenced by politics, even during the romantic period. The energies of both liberal and conservative intellectuals were turned outward; they were forever in the process of "rebuilding" their nation. Thus, the best Portuguese prose was in essay form, the best poetry and drama was in satire, and historical writing flourished. Among the celebrated literati of the era were Alexandre Herculano, who wrote both historical fiction and a monumental history of Portugal, and the brilliantly versatile Almeida Garrett, best known for his drama, but also a writer of poetry, novels, and essays.

The conflicts of the 19th century were encapsulated in the "Coimbra question". Two groups of university scholars stood divided. The older group, led by the blind poet Castilho, advocated the virtues of the status quo, while the "generation of 1870", as they became known, called for revision of both intellectual and spiritual values. They were rationalist, anticlerical, and antimonarchist. In their writing could be heard the first strains of emerging socialist thought. Their daring critiques, however, were suppressed by the government in 1871.

But the rising tide of republicanism could not be stopped. As the century drew to a close, the democratic ideal was combined with a nationalistic utopian vision, a shift that was hoped would return Portugal to its long-lost glory. The national anthem adopted in 1910 echoed the theme: "Oh sea heroes, oh noble people… raise again the splendour of Portugal… may Europe claim to all the world that Portugal is not dead!"

The assassination of Carlos sealed the victory of republicanism; but it took time for the

Left, the first Republic is proclaimed in 1910 and Joaquim Teófilo Fernandes Braga forms an anti-clerical government.

SALAZAR

António Oliveira worked as an overseer for absentee landlords around the village of Santa Comba Dão, halfway between Viseu and Coimbra. He was known for his austerity, strong faith and stringent supervision and was known as *O Manholas* – "The Crafty One". His only son, António de Oliveira Salazar (born in 1889), took the conservative values of his father far beyond the small rural world that formed them, ultimately transforming the whole nation of Portugal into his image of what it should be.

Salazar, as a professor of economics at Coimbra, was an active polemicist for the right, expressing

his political faith in the slogan "Nothing against the nation, all for the nation."

He had made his first political impact as the youthful leader of the Centro Académico de Democracia Crista (Academic Centre for Christian Democracy), a Catholic intellectual group that opposed the anticlerical and individualistic philosophy of the Republic. He made a brief foray into national politics but only accepted political position when he could be assured of complete control. In 1928 General Carmona, as Prime Minister, offered Salazar the role of Finance Minister with absolute power over national finance. In 1932, he was appointed President of the Council of Ministers – Prime Minister.

Although there was scattered opposition, and various plots on the dictator's life, his pervasive influence on Portugal would not truly lift until the April revolution of 1974, six years after a disabling stroke and four years after his death.

Salazar's character is best read in the character that he imposed upon the nation. An introvert, he seldom travelled out of Portugal, perhaps taking some pride in that mark of cultural purity. In the same way, Portugal steered through international affairs with neutrality where possible.

Portugal accepted Salazar's fascism as a kind of defensive posture to the worldwide technological explosion of the 20th century. His conservative and at times reactionary attitudes toward industrialisation, agricultural reform, education and religion kept Portugal out of the traumatic turbulence of the age. His attitude that Portugal was a naturally poor country – good for living but not for producing anything – was widely held. Catholic cults, like that of Our Lady of Fátima, were encouraged and turned into propaganda for the regime.

Salazar also drew upon the romanticised history of the Portuguese exploration and trade, inculcating a generation of schoolchildren to the self-aggrandising idea of Portugal's manifest destiny as an "empire". They turned inward, though still holding their colonies where possible, and tried to ignore the changing face of world politics. It was a comforting if finally debilitating attitude. Portugal, after all, would eventually have to catch up.

He lived quietly, taking modest vacations by the shore or in his beloved Beira countryside. He remained unmarried, though he had a close but apparently celibate relationship with his lifelong housekeeper, Dona Maria de Jesus Caetano, who raised his two adopted daughters.

On 3 August 1968, in his fortress sanctuary in Estoril, Salazar's chair collapsed. The Prime Minister hit his head, developing a stroke that left him an invalid. With little turmoil, Marcelo Caetano, a brilliant lecturer, though weak politician, was made Prime Minister.

For the rest of Salazar's life, which lasted less than two years, he enjoyed few visitors and little public attention. Strangely, those close to him chose not to tell him the truth about the succession of Caetano. They fabricated a Portugal still led by Salazar. When Dona Maria tried to convince him to retire, he refused and, in a last pathetic boast, said that he had no choice because there was no one else. ∎

various parties and coalitions to sort themselves into a workable government – practically speaking, they never did. Between 1910 and 1926 there were 45 different governments, with most of the changes being brought about by military intervention rather than parliamentary procedure. The early leadership pressed their radical anti-church and social reforms too hard, causing a reaction that revived the influence of the Catholic church. Labour movements sprang up with the best intentions, but often paralysed industry. First and foremost, the republicans were unable to deliver promised financial reforms and stability, both through their own ineptitude and, later, because of the interna-

Portugal, initially neutral, joined the Allies under Britain's influence in 1916, but World War I meant little to the nation except further financial upheaval. In 1926, the democratic government was overthrown by military forces and the constitution was suspended. Leadership passed through various hands and finally to General Oscar Carmona. He would remain as president until 1951, but it was not his leadership but that of his most influential appointee that made stability possible. In 1928, Carmona appointed António de Oliveira Salazar to the post of Finance Minister, with wide-ranging powers. By 1932, Salazar was effectively Prime Minister.

Salazar's regime: Salazar immediately

tional depression of 1920s. It was their economic failure that most significantly eroded their popular support.

Afonso Costa rose to leadership of the Republican factions, but the hard stance of anticlericalism caused too much ill feeling to allow stability. Coups became standard. General Pimenta de Castro grabbed control briefly, but democratic forces deposed him. Sidónio Pais formed a dictatorial government in 1917, but was assassinated in 1918.

Left, Salazar makes a speech. **Above**, shrine of Fátima, the focus of a Catholic cult which produced propaganda for the Salazar regime.

straightened out the country's disastrous financial morass, mostly through narrow-minded austerity reflecting his personal habits. Having done what no leader had been able to do for a century, Salazar used his political capital to form what amounted to a dictatorship, taking Mussolini's Italy and fascists in general as his models for national order and discipline.

The "New State", though nominally a corporative economic system under a republican government, was a fascist regime, with National Union its only political party. It was authoritarian, pro-Catholic, and imperialist. A state police organisation, the PIDE, was notorious in its suppression of subversion. A rigid and effective censorship settled like a thick fog over art, literature and journalism. Nothing negative or critical could find its way into print. An example of the absurd extremity of the New State's repression was when a censor in Mozambique replaced the word "muddy" with "blue" in the sentence "...the South African fleet had arrived in the muddy waters of the bay on a courtesy visit to Lourenço Marques." The formerly lively national journalism withered away. In blatant doublespeak, the government often referred to itself as a dictatorship without a dictator.

There was some resistance. In reaction to

The minor flourishing of culture of the republican era, when democratic ideals had encouraged efforts at mass education, a proliferation of journalism, and a few writers of modern fiction and poetry, was slowed by political upheavals, and effectively quelled with the advent of the New State. The greatest writer of the period, the poet Fernando Pessoa, was not "discovered" until after World War II, when most of his works were first published, posthumously. Few others transcended the romantic nationalism of the era, as formidable barriers to the larger currents of European culture were created. In any case, the censorship of the New State slowed original thinking to a trickle, and

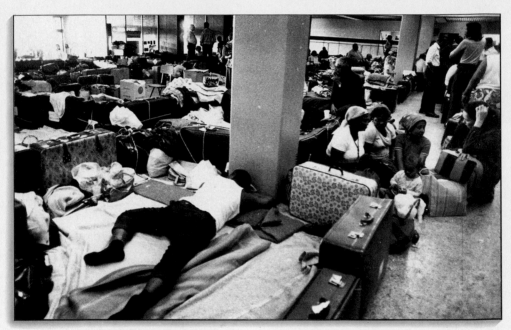

the powerful militaristic control of the country, there were numerous attempted coups and an underground Communist party that grew in power, leading the clandestine opposition. However, Salazar's leadership was never strongly challenged.

Putting self-preservation ahead of ideology, Salazar pretended to adhere to the League of Nations' nonintervention policy during the Spanish Civil War, because he could not afford international censure, but actually sent a great legion of soldiers – as many as 20,000 – to aid Franco's Nationalist forces. Franco's victory served to validate the authority of Salazar's own regime.

most of that was devoted to political subversion. Of course, this was nothing new to a country that had been dominated by the Inquisition for so many years. In the whole 500-year history of Portuguese publishing, little more than 80 years have been free of oppressive censorship.

After the war: During World War II, the New State again sensibly concentrated on self-preservation. Though Salazar admired Hitler, Portugal's traditional political and economic ties with Britain demanded at least

<u>**Above**</u>, the *retornados* pour into Lisbon after the end of the colonial wars.

neutrality. However, Portugal did supply the Axis with much needed wolfram (the ingredient necessary to alloy tungsten steel) almost until the end of the war. On the other hand, the Allies were granted strategic bases in the Azores. In fact, the war's main effect – though it was not widely advertised – was to replenish Portugal's coffers as they did business with both sides. The defeat of the fascists did serve as a signal to Salazar, a warning to mute his totalitarianism, but he was by now firmly entrenched. The changes over the next decade served primarily to protect the dictatorship still further from democratic insurgency.

In the 1950s, opposition to the New State solidified into two blocs. The one, legal, took advantage of the relaxed censorship in the month preceding elections (the state's way of giving the impression of free elections) to run independent candidates. The other, furtive, organised various protest actions and engaged in what propaganda they could. These means kept resistance alive, forcing Salazar's hand. Their actions required new rounds of repression, deceit, and constitutional changes that eroded both Salazar's authority and popularity.

In 1958, General Humberto Delgado, a disenchanted member of the regime, stood for President, announcing among other things that he would use the constitutional power of that position to dismiss Prime Minister Salazar. Despite the mass demonstrations in his support, the "official count" elected instead Admiral Américo Tomás, a Salazar loyalist. Afterwards, constitutional decrees were enacted to prevent the repetition of such an election. The President was to be elected not by popular vote, but by an electoral college of the National Assembly, which was Salazar-controlled. Delgado was assassinated in 1965 by state police, while attempting to cross the Spanish border into Portugal.

Portugal's entry into the United Nations had been prevented by the Soviet bloc and by opponents of Salazar's imperial colonialism until 1955. Membership was finally granted not because of any real change, but by a successful diplomatic effort to whitewash his despotism. Salazar would not actually alter his policies because, despite the increasingly higher cost of maintaining military rule in the colonies, they were very profitable for the homeland. Subsistence crops were increasingly neglected in favour of crops like cotton, to feed the mills of Portugal while the native Africans went hungry. The policy of *assimilado* – claiming that the national goal was to assimilate the local culture into Western, Portuguese culture – allowed Portugal to exploit these "citizens" as virtually free labour.

Despite international pressure, and increasing agitation within the colonies, the regime fiercely resisted any incursions on its colonial outposts, to extreme and sometimes ridiculous lengths. For example, in 1961, the territory of São João de Ajuda consisted of a decrepit fortress and the governor's estate, a tiny enclave surrounded by the country of Dahomey. That year Dahomey had become independent from France, and had delivered an ultimatum to Lisbon to return Ajuda. Waiting until the last possible minute to surrender this tiny sliver of territory, the Portuguese governor spitefully burned down the buildings before departing.

Salazar's imperial intransigence had far more serious consequences elsewhere. An explosion of African nationalism was set off by the violent 1961 Angolan uprising that was brutally crushed in a Portuguese military reaction. Throughout the 1960s, the government was more and more economically and militarily involved in maintaining the colonies, which had been renamed "provinces" in a 1951 decree that semantically underscored the insistence on a permanent Portuguese settlement. Meanwhile, the stagnation of Portugal's home economy grew more oppressive. Hydroelectric power projects were successful, but industry and agriculture fell more and more behind compared with international standards. Emigration, a national issue for more than a century, once again began to take a serious toll on the country's demographic resources.

Many young men were conscripted, and popular support for the wars in Africa waned quickly. Angola continued to be an economic boon, but the other colonies were a drain. Salazar, in response, trusted fewer and fewer members of the regime, taking on more direct responsibilities for continuing the wars. He also relaxed his policy of fiscal austerity, and increasingly relied on foreign credit to finance the overseas operations.

Acting Prime Minister: In 1968, a chair collapsed under the 79-year-old Salazar. He suffered an incapacitating stroke, and the long awaited succession had arrived. Because Salazar had made no provision for a successor – unwilling to face his own mortality – major upheavals were expected. But the transition to "acting" Prime Minister Marcelo Caetano (while Salazar lived his final years in seclusion) was relatively smooth.

Caetano, once a protégé of Salazar, had resigned seven years earlier over conflicts with his superior. Now called upon to resolve the national crisis, he saw the need for balanced change and stability. But he was not bold enough. Though many of the gravest injustices of the old regime were righted,

the power structure. Though many factors had built toward the revolution, this famous publication lit the fuse. Caetano himself felt its importance, saying later that he began reading it in the late evening and "did not stop until the last page, which I read in the small hours of the morning. And when I closed the book I understood that the military coup, which I could sense had been coming, was now inevitable."

Bloodless coup: Two months later, on 25 April 1974, after a few premature uprisings, a nearly bloodless coup began in Lisbon. Involving Spínola and fellow General Costa Gomes, it was conducted by angry "young captains" who commanded the 27 rebel units

other changes were superficial, and the colonial issue was not confronted. And when his early efforts at liberalisation failed to appease opposition unrest, Caetano returned to oppressive hostility.

Discontent among all ranks of the military over the continual and ineffective wars in the colonies led to the formation of the Armed Forces Movement (MFA) in 1973. In 1974, General António de Spínola published *Portugal and the Future*, a stinging and comprehensive critique of the current state of affairs that recommended a military takeover to save the country. The book's messages had been heard before, but never from so high up

that seized key points throughout the city. One of the signals used to coordinate the coup's launch was the playing of a song on the radio. The song "Grândola, Vila Morena", about a town where the people governed themselves, became an unofficial anthem of the movement. Caetano and other ranking government officials took refuge in the barracks of the National Republican Guard, a building that was once a convent. The formal surrender came after a young officer threatened to crash a tank through the gates. The rebel takeover was quickly accepted throughout the country. The revolution, taking the red carnation as its symbol, sparked nationwide celebration culminating in joyous demonstrations on the first of May.

The initial government was a National Salvation group of military men, designed to give way to a constituent assembly as soon as it was practical. A provisional government was soon in place, and negotiations with African liberation movements went ahead. The government was divided over the new overseas policies, and an odd coup within the coup developed, with Spínola attempting to wrest control from his opponents. It was unsuccessful and liberal forces continued to divest Portugal of its colonies. Guinea-Bissau, Mozambique, the Cape Verde Islands, São Tomé and finally Angola were granted inde-

pendence. One of the disastrous results of this sudden change was a mass immigration of Portuguese nationals back to their homeland. As many as 500,000 people flowed into Lisbon and other urban centres.

In 1976, with the economy in dire straits, a socialist-influenced constitution was adopted, and Mário Soares, leader of the Socialist party, was appointed Prime Minister. The next decade brought little stabilisation. The Socialists fell in 1977, then

Left, Prime Minister Mário Soares signs the entry of Portugal into the EC in 1986. Above, the Chiado area was ravaged by fire in 1988.

rose again as part of a coalition government with the Social Democratic Central Party. But it fell again the next year, replaced by a government of technocrats that lasted just 17 days. Small, powerful groups were ranged throughout the political gamut, keeping the government in turmoil. Among the various short-lived governments was an interim period led by the first woman Prime Minister, Maria de Lurdes Pintassilgo. At the end of 1979, a coalition of the right took power.

In 1982 the long-awaited revision of the constitution finally arrived. The Democratic alliance and the far right were determined quickly to rid that document of its Marxist taint. They were partially successful after a period of nationwide demonstrations, strikes, and resignations. The Council of the Revolution, a powerful overseeing branch of the former arrangement was eliminated, but the hope for a truly classless society remained a signal goal, mentioned in Articles 1 and 2 of the document.

In the next few years, the country witnessed a shift away from socialism toward capitalism. Although the veteran socialist leader Mário Soares was elected President in 1986 (the first civilian to hold the post in over 60 years) and re-elected by a landslide in 1991, the capitalistic Social Democrats under youthful economist Anibal Cavaco Silva won an overall majority in July 1987. In 1991, after a campaign based largely on his own forceful personality and on his claims that his government has wrought nothing less than an economic miracle, he won another resounding electoral victory.

Such stability allowed Portugal to emerge from being the most backward economy in Europe to being by the early 1990s one of the most buoyant. In 1986, it joined the European Community and in 1992 proudly took its turn at assuming the presidency of the EC.

Among Cavaco Silva's most successful programmes has been the reprivatisation of many companies and industries that had been nationalised under Communist pressure after the Revolution. These poorly managed national resources are regaining vitality as private enterprises. For a change, the Portuguese are looking within for economic viability – expanding industry, agriculture, education – and putting behind them their glorious but obsolete history of adventuring and colonising.

Defining a national character is never simple. The Portuguese themselves, with considerable self-mockery, endlessly profess despair at facets of national identity – if there is such a thing. Travel writers tend to portray the Portuguese as easy-going, smiling, patient, good-natured but imbued with an inner *saudade*, a feeling variously defined as nostalgia or melancholy. Certainly the local people offer a relaxed welcome to foreigners seeking sunny beaches, medieval architecture, the joys of the countryside, and Portugal's food and wines.

A natural courtesy tolerates cross-cultural *faux pas* and halting, phrase-book Portuguese (though English or French is quite widely spoken). For the visitor in a hurry, the worst Portuguese character flaw seems a resistance to consider passing time, though no discourtesy is intended when appointments are not kept.

The Portuguese have also faced more serious criticism. Writing in the 1930s, the great modern poet Fernando Pessoa criticised their "provincialism", meaning their naively uncritical appreciation of all things "modern" and "civilised": big cities, new fashions, and so on. Prime Minister Salazar, whose 40 years of oppressive rule still affect Portugal's character today, once commented bluntly, and unfairly: "The Portuguese are not a very intelligent people."

Paul Descamps, a Frenchman writing earlier this century, isolated permissive child-rearing as a key to understanding the national character. Though this may seem a specious argument, its conclusions make sense. Portugal is a matriarchal society and having been spoiled by mother, the Portuguese learn to operate by cajolery rather than diligence, to favour patience over perseverance. Raised permissively (in other words, with a lot of personal freedom), they grow up without great self-discipline, with only the vaguest sense of time constraints, and generally with

a streak of independence and an unsinkable self-esteem.

Generalities are great liars, however. Ten million individuals live in this country from whose ancient roots – its national boundaries are the oldest in Europe – has emerged, since the 1974 Revolution, a newborn fervour. Even the tempo is changing: Portugal is recently listed as having the fastest growing economy in the European Community.

In the bucolic backways of Trás-os-Montes and the Beiras, however, you may well feel

that you have stepped back in time. There are windmills on grassy knolls, cobbled roads from Roman times, and horse-drawn farmer's carts – some with handmade wooden wheels – that look extremely picturesque when piled high with the grape harvest.

Rural people generally distrust Lisbon and all that it stands for: social turmoil, taxes, bureaucracy, centralised education. They would rather keep their distance. Able to sustain themselves, if sometimes meagrely, by their harvests, they are fully aware of EC grants but have little interest in inflation or trade deficits. They are self-reliant.

This is not to say that national pride is any

Preceding pages: a Portuguese-French immigrant in the Upper Minho; Maria Lusa, Bruno, Marco, Eva and friend in Grandola; a lone traveller in Monsaraz; Cup Final day. <u>Left</u>, traditional dancer by the Douro. <u>Right</u>, a couple in Aldeia Solveira.

less vigorous here. Even the smallest town will boast its own museum, pretty church, or historical monument, and the residents are anxious that you visit and appreciate them.

In both city and country, there are ingrained social classes, but there is also a broad sense of equality. Every man expects to be treated with dignity. Manners tend to be elaborate, especially in forms of address. "Your excellency" is a standard form of address. Handshakes are exchanged at every encounter.

The fairer sex: Women, on the other hand, are on a separate footing. Feminist ideas are only beginning to be heard. A ground-breaking feminist collection of poems, letters and stories, *New Portuguese Letters*, was written

national mood – and of convoluted politics. It's true that the country, helped by EC funding, took a big leap forward in social, commercial, industrial and communication terms. But stability also saw the return of a familiar indifference to the shifts and turns of policy and to sharp-suited, self-seeking politicians whose doings helped fill the daily papers and, by 1993, four TV channels.

Beneath the face of contemporary life are the proud contours that are Portugal's history. Camões's *Os Lusíadas* is hailed as the seminal Portuguese work not only for its beauty and literary influence, but for its paeans to the discoveries and to national pride. In fact, this Portuguese identity – as

in 1972. There is legal equality, but a long way to go before attitudes change.

If in many ways the rhythm is slow and habits cautious, this is less to do with Latin temperament or sunny climate but more the effect of the Salazar era, even after some 20 years of democratic government. When the nation awoke from its long sleep, it experienced years of instability as governments rose and fell – 16 in the first 13 years after the Revolution. But when Social Democrats led by Anibal Cavaco Silva won an overall majority in 1987 (repeated in 1991), it was as if all Portugal, with a sigh of relief, could relax.

This is, of course, a simplification of the

explorers, colonisers, a world power – lent itself to dangerous illusions during Salazar's regime. The tendency to look overseas for answers to internal woes is only now being overcome.

Work: The control of many industries was usurped by the state in 1974, and though the policy over the last few years has been toward reprivatisation, a few remain stateowned. Unemployment, rampant in the 1970s, is relatively low, except among young people seeking first jobs. Long-term emigration in search of steady work causes strange demographics; almost as in wartime, young and old are left behind as workers part from their families and send home wages. Well over half the population, around 65 percent, lives a rural life. In industry and commerce, there are a few conglomerates; the large majority of companies are small- and medium-sized businesses employing, for the most part, fewer than 10 people – textiles and shoes topping manufacturing activities.

With a long coastline, fishing remains a strong vocation, as it has been for centuries. Agriculture has never been more than basically productive, despite the rustic image. Portugal's olive oil production, for example, just meets its own needs. Forestry is profitable (the spread of eucalyptus an ecological issue), with cork still a major traditional

tional product per capita at the beginning of the 1990s was $5,760, a figure expected to double within five years but still painfully low. Statistics on literacy or health services are also revealingly grim, though improving. A faster growth than its EC neighbours is a source of pride. More interesting, perhaps, to travellers is the fact that Portugal has the lowest pollution in the industrial world.

Family ties: Home and family life is a strong, stable framework of all Portuguese society. At the top everyone knows everyone, even across political boundaries. Families, especially in the north, tend to be large. The extended family is a common living situation, as grandparents help care for the

harvest. If port wine from the Douro river is among Portugal's most famous products, table wines from many newly designated areas are reaching new peaks of quality. Tourism contributes a high proportion of foreign earnings.

Salaries, though rising, are about a third of the European average, and Portugal remains at or near the bottom of the list of Europe's poorest countries with nearly 70 percent of the population living in poverty. Gross na-

children, and young adults – without any other housing option – often live at home until they are married.

Portugal is predominantly a Roman Catholic country, with a few Protestant communities, and a few Jews and Muslims, too. One interesting group is the so-called *Marranos*, hereditary Jews who converted during the 16th- and 17th-century prosecutions, and who retain some Jewish rituals sometimes in combination with a nominal Catholicism.

The Portuguese are sympathetic to unmarried couples. They adore babies and small children. They can be deeply superstitious: wax images in churches and herbalist witch-

Left, a carrier in Caria; time out for the latest gossip. **Above**, graduation day at the University of Coimbra.

ery in villages are commonplace. They love a rude joke and earthy gossip. With books, cinema, the arts in general the solace of a small minority, television is viewed by many – even the advertisements count as culture. More homes in Portugal, a 1991 census revealed, have television (94.8 percent) than a refrigerator (94.2 percent). Computers are commonplace in business; 8.4 percent of all homes had a personal computer.

Tolerance might be considered Portugal's prime virtue – capital punishment for civil crimes was abolished as long ago as 1867 and violent crime is rare. But behind the wheel of a car the easy-going nature turns too often to dangerous bravado. The urge to overtake has

given the Portuguese the dismal distinction of one of the highest accident rates in Europe.

Who owns these cars? Statistics state there is one car for every 6.5 people in Portugal (compared with one for every 2.5 people in the EC, and one to 1.5 in the United States). You will also see – and hear – numerous motorbikes and under-powered, overladen scooters. Laws, in theory, forbid high levels of noise or small children on bikes. These laws are frequently ignored by traffic police, who may well charge you steeply for not wearing the mandatory seat belt.

Traffic or judiciary police, the GNR – the National Republican Guard – continue to

have a role in a peaceful society. Uniforms that are disappearing are those of the Armed Forces, gradually being reduced to below 20,000 by 1996. Even compulsory service, still applicable, is being reduced, in many cases to periods of only four months. Women, for some time, have been welcomed in all three forces – Army, Navy and Air Force – whose pilots have publicly yearned for the better pay of civil airlines.

Education has been thoroughly modernised. Pre-school is an option for three-to-six-year-olds, while basic mandatory education is six years during the ages six to 14. In the age group six to 12 enrolment is 97 percent. Secondary education is not compulsory. Competition to enter university has become intense, as secondary school graduates have increased. A major issue in this volatile generation is a qualifying entry exam that many consider unrelated to their years of study.

To the Portuguese, their nation is an entity calling for a proper patriotism. Their *terra*, or homeland, is the place they truly love. A *lisboeta* cannot believe there is a city more beautiful than lovely, hilly Lisbon. The citizens of Oporto dote on their own granite city on the banks of the Douro river. The country displays surprising variations from region to region and quite clearly between north and south. Some of the differences are physical: in the north the basic Iberian strain – dark, thick-set – has been leavened with Celtic blood, while in the south, Jewish, Moorish and African ancestors are evident. The north is generally more conservative, both politically and culturally. It is the bastion of Portuguese Catholicism. The south has a tradition of liberalism and adaptation.

The two temperaments – the warm Mediterranean and cool Atlantic – wash over each other across Portugal. The people are as varied as the land that drinks at the banks of the Tagus and Douro rivers: bursting with verdure in Sintra, rippling with stark beauty in the Alentejo, and thundering up into the craggy Serra da Estrela. There is a saying that "Coimbra sings, Braga prays, Lisbon parades, and Oporto works." Nothing is that simple, but it is true that travelling here unveils not only a beautiful landscape but a rich panorama of humanity.

Left, Portuguese children have a lot of freedom, which produces (right) self-confident adults.

Early in the 6th century a young monk named Martin arrived in Braga. This former Roman city was now the political and religious stronghold of the Suevi, the barbarian tribe that had adopted Arianism, a heretical form of Christianity. Martin, inspired at the shrine of St Martin at Tours, was determined to convert these rulers to Catholicism.

Martin's parents came from Panonia (modern-day Hungary), the original home of the Suevi, so he was well suited for this particular mission. He founded an abbey at Dume, became a bishop, and, in 559, converted the Suevi king Theodomirus.

Martin found a further challenge, however, among the general population. Although Catholics since their conversion under the Roman Empire, the people had incorporated many local beliefs and customs into their religion. To Martin, this amalgam was unacceptable, and in a written sermon entitled *De Correctione Rusticorum* (On the Correction of Peasants), he called for the cessation of the use of charms, auguries and divination, of the invocation of the Devil, of the cults of the dead, fountains and stars.

In this St Martin of Dume did not succeed, nor have 14 centuries of similarly inclined zealots and reformers. All these elements are present to this day as an obstinate strain within the orthodox Catholic traditions. The north, in general, is the most devout section of Portugal – over 40 percent of adults attend Sunday Mass as opposed to about 10 percent in the south.

Naturally, there is still much wrestling over these issues between the church hierarchy and the parishes – the bishops have banned a certain Padre Miguel, a priest from an isolated northern mountain parish who was supposed to have healing powers. Yet, though frowned upon by the orthodox church, this spontaneous, independent Catholicism should not be seen as a form of pagan superstition or magic; rather, it is evidence of a vigorous religious tradition.

What are some of these still-current be-

liefs? When a newborn child proves healthy, it is said that it was conceived when the moon was waxing. The states of the moon are believed to be very influential in the way all vegetables, animals and humans grow. Similarly, certain fountains are reputed to have particular healing powers. And under many of these, Moorish princesses are said to be hiding, watching over treasures.

A variety of beliefs function to reassure people during the most frightening moments of the human life cycle. For instance, many

practices have evolved that are meant to protect children as they gestate in their mothers' wombs, or just after they are born. Thus, a newborn should not be taken out of the house during certain hours, to protect it against the "evil air"; and its father's trousers should be placed over the cot to frighten away witches; and the mother should not eat at the same time as breastfeeding, or the child may grow up to be greedy.

Around midnight: One of the more dramatic folk practices is the Midnight Baptism. This happens when a pregnant woman is prone to miscarriages or when her previous child was stillborn. The "baptism" takes place at mid-

Preceding pages: the Fátima devout in a candlelit procession. Left, solemnity at Good Friday in Braga. Right, St Anthony's festival in Lisbon.

night in the middle of a bridge that divides two municipalities – a powerful place that is neither one place nor another, at the moment that is neither one day nor the next. Certain bridges, such as the Ponte da Barca in the Minho, are famous for this. When all is ready, the father and a friend, armed with sticks, stand guard at the ends of the bridge. They are warding off cats and dogs – which may be witches or the Devil in disguise. The first person who passes after the church bells strike midnight must perform this rite. He pours river water over the expectant mother's belly and baptises the child "in the name of the Father, the Son and the Holy Ghost…" but the final "Amen" must not be uttered.

strongly felt sense of continuation with the past, praying together for "their" dead.

Perhaps the strongest evidence that the feeling of community extends beyond this life is the common belief in the "procession of the dead". Certain people claim that they have the power to hear or see a procession of the ghosts of those parishioners who have recently died. This procession is seen leaving the cemetery, with a coffin in its centre. When it returns, the ghost of the parishioner who will be the next to die will be in the coffin. Thus these seers predict how many people are going to die soon – but they cannot reveal their names if they themselves want to remain alive.

The child must wait to be born to be properly and baptised by the priest in church.

The church is the central meeting place of the whole parish. At Easter, the cross that represents the resurrection of Christ is taken out of the church to visit all the households. The cross is kissed as it enters each house, and when it returns to the church, it is a symbol of the new life shared by all in the community.

Similarly, on All Saints' Day and All Souls' Day (1 and 2 November), the celebrations at the parish cemetery are attended by all. Lamps are lit, tombs are cleaned and decorated with flowers. The whole parish celebrates this

The use of religion to establish a communal identity is most clearly shown by the celebration for the local patron saint. An organising committee busies itself all year collecting money, planning decorations, arranging events. The importance of these celebrations is immense. They represent and solidify local pride. The *festa* is a joyful occasion heralded by firecrackers and by music blaring from loudspeakers placed on the church tower. The pivotal event is the procession after the Mass, when the image of the patron saint is carried with great pomp on a brightly decorated stand in a roughly circular, traditional path.

After that, the lay celebrations begin. These usually involve a great deal of dancing to traditional brass bands, folk-dance groups and, nowadays, rock bands. Much wine is consumed and the festivities are a focus for young people, who use these opportunities as social mixers. It is this section of the celebration that the priests have opposed.

Popular attitudes to saints differ from church doctrine not so much in content as in emphasis. The people place great importance on material benefits and personal, reciprocal relationships with saints. They pray to specific saints for specific problems – St Lawrence for toothache, St Bráz for a sore throat, St Christopher for travelling, Our

gion is also more loosely interpreted than in the church. Essentially, a miracle is considered to have taken place every time a specific prayer is positively answered. The believer must then "pay" the saint whatever he or she had promised.

Wax offerings: When a prayer to St Anthony asks that a loved one, or even a pig, recover from a bout of ill health, a promise is made to give the saint something in return. A wax heart might be given for a successful engagement or a wax pig if the pig has fully recovered. If the promise is not fulfilled, punishment may follow.

If you visit churches in northern Portugal, you will often see these offerings hanging on

Lady of the Conception for infertility, the Holy Family for family problems, and so on. Also, people will have personal prayers to particular saints. If the believer's prayer has been answered, this proves that the particular image addressed is a singularly sacred one, a favoured line of communication. In this way shrines develop, whether individual, family, or even national, with images famous for their miraculous powers.

The notion of the miracle in popular reli-

the walls alongside other gifts such as bride's dresses, photographs, written testimonies or women's braids. Shrines of great fame such as Bom Jesus and Sameiro, near Braga, have large displays. At Fátima, the best known shrine in the country, wax gifts accumulate so quickly that special furnaces have been installed to burn them.

There is also another kind of gift: a personal sacrifice. Recently, the church has been strongly critical of this, but until the late 1960s, it was strongly encouraged. If you visit the shrine of São Bento da Porta Aberta (St Benedict of the Open Door), in the beautiful mountain landscape of Gerês near the

Left, the much-kissed crucifix makes another stop on its Easter Sunday rounds. **Above**, cemetery candle-burning on All Saints' Day.

dam of Caniçada on 13 August, you will find men and women laboriously circumambulating the church on their knees.

This scene is even more striking as these people are surrounded by others celebrating the day with song, dance, eating and drinking. Those on their knees are celebrating, too – because the saint answered their prayers.

Another shrine associated with such practices is the aforementioned Fátima, near the town of Leiria, in the centre of Portugal, one of the largest shrines in Western Europe. On 13 May 1917, the Virgin is supposed to have appeared to three children on top of a tree (two died young; the third, a Carmelite nun, was re-affirming her vision in the 1990s).

The event is said to have been repeated on the 13th of each month until October of the same year, and each time the Virgin spoke in a vague and allegoric way about peace in the world. Fátima soon became a rallying point for the revival of Catholicism in the 1930s and 1940s. Today, from May to October the roads around Leiria are lined with pilgrims, many of whom have come on foot from great distances to "pay" the Virgin for her favours.

Another kind of "payment" to the saints has all but disappeared now due to strong church opposition. In the parish of Senhora da Aparecida in Lousada, for example, before the main procession leaves the church,

another procession takes place. This is the procession in which 20 or so open coffins are carried – containing live people, their faces covered with white handkerchiefs. Those who ride in the coffins are offering a false burial to the saint who saved them from having to participate in a real one. The occasion, therefore, is a joyful one. There are plenty of light-hearted comments, and the participants mingle with the others afterward, drinking and dancing.

The cult of the dead, another morbid religious tradition, and one of the targets of St Martin of Dume during the 6th century, remains the object of popular fascination in the 20th. Occasionally, a body is buried but does not undergo the normal process of decay. Such people often are considered by the northerners to be saints. There are a number of such grim shrines where the corpses are exposed. The Church nearly always opposes these cults at first, but eventually tolerates them as they grow in popularity – three such are the Infanta Santa Mafalda in Arouca, the São Torcato near Guimarães, or the Santinha de Arcozelo near Oporto. Even in an unlikely spot like the small urban cemetery of the elegant neighbourhood of Foz in Oporto, a shrine of one of these "saints" can be found.

Along rural roads one will frequently find pretty little shrines. These contain an image of Christ or the Virgin or a saint. At the bottom, little moulded flames surround barely dressed figures who represent the souls of sinners suspended in Purgatory. These shrines are there to protect travellers.

Portuguese history is full of examples of the continuing conflict between the spontaneous and all-embracing religiosity of the less educated class and the more restrictive attitudes of the theologically learned. From the early days of the "western crusade" to the Knights Templar and their ilk to the dark days of the Inquisition, religion has vied with national authorities. Imperialism, like the early exploration, was seen as a form of religious crusade – each victory along the way was considered a miracle. Even Salazar's regime presented its policy of neutrality during World War II as based on the reported soothsayings of the Virgin at Fátima.

Left, the plaques are gifts given by grateful supplicants. **Right**, a floral offering to the Virgin in Lamego's cathedral.

"For me Lisbon was a very agreeable surprise," Evelyn Waugh wrote in his travel book *A Bachelor Abroad*. "There is no European capital of antiquity about which one hears so little." Without realising it, Waugh was echoing the impressions of others before him, among them Dorothy Quillinan, daughter of the poet Wordsworth. In 1845, she had written, "There is, I believe, no country in Europe that is less thoroughly familiar to me." The visitor to Portugal has always believed himself to be a discoverer of the one exotic land left in well-visited, well-described Europe.

Crusaders: Those ancient Greek and Roman sailors who made it to fair Lusitania left few written records of their impressions or opinions, noting only their belief that the sun hissed when it set off the Atlantic coast. In the centuries before Christ, the Greek historian Polybius remarked upon the fat tuna off the coast of Lusitania, and the geographer Strabo reported that the Cabo de São Vicente, the westernmost point of continental Europe, was shaped like a ship. Both these men were unknowing oracles of Portugal's future maritime greatness.

The 4th-century poet Avienus left us *Ora Maritime*, iambic verses in Latin about his sea journey along the Atlantic and Mediterranean coasts of Iberia. This poetic sea log would inspire the intrepid English writer Rose Macaulay more than 1,500 years later to retrace part of his route in *The Fabled Shore*, her book about Spain and Portugal.

The earliest full-scale account of travel to Portugal dates from the crusades, reputedly jotted down by, or addressed to, a British priest named Osbern. Before this bard ever set eyes upon Portugal, he had to make the crossing from Britain to the Iberian peninsula, a trip that was legendarily unpleasant. Frequently, on their way to the Holy Land, crusaders would stop at Santiago, in western Spain, to visit the shrine of St James of Compostela. The discomforting effect of the voyage on the constitutions of the pious

Left, early tour groups, like these crusaders, did not have the luxury of buses and occasionally kicked up a fuss about their accommodation.

through what Byron would later called "Biscay's sleepless bay", is depicted graphically by one unnamed medieval poet:

Men may leve all gamys,
That saylen to seynt Jamys!…
Thys mene whyle the pylgryms ly,
And have theyr bowlys fast theym by,
And cry aftyr hote maluesy,
"Thow helpe for to restore."

After the physically and spiritually restorative visit to the sacred bones of St James, the pilgrims would continue south, eventually entering the Mediterranean through the strait of Gibraltar.

In 1147 a band of crusaders – English, German and Flemish – broke their Atlantic journey in Oporto (some may have been shipwrecked), and were then persuaded by the new king of Portugal, Afonso Henriques, to join him on a side trip to seize Lisbon from the Moors. The Osbern chronicles sang the beauties of Lisbon first seen by the Britons – from the sea, of course. Its fertile countryside, lush with figs and vines, epitomised the seductive pleasures of the south. The 17-week siege led to victory for the Christians.

A number of English settled along the Tagus: the first Bishop of Lisbon, Gilbert of Hastings, was an Englishman. This was neither the first nor the last of such stopovers for the crusaders, but it was the most celebrated. It even became the subject of a poem written by the 18th-century translator of Camões, William Mickle:

The hills and lawns to English valour given
What time the Arab Moors from Spain were
    driven,
Before the banners of the cross subdued,
When Lisboa's towers were bathed in
    Moorish blood
By Gloster's Lance – Romantic days that
    yield
Of gallant deeds a wide luxuriant field
Dear to the Muse that loves the fairy plains
Where ancient honour wild and ardent
    reigns.

The Portuguese themselves had less happy memories of the crusaders from the north, whom they generally considered a loud drunken lot, given more to piracy than to piety. But the British, with their superior size and martial skills, would long feel a condescending pride in their Portuguese achievement, expecting gratitude and not a little obsequiousness from their allies to the south.

If the British crusaders were given bad marks for their plundering and their fondness for the local wine, the Portuguese could not be praised for their later persecution of British "heretics". From its establishment in 1536 to its final dismantling in the 19th century, the Inquisition got its unpleasant hands on a number of Englishmen. One of the first of these was the 16th-century Scottish humanist George Buchanan, who went to Portugal in 1547 to join the colony of educated men at the recently established

University of Coimbra. The death of his protector, André de Gouveia, left Buchanan vulnerable to the attacks of his enemies. He was then made to suffer many months in a squalid prison, ignorant of both his accusers and his crimes. He was brought before the inquisitors and interrogated numerous times. His crimes, he finally discovered, were writing impious verses against Franciscans, eating flesh during Lent, and being critical of the monks. After a year and a half he was sentenced. In his autobiography (written in the third person) he sounds surprisingly forbearing about the whole affair: "They enclosed him several months in a monastery, so

that he could be taught by the monks, men indeed neither inhumane nor evil, but completely ignorant of religion."

Buchanan fared better at the hands of the Inquisition than others who were unwilling to deny their religion to escape the horrors of the torture chamber. The Roman Catholic church was not, after all, Buchanan's sworn enemy, as it would be for later visitors from Great Britain. While the Enlightenment, with its principles of reason and tolerance, lit up England, the fires of the *auto-da-fé* still raged in Portugal. In 1770, John Marchant compiled an anthology of monstrous experiences of the Inquisition in Spain and Portugal called *The Bloody Tribunal*, or *An Antidote Against Popery*. In it he states the rationalist view of the Inquisition: "Conviction can only be wrought by reason and argument; a convert by necessity is no better than a hypocrite."

Marchant includes the horrifying account of Mr John Coustos, a British entrepreneur. Coustos came to Lisbon in 1743 to get a passage to Brazil, where he wanted to trade diamonds. His fierce loyalties to Protestantism and freemasonry inspired the wrath of the inquisitors. Coustos wrote:

"I considered that, being a Protestant, I should inevitably feel, in its utmost rigor, all that rage and barbarous zeal could infuse in the breast of monks; who cruelly gloried in committing to the flames great numbers of ill-fated victims, whose only crime was their differing from them in religious opinions; or rather who were obnoxious to those tygers, merely because they thought worthily of human nature."

Coustos, willing to die in the claws of these "tygers" rather than renounce his religion, managed to survive being tortured nine times.

For the most part Portugal was not a popular stopping place of the Grand Tourists of the 18th century. The modest list of ladies and gentlemen who published accounts of their travels in Portugal cannot compare with the massive catalogue of writers offering narratives about France or Italy. Henry Fielding, who might have left a worthy literary tribute to the Portuguese, instead bequeathed only his grave to Lisbon. The novelist, who went to Portugal in 1754 hoping the mild climate would help his dropsy, survived only two months. His lengthy *Journal of a Voyage to Lisbon* is devoted to the journey itself and offers no impressions of the country, except to say that Lisbon was "the nastiest city in the world". Not very charitable, but then, he was dying. Nevertheless, his grave in the English Cemetery in Lisbon has been a pilgrimage spot for generations of travellers. The 19th-century missionary George Borrow wrote in his idiosyncratic and brilliant travel book *The Bible in Spain* that the cemetery was "Père-la-chaise (the famous burying place of Paris) in miniature". He added that travellers, "if they be of England... may well be excused if they kiss the cold tomb, as I did, of the author of *Amelia*."

The grandest tourist: Without a doubt, the most flamboyant of 18th-century visitors to Portugal was William Beckford, who set up a sumptuous house in Ramalhoa near Sintra in 1787. He inspired Byron's Childe Harold, whose first stop on his pilgrimage to Portugal was to wander through Sintra conjuring Beckford's ghost and meditating on the brevity of life and pleasure:

There thou too, Vathek! England's
*   wealthiest son*
Once formed thy Paradise, as not aware
When wanton Wealth her mightiest deeds
*   had done,*
Meek Peace voluptuous lures was ever
*   wont to shun.*
Here didst thou dwell, here schemes of
*   pleasure plan*
Beneath yon mountain's ever beauteous
*   brow:*
But now, as if a thing unblest by man,
Thy fairy dwelling is as lone as thou!

Beckford first visited Iberia in 1787 shortly after the publication of his Gothic novel *Vathek*. The unorthodox Englishman, who had left England in the wake of a scandal over a homosexual affair, caught the fancy of the extremely pious Marquis of Marialva, who was convinced Beckford would convert to Catholicism. Beckford, meanwhile, as we learn from his diary, was desperate not for the salvation of his soul but for an introduction to the court of Queen Maria. England's ambassador Walpole had refused to perform this service for his disgraced countryman. The Marquis guaranteed an introduction if Beckford would become Catholic and abandon England. Beckford had no such inten-

tion and he left, petulant, without being presented to the Queen. By the time he was finally presented at court in 1795, Maria had long been insane.

Beckford's *Sketches of Spain and Portugal, Recollections of An Excursion to the Monasteries of Alcobaça and Batalha* and his diary give an idiosyncratic, slightly bitchy, aesthetically sensitive view of Portuguese art, music, nature and society. Beckford's Portugal is a land of the senses – he describes the haunting, erotic song called the *modinha* and the luxuriant beauty of the vegetation. (English plants he imported to his *quinta* in Ramalhoa grew strangely large and luxuriant in the southern clime.) Beckford's dia-

ries and travel journals provided a brilliant, if haphazard, guide to aspects of the art and climate of Portugal.

Byron: Beckford offers a pleasant alternative to the vitriolic portrait of Portugal left by the 19th century's greatest promoter of travel outside of Thomas Cook: George Gordon, Lord Byron. The poet left two accounts of Portugal, neither favourable: one in his letters home during his visit there in 1809, the other in Childe Harold's pilgrimage, *Canto I*. His hatred for the Portuguese has mystified and disturbed scholars and admirers of Portugal since it first appeared in print in 1812. There is no record of any encounter during his brief stay there that would have led to such dislike. Some of Byron's criticisms reveal a typical Anglo-Saxon ambivalence toward the South. Robert Southey, a romantic and the future English Poet Laureate, visiting Portugal 25 years earlier, had also been torn between his disapproval of the filth of Lisbon, the discomfort of the country inns, and the corruption and superstition of the priests; and his delight in the sensual orange groves, long lazy days and lush, fertile fields. William Mickle, an unqualified admirer of Portugal's "genial clime" contrasted the "gloomy mists" of England to the "sun-basked scenes... where orange bowers invite". This view of Portugal differs little

fair land that has been peopled by beasts. The most likely explanation for his anger is that the Portuguese felt resentful rather than grateful towards the British for their help in expelling the French invader, "Gaul's locust host", from their country during Napoleon's Iberian campaign. Byron probably, like many of his countrymen, also felt shame that at the Congress of Cintra (Sintra), Arthur Wellesley (later the Duke of Wellington) allowed the defeated French to evacuate with their loot, including many of Portugal's treasures.

That the Portuguese felt resentment rather than gratitude toward their northern liberators is testified to by another Englishman, George Borrow. Travelling in 1835, he was

from reflections on other southern lands – Italy or Spain or southern France. But while elsewhere Byron admires the southern spirit, his image of Lisbon is of a false and faithless harlot of a town, a southern siren who glitters beautifully from the water but who reveals, on closer contact, only filth and treachery:

But whoso entereth within this town,
That, sheening far, celestial seems to be,
Disconsolate will wander up and down,
Mid many things unsightly to strange see;
For hut and palace show like filthily...
Poor paltry slaves! yet born midst noblest
  scenes.

Byron's summary of Portugal is that it is a

miffed by the ingratitude of the Portuguese. Borrow, an eccentric itinerant minister, once left New Testaments and tracts next to the smouldering charcoal and broken bottles of a bandit campsite in the wild back country of Portugal. His impatience with Portuguese hostility to the English is similar to the way many Americans felt after World War II about French criticism of the United States: "I could not command myself when I heard my own glorious land traduced in this unmerited manner. By whom? A Portuguese! A native of a country which has been twice

Above, **invasion by the crusaders.**

liberated from horrid and detestable thraldom by the hands of Englishmen." He complains that the English "who have never been at war with Portugal, who have fought for its independence on land and sea, and always with success, who have forced themselves by a treaty of commerce to drink its coarse and filthy wines… are the most unpopular people who visit Portugal." But, unlike Byron, the pious if irascible Borrow attributed this not to the Portuguese nature but to "corrupt and unregenerate man".

Borrow is a wonderfully comic traveller, especially in his belief that after just two weeks he could speak fluent Portuguese. His advice to novices speaking a foreign language is the sort of wrong-headed lesson that tourists of all times can never seem to forget. "Those who wish to make themselves understood by a foreigner in his own language should speak with much noise and vociferation, opening their mouths wide."

Borrow's account of Portugal, less famous than the nasty stanzas from Byron, is a most original, entertaining and evocative description. He is a great reporter of human eccentricity. He is also quite enthusiastic about the beauties of Portugal, comparing them favourably to other more visited countries. Lisbon, he claims, "is quite as much deserving the attention of the artist as even Rome itself". Sintra, praised lavishly even by Byron, is "a mingled scene of fairy beauty, artificial elegance, savage grandeur, domes, turrets, enormous trees, flowers, and waterfalls, such as is met with nowhere else under the sun". It is truly, Borrow writes, "Portuguese Paradise".

Byron's attacks on Portugal led predictably to a positive reaction. In 1845 Dorothy Quillinan, William Wordsworth's daughter, set out to contradict "Childe Harold's rash and unlordly sneer". Her *Journal of a Residence in Portugal*, she had hoped, would "assist in removing prejudices which make Portugal an avoided land". Unfortunately her call was not heeded by many, and with the exception of the Danish Hans Christian Anderson's *A Visit to Portugal 1866*, which was never very popular in his time, none of the great 19th-century travel writers put down their thoughts about Portugal.

Dorothy Quillinan was hoping to inspire Americans to visit as well, but the closest any 19th-century American writers came was when Mark Twain visited the Azores. Read today, *The Innocents Abroad* displays Twain's deep streak of jingoism and blustery intolerance. Every land he visited crumbled when compared to the United States. He also tends to look at the natives as if they were the foreigners, not him. He comments upon the backwardness of the Portuguese islanders: "Oxen tread the wheat from the ear, after the fashion prevalent in the time of Methuselah." He continues with the real horror: "It is in communities like this that Jesuit humbuggery flourishes." The phony relics irk him. To Twain, backwardness is neither quaint nor romantic, but ignorant and un-American.

For 20th-century travellers, disenchanted with the progress which Twain touted with such vehemence, Portugal has provided an escape from modernity. Close to a hundred years after Twain visited the Azores, the Irish writer Leonard Wibberly would also comment on the backwardness of the Portuguese agricultural methods, in his charming and funny account of a year in Portugal, *No Garlic in the Soup*. He found much wisdom in sticking to the old ways.

For the 20th-century visitor, Portugal satisfies a nostalgia for the past. It is, after all, the last country in Western Europe to engage in full-scale modernisation and industrialisation. Wibberly devotes an entire chapter to "The Language of Oxen" in which he describes the mysterious way the farmers talk to their oxen when they're ploughing the fields: "Here was one of the most ancient agricultural cries in the world… It was a cry which Vasco da Gama, should he return to Portugal, would recognise immediately." The plough, he also notes, resembles those used by the Saxons in the dark ages. Wibberly cannot resist asking a farmer why he doesn't use a metal plough. His answer: "There must be work for the oxen to do." What may seem to be charming and quaint to the traveller is often the source of hardship and poverty to the native.

Portugal is fast modernising. The traveller will have to look a little harder for the land where Moorish minarets inspired the bloodlust of the crusaders or where William Mickle wandered through orange groves that stretched to the horizon, or where Beckford "trifled away the whole morning, surrounded by fidalgos in flowered bee-gowns and musicians in violet-coloured accoutrements…"

To dine in Portugal is to taste the presence of other countries, other cuisines. It is to conjure up images of empire. Brazil, Angola, Mozambique, Goa – these and others all belonged to Portugal once; in a manner of speaking, each helped to stir the pot.

The period of Portuguese Empire, when this small nation reached out across the terrifying "Green Sea of Darkness", as the Atlantic was called, has long passed. Yet Portugal, left with only Macau (until 1999), the Azores, and Madeira, has preserved the

in 1497–98, five years after Christopher Columbus's discovery of the West Indies.

Black pepper was what Vasco da Gama sought, but cinnamon, which he also found in Calicut, would soon become equally precious to Portuguese cooks. Indeed, one boatload of cinnamon sticks fetched enough money to pay for an entire expedition to India. Cinnamon is perhaps the most beloved spice in Portugal today, certainly for the famous egg sweets (*doces de ovos*). Spaniards, on the other hand, prefer vanilla for

flavours of other cultures in its cooking.

Prince Henry the Navigator, less than 30 years old when he began to promote exploration, was a true scientist in an age of superstition. He ordered his 15th-century explorers to bring back from new lands not only riches and wild tales, but also fruits, nuts and plants. In 1420, he sent settlers to colonise the newly discovered island of Madeira. With them went plants he believed would thrive in Madeira's volcanic soil and subtropical climate, including grapevines from Crete and sugar cane from Sicily. Even more significant for Portuguese cooking was Vasco da Gama's discovery of the sea route to the east

their puddings and flans. There's good reason for this. It was the Spaniards who found Montezuma sipping vanilla-spiked hot chocolate in Mexico and learned the trick of curing vanilla beans, the seed pods of a wild orchid. Perhaps this is why chocolate, too, is more popular in Spain than in Portugal.

More surprising than the Portuguese appetite for cinnamon, however, is their fondness for curry powder (another bonus of Vasco da Gama's voyages). In the beginning, only the rich and the royal could afford the precious yellow stuff, which pepped up the blandest dish – and also retarded spoilage.

Today, curry powder can be found in

supermercados everywhere. Its function, rather than to set food afire, is to mellow and marry the other ingredients, and add a muskiness to a large repertoire of soups and stews. The spiciest Portuguese dishes, incidentally, are not found on the mainland but in the Azores and Madeira. These islands were ports-of-call for the navigators, who would barter with the natives – offering spices in exchange for fresh fruits, vegetables and meat (and no doubt the local brew, too).

New food for old: During Portugal's lavish

and tender to the core, are teamed today with rosettes of Portugal's mahogany-hued, air-cured *presunto* (prosciutto-like ham) and served as an elegant appetiser in fashionable Lisbon restaurants.

Tiny, incendiary Brazilian chili peppers took root in Angola, another important Portuguese colony, early on, and became so essential to cooks there that today they're known by their African name, *piri-piri*. Since Angola ceased to be a Portuguese colony in the mid-1970s and the subsequent influx to

Age of Empire, Portuguese navigators became couriers, bringing New World foods to the Old and vice-versa. Mediterranean sugar cane, for example, was cultivated in Brazil. Brazilian pineapples were introduced to the Azores, a colony established under Prince Henry. They still flourish there in hot-houses, ripening under waftings of wood-smoke. Azorean pineapples, chunky, honey-sweet

Preceding pages: *al fresco* refreshments at Cascais; more elegant dining in Pousada Nossa Senhora de Oliveira in Guimarães. **Left**, sweet fried dough, and eating in the Alfama streets at festival time. **Above**, *carne de porco à alentejana*.

Lisbon of thousands of Angolan refugees, *piri-piri* sauce (an oil and vinegar mixture strewn with minced chilies) is as popular a table condiment in mainland Portugal as salt and pepper.

Other exchanges thanks to the Portuguese: African coffee was transplanted in Brazil, which today produces about half of the world's supply; Brazilian cashews landed in both Africa and India; and Oriental tea plants arrived in the Azores (interestingly enough, the Portuguese word for tea – *chá* – is almost identical to the Cantonese one – *ch'a*).

All of this fetching and toting of seeds, leaves, barks, roots, stems, stalks and cuttings by Portuguese explorers across oceans and continents dramatically affected Portuguese cooking. New World tomatoes and potatoes came to Portugal about as early as they did to Spain – in the 16th century. But Portuguese cooks, unlike the Spanish, might drop a few garlic cloves into the soup or stew along with the tomatoes and potatoes, or tuck in a stick of cinnamon.

It's unlikely that anyone grows nuttier, *earthier* potatoes today than the Portuguese. Indeed, along the New England coast in the US, where so many Portuguese families have settled, there's an old saying: "*If you want your potatoes to grow, you must speak to them in Portuguese.*" Tomatoes respond to

it's known that the Romans were making wine there as early as the 2nd century AD.

The Moors, who occupied a large chunk of Portugal from the early 8th to the mid-13th centuries, enriched the pot even more than the Romans. The southern provinces were the Moorish stronghold – the Algarve and Alentejo, in particular – and many visual echoes of North Africa can still be seen.

It was the Arabs who dug irrigation ditches, who first planted rice (it now grows up and down the west coast), and who covered the Algarve slopes with almond trees. The Algarve's almonds were ground into paste, sweetened, and shaped into miniature fruits, birds and flowers of intricate detail, still

the Portuguese touch, too, and those harvested in the vast Alentejo province, east of Lisbon, are as juicy, red and deeply flavourful as any on earth. Not for nothing does that French menu phrase, "*à la Portugaise,*" mean a dish that is richly sauced with tomatoes.

Onions and garlic, indispensable to any respectable Portuguese cook, were probably introduced by the Romans, who established colonies in Portugal. The Romans are believed to have brought wheat to Portugal, too. They aimed to make Iberia the granary of Rome. They also probably introduced olives (a major source of income today), and grapes. From shards found in the Alentejo,

produced today.

The Moors also introduced figs and apricots to the Algarve together with the tricks of drying them under the relentless sun. They planted groves of lemons and oranges and, as was their custom, they combined fish with fruit and fruit with meat.

Innovative cooks: Finally, it was the Arabs who invented the *cataplana*, a hinged metal pan, a sort of primitive pressure-cooker shaped like an oversize clam shell that can be

Above, *Bacalhau à Gomes de Sá*, one of the 365 recipes that keep Portuguese eating salted cod all year round.

clamped shut and set on a quick fire. The food inside – fish, shellfish, chicken, vegetables or a medley of them all – steam to supreme succulence. What goes into a *cataplana* depends upon the whims of the cook (and on what's available), but the most famous recipe is *amêijoas na cataplana*, clams tossed with rounds of sausage and cubes of ham in an intensely garlicky tomato sauce. This unlikely pork and shellfish combination was supposedly created at the time of the Inquisition to test Christian zeal. Pork and shellfish, of course, were forbidden to Jews and Moslems alike.

There is no shortage of examples of Portugal's culinary ingenuity. No one but a thrifty Portuguese cook with an eye on her *escudos* would have made bread a main course by layering yeast dough into a pan with snippets of chicken and sausage and two kinds of ham (this classic from the remote northern Trás-os-Montes is called *folar*).

Or who would have thought to crumble yesterday's bread into shrimp cooking water and come up with another favourite, the Estremadura classic known as *açorda de mariscos*. Or to braise duck with bacon and rice as it's done in the Serra da Estrela, or to smother red mullet the Setúbal way with tiny tart oranges, or to scramble flakes of salt cod with eggs and shoestring potatoes, as is done all over the country?

Cod country: Dried salt cod, or *bacalhau* (pronounced buckle-YOW), is a purely Portuguese invention. António M. Bello, first president of Portugal's gastronomic society, wrote in his *Culinária Portuguesa,* published in Lisbon in 1936, that the Portuguese were fishing Newfoundland's Grand Banks for cod within just a few years of Columbus's discovery of America.

The cod-fishing continues today, with the men putting to sea in spring and not returning until autumn. Sometimes, of course, they do not return; to see their widows dressed in black, some of them barely 20 years old, is to understand why so many of Portugal's poems, stories, folk sayings, even *fado* songs focus upon the nation's bittersweet seafaring tradition:

O Waves from the salty sea,
From whence comes your salt?
From the tears shed on the
Beaches of Portugal.

It was as early as the 16th century that Portuguese fishermen learned to salt cod at sea to last the long voyage home, to sun-dry it into board-stiff slabs that could be kept for months, later to be soaked in cool water before cooking. Cod is still sun-dried on racks the old way on the beach at Nazaré, although much less of it now. The Grand Banks have become so overfished that the Portuguese have taken to importing *bacalhau* from Norway just to be able to meet their annual demands. This puts the price of salt cod beyond the reach of the very people it sustained for centuries – the poor.

Someone once said that the Portuguese live on dreams and subsist on salt cod. They do claim to know 365 ways to prepare it, one for each day of the year. The best and most famous dishes are *bacalhau à Gomes de Sá* (cooked in a casserole with thinly sliced potatoes and onions, then garnished with hard-boiled eggs and black olives), *bacalhau à Brás* and *bacalhau dourado* (two quite similar recipes composed of scrambled eggs, onions and shoestring potatoes), *bacalhau à Conde de Guarda* (salt cod creamed with mashed potatoes) and *bolinhos de bacalhau* (cod fish balls, a particularly popular hors d'oeuvre). All of these once-humble recipes are served today even in the most expensive restaurants.

Very nearly as popular as salt cod are the sardines netted off the Portuguese coast. These are what the tartan-clad fishermen of Nazaré go out for day after day. Portuguese sardines are considered the sweetest and fattest in the world and Portuguese women grill them right on the streets in every town and village, using little terracotta braziers – but only in spring, summer and early autumn, the unofficial "sardine season". As every Portuguese knows, sardines are too bony to eat between November and April.

If salt cod and sardines share top billing as the favourite fish, pork reigns supreme as the king of *carne* (meat). Portuguese pork is incomparably sweet and tender because of its life of leisure and diet of acorns, truffles and chestnuts. In the northerly Trás-os-Montes province, they say if you want good pork in the autumn you must feed your pigs twice a day in August. Some farm women even go as far as to cook potatoes for their animals. Small wonder the hams (*presunto*) and sausages (*salsicha*) are so highly prized here (the best of all are said to come from

Chaves). Small wonder, too, that *charcuterie* figures so prominently in the regional soups and stews. Cooks here even wrap freshly caught brook trout in slices of *presunto*, then bounce them in and out of a skillet so hot the ham is transformed to a crisp, deeply smoky sort of "pastry".

But Portugal's most famous pork dish comes from the Alentejo. It's *porco à alentejana* for which cubes of pork are marinated in a paste of sweet red peppers and garlic, browned in the very fruity local olive oil, then covered and braised with baby clams, still in the shell. The clams open slowly under the gentle heat, spilling their briny juices into the ambrosial red muddle. The

secret behind achieving the distinctive nut-like flavour of Alentejo pork is that the pigs are turned loose each autumn to forage in the cork orchards. Here they are able to nibble on acorns and wild herbs, as well as the occasional truffle.

Sausage-making is also highly-prized in the Alentejo and this region's garlicky *chouriços, linguiças, farinheiras* (porridgey sausages plumped up with cereal) and chunky, smoky *paios* are without peer. As Portugal's food authority, Maria de Lourdes Modesto, writes in *Cozinha Tradicional Portuguesa*, "The grand destiny of the pig in the Alentejo is to become sausage."

Here, every part of the pig is used – ears, snouts, tails, feet – even, it would seem, the squeal. At carnival time, for example, the centrepiece of each banquet *festa* is *pezinhos de porco de coentrada*, dainty pig's feet braised with onions, garlic and fresh coriander.

Another province famous for its pork is the coastal Beira Litoral, particularly the little town of Mealhada, which is not much more than a wide place in the road about 20 km (12 miles) north of Coimbra. Here both sides of the highway are lined with restaurants that make suckling pig (*leitão assado*) a speciality. The piglets are rubbed with secret blends of oil and herbs, skewered from head to tail, then spit-roasted over white-hot hardwood coals until their skin is as crisply brittle as an onion's and their milk-white flesh so meltingly tender it falls from the bones at the touch of a fork.

Cabbage patch: The Portuguese national dish, ironically, is built neither upon salt cod nor pork. Its key ingredient is cabbage, specifically a richly emerald, tender-leafed variety (*couve gallego*). The dish itself is *caldo verde*, a bracing, jade-green soup which is brimming with potatoes, onion, garlic and filament-thin shreds of green cabbage. Sometimes the soup is fortified with slices of *chouriço* or *linguiça* although in the humblest Minho versions (it's here that the recipe originated), it often contains nothing more than water, potatoes, onion, garlic, cabbage and perhaps a tablespoon or two of robust olive oil.

To some people, "robust" may seem a euphemism. Portuguese olive oil, *azeite*, is richly aromatic – to critics, "rank". The distinctive flavour comes from harvesting methods. The festive December olive harvest is a casual event. The olives, once they are beaten down from their branches, are left to age lying on the ground, only gathered after a week or so. That, in addition to the hot-water pressing methods, accounts for their intense flavour.

Every Portuguese province now calls *caldo verde* its own, and it's not unusual to find kettles of it steaming in every kitchen. Indeed, *caldo verde* is such a staple in the Portuguese diet that plastic bags of minutely shredded *couve gallego*, ready to drop into the pots of potato broth bubbling at home, can be bought at Lisbon's Mercado da Ribeira and other markets – the ultimate in convenience food.

Country women, whether they grow their own cabbage or buy it at the local market, must cope with the whole head. A purely Portuguese sight is a small, ramrod-straight woman balancing cabbages on her head, sometimes six or eight of them at a time, as she goes about her shopping or chats with friends, completely oblivious to the burden she carries. Anyone who drives the back roads of Portugal will be awed by the inventory of items that Portuguese women balance atop their heads: crates of squawking chickens, baskets of laundry, terracotta water jugs, tables, chairs, even sewing machines!

tossed into the pot just minutes before serving so that its colour intensifies but does not "turn" to a paler shade.

Soups and others: The food of Portugal has often been referred to as the food of farmers and fishermen. Fishermen brew giant drums of *caldeirada* (literally, "kettle of fish") on the beaches at Sesimbra, Nazaré, Albufeira and Sagres, beginning with water (sometimes sea water), adding tomatoes, onions and garlic, then lean and oily fish in roughly equal proportion, and if their catch has been especially good, squid and/or octopus, too. No two *caldeiradas* are ever alike. One of the pleasures of visiting a deserted *praia* (beach) in Portugal is the chance of running into a

As for the preparation of *couve gallego*, every country girl learns, by the time she's grown head-high to the kitchen table, to shred it with the speed of light. The leaves are stacked, perhaps five or six deep, rolled into a fat cigar, then literally shaved as a razor-sharp knife is whisked back and forth across the end of the cabbage roll so fast the movements are scarcely visible. The fineness of the cut is what makes a bowl of *caldo verde* resemble molten jade; also the cabbage is

Portuguese cooks demand fresh food, which keeps the markets hopping. <u>Left</u>, Ribeira Market in Lisbon. <u>Above</u>, the fish market in Setúbal.

group of fishermen boiling up their latest catch. They're always willing to share.

Farmer's soups and stews are ever-changing, too, as country women constantly improvise with odds and ends – a bit of chicken from the Sunday dinner, a few *favas* (beans) left over from lunch, a handful of carrots, a dab of rice, some crumbles of yesterday's bread, and maybe some freshly minced mint or coriander. This is the way many of Portugal's great classic recipes were created.

Next to *caldo verde*, Portugal's most famous soup is probably *açorda à alentejana*, a coriander-strewn, bread-thickened, egg-drop soup seasoned, as someone once quipped, "with enough garlic to blow a safe". The soups and stews of Portugal – whether they're made of chick-peas and spinach (another Alentejo classic), of tomatoes and eggs (a Madeira speciality), of pumpkins and onions (a Trás-os-Montes staple), or of dried white beans and sausages (the universally beloved *feijoadas*) – are frugal and filling, nourishing and soul-satisfying. All they need for accompaniment are a glass of wine, a chunk of cheese and a crust of bread.

Bread and cheese: Does any country bake better bread? The simple country breads usually contain only four ingredients – flour milled from hard wheat, water, yeast and salt – but they're kneaded until their dough fairly

one for fresh produce (everything from potatoes to poultry); one for farm and winemaking equipment, and the fourth for the lace tablecloths, fancifully painted brown pottery and exuberantly decorated ceramic roosters of the region (these have become a national symbol).

Cheeses can be bought at country markets everywhere. The queen of them all is the ivory-hued *queijo da serra*, a cheese so strictly demarcated it can be made only from the milk of sheep grazing on the wild mountain herbs of the Serra da Estrela. At the peak of its season – winter – a properly ripened "*serra*" is as biting, buttery and runny as the finest Brie.

springs to life. And because they're baked in wood-stoked brick or stone ovens, they have a faintly smoky flavour. There are fancier breads, to be sure, notably the sweet festival breads, *pão doce* of Easter and fruit-studded *bolo rei* of Christmas. There are huskier breads, too, the rough round barley breads and, most famous of all, the *broas* – yeast-raised corn-breads of the Minho that are sold by the truckload at the merry market in the river town of Barcelos.

This country market is Portugal's biggest and best. Held every Thursday in a vast tree-shaded square, it's divided into quadrants: one for breads, cakes and other baked goods;

Portugal also produces a number of other cheeses that are a match for the world's best: the nutty, semi-dry *serpa* from the Alentejo town of the same name, which connoisseurs rank as the nation's second best (it's cured in caves and brushed regularly with paprika-laced olive oil); *beja*, a buttery semi-hard cheese from Beja, near Serpa; *azeitão*, lovely little rounds of gold, tangy and creamy, that come from the village of Azeitão on the Arrábida Peninsula just across the Tagus river from Lisbon. Finally, there are the *queijos frescos*, snowy, uncured cheese much like cottage cheese, which calorie-conscious Portuguese sprinkle with cinnamon.

Egg sweets: The Moors are thought to have introduced egg sweets to Portugal during their 500-year occupation. But it was the 17th- and 18th-century nuns of Portugal who glorified them – one reason, no doubt, why so many egg sweets bear such amusing names as "bacon from heaven" (*toucinho do céu*), "nun's tummies" (*barriga-da-freira*) and "angel's cheeks" (*papos d'anjo*).

Regardless of their names, what the dozens of different egg sweets share in common is a prodigious use of egg yolk and sugar. Many are flavoured with cinnamon, others with lemon or orange or almonds. Each, moreover, is shaped in its own traditional way – like little bundles of straw, for example, or miniature haystacks, even like lamprey eel. The Portuguese so love this ugly river fish they make golden egg effigies of it for festive occasions. A ritual practised at nearly every Portuguese restaurant, no matter how simple or sophisticated the presentation, is the pastry cart, a glittering double-decker trolley laden with *doces de ovos* (egg sweets) brought round at the meal's end.

Usually there are at least five or six choices – sunny little hillocks bathed in clear sugar syrup, flans decorated with siftings of cinnamon, individual goblets of rice pudding (*arroz doce*) as radiant as molten gold, flat yellow sponge cakes twirled up around orange or lemon custard fillings, tiny translucent tarts (*queijadas*) and a snowy poached meringue ring known as *pudim molotov* (one of the few egg sweets made out of the whites). All are beautifully presented.

The egg sweets of Portugal look irresistible. However, most of them, alas, are excruciatingly sweet and far too rich for non-Portuguese, contemporary, palates. The Portuguese, on the other hand, find that nothing complements – or follows – an egg sweet like a silky, syrupy wine. A vintage port, or a madeira.

Left, a hearty, but simple, lunch. **Above**, no shortage of fruit and vegetables.

Welcome relief: When you do choose a *doce* from the cart, you can at least be assured of a good cup of coffee to cut the sweetness. Coffee houses are a national institution, a gathering place morning, noon and night. It's actually not surprising for a country whose former colonies – Brazil and Angola – still produce some of the world's finest coffee beans.

The choice is usually a *bica*, a powerful espresso-like brew. *Café* is closer to American standards, but if you really miss your morning coffee, order *carioca*: half-café, half-hot water; it will still be pretty strong and very good.

The Romans first grew grapes and drank the wines of Portugal. They were followed by crusaders who, in 1147, helped Portugal's first king Afonso Henriques take Lisbon from the Moors, but they left a lasting distaste for their bibulous excess – these "holy warriors" had agreed to join the king's forces only after the Bishop of Oporto entertained them with "good cheap wine and other delights". Today, Portugal's port, the fortified wine that's virtually a national emblem, scintillating *vinhos verdes* and a range of first-class table wines are widely enjoyed. Sogrape, the largest wine-producing company, exports Mateus *rosé* – a brilliant marketing success – and other wines to more than 150 countries.

What's new above all, though, is the expanding range of excellent wines. Under European Community (EC) regulations, closely supervised by the Instituto da Vinha e do Vinho (Vineyards and Wines), wine areas are "determined" or "demarcated" under the code-like initials VQPRD, standing for Quality Wines Produced in Demarcated Regions. Twenty-eight newly "determined" areas mean that fanciers familiar with classic Bairrada or Dão wines can look with fresh interest to *zonas viticolas* like the exhilarating Douro, to little Cartaxo or Tomar in the Ribatejo, or the always popular Alentejo. The scene is an exciting one, but still port leads the field.

Port wine: Port as it is known today has been made since the 1830s. It developed by dint of the historic commercial alliance between the British and Portuguese. The British invested considerably in both its research and development, thus controlling the industry. Needless to say, the British populace acquired a healthy thirst for it and for hundreds of years were the primary bottlers and consumers of the product. Today, among the port lodges of Vila Nova de Gaia, the blending and storing place for these wines, you still find a high percentage of British names represented.

Port wine begins its life in the Upper

Left, a classic wine in the making? Young grapes ripening on the vine in Estremadura province.

Douro, an officially demarcated region whose boundaries cling to the banks of the Douro and its tributaries. A number of approved grape types grow here. The reds include Tinta Roriz, Tinta Francesa (a descendant of the French Pinot Noir), Touriga Nacional and Bastardo; among the whites, Malvasia, Esgana Cão and Rabigato.

The earth of the Upper Douro is the slate and granite "soil" of the river's banks, a craggy terrain that often approaches a slope of 60°. Into this unpromising territory countless hours of manual labour have been spent to create the terraced grounds in which the vine can prosper. The slate and granite first had to be broken up. Support walls were then built with the shattered stone to harbour the soil from erosion. Driving along the river, you see thousands of these walls, many of them nearly 300 years old. A haunting sense of timelessness pervades the area.

Come October, the silence on the great terraced slopes is broken when the harvest – *vindima* – begins. Groups of grape pickers, mainly women and girls, are specks in a vast landscape. Strong young men stride the terraces to carry 50 kilo (112 lb) baskets of grapes to waiting containers. At night, in some wineries, platoons of barelegged treaders tread the grapes to a purple must, accompanied by an accordion and encouraged by watching, dancing girls. In other wineries, rows of shining auto-vinificators silently perform the same function.

As new vineyards are planted, modern techniques – bulldozing and dynamiting – have made expansion economically feasible. Virtually all of the new area has been forged upriver, in the valleys of the Douro tributaries: the Pinhão, Tua, Torto and Távora. The products from around Régua and the Rio Corgo are now thought of as lesser wines. The regions producing the finest ports presently centre around Pinhão, some 20 km (14 miles) east of Régua, and extend to the Spanish border.

The famous shipping houses have their *quintas* in the hills of the Douro. These are often spacious white houses, clad in vines, that offer sanctuary from the heat and glare of summer, the dark chill of winter. It is here in autumn that the fermentation process takes place, interrupted by the addition of grape brandy, to create the raw, fortified wine. Young port then spends the winter at the *quinta*. In springtime, it is transported to the port lodges in Vila Nova de Gaia by truck, where it is blended and matured into a variety of styles. In times past, the port was shipped to the lodges in the lovely *barcos rabelos*, boats with large square sails. Restored *barcos rabelos* adorn the Douro's southern bank at Vila Nova de Gaia. During the São João *festas* in June these boats show their stuff in a cheerful regatta.

Vila Nova de Gaia, facing Oporto, has more than 80 port lodges; many may be all other ports: the majority of its ageing takes place in glass, not wood. From a legal standpoint, vintage port must identify itself as such, stating the name of its maker, the year of the vintage and carrying the governmental seal.

As bottle ageing progresses, vintage port "throws" a heavy sediment as heavier particles in the wine succumb to gravity. So it is important that the wine is stored correctly: horizontally, yet at a slight incline, wine in contact with the cork. When vintage port – or any ageing red wine, for that matter – is then opened, its contents will be disposed to decanting, a simple procedure whereby the clear wine is poured away from the accumu-

visited. It is here that you can learn the basic differences of port styles, aided, delightfully, by sampling the product itself.

Vintage port: The most famous and most expensive of the ports is the vintage variety. Representing only two percent of the entire annual port production, it is the crown jewel of Portuguese wines. It is produced from a single harvest's grapes and is "declared" only in years when the quality is deemed extraordinary. Vintage port is bottled after two or three years in wood. For example, the great 1963 vintage must, by law, have been bottled between 1 July 1965 and 30 June 1966. This is what distinguishes vintage from lated dregs. A properly stored bottle will facilitate this procedure.

Vintage port can be drunk as soon as 10 years after its vintage date, but most wines hit their stride after 15 to 20 years. 1991 was a year when several shippers "declared". 1985, 1983, 1980, 1977, 1966 and 1963 produced classic wines. Taylor, Graham, Croft, Noval and Ferreira are among a host of eminent port wine makers.

Crusted port: Crusted port differs from vintage port in that it needn't be from a single year, or vintage, but is mostly created from

Above, vineyards of the Ribatejo.

two or three different harvests. Crusted port spends extra time in wood, accelerating the wine's maturation. This extended ageing makes for a lighter-bodied wine. Like vintage port, however, crusted port throws a sediment and needs to be decanted.

Late bottled vintage (LBV) sees even more time in wood – from four to six years. As its name implies, the wine comes from a single year's harvest, but is much lighter in colour than vintage port and need not be decanted. Both the date of the vintage and the date of bottling must appear on the label. It is worth remembering that shippers generally do not offer late bottled vintage in the same years as real vintage port.

A confounding offshoot of the vintage-dated wines, "Port of the Vintage" or "Port with Date of Vintage" come from a single year, but will have been aged in wood for no less than seven years. The bottle will often say *Colheitas* (which means "vintage") and give the year; it will have the date of bottling and some indication that the wine has been aged in wood. The house of Nierport has a wonderful stock of these *Colheitas* wines. For all intents and purposes, these wines are the first step into tawny ports; that they are from a single vintage, however, prevents them legally from being so titled.

Wood ports: Wood ports are the bread and butter of the port trade. They are blended wines – from several harvests – that are matured in cask until they are ready for drinking. Because they are blended, it is the goal of the shipper to define his style through this wine so that year after year the customer can expect a consistent product. Three main types are ruby, white and tawny.

Ruby is young and hearty, not complex and not expensive. To a port drinker, it is the staple wine, attractive for its full, overt flavour. It is aged for two or three years in cask before bottling. One offshoot of ruby port is called "Vintage Character" port. This wine will have the same general features of ruby, but will be of a higher quality, usually older, and certainly more expensive.

White ports are also matured in wood. They can come from either red or white grapes. A white or clear colour can be obtained from red grapes by separating the juice from the skins during fermentation before the colour has been extracted. Winemakers have sought to popularise them by fermenting out the sugar, adding brandy, and marketing them as dry, aperitif wines.

Last, but by no means least, there is tawny port, a special blend of port wine from different vintages which sees many years in cask. Through the more rapid oxidisation process within a barrel, this wine matures rather quickly, evolving its tawny colour and fabulously scented bouquet. Tawny port is thus more mellow in style than the "vintage-dated" ports, but it is refined, pensive and self-esteeming.

Old tawnies are rather expensive, priced in correlation to the long years the wine has spent ageing in barrel. They should not be confused with the cheap tawny port available abroad. Cheap tawny port owes its existence to the strong world demand for a less concentrated, eminently drinkable port wine. The port shippers have handled this demand by concocting a blend of ruby and white port. The product is a simple wine of pinkish hue, in contrast to the fading russet of a true tawny. It will have none of the complexity that real tawny port gains through long ageing. Since the name "tawny" can apply to either wine, the consumer must rely on colour and price to distinguish between the two. Real tawny is not cheap; cheap tawny should never be expensive!

Among a wide choice, Ferreira, Noval and Taylor 10, 20 and 30-year-olds are fine examples of tawny port. Only the "real thing" will reveal why this is the wine which many port houses most prize and which many blenders enjoy as an all-day drink (and have even been seen to add ice cubes to).

Vinho Verde Country: The lush, green Minho area occupies just under 10 percent of continental Portugal, in the northwest corner. It is the country's oldest and most intensively cultivated wine land, the region of *vinho verde*. The Minho is a densely-populated province of cramped smallholdings – some 150,000 people are involved in viticulture. And the vine seems everywhere – along narrow roads, framing houses with pretty bowers called *ramadas*, across new, neat plantations of *cruzetas*, crosses with wire supports a tractor can reach, and still, in places, clinging to tall trees – though *vinho verde* does not, as a cheerful promotion had it, grow on trees. Nor, as its name suggests, is *vinho verde* a green wine.

Though no-one knows for sure, the eloquent phrase is believed to derive from the Minho's green, well-watered landscape, which receives up to 200 cm (78 inches) of rain a year.

Vinho verde, light and refreshing with an alcohol content of only 8 to 11 percent, is white or red, *verde branco* or *verde tinto*. It is made from fully matured grapes from varieties that include Azal, Trajadura, Alvarinho and Loureiro for the whites, and Brancelho, Pedral and Tinto Cão for the reds. The taste is dry, with many subtle shadings. The fizz – the *pétillance* of wine buffs, *agulha* to the Portuguese – is not added, but appears in the making.

First, the grapes are fermented to convert

spritely carbonation, the hallmark of *vinhos verdes*.

The *vinho verde* region was demarcated in 1908, and has six sub-zones. The differences in taste from grower to grower reflect vineyard setting, climate, the grape itself, but are also a result of the growing number of single-*quinta* producers. Notable estate-made *vinhos verdes* come from over 50 members of the Association of Producers and Bottlers of Vinho Verde who must produce wine only from their own grapes (not buy them, as bulk producers do). The effect is a range of wines produced in small quantities but with individual characteristics.

Much admired among single-estate wines

their natural sugars into alcohol. Then a secondary fermentation, called the malo-lactic, takes place, induced by naturally occurring bacteria. As you might guess from its name, this process converts malic acid to lactic; a harsher, more unpleasant acid into a milder, more palatable one.

While this secondary fermentation is common to wines made in many countries, the *vinhos verdes* are distinguished by their retention of the fermentation's by-product: carbon dioxide. From this comes that characteristic sparkle in the wine, which can vary – depending upon age, technique and storage – from a light tingle on the tongue to a

is the Palácio da Brejoeira *vinho verde* produced from a single grape variety, Alvarinho, in Monção. It is also the most expensive. You can, though, taste a good, and cheaper, Alvarinho made by the Adega Cooperativa of Monção.

Labels on Association bottles show their origin, often elegant ancestral homes in which you can stay in considerable comfort. These include Casa de Sezim near Guimarães, which dates to 1375 and has been in the family for 22 generations; and Paco d'Anha, near Viana de Castelo. Both distinguished houses make an estimable *vinho verde*. You will also find good quality *verdes brancos* from large producers like Sogrape or the Quinta da Aveleda. They are delicious, particularly with seafood or light meals.

Red *vinho verde* – it used to amount to more than half of all production – is much enjoyed by *minhotos* (people of Minho) but scorned by connoisseurs. A Portuguese oenologist, trying to explain its appeal after a tasting in which, yet again, it failed to please, once invited his foreign colleagues to a hefty dinner, accompanying it with a *verde tinto*. The wine went down surprisingly well, and the message was clear: you shouldn't try to taste it in isolation, but drink it with a generous meal, a heaped plate of meat or grilled sardines.

in Portugal. From the once-cherished Dão area, which in recent years has tumbled from its pedestal, comes Caves São João's good red Porto dos Cavaleiros (its Reserva among the very best Dão wines) or the Sogrape Dão Reserva; and, from Sogrape's technologically advanced winery, the old favourites Grão Vasco and Terras Altas.

Bairrada, a small area north of Coimbra, has held its reputation for classic wines, more than 80 percent red, mainly from the Baga grape. The whites include a pleasant *espumante*, or sparkling wine. Good Bairrada wines are made by Sogrape, Messias and Caves Aliança.

For something really special, though, you

Wine lists in many restaurants are helpfully divided into region as well as types of wine, and a knowledgable wine waiter can guide you. Among Portugal's best table wines are *vinhos maduros*, mature reds. All restaurants, whatever they stock, must also offer a house wine. Usually it will be considerably cheaper than others listed, but it will also be quite acceptable.

Wine regions: Truly superb wines, a few eccentric and many sublime, are to be found

Left, the older the better: vintage 1863 bottles of Ferreira port wine. **Above**, barrels of port await the next stage in production.

might head for the bizarre and extravagant neo-Manueline Palace Hotel do Buçaco, whose cellar of its own Buçaco wines, dating to the 1920s, is virtually a national treasure. Reasons to visit this unusual palace are numerous – the forest is enchanting, historical aspects intriguing, and you can stay in the suite occupied by the last king of Portugal. But if wine is your pleasure, and you have the resources, you can luxuriate for days eating classy food and sampling 30-year-old whites and 40-year-old reds.

You can also taste perfectly good Bairrada wines at the cluster of down-to-earth roadside restaurants that can be found in nearby

Mealhada, all offering the local speciality, *leitão*, suckling pig.

The Douro is the source of many of Portugal's finest table wines (even in the port region only 40 percent of the grapes go into port). Ferreira, a distinguished port wine producer, also makes the legendary Barca Velha, probably the finest of all Portugal's red wines. Other Ferreira reds include their Reserva Especial or the more accessible Esteva. Other top-ranking Douro wines are under the Quinta do Cotto label – Grande Escolha is one. As in other areas, Sogrape are conspicuous – Planalto is just one of their good Douro wines.

From nearer to Lisbon comes a variety of

good wines – the white from Bucelas a consistent favourite. Pleasant wines, too, come from the Colares area, just beyond Sintra, which is interesting, moreover, as its rootstocks are among the very few survivors of the phylloxera plague that struck all Europe in the 19th century. (Today's rootstocks for Portugal's own grape varieties are American, something of an irony because the catastrophic vine-devouring louse also originated in the United States.)

To the south of Lisbon two major wineries, confusingly with much the same name, are in Azeitão, near Setúbal. One, José Maria da Fonseca, makes a very popular red Periquita

and the excellent dry Branco Seco. If you care for sweet muscatel dessert wines, this is the place for Moscatel de Setúbal. The second and more modern winery (both may be visited) is J.M. Fonseca International, widely known for its very successful Lancer's red, white and *rosé* in their distinctive clay jars. Two eminent wines from the Setúbal area are João Pires and the deep red from the Quinta de Bacalhoa, both developed by the skills of Australian oenologist, Peter Bright.

Wines from Portugal's southernmost province, the Algarve, have never won much respect overseas (they are largely consumed on the spot by *Algarvios* and tourists) but the range of good wines made in the eastern Alentejo is another thing altogether. The quality of wines made in such towns as Borba, Reguengos and Vidigueira (from where comes a very good white *reserva*) is higher than ever these days.

Look, too, for the deep red and distinctive Esporão. In good Lisbon restaurants you will very likely be recommended an Alentejo red, not white, if you choose a dish of *bacalhau* (cod), the national favourite.

On the label: Changes in labelling may easily confuse you, if you are both a frequent visitor to Portugal and an interested observer and taster of wine. No winery these days is permitted to use its town name as a wine name, so you may have to look for wines you've enjoyed before – from the Alentejo towns of Borba or Reguengos, say – under new names with the estate and town name in small print below.

From a bottle of wine can come purest joy. The label too often needs explaining: *vinha* is vineyard, *quinta* farm or estate, *colheita* vintage or harvest, *região demarcada* demarcated area, *denominação de origem*, denominated area, *reserva* good quality wine, *garrafeira* top quality from a single private cellar, *engarrafado na origem* estate-bottled.

There's another word to look for: *aguardente*, brandy made by numerous wineries. Like many Portuguese, you may find an *aguardente velha*, a well-aged brandy, the perfect end to a meal.

Left, a tawny port, so called because of its relatively light colouration, the result of being left in the cask for at least seven years. **Right**, wine casks must be tended with care; blends are added at specific times over the years.

ESCOLA do MESTRE do TOMAR

Portugal's unique geographical position, cut off from Europe by Spain on one border, facing out toward the New World on the other, is reflected in its art and architecture. In order to counter the natural tendency towards isolation, Portuguese artists and architects have for centuries looked outside for influence and affirmation. Thus, a kind of filtering process has occurred, where local traditions have blended with imported ideas.

Romanesque: In Europe, the reinforcement of Christianity in the face of encroaching Moslem faith was represented not only by the crusades, but also by the reforms introduced by the new religious orders, especially those of Cluny and Cister, whose influence spread far and wide.

In Portuguese art, a discussion of the Romanesque period, the period that began with the 12th century, is essentially a discussion of religious architecture. The predominance of religious architecture is hardly incidental: the founding of the kingdom corresponds to the reconquest of Portugal from the Moors, a period in which Christianity was strongly felt. The construction of cathedrals during this period followed the path of reconquest from Braga to Oporto, southwards to Coimbra, Lamego (reconstructed in the 18th century), Lisbon and Évora.

The man who, enlisting the aid of the crusaders, led this sweep of Portugal and became its first king was Afonso Henriques. His father, Henri, had arrived from Burgundy in the late 11th century. These Burgundian roots of the kingdom were instrumental in the development of Portuguese Romanesque. Romanesque cathedrals, especially those in the west of the country along the route to the pilgrimage church of Santiago de Compostela (in what today is Spanish Galicia), have an affinity with the churches of Auvergne and Languedoc.

The building of Romanesque churches continued into the 14th century in the north,

Preceding pages: detail from the six-panelled masterpiece, *The Adoration of St Vincent* by Nuno Gonçalves. **Left**, *Calvário* by Gregório Lopes, from the School of the Master of Tomar. **Right**, the Romanesque Old Cathedral at Coimbra.

at which time the Gothic style was already spreading throughout the rest of the country. Portuguese Romanesque is an architecture of simple, often dramatically stark forms, whose sturdiness is frequently explained by the need for fortification against the continued threat of Moorish or Castilian invasion. This fortified appearance is enhanced in the cathedrals of Lisbon and Coimbra by the crenellated facade towers.

Most of these buildings are of granite. The hardness of granite renders detailed carving

impossible, thus favouring a simplicity of form. In areas where the softer limestone abounds, such as the central belt of the country (including Coimbra, Tomar and Lisbon), carved decorations are more common.

These Romanesque churches share a certain robustness; a method of construction based on semi-circular arches and barrel vaults; a cruciform plan; and a solid, almost sculptural sense of form in the interior which allows for a play of light and shade. This sobriety is accentuated by the paucity of decoration, which is frequently reduced to the capitals of columns and the archivolts surrounding the portals. When the tympana are not bare, the simplified carvings are usually stylised depictions of Christ in Majesty, or the *Agnus Dei* (Lamb of God) or simply of a cross. In some cases, animals and serpents climb up the granite columns, as in the Sé Velha (Old Cathedral) of Coimbra or in the unusually richly decorated principal portal of the early 13th-century church of São Salvador in Bravães in the Minho.

Gothic: In France, new methods of construction involving pointed arches and ribbed vaults allowed for lighter, taller architectural forms. As the main weight of the building was now borne outside at fixed points by flying buttresses, the walls could be pierced at frequent intervals. The light filtering into these Gothic interiors became a metaphor for Divine Light replacing the Romanesque emphasis on Mystery.

The first building in Portugal to use these new construction methods was the majestic church at the abbey of Alcobaça, commissioned by Afonso Henriques. With its great height and elegant, unadorned white interior bathed in a milky light, Alcobaça is one of the most serene and beautiful churches in Portugal. Begun in 1178 and consecrated in 1222, it is almost purely French in inspiration: its plan echoes that of Clairvaux, the seat of the Cistercian Order in Burgundy – a nave and two side aisles of almost the same height, a two-aisled transept, and an apse whose ambulatory fans out into chapels.

The true affirmation of the national Gothic style came after the Portuguese armies defeated the invading Castilians at the Battle of Aljubarrota. In fulfilment of a religious vow made prior to the battle, King João I commissioned the construction in 1388 of the now famous Dominican Monastery of Santa Maria da Vitória (St Mary of the Victory), better known as Batalha, which means "battle".

The stylistic heterogeneity of Batalha is due to the many years it took to build. Its construction can be divided into three stages. The first, lasting until 1438, was initially supervised by architect Afonso Domingues, who died in 1402, and then by a figure known as Huguet, whose nationality is unknown. Domingues's plan was entirely Portuguese in inspiration, following the general scheme of the churches of the Mendicant Orders (Franciscans and Dominicans). The central nave is illuminated by windows; simple ribbing supports the vault; and the chancel gives on to two pairs of chapels, without ambulatory.

Offset by Domingues's scheme, Huguet's contributions, which include the Founder's Chapel and the famous chapterhouse vault, have a greater refinement and elegance, influenced by English Gothic architecture. Indeed, similarities have been noted between Batalha and the cathedrals of York and Canterbury. Contact with England was close at this time as João I's wife, Philippa of Lancaster, was the daughter of John of Gaunt.

The second stage, under Martim Vasques and Fernão de Évora, lasted until 1481, during which time a second cloister was built. The third stage was supervised by Mateus Fernandes and Diogo Boytac, and corresponded to the Manueline phase of the building, culminating in the arcade of the incomplete chapels and the Royal Cloister.

The stylistic influence of Batalha is felt in various churches throughout the country, examples being the cathedral at Guarda and the ruined church of Carmo in Lisbon, which were both begun at the end of the 14th century. The state of ruin in which Carmo stands today is a poetic if sombre commemoration of the Lisbon earthquake of 1755.

In general, the austerity imposed by the Mendicant Orders meant that the national Gothic style leaned toward temperance rather than flamboyance. Soaring pinnacles and the dissolution of form into light did not suit the national temperament either.

Sculpture: If Portuguese Gothic architecture retains something of Romanesque sobriety, this is not the case with its Gothic sculpture. In free-standing pieces in both wood and stone, the image of the Virgin presides. Emphasis is given to those aspects of her relationship with her Son that are most human and tender – from pregnancy in the *Senhora do O* (such as the beautiful example by the renowned Master Pero, now at the Machado de Castro Museum in Coimbra), to suckling, or carrying the Infant on her raised hip, as at the cathedrals of Braga and Évora. The hieratic sternness of Romanesque carvings is replaced by the humanisation of Christ and his mother. The handling of the drapes also becomes less stylised: now ample, they follow the curves of the body they clothe.

By far the most important category of sculpture in the 14th and 15th centuries was that of tombs, often carved with representations of their inhabitants. It was only well into the 13th century that sculpted sarcophagi began to proliferate. Coimbra was the most important focus for this tradition, as a result of its abundance of soft limestone. While the sarcophagi of Lisbon and Évora tend to the archaic style, the tomb (1330) at the Church of Santa Clara-a-Nova in Coimbra of the Rainha Santa (Holy Queen) lying serenely, clothed in the Franciscan habit of the Order of St Clare, is a moving example of early Gothic naturalism. The sculpture has no Portuguese precedents. It is thought that it was inspired by the School of Aragon, which was then the most important centre for sculpture in the Iberian peninsula.

The two tombs that together emerge as the crowning glory of Portuguese 14th-century funerary sculpture are those of King Pedro and his lover, Inês de Castro, in Alcobaça. The illicit, passionate love affair, the brutal murder of Inês, Pedro's unmitigated sorrow and horrible revenge – this sad and beautiful story has been sung by the nation's greatest writers and poets (see page 34). The sarcophagi do justice to the dramatic tale. Of unknown authorship and hybrid influence, they outshine all preceding funerary sculp-

Above, detail from the great polyptych showing Prince Henry the Navigator and the future João II.

ture in their monumentality, plasticity, refinement of naturalistic detail, and richness of symbolism.

Inês lies calmly, surrounded by angels and crowned at last, in earth as never in life, as Pedro's queen. The sides of her tomb are carved with scenes from the life of Christ and the Virgin, while the head and foot depict scenes of Calvary and the Last Judgment respectively. The latter, a favoured theme of European portal sculpture, is the only one of its kind in Portugal.

The sides of Pedro's sarcophagus display incidents from the life of St Bartholomew. Carved on the head of this tomb is a magnificent rosette. Some scholars see in them the narration of the story of Pedro's love for Inês; more frequently, the rosette is considered to be a wheel of fortune, representing life's vicissitudes.

Of a later date (circa 1433) is the double tomb in the Founder's Chapel at Batalha of King João I and Philippa of Lancaster. The tomb itself is unadorned but for a Gothic inscription. The King clasps the sword of Aljubarrota, and his armour bears the crest of the House of Avis, the dynasty he founded. The crowned couple lie open-eyed and hand in hand. Although common in England, this type of double tomb was rare in the Iberian peninsula.

Painting begins: The 15th century was the first great age of Portuguese painting. Almost no paintings of the 12th to 14th centuries have survived, although frescoes were certainly painted in churches. One fragment of an early 15th-century fresco is an interesting, rare example of secular painting – the allegory of justice entitled O Bom e o Mau Juiz (The Good and the Bad Judge) in a Gothic house in the town of Monsaraz.

The most notable surviving religious fresco of the same period is the Senhora da Rosa in the sumptuous Church of São Francisco in Oporto. It has been attributed to an Italian painter, António Florentino, who, it is thought, may also have painted the portrait of João I now at the Museu Nacional de Arte Antiga in Lisbon.

By far the most brilliant contribution to painting during this period was the introduction of retábulos – painted panels, or altarpieces, with Flemish influences. In 1428, the Flemish master Jan van Eyck was invited to the court of João I to paint the portrait of the

Infanta D. Isabel, future wife of Philip the Good (1396–1467), Duke of Burgundy. The Netherlands were, at the time, under the control of the dukes of Burgundy who were renowned for their excellent taste in art. When the Flemish artists turned from illumination to the painting of altarpieces, they added to their own love of realistic detail the Burgundian passion for gemlike decoration.

The most outstanding 15th-century Portuguese *retábulo* is the polyptych of St Vincent attributed to Nuno Gonçalves, in Lisbon's Museu Nacional de Arte Antiga. The mystery that enshrouds this work has increased its aura. The panels were "lost" for some centuries, and there are various conflicting

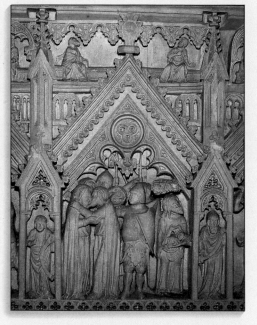

accounts of their reappearance at the end of the 19th century. No sooner were they cleaned and hung publicly than an angry controversy arose as to the identity of their author as well as of the figures depicted. A touch of drama was added when one eminent scholar committed suicide after a dispute concerning two documents which radically altered the direction of the research. The documents were later proved false.

The eminent Portuguese art historian José de Figueiredo, who was responsible for the polyptych's attribution to Gonçalves, based his argument on the 16th-century *Treatise on Ancient Art* by Francisco de Holanda, which mentioned that a great Portuguese artist had painted the altar at the Church of St Vincent. Holanda later praised one Nuno Gonçalves, royal painter at the court of Afonso V, for his panels depicting St Vincent. The work includes a portrait of King Afonso V, and it is known that in 1471 Gonçalves was still a favourite royal painter.

The theme of the polyptych has also given rise to dispute. Some see in it the veneration of the *Infante Santo* – Fernando, uncle of Afonso V, who died at the hands of the Moors. But nowadays, it is generally thought to represent the adoration of St Vincent, patron saint of the kingdom and of the city of Lisbon. The important point of departure was the identification of the Infante Henrique (Prince Henry the Navigator) to the left of the saint in the third panel from the left.

The panels, from left to right, are known as the Panel of the Monks (of the Cistercian Order), the Fishermen, the Infante, the Archbishop, the Calvary and finally, the Relic Panel.

The polyptych uses neither the linear perspective of the Italians nor the aerial perspective of the Flemish, who often included landscapes in their altarpieces. Instead, the composition of figures echoes tapestry design. While the chromatic richness and exquisiteness of handling seem of Flemish influence, the drawing of the heads and the almost sculptural drapes is Italianate – broader and more synthetic than that of the northern masters.

The work's real genius and originality lie in the fineness of the portraiture – its masterful attention to realistic detail as well as its psychological dimension. It reads like an epic poem of King Afonso's dreams of conquest and of the magical world of the Infante Henrique's navigations – blessed, as it were, by the patron saint of the kingdom.

Manueline: The exhilaration of Portugal's overseas discoveries had a marked effect on art, architecture and literature. The term "Manueline" was first used in the 19th century to refer to the reign of Manuel I (1495–1521) during which Vasco da Gama reached the coast of India (1498), and Afonso de Albuquerque conquered the Indian city of Goa (1510). The term is now used more broadly to refer to certain stylistic features predominant during the Avis dynasty (1383–1580), especially in architecture.

Manueline architecture does not have major innovative structural features – the twisted columns, such as those at the Church of Jesus in Setúbal, perform the same function as do plain ones. Rather, Manueline can be seen as a heterogeneous late Gothic, its real innovation lying in its stone decoration, the exuberance of which reflects the optimism and wealth of the period. Inspired by the voyages to the New World, it is ornate and imposing, uniting naturalistic maritime themes with Moorish elements and heraldic motifs: during the reign of Manuel I, the king's own emblems are usually included. These emblems were also used in the churches built in the newly "discovered" overseas territories.

The Monastery of Santa Maria de Belém in Lisbon, better known as Jerónimos, is one of the great *hallenkirchen* of the period – that is, a church whose aisles are as high as its nave. The construction was at first supervised by Diogo Boytac, also responsible for the Royal Cloister at Batalha, and the Church of Jesus at Setúbal. The apse of Jerónimos was rebuilt along more classical lines after an earthquake destroyed the original in 1571.

Perhaps the most notable feature of Manueline architecture is the copious carving surrounding portals and semi-circular windows. The imposing southern portal of Jerónimos and the window of the chapterhouse at the Convent of Christ in Tomar well deserve the acclaim they receive. Construction on the Tomar window began in the 12th century with the Templar *Charola* a chapel with a circular floor plan. During the 16th century, the conventual buildings, including four cloisters, were added. The lavish Manueline decoration of the church culminates in the famous window, which is designed with two great ship's masts on either side, covered with carvings, topped, like the southern portal at Jerónimos, by the cross of the Order of Christ.

Cloisters were now also richly ornamented, with many fine examples, such as: Batalha's Royal Cloister, the Cloister of Silence at the Santa Cruz Monastery in Coimbra, and the cloisters of Jerónimos, as well as those of the elegant churches of Jesus at Setúbal and Lóios at Évora.

Left, detail from the sepulchre of Inês de Castro. **Right**, the fantastically ornate Manueline window at the Convent of Christ at Tomar.

Manueline architecture also adopted and modified certain Moorish features, known as *morisco*. At the Palácio Nacional at Sintra, for instance, restored during Manuel's reign, *morisco* features include the use of tiles, merlons, and windows divided in two by columns reaching the parapet. Another *morisco* feature is the horseshoe arch, as in the chapterhouse at the Convent of Lóios in Évora. In Alentejo province numerous palaces are strongly *morisco* in their decoration, which includes flat lattice-worked ceilings.

During the reign of João II (1481–95), when voyages occupied the energies of the nation, there was a lull in painting activity. However, with the discovery of the sea-route

to India and the consequent prosperity, painted *retábulos* again became a dominant form of expression. At the end of the 15th century, Portugal was one of the largest importers of Flemish paintings. Many of the altarpieces in Portuguese churches were Flemish, and some can still be seen today, such as the *Fons Vitae* at the Misericórdia Church in Oporto.

Nevertheless, Portuguese painting maintained local features, giving rise to the "Luso-Flemish" style. Manueline painting has been characterised by the following features: monumentality, a fine sense of portraiture, brilliant gem-like colours, a growing interest in the naturalistic depiction of architectural and landscape backgrounds and an increasing preoccupation with expressive detail.

At this time painting was not the expression of an individual sensibility, but more often the collaborative effort of a master and his assistants. Attribution, then, is extremely difficult, and often paintings are known as the products of particular workshops. The two principal Portuguese workshops were that of Vasco Fernandes in Viseu and that of Jorge Afonso in Lisbon.

Vasco Fernandes, better known as Grão Vasco, is doubtless the most celebrated regional Manueline painter. For many years, the myth of "Grão Vasco" obscured his real work in a plethora of attributions – he was thought to be the author of Gothic and Renaissance paintings, although a single lifetime would not have sufficed for so large an output. He was responsible for the altarpiece originally at the Lamego cathedral (now in the Lamego Museum), dating 1506–11, as well as the one for the Viseu cathedral (Grão Vasco Museum, Viseu) of a slightly earlier date. The stylistic differences between the two works befuddled scholars for some time, but it is now assumed that Flemish assistants at Lamego account for the differences. The panels for the chapels of the Viseu cathedral (also in the Grão Vasco Museum), of which those of the *Calvary* and *St Peter* are the most renowned, are also attributed to him, although dating to his mature phase (1530–42). Noteworthy for their emotional strength and drama, these works are also characterised by a denser application of paint than that of the Flemish masters. Furthermore, the faces of the Portuguese works tend to be less stylised, more expressive, and, it would seem, often drawn from specific local models, just as the landscape backgrounds are drawn from the Beja region rather than being imaginary or purely symbolic.

The Lisbon workshop was under the aegis of Jorge Afonso, royal painter from 1508. Many artists are known to have worked there, including Grão Vasco himself, Francisco Henriques, Cristovão de Figueiredo, and Gregório Lopes, whose works can be seen in churches and museums in various parts of the country. As for Jorge Afonso himself, documents from the reign of Manuel I show that he was involved in various royal projects, but none has helped to identify

which works were actually by him. It is possible that he painted the "anonymous" panels at the Tomar *Charola.*

Two of the most important artists to emerge from Jorge Afonso's workshop were his son-in-law Gregório Lopes, royal painter to Manuel I and João III, and Cristovão de Figueiredo. Of all the works attributed to the former, the one that is in the best state of repair is the *Martyrdom of St Sebastian* (Museu Nacional de Arte Antiga) painted for the Tomar *Charola.* As for the latter, little is known about his life except that between 1515 and 1540 he was extremely prolific and exercised great influence on Portuguese painting. One of his most impressive works is the

Deposition (also in the Museu Nacional de Arte Antiga in Lisbon), remarkable for its emotional power and its portraiture.

The discussion of Manueline painting would not be complete without mention of the *Santa Auta* altarpiece, whose panels now hang separately in the Museu de Arte Antiga. This work was commissioned by Queen Leonor; a case has been made for the authorship of Cristovão de Figueiredo. The central panel represents the martyrdom of 11,000 virgins pierced by the arrows of the Huns, and includes a shrimp net, which was Leonor's emblem. One of the side panels depicts the arrival at church of the saint's body, and includes what is assumed to be a portrait of the queen. The Manueline portal with Leonor's coat of arms and the Della Robbia medallion identify this as the Church of Madre de Deus in Lisbon, which indeed is where the work originally hung.

Renaissance and Mannerism: The Renaissance has been described as a narrow bridge crossed the moment it was reached. This was certainly the case in Portugal. In their art and architecture, the Portuguese shied away from the Renaissance rationalism, instead inclining toward naturalism or toward the drama of the Romanesque – and later the baroque. The Renaissance in Portugal, then, was best represented by foreign artists. Foreign sculptors

were frequently invited to decorate the portals and facades of Manueline buildings, introducing elements of Renaissance harmony and order within the general flamboyance of the Manueline decorative scheme. The coincidence of Manueline and Renaissance influences and later of Renaissance and Mannerist forms explains the hybrid style prevalent during this period.

Mannerism uses elements of Renaissance classicism but the sense of an ordered, har-

Left, *Calvary*, by Grão Vasco. **Above**, a 16th-century portrait of the reckless and ill-fated King Sebastião by Cristovão de Morais.

monious whole gives way to an exaggeration of these elements. Applied to painting, this often means a certain elongation, which is considered the most characteristic feature. It can also mean unexpected highlighting of a seemingly incidental section of the work. In architecture, Mannerism is characterised by a stress on detail, a shift away from the basic classical proportions.

To the drama of the art of the discoveries, the French sculptors Nicolau de Chanterène and João de Ruão added a touch of Mediterranean rationalism and sobriety. The heraldic motifs and abundant foliage of the former were transformed into the plaques, medallions, and symmetrical foliate arabesques typical of the latter. Chanterène's work includes the portal sculptures of Manuel I and his second wife, Queen Maria, on the western portal of Jerónimos. The pulpit at the Church of Santa Cruz in Coimbra has been variously attributed to both Chanterène and João de Ruão. The latter was most prolific and introduced classicising elements to Portuguese carving, especially in the region around Coimbra, in works such as the altarpiece at Varziela.

Architects, too, immersed themselves in an Italianate vocabulary. The Spaniard Diogo de Torralva is thought to have designed one of the finest examples of Renaissance construction in the peninsula – the Chapel of Nossa Senhora da Conceição (Our Lady of the Conception) in Tomar (*circa* 1530–40), with its simple exterior and diffusely lit, barrel-vaulted interior. Also in Tomar, Torralva's Great Cloister at the Convent of Christ evokes the balance and harmony of Palladian classicism. After Torralva's death in 1566, this majestic cloister was completed by the prestigious and skilled Italian architect Filipo Terzi.

Terzi, a specialist in military architecture, had been invited to Portugal by Philip II of Spain, who acceded to the Portuguese throne in 1580 after the tragic battle of Alcacer-Quiber, which lost Portugal its king – the young Sebastião – and its independence.

The imposing Church of St Vincent in Lisbon, previously attributed to Terzi, is now thought to be by Herrera, architect of the Escorial. The plan is in the shape of a Latin cross, with intercommunicating chapels. The huge central nave is spanned by a barrel vault. The exterior, dominated by two towers and three equally sized portals, is divided into two storeys, the bottom with Doric arcades, the top with Ionic, in the manner of an Italian *loggia*. This facade became a prototype for many other Portuguese churches, especially those of the Benedictine and Carmelite Orders.

From the late 16th to the 17th centuries, the spirit of the Counter-Reformation was pervasive, and another type of church became predominant. The Jesuit Order of St Ignatius Loyola insisted that the interiors of its churches should be ample, and that the pulpit should be clearly visible. This meant a broadening of the central nave, disposing of the side aisles and giving rise to a centralised plan with ambulant chapels.

The first church to be built along these lines in Portugal was that of Espírito Santo (Holy Ghost) in Évora, whose construction began in 1567, one year before that of the Church of Gésu in Rome, long thought to be the first of its type.

The magnificent Jesuit Church of São Roque in Lisbon, which unfortunately suffered much damage during the 1755 earthquake, was begun in the late 16th century, following a plan by Terzi. Simple and austere on the exterior, the interior is richly decorated with tiles and gilded woodwork. It is, nevertheless, extremely spacious and sober, in keeping with the Jesuit tradition.

With the death of Gregório Lopes (*circa* 1550), the great age of the Manueline *retábulo* had come to an end. During the reign of João III, many artists went to Rome, and Italian influence replaced that of Flanders. Altarpieces, for instance in the cathedral of Portalegre, became overtly Italianate, with their emphasis on modelling and *chiaroscuro*. This was also the period in which portrait painting came into its own. The fine, aristocratically elongated portrait of King Sebastião (Museu de Arte Antiga), attributed to Cristovão de Morais, is but one example.

Baroque and Rococo: The baroque is considered to be that stylistic range which, although it uses a basic classical vocabulary, strives for dissolution of form rather than definition. Emphasis is given to motion, to the state of becoming rather than being. This obliteration of clear contours – whether by brushstrokes or as an optical illusion in sculpture and architecture – is further enhanced by a preference for depth over plane. These features all stress the grand, the dynamic and the dramatic.

The first truly baroque Portuguese church is Santa Engrácia in Lisbon with its dome and undulating interior walls. This building, begun in 1682, was not completed until 1966. The octagonal plan, like the oval used in Italy, dispenses with axiality. The richness of the coloured marble lining the walls and floor, the dynamic interior space, and the general sumptuousness of the edifice are typical of construction during the reign of João V (1706–50).

The wealth from Brazil and the munificence of João V rendered the early 18th century a period of great opulence. It was this

king who commissioned the Chapel of St John the Baptist at the Church of São Roque in Lisbon. The entire chapel was built in Rome, blessed by the Pope, shipped to Lisbon and reassembled in the church, where it shines with bronzes, mosaics, rare marble and precious stones.

The most extravagant project launched by João V was the construction of the huge complex of church, palace, and convent at Mafra, near Sintra. The king commissioned the German silversmith-turned-architect, Johann Friedrich Ludwig (Ludovice), and construction began in 1717. The plan of the complex is a huge square; the church is at the centre of the principal facade, flanked by wings belonging to the palace, with a monumental turret abutting at each end. Hybrid influences are particularly evident in the imposing Italianate facade and the Germanic bulbous domes.

In the north the major centres for the development of the baroque were Oporto and Braga. Here, the influence of the Tuscan architect-decorator Nicolau Nasoni, who came to Portugal in 1725, predominated. He introduced a greater buoyancy and elegance, and rich contrasts of light and shade. Unlike Ludwig, he incorporated local characteristics as well. His elliptical-naved Church of Clérigos in Oporto was without successor.

But his secular buildings, such as the Freixo Palace in the same city, with their interplay of whitewash and granite, established a large following.

The Chapel of Santa Madalena in Falperra and the Casa do Mexicano in Braga, although following Nasoni, are already rococo – drama is replaced by fantasy and a love of flourish and ornament. In the former, the portal is bordered by exuberant granite vo-

Left, the pilgrimage church of Nossa Senhora dos Remédios in Lamego (1750–60) is a fine example of baroque architecture. **Above**, *azulejos* became popular in new church buildings.

lutes playing against the white wall; this sense of contrast is less effective in the latter, whose facade is dressed in tiles. In addition to the love of fanciful, sensuous ornament, the rococo was also marked by a growing interest in landscaping. The type of church represented by Bom Jesus in Braga became popular: surrounded by gardens, it sits atop a hill, and is reached by a sweeping succession of stairways which at a distance seem to cascade downward.

In Lisbon the rococo was more sober than in the north. The architect Carlos Mardel designed many of the city's public fountains, including those of Rua do Século and Largo da Esperança. He was also responsible for a section of the Aguas Livres Aqueduct, which was commissioned by João V and has been for over two centuries a handsome and familiar part of the Lisbon cityscape. Mardel was one of the architects involved in the Pombaline reconstruction of Lisbon after the 1755 earthquake. Much of what characterises the Lisbon of today dates to this period. The masterpiece of the reconstruction was Praça do Comércio, the majestically proportioned, arcaded square giving on to the Tagus river. The square is a kind of symbol of the nation itself. From its centre, mounted on his horse, King José, immortalised in bronze, casts his eye towards the horizon. The square is commonly known as Terreiro do Paço – the Palace Square – for the royal palace was here, until it was destroyed by that fateful earthquake.

One of the truly singular features of this period was the use of *azulejos* – ceramic tiles. They were first used in the mid-15th century, gained importance in the mid-16th century, and by the 17th century were nearly indispensable. Impressive examples are in the Church of Marvila at Santarém or São Lourenço in Almancil in the Algarve. At the end of the 17th century, the improved economic conditions allowed for much restoration and reconstruction of older buildings, and many *azulejo* panels date from this period. Both Oriental and Dutch porcelain, in blue-and-white, temporarily replaced the local polychrome tradition. While vast decorative schemes of *azulejo* panels filled churches and palaces – a notable instance of the latter is the Palace of the Marquês de Fronteira in Lisbon – the tile also enjoyed humbler use in settings such as kitchens and stairways. In

addition to the murals, the use of small floral panels, or single tiles, in the Dutch manner, adorned with motifs such as flowers, birds or human figures, was also popular. In the 18th century, decorative *azulejo* panels sumptuously adorned gardens such as those of the Palace of Queluz.

In religious architecture, exteriors continued to be quite austere until relatively late. Interiors, however, became increasingly ornate: the use of *azulejos* was often accompanied by that of carved and gilded woodwork known as *talha dourada*, which had been used mainly on altars. This was particularly the case in the north. The Convent of Tibães near Braga, for example, and the smaller Church of São Francisco in Oporto, have walls encrusted with an overwhelming confection of gilded putti and floral arabesques.

The reign of João V saw another influx of foreign artists. The first of these was the French sculptor Claudio Laprade. His tomb of Bishop Manuel de Moura at the Chapel of Nossa Senhora da Penha in Vista Alegre, with its angels securing a billowing drape, is the most baroque of Portuguese funerary monuments.

Laprade spent his last years at Mafra, where João V had also commissioned numerous works from Italian sculptors, all in the tradition of Bernini – swirling drapes and suspended motion were the order of the day. Alessandro Giusti, who came to Lisbon from Rome in 1747 in order to reassemble the St John the Baptist Chapel at São Roque, was commissioned to carve a marble altarpiece at Mafra; there he formed a school which attracted a large following. Undoubtedly the most gifted Portuguese sculptor to emerge from Giusti's school was Joaquim Machado de Castro, the author of the first Portuguese equestrian statue, King José in the Praça do Comércio. He also made polychrome clay figures – a popular tradition which flourished in the 17th and 18th centuries – such as those at the Regional Museum of Aveiro.

This period saw the flourishing of portrait painting in Portugal as elsewhere in Europe. Perhaps the most celebrated 17th-century portraitist was Domingos Vieira (1600–78), known as "the Dark" to distinguish him from his contemporary Domingos Vieira Serrão. His nickname stemmed from his predilection, in works such as the *Portrait of Isabel de Moura* (in the Museu de Arte Antiga in Lisbon), which dramatically contrast the deep, velvety backgrounds and the rich, creamy whites of ruffs and headgear.

Neoclassicism: The Pombaline style of the reconstruction of Lisbon is closer in many ways to classical models than to the contemporaneous rococo constructions in the north of Portugal. The neoclassical style proper, with its interest in Greco-Roman colonnades, entablatures and porticoes, was introduced in Lisbon in the last decade of the 18th century. It was given court approval when used for the Royal Palace of Ajuda, begun in 1802 (and never completed) after a fire destroyed the wooden building that had been the residence of the royal family since the 1755 earthquake.

The Basilica of Estrela in Lisbon (1789) was the last church to be built in the baroque Grand Style. With the dissolution of the monastic orders in 1834, religious architecture lost its privileged position in Portugal. This had a negative effect on the development of large-scale public architecture. In Lisbon, after the Palace of Ajuda, perhaps the only noteworthy public building to be built in the first half of the 19th century was the Theatre of D. Maria II (1843), with its white Greco-Roman facade.

In the north, the middle-class ambience of Oporto proved fertile ground for conservative neoclassicism to take root. The large English community connected with the port-wine industry favoured this style, perhaps because of its affinities with the architecture of Richard Adam. The British Consul John Whitehead commissioned not only the *Feitoria Inglesa* (the English Factory House, actually more of a club) in Oporto, but also the Hospital of Santo António – perhaps the finest neoclassical building in the entire country.

The return to the Greco-Roman aesthetic principles of neoclassicism is also evident in such works as João José de Aguiar's statue of Queen Maria I, flanked by allegorical figures representing the four known continents, now presiding over the driveway at the Palace of Queluz, itself neoclassical.

At this time, two painters emerged as especially outstanding: Francisco Vieira, known as Vieira Portuense (1765–1805), and

Left, the work of Domingos António Sequeira offers an ideal study in the transition from neoclassicism to Romanticism.

Domingos António Sequeira (1768–1837). The two met in Rome, which was the essential venue for any serious artist. Vieira Portuense also spent some time in London, where the classicising Roman influence was tempered by that of Sir Joshua Reynolds.

The work of Sequeira is a study in the transition from neoclassicism to Romanticism, a rare example of a single life encapsulating two eras. He was nominated court painter in 1802 by João VI, and was commissioned to provide paintings for the rebuilt Palace of Ajuda. Political turbulence forced Sequeira to emigrate to France and then Italy, where he died. His work can be divided into three stages: the first, largely academic

and neoclassical in inspiration, corresponds to his first sojourn in Rome and to his work as a court painter; the second stage (1807–23) which includes the *Alegoria de Junot* (Soares dos Reis Museum, Oporto), is stylistically freer and more individualistically inspired, with Goyaesque contrasts of dark and light, rapid brushstrokes and sudden bursts of luminous white; the last phase corresponds to his visits to Paris and Rome. The late works show great painterliness and luminosity. The four cartoons for paintings in the Palmela collections, again in the Museu Nacional de Arte Antiga in Lisbon, are some of his most inspired, mystical works.

Romanticism: If neoclassical art and architecture represented an escape from the turmoils of the present into a restrained, harmonious classical ideal, another form of escapism became an important ingredient in Romanticism. The flight into the past (medievalism) or into other cultures (orientalism), or into other states – the dream, madness, trance – are all forms of escape. The most extraordinary architectural manifestation of this was the Pena Palace in Sintra, commissioned by the Prince Fernando of Saxe-Coburg-Gotha (consort of Maria II). The building is a strange agglomeration of medieval and orientalising forms, including Manueline, Moorish, Renaissance, baroque, and incorporating parts of the site's original structure, a 16th-century monastery. The whole is an overwhelming pastiche of English neo-Gothic revivalism.

In painting, heroic, religious and ceremonial works gave way to more intimate and personal pieces. This also corresponded to the rise of the middle class. Courtly art had breathed its last. The liberal revolutions questioned the long upheld notion of history as the unfolding of a predetermined order, in favour of a relativism which heralded our modern times. Similarly, the idea that art expresses timelessly valid principles gradually gave way to the subjectivist and individualist notions which continue to hold sway in art today.

Sequeira represented the mystical, religious side of early Romanticism. With his death, Romanticism took a turn: nature became the new religion. The humbling of man before the larger, inscrutable forces of nature was already a contemporaneous theme elsewhere. In Portugal, Tomás da Anunciação became the foremost romantic landscapist of his generation, along with Cristino da Silva.

Not surprisingly, portraiture not only became the art form of the bourgeoisie par excellence, but also gave increasing emphasis to the sitter's inner life. In Miguel Lupi's *Sousa Martins' Mother*, which is now in Lisbon's Museu Nacional de Arte Contemporânea, the illuminated areas correspond to the face and hands – the most expressive parts of the body – and convey a sense of dignified pensiveness.

The foundation of the Artistic Centre in Oporto (1879) and of the Lion Group in Lisbon (1880) were of seminal importance, especially as contact was established between them and the artistic milieu in Paris. Whether settling in as members of the vivacious émigré culture, or simply sampling the new ideas bursting everywhere in the newly recrowned capital of artistic innovation, the Portuguese joined the rest of the world in turning toward France. The individualism which coloured the late 19th century makes any stylistic generalisation difficult; this is true again in the 20th century. As in France, in landscapes and portraits, Romanticism gave way to naturalism: the difference between them is often merely one of emphasis.

At the end of the 19th century, Silva Porto, José Malhoa, and Henrique Posão were the

illumination in no way conflicts with the naturalistic observation. On his return to Portugal, he joined the Lion Group, and painted a group portrait of its members in 1885. His later portraits especially reveal him as a colourist; they are lighter, airier, with a masterly quick touch.

Columbano's brother, Rafael Bordalo Pinheiro, was perhaps a figure of even greater popularity in his day. A celebrated ceramicist working within popular caricatural traditions, he founded a porcelain factory in 1884 which became a veritable school for ceramicists. He was also a sketch artist known for his biting political caricatures.

Modernism: The first few decades of the

foremost naturalists. As opposed to their loose, painterly, luminous outdoor scenes, Columbano Bordalo Pinheiro (1857-1929) continued in the tradition of studio painting. Columbano, as he is known, is considered the Grand Master of Portuguese 19th-century art. He studied under Miguel Lupi at the Academy of Fine Arts (founded in 1836) and then spent three years in Paris.

There, in 1882, he painted the renowned *Concert of Amateurs* where the dramatic

Left, *Sousa Martins' Mother*, **by Miguel Lupi.**
Above, **portrait of the poet Fernando Pessoa by Almada Negreiros.**

20th century saw an unprecedented ferment of artistic activity and invention, first in Europe and then in America. In Portugal, the political turmoil that resulted in the end of the monarchy (1910) did not provide a propitious context for this artistic revolution. Not long afterwards, the absolutist regime, which governed the country from 1926 to 1974, closed the doors to external cultural influence. For these reasons, many of the modern movements arrived late or in diluted form to Portugal. Indeed in architecture, the most interesting works were those which reappraised local traditions such as the Pombaline style. Predictably, this was a period not only of reappraisal of what constitutes "Portugueseness" but also of urban expansion and extensive renovation.

For painters, 1911 was a turning point, for it saw the founding of the Museu Nacional de Arte Contemporânea in Lisbon, the transformation of the Academies into Schools of Fine Arts, and the establishment of the first Salon of Humorists in Lisbon – a turning away from conventional salon painting. Paris remained an important venue for forward-looking artists, and the point of contact with the Modernist avant-garde. Of this generation of painters, the most daring and interesting were Santa-Rita and Amadeo Souza-Cardoso. The premature deaths of both these

artists within six months of each other in 1918 signalled the end of a key phase.

Santa-Rita was an eccentric personality who brought Futurism, with its talk of speed and dynamism and progress, to Portugal. Almost none of his work survives, as it was destroyed by his family, according to his wishes, after his death. Amadeo, many of whose works are in the collection of the Centre of Modern Art at the Calouste Gulbenkian Foundation in Lisbon, was deeply influenced by Cubism, and by Robert and Sonia Delaunay, whom he met in Paris. In his works of 1913–14 this is particularly clear, as the figures delineated are a pretext

for interplay of the brightly coloured arcs.

One of the brightest lights of the 1911 exhibition of Humorists was José Almada Negreiros (1893-1970), who was to become one of the most fascinating, charismatic and energetic cultural figures in Portugal in the 20th century. Painter, draughtsman, poet and playwright, he also flirted with choreography and dance. He was a polemicist and theoretician of some import, and wrote, among other texts, an explication of the 15th-century Polyptych of St Vincent, with which he was obsessed. His early caricatures drew the attention of the poet Fernando Pessoa, who became a friend and whose celebrated posthumous portrait he painted in 1954 (in Lisbon's City Museum) and again in replica in 1964 (now in the Calouste Gulbenkian Foundation).

One of Negreiros's most important commissions was that for the frescoes for the port of Lisbon in 1943-48. His last major project was the mural for the lobby of the Calouste Gulbenkian Foundation in Lisbon. While for most of his life Almada Negreiros painted the world he saw about him, in later years he turned to abstraction which he based on geometrical and metaphysical precepts. The title of this last work – Começar (Beginning) – indicates a sense of spiritual rebirth at the end of his life.

Although all the major modern movements found expression in Portugal, Salazar's regime actively prevented outside stimulus so that forward-thinking, confrontational intellectual and artistic exchange was either clandestine or short-circuited in cultural circles. The military coup and return of democracy in April 1974 breathed new life into the arts, which were invested with a great exploratory energy. Fervent activity echoed the sense of exhilaration after years of repression and censorship.

With access to external artistic events, Portuguese artists have been able to enter the contemporary artistic discourse, often modestly, sometimes boldly. The conflict between the relative value of imported and indigenous ideas – the conflict between "in here" and "out there" is now, as it has been for centuries, one of the central concerns of Portuguese art.

Left, Lalique plaque from the Calouste Gulbenkian Foundation. **Right**, Lisbon by Almada Negreiros.

See the Where to Stay section of Travel Tips for contact details of places mentioned.

If waking up in a bed that once belonged to a Portuguese queen, or staying in an opulent remodelled convent, or even eating home-made bread and cheese in a shepherd's cottage sounds like an appealing change from standard hotels, then you should head for the national *pousadas* (inns) or privately-owned *turismo de habitacão* ("manor house") accommodation. The *pousadas*, now numbering more than 30, have earned a high reputation for comfort, service, and are often architecturally and historically fascinating – many are former castles or monasteries. They are also easily located. The quality of the private lodging varies widely but they are all government-approved – and, moreover, often situated in beautiful settings.

If you are travelling in the lush green northwestern corner of Portugal, in the medieval town of Valença do Minho you will find the **Pousada de São Teotonio**. It sits on a high point inside the ancient walled city and has a spectacular view of the Minho river across to Spain and the Galician mountains. It is also perfectly located for walks around the winding streets and stone houses.

The **Pousada D. Diniz**, named after a 14th-century Portuguese king, is in Vila Nova da Cerveira, just west of Valença, and also overlooks the Minho river. The inn is built into the town's ancient castle and has a small 18th-century chapel around the corner. The rooms, housed in several separate buildings, are large with handsome carved beds.

To the east is the **Pousada de São Bento**, a chalet-style building on a hill just south of the **Peneda-Gerês National Park**. Its floor-to-ceiling windows overlook the Caniçada Dam and a forest. The *pousada* has its own swimming pool and tennis court.

The **Pousada de Santa Marinha da Costa** is further south on a hillside just outside Guimarães, the town known as the "cradle of Portugal", because the first king of the country was born here. The Santa Marinha is a vast 12th-century monastery, with all its stone walls and windows, including a long, long central hallway where the

last owner is said to have exercised his horses! Some of the small rooms used to be monks' cells. Many have balconies with a view of a charming courtyard. In the heart of old Guimarães is another *pousada*, the more modest but charming **Santa Maria**.

At Nespereira, just 5 km (3 miles) from Guimarães, you can stay in luxurious manor house accommodation in the handsome **Casa de Sezim** owned by the same family since 1376. With a monumental facade, the buildings are set around a courtyard. The

Casa de Sezim today makes an award-winning *vinho verde*.

Some 3 km (2 miles) from the coastal town of Viana do Castelo, another ancient residence, **Quinta do Paço d'Anha**, is both a notable maker of *vinho verde*, and has comfortable guest accommodation – four apartments, each for four people.

The manor house scheme, to which such gracious houses belong, began in the north of Portugal. The scheme was created to conserve some of the country's most beautiful private manor homes and palaces. The owners of these magnificent homes can no longer afford the expensive maintenance and have opened them up to tourists, who are quite often treated as guests of the family.

Some are luxurious and historic *casas antigas*, stuffed with antiques, others sturdy old country homes which have sensibly added modern apartments, and some are charmingly rustic (but with all mod cons) like the **Casa do Adro** in Soajo, a perfect base to explore the Peneda-Gerês National Park. One of the most impressive manor houses is 5 km (3 miles) from Ponte de Lima, where you have a considerable choice. In

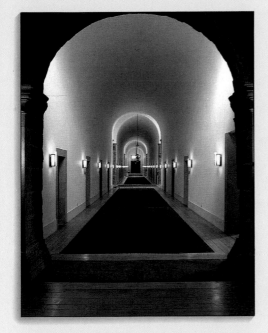

this lovely northwest corner of the Minho, the **Paço de Calheiros** has been the home of the Count of Calheiros since 1336; the present count now lives here.

Accommodation ranges from double rooms within the manor house to apartments to one side, all furnished with antiques and in impeccable taste. Be sure to sample the homemade jams as you dine using the fami-

ly's heirloom silverware. The bedrooms are all delightful, but perhaps the most thrilling experience is to sleep on Portugal's Queen Carlotta Joaquina's original bed; a precious antique whose legs are carved in the shape of dolphins crowned with flowers.

Just 2 km (1 mile) from Ponte de Lima is the 18-century **Casa do Outeiro**, a large, comfortable house framed by trees. Although modernised, it has lost none of its original charm. Not far away is **Casa do Antepaço**, tucked away in a lovely *quinta*, or estate, still with a Roman milestone. Rooms are in a rustic stone Minho-style building.

In the same area, 7 km (4 miles) from Ponte de Lima, rising suddenly out of a curve in the road, is **Casa das Torres**, a magnificent example of King João V (1706–50) architecture, with stone-framed windows, thick white-washed stone walls and gracefully tiled tower roof-tops. There is one double room in the main house and a separate annexe apartment for four. Visitors are welcome to use the swimming pool and gardens.

Only 500 metres from Ponte is the 17th-century **Casa de Crasto**, a two-storey arcaded house built in the Minho granite. It has its original kitchen and five double rooms for guests.

Your own watermill: Also near Ponte de Lima, **Minho de Estoroes** is a small, old stone watermill on the banks of the Estoroes brook that has been refurbished to fit one family. Don't be surprised if you share the brook with a group of local women kneeling at the rocks to wash their family's clothing.

These are just a few of the 50 or so houses in the area, known as the *Costa Verde* or "Green Coast". In the Douro Valley there are a few houses, two contrasting examples being the **Vila Hostilina** in Lamego and **Casa de Marrocos** just 2 km (1 mile) from Régua. The villa overlooks the old city of Lamego and has been totally refurbished to include a gym, sauna, massage room, tennis courts and a pool. In the Casa de Marrocos, a rustic house built of schist, dating to the 17th century, you can enjoy the full beauty of the Douro. This house has three double rooms.

Heading south in the heart of the Serra da Estrêla is the **Pousada São Lourenço**, a modern building of stone with a red-tiled roof. The rooms are plain but comfortable with wooden four-poster twin beds. Rooms on the upper floor have verandas with dramatic views of the mountains and the town of Manteigas below. It can be cold up here; accordingly a fireplace warms up the dining-room. Regional specialities, such as the famous Serra da Estrêla sheeps' milk cheese, are served.

For outdoor activities in the Serra, Sabugueiro is a tiny mountain village of narrow cobblestone and mud streets and granite houses. Any villager can show you the way to the **Casas do Cruzeiro** tavern, with the village shop beside it and shepherds

the eastern village of Monsanto and other Beira interior villages. Turn right off the main street and you will come to a 19th-century-style house called **Casa do Barreiro**. Here you will be ushered through several rooms full of overstuffed chairs, pianos, thick carpets, and numerous knick-knacks and antiques. The walls of the houses are decorated with antique fans, tapestries and tiny crowded vitrines.

Southeast of Tomar, with its intriguing Convent of Christ, is the *pousada* of **Castelo do Bode**, beside a large dam on the Zêzere river. The bedrooms are smallish but comfortable. The breakfast room is full of sunlight in the morning and looks out over the

resting outside. This is a real taste of rural Portugal (although with considerably more comfort). Expect to wake up to the tinkle of sheep bells and the low calls of the shepherds before sunrise.

Dona Teresa, who runs the tavern, and her doctor son, have remodelled the inside of two granite houses into charming white-walled bedrooms, neat bathrooms and sitting-rooms with small corner fireplaces. There is also a small dining-room where you may eat home-made bread, cheese and plate-fuls of the meal of the day.

Just south of Fundão at the foot of the Serra is Alpedrinha from where you could explore

dam. Regional dishes in this unpretentious *pousada* are tasty, the Tomar wine very pleasant.

Just south of Batalha is Porto de Mós, with its massive castle. The rambling **Quinta do Rio Alcaide**, recently remodelled, is set in the side of the mountains, with columned terraces and red-tiled roofs overlooking the wide gardens. The *quinta* has four sections: the main house, the "middle" house, the old "bread-oven" house, which has been transformed into a self-contained apartment, and the "windmill" house that sits on a hill overlooking the *quinta*.

Southwest is the graceful walled town of

Óbidos. The **Pousada do Castelo**, which is built into a section of the old castle, is very small and popular, and therefore difficult to reserve. It's still worthwhile to stop in and have a drink.

It's often been difficult to find accommodation in the Ribatejo. In Santarém itself you can stay privately in a modest house, **Casa da Pedra**, at 16 Rua das Pedras Negras; or in the comfortable **Casa dos Cedros** which is nearby in Alcanede; or in the very attractive l9th-century **Quinta da Sobreira**. In the Vale de Figueira, 15 km (9 miles) from Santarém, the latter offers three double rooms and a swimming pool.

Heading east, you could arrive at the bor-

this tiny town. One is in the **Travessa do Terreirinho**, owned by Margarida Lcite Rio. The house is typical, with a huge fireplace (the hostess will provide large logs in winter) in the open sitting-room, a cosy loft bedroom with a lovely arched window seat. There are two more bedrooms downstairs, so the house is big enough for three couples or a family.

Around Lisbon: A few of the houses in the greater Lisbon area live up to the beauty and grace of the houses in the north of the country. One example is the **Quinta da Capela** in Sintra, an exquisite place that fits in perfectly with the Byronesque setting of the Sintra hills. The palace belongs to the Marchioness

der town of Marvão, a 14th-century whitewashed walled town perched like an eagle's nest at the top of an escarpment. Inside the medieval walls is the **Pousada Santa Maria**, simply decorated with red tile floors, wood-beamed ceilings and fireplaces, and a glassed-in terrace with a panoramic view across into neighbouring Spain. The bedrooms are comfortable but small, and the restaurant's menu includes local game.

You may rent rooms or a whole house in

Left, the vaulted ceilings of Pousada dos Lóios in Évora. **Above**, the dining-room of Pousada da Rainha Santa Isabel in Estremoz.

de Cadaval and is arranged in perfect taste with fresh flowers on the windowsills; the dining-room in soft shell-pink tones; and the extensive gardens carefully tended. The *quinta* has 10 rooms.

Directly south of Lisbon is Palmela and the impressive **Pousada Castelo de Palmela**, part of a 15th-century monastery built in the reign of King João I, facing the Palmela Castle. All the large airy bedrooms have sweeping views over the countryside. The food here is imaginative and elegantly served in the long dining-hall. The old cloister is a pleasant lounge area.

Only 10 km (6 miles) away is Setúbal,

whose **Pousada de São Filipe** is within the walls of the São Filipe Castle. Most of the high-ceilinged rooms have a view of the bay, as does the restaurant, which specialises in regional dishes. The old stone terrace is a splendid setting for a drink before dinner.

Travelling toward Spain from here you would come to Elvas and Estremoz. The **Pousada de Santa Luzia** in Elvas is known for its cuisine and lavish servings of food. Many people just stop in for lunch. The rooms are adequate; those near the road can be noisy. Be sure to see or stay in the fantastic **Pousada Rainha Santa Isabel** in Estremoz, which dominates the small town. The *pousada* is furnished with 17th- and 18th-

full of antiques. Just 20 km (12 miles) south, in the village of Terena, you can find accommodation in the 17th-century **Casa de Terena** and a meal in the restaurant run by the owners. Quite new there, too, is the **Herdade Dom Pedro**, a farmhouse with several rooms which have been renovated by an English family.

In Évora, the **Pousada dos Lóios** was originally a 15th-century monastery, with high ceilings and granite and marble arches. A carved marble staircase leads upstairs to the bedrooms – small, but then they were once monks' cells. The sitting-room is decorated with antiques, and the dining-room has been set around the glassed-in interior gar-

century antiques. A majestic marble staircase leads to the bedrooms upstairs, often somewhat small but in deep rich colours. The dining-room is a huge hall with a series of low arches and stone pillars. The menu branches out from local specialities to include Steak Diane and Crêpes Suzette, cooked at your table.

In between Estremoz and Elvas, just south of Borba, is **Vila Viçosa**. Since you would probably wish to spend a little time visiting the Ducal Palace as well as the many charming small towns around here, a very comfortable base could be the luxuriously furnished **Casa de Peixinhos** – six stylish bedrooms,

den and fountain. If it's fully booked, as often it is, you should find accommodation in one of Évora's smaller hotels.

Not far from Évora and just a few kilometres from the village of Redondo is the magnificent **Convento da Serra D'Ossa** which has been in the family of Sr Henrique Leotte for more than 150 years. It was originally built by monks of the Order of Saint Paul around 1070, but other sections were added in the 14th and 18th centuries. The surrounding countryside is covered in olive, pine and eucalyptus trees. The rooms are converted monks' cells which branch off a main corridor, itself a work of art, with panels of blue-and-white tiles dating from the 18th century.

A wonderful outdoor patio, also decorated in original tiles, faces a Florentine fountain with archways crossing overhead. The original chapel has frescoes dating from the 17th and 18th centuries and tiles depicting biblical scenes, which have the rare feature of being signed.

On the west side of the Alentejo, not far from the Roman ruins of Miróbriga, is Santiago do Cacém and the **Pousada de São Tiago**, a small ivy-covered building with a garden full of flowers and a swimming pool. There are four bedrooms in the original part of the inn, all with a pleasant rustic flavour,

lake; at night, this tranquil place is a stargazer's heaven.

In Portugal's southernmost province, the Algarve, are two *pousadas*. The **Pousada de São Bras** is a quiet country house strikingly set on a high hill 3 km (2 miles) above the small town of São Bras. Rooms have a view over the valley below and beyond to the coast. The **Pousada do Infante**, named after Prince Henry the Navigator, on the west coast at Sagres, is a sprawling modern building on a coastal cliff with airy rooms overlooking the swimming pool and out to sea. It's a comfortable base to explore the wilder reaches and splendid beaches of the Algarve coast. Linked to this *pousada* is a small

with wood floors and whitewashed walls, and additional bedrooms in an annexe. This *pousada* has a calm and welcoming air.

To the south, almost on the border with the Algarve, is the **Pousada Santa Clara** overlooking the lovely lake of the Santa Clara dam and the golden hills framing it. The dining-room looks out on to a stone terrace and a fine sloping garden planted with orange trees. During the day you can choose to sail, swim, fish or go for walks around the

Left, exterior of Pousada de Santa Marinha da Costa outside Guimarães. **Above**, Pousada do Castelo in the walled town of Óbidos.

fortress (*fortaleza*) annexe at wind-tossed Cape St Vincent.

Privately-owned tourist accommodation handily near Tavira in the eastern Algarve is the **Quinta do Caracol**, a low white house bedecked in purple bougainvillaea, with a tennis court and small pool. A quiet and classical manor house where you may also stay in the Algarve is the **Quinta de Benatrite**, 3 km (2 miles) west of Santa Bárbara da Nexe (some 10 km/6 miles inland from Faro). In the heavily-developed central Algarve it is an oasis of calm with a pool, excellent food, and delightful accommodation for a maximum of six.

The Portuguese are a people of the earth: they describe their country as a garden which has been sown on the edge of the sea; they weave their ancient legends around roses and almond blossoms; and a flower – the red carnation – is the symbol for the 1974 Revolution, which restored democracy to Portugal. Many people still cherish the flowers, now pressed and dried.

But the land that the Portuguese have inherited does not make cultivation easy. Nowhere in the country is this more true than in land is really suited to agriculture. Economic planners argue that the labour expended on raising sparse crops from barren soil could be turned to more productive account by using the land in a different way. The agronomists' answer to Portugal's farming problems is a return to the country's historic wealth – forests. For the Portuguese, the cultivation of trees is a growth industry on a par with vineyards.

Centuries ago dense oak woods covered most of Portugal. One third of the country,

the toilsome soil of the large, parched plains and craggy coastline of the Alentejo.

Alentejo balconies brim with hydrangeas and the white walls of houses are cloaked with purple bougainvillaea in the late summer. But Portugal must work its land to produce useful crops, not decorative blossoms. Almost a quarter of Portuguese workers are engaged in farming, more than double the European average. But poor soil, a difficult climate and outmoded methods mean that most crops yield less than half the average per acre in other parts of Europe.

About half the surface of Portugal is devoted to farming, although only half of that about 3 million hectares (7½ million acres), is now forested. Massive planting projects are underway to double that amount, including a plan funded by the World Bank to reforest a huge area of central Portugal north of the Tagus river. Similar plans will surely be instituted in the Alentejo before long.

Pulp: Even now trees are big business. The forestry industry employs some 100,000 workers in a sector that earns nearly $2 billion a year in export revenue. Pine, said in Portugal to be of use to man from cradle to coffin, is used to produce timber for furniture and construction, as well as resin for pitch and turpentine. Pine accounts for about 40 percent of the country's wooded land. Driving through pine forests, you will see metal cups strapped below holes to collect sap. Each mature tree is tapped for resin once or twice in each of the last two years before it is felled and each tapping takes about a month.

The main product of Portuguese forests is pulp used for manufacturing paper and cardboard. The Australian eucalyptus, whose distinctive aroma fills the air, was introduced into Portugal in 1856 for this industry. Today it accounts for 15 percent of all forested

About half the cork in the world, from stoppers in bottles of the finest champagne to the linings of spacecraft, is supplied from these fields where pigs, turkeys and sheep amble between the trees, feeding on the acorns as the bark slowly matures to readiness.

Cultivating cork is not a trade for the impatient. From the acorn, the spreading tree with its heavy, twisted branches grows for about 25 years before it is ready to yield its bark. The branches of shiny dark-green evergreen leaves with a grayish underside are

land. Eucalyptus oil is also used for various pharmaceutical products. Pulp manufacturers are lobbying to extend the cultivation of the eucalyptus, which grows very fast, but some farmers oppose this move on the grounds that, if not managed correctly, the trees rapaciously draw up water which is needed for other crops.

Cork: Alentejo province is famous for its sprawling cork-oak trees with their raw, stripped trunks spread over the grasslands.

Preceding pages: the Alentejo plains. **Left**, the groves that produce the piquant Portuguese olive oil. **Above**, distinctively knotted cork trees.

carefully pruned to admit the sunlight and make the bark accessible to the cutters. What underbrush there is on the plains is periodically burned away.

At the height of summer, when the trunk has shrunk away from the gnarled, dull-gray outer skin, workmen skilfully begin the stripping. Using special axes ground to razor sharpness, they first make horizontal cuts around the circumference of the trunk and the lower branches. These are linked with vertical incisions and the roll of bark is stripped off, leaving the rich red, bare trunk beneath. Machines cannot replace the expertise of the strippers, who cut the bark with such skill that the tender trunk below is left undamaged.

The first stripping yields virgin cork that is used for specialised purposes such as life-jackets. Each tree gives between 27–45 kilograms (60–100 lbs) of cork at a cutting. It will be another nine years before a sufficiently thick layer of bark has grown back. A tree is usually stripped 12 to 15 times in a life of around 200 years.

After sorting, the cork strips are transported to 700 processing plants distributed across the country. They are dried for up to a year to remove any viscous residue that might remain in the millions of minute, air-filled cells that make cork so light. An im-

crafting the perfect fits that are needed to cork fine wines and champagnes. Nor are artificial materials, which do not allow wine to breathe, ever likely to replace bottle corks.

Portugal produces around 150,000 tons of cork a year, with an export value of some $200 million.

Olives: Older still than cork oaks are many of the olive trees found across all of southern and central Portugal and along the Douro Valley in the north. Experts believe some Portuguese olives are as old as the trees in the Garden of Gethsemane, shown by carbon-14 tests to date from the time of Christ.

Olive oil, called "the thread of life", is as basic to Portuguese cooking as salt and pep-

properly dried cork could spell disaster for a vintage port! The strips are then boiled in water for a day to bond the cells and make the cork more flexible, and afterwards are smoothed out into flat sheets and dried again in the sun.

Cork is graded into almost 50 different categories. Uses include heat insulation, floats, tiles, sound-proofing, containers for radioactive materials, badminton shuttle-cocks, table tennis bats and, of course, corks. Workmen who manually punch out thousands of stoppers a day from strips of cork are now being replaced by machines. But mechanisation cannot match their skills for

per in other countries. The starting point of most dishes is a *refogado*, a base of chopped onions and garlic browned in olive oil. The oil is also poured on to boiled fish, potatoes and vegetables and into some soups.

Much of the olive oil produced in Portugal, which has a slightly more tangy taste than in other countries, is used in the canning of sardines and tuna. Some olives are preserved in salt water and served as an appetiser or a garnish.

A great deal of labour goes into producing the oil. The tree, which reaches between 3–12 metres (10–40 ft) in height, does not bear fruit during its first 25 years of life. The olives are picked in November, just before they ripen fully, between six and eight months after the tree flowers. Crops are erratic, varying from heavy one year to sparse the next. A sheet is spread beneath the tree, and the pickers shake the fruit on to the sheet with long poles, then climb into the tree to glean the rest. Today, some farmers use machines that grip the tree trunk in a large clamp and shake it mechanically.

Between 20 and 30 percent of the weight of the fresh fruit is oil. Most farmers today sell their olive crops to cooperatives who use modern, mechanical presses to produce and refine industrial quantities. Lightweight, dark-green virgin oil of the highest quality is

the south. Around the bursting almond blossom, in snowy white and soft pink, linger legends of the Moorish prince who restored the health of his northern wife with his visions of "winter snow". The almonds themselves are harvested in the heat of summer – you will hear the tap-tap-tap of the pole that topples the last almond to the ground. Figs, green, black, lush and delicious, are sundried to preserve them and press them, with nuts, into delicious nibbles.

Yet more than any other tree it is the evergreen carob with its long, dark, wizened beans that is the true "tree of life". Those beans sustained John the Baptist in the desert, fed the Duke of Wellington's cavalry in the

produced from the first pressing. The second pressing delivers a heavier oil, also of excellent quality, which is blended to make the olive oil most commonly used for cooking. Third pressings are usually refined for industrial uses. Complex methods of repressing and processing are used to produce other grades of oil.

Almonds and carob: The trees of the Alentejo are perhaps not as strikingly exotic as the lovely almond and carob of the Algarve to

Far left, aromatic eucalyptus trees. **Left**, a cork trunk shorn of its bark. **Above**, working at Robinson's cork factory in Portalegre.

Peninsular War, and altogether yield a greater harvest of food than any other tree – as well as providing a fine oil from the seeds. So consistent in size are these seeds they were the original qirats, or carats, still used as a measure of weight.

And there are other native beauties to be found. The *loquat*, another southern tree, is an evergreen of the rose family that originated in China and Japan. You can tell the tree by its stiff leaves and small, fragrant, white flowers. The oval, yellow, plum-like fruits grow between one and three inches long in large, loose clusters. Eaten raw, the juicy white flesh has a tart but pleasing taste.

"Somos o gente do mar" ("We are the people of the sea"), proclaimed Vasco da Gama on his return to Lisbon after discovering the sea route to India in 1498. Using small, light, high-prowed caravel sailing ships based on an ancient Mediterranean design, 15th- and 16th- century Portuguese explorers voyaged the world and became the greatest maritime nation on earth.

A generation later Portugal was defeated and driftwood was all that was left of the caravels. Nevertheless, the numerous seafaring traditions which history had thrust on Portugal were still in place. And curiously, as Portugal retreated into centuries of introspection, some of the boat-building techniques and traditions left by ancient mariners were absorbed up her rivers and on to inland waterways. Several examples survive today.

Port boats: Best known are the flat-bottomed, square-rigged *barcos rabelos*, familiar to anybody who has ever visited Oporto. A flotilla of them lines the quayside of the River Douro at Vila Nova de Gaia opposite the city, their sails emblazoned with the motifs of the port-wine firms whose warehouses are scattered around the wharfs: Cockburn's... Dow's... Calem... Graham's. The boats have become a symbol of the product with whose destiny they have been entwined for hundreds of years, and of Portugal's second city.

Less appreciated, however, are the similarities in design with Viking longships which sailed along the Portuguese coast from the 9th century to the 11th century on their way to the Mediterranean, making contact with Galician and Portuguese noblemen en route. The saga of the *barco rabelo* pre-dates the Vikings to the extent that boats are known to have existed on the Douro in Roman times and earlier; but experts in the origins of the *rabelo* find very little which can be traced to the Mediterranean.

In traditional *barco rabelo* building the hull's shell is laid first, then the ribs are placed. This is the nordic "clinker building" method which, very plausibly, is a direct Viking legacy. A comparison between the bare hull of a *rabelo*, and that of a reconstructed longboat in the Norwegian capi-tal Oslo's Viking Museum, shows striking similarities; the square-rigged sail is also common to both.

Other features of the *rabelo*'s design evolved in the early 17th century, the nascent period of the trade in port wine. Ever since then the fortified wine has been grown in the upper reaches of the Douro Valley from where it is transported to Vila Nova de Gaia for shipment abroad. The adapted indigenous boats of the Douro were constructed in large numbers and put to this use on the treacher-

ous river, stacked with casks or "pipes" of wine. Flat bottoms were needed to shoot the rapids, negotiate the shallows, and also to achieve high loading ratios. A tall platform at the stern gave the helmsman a clear view over the rows of pipes and a huge steering oar, or *espadela* – effectively a rudder – was needed to change course rapidly; the rudder also had to be capable of being levered out of the water to avoid smashing in the rapids and rocky shallows. Intrepid boatmen slept and ate on board, suspending cauldrons from a beam and boiling their traditional dishes of pungent *bacalhau* (dried cod).

Up until the 1960s accidents were frequent

with lives lost as laden boats headed downstream. Back upstream, they sailed through the placid stretches pushed by the prevailing westerlies, and were hauled up rapids by teams of bullocks. One of the most famous casualties was the pioneering Scots port shipper and cartographer of the Douro, Baron Forrester, who in 1862 was travelling by *rabelo* between various wine-growing *quintas*, paying their farmers in gold coins. The *rabelo* capsized and Forrester, weighed down by his beltful of gold, was drowned.

contested but without much store set by winning or losing, is held on 24 June – the festival of São João (St John the Baptist and Oporto's patron saint) when the city erupts in revelry. The boats set off from the mouth of the Douro, with the race climaxing at Oporto's double-decker Dom Luís I bridge.

What *is* taken absolutely seriously is the set of rules ensuring that the *rabelos* are constructed precisely according to the specifications evolved during their heyday. The craft have to be built in boatyards along the

The damming of the Douro for hydroelectric power brought to an end the era of the *rabelo*'s interdependence with the port trade. Or so it seemed. Although for nearly 30 years port has made the journey down from the Upper Douro by road, the *rabelo* has proved to be an irrepressible symbol of the product. Boats are still constructed, at great expense, to compete in the heralded annual race between *rabelos* owned by the various port-shipping firms. The regatta, enthusiastically

banks of the Douro, with the hull constructed from maritime pine, forests of which cloak the north coast of Portugal, and laid down by the shell-first "clinker building" technique. The largest *rabelos* are around 24 metres (80 ft) long by 5.5 metres (18 ft) wide with 80 sq. metres (860 sq. ft) of sail billowing in the wind, and need at least a dozen crew members. Payloads are up to 65 pipes, each one holding 522 litres of port.

The São João regatta provides proof that the boats – which for the rest of the year line the Vila Nova de Gaia quayside – are more than simply advertisements for the wares of their owners. The boatyards and skills of the

Preceding pages: *barcos rabelos* **are still raced by port companies.** **Left**, **weed-gathering with a** *moliceiro*. **Above**, **hauling a** *traineira* **home.**

craftsmen have not been drowned by one hydroelectric project.

Weed boats: Fewer visitors to Portugal come across the *moliceiro*, another craft of ancient ancestry which has been adapted for a specific commercial use and survived the changes of centuries. *Moliceiros* are the seaweed-gathering boats of the Ria de Aveiro, a 45-km (28-mile) long lagoon, linked to the Atlantic by a narrow breach in the dunes, which spreads over the misty, marshy wetlands of the Beira Litoral province.

The seaweed, or *molico*, which grows in profusion along the shallow bed of the Ria, is used as fertiliser on the fields of the Beiras. The high, curling "swan-neck" prows of the

throughout the Mediterranean. On them are painted motifs of flowers, saints, bulls, horsemen or mythical heroes, in bright colours.

Moliceiros are between 10–15 metres (33–50 ft) long, and are usually crewed by two men, who may spend a few days sailing the lagoon, sleeping on board, before returning to their bases at Aveiro, Ovar or Torreira. At the stern is an enormous rudder operated by means of ropes, and at the centre a mast on which a white, trapezoidal sail of about 24 sq. metres (260 sq. ft) is rigged. Hefty oars are also kept on board; but when becalmed or in reeds, a punting pole is usually preferred. Boatmen stand on the prow, thrust the wooden pole into the mud which is never far from the

moliceiros emerge noiselessly from the somnolent marshes, where the stillness is broken only by the splash of a flock of waterfowl, or the cry of one boatman to another.

It is sometimes suggested that the dark features characteristic of some of the communities living around the Ria, as well as a few obscure words which have survived in local dialects which may have Middle Eastern origins, are evidence that the Phoenicians settled here. Whatever truth there may be in this, there is no doubt that the design and decoration of *moliceiros* owe a great deal to the Phoenician traders. Similar influences, particularly the swan-neck prows, are found

surface, and push their way down the side of the craft to the stern, deftly propelling the flat-bottomed boat through the reeds.

The other all-important pieces of equipment aboard *moliceiros* are the multi-pronged rakes known as *ancinhos,* whose heads are hung over the prow as they travel towards the patch of seaweed to be harvested. The weed is then scraped from the floor of the lagoon, and deposited on the floor of the boat. The chemically-rich harvest is then taken ashore to be dried and sold to farmers.

As with the *rabelos,* the number of *moliceiros* has dwindled. In the earlier half of the century over 1,000 harvested the fruits of the Ria, but artificial fertilisers have largely replaced *molico*, leaving only enough demand for the natural stuff to sustain just a handful of working *moliceiros*. Other boats of a similar, though less extravagant, design are also occasionally seen on the lagoon, usually looking equally over-laden. These are known as *mercanteis*, used for transporting cargo such as the salt collected in conical heaps in the pans at the Ria's fringes. An annual regatta keeps alive the skills of *moliceiro* sailing and brings scores of redundant boats out of retirement. The event is held in Torreira at the port's annual festival, the Romaria de São Paio da Torreira, on the first weekend in September.

Off-shore: More high prows and motifs with claims to Phoenician ancestry are found drawn up on the beaches of Praia da Mira west of Ria, and down the coast of the Beira Litoral and Estremadura to Nazaré. Instead of sails and flat bottoms, however, these offshore fishing boats are driven by brawny arms heaving oars, and have arch-shaped hulls built to ride the Atlantic swell.

Designs vary between the fishing villages scattered up and down this coast of expansive, wind-swept beaches and dunes leading down to the cold, rough Atlantic; but typi-

<u>Left</u>, a source of pride. <u>Above</u>, racing *moliceiros*.

cally, they are about 5 metres (16 ft) long with their prows tapering up to a peak. A common motif is the pair of eyes painted on to the bows to ward off evil spirits, almost identical to those found on other Phoenician-influenced fishing vessels, such as the *luzzus* of Malta. The bright colours, with each boat painted differently, help fishermen recognise each other from afar.

Because the rough sea and wide beaches allow few ports or harbours along this coast, the boats are launched into the surf over tree-trunk rollers, before being rowed out to lay nets for sardines or pots for lobsters, octopus and squid. The boats are often out all night, before returning to shore at dawn to be hauled by bullocks or tractors over the rollers back on to the sand. The catch is then auctioned on the beach.

These *barcos da Praia de Mira* and *barcos de Armação da Nazaré* hark back to Portugal's intrepid days of discovery.

Traineiras also have a long pedigree. These are the wooden trawlers, large fleets of which are based in Portugal's major fishing ports such as Matosinhos (near Oporto), Peniche, Setúbal and Portimão. Again, it is to the Phoenicians that the broad prows, bright colours and cryptic motifs can be traced. But battered and weather-beaten as they invariably appear, these are deep-sea fishing boats, of the kind which for centuries have been voyaging to distant waters – the North African coast, Greenland, the Grand Banks of Newfoundland – in scarch of cod which, dried, becomes the national dish, *bacalhau*. Some believe that *traineiras* from Cascais on the Lisbon coast reached America in 1482, and that it was thanks to the ensuing rumours that Columbus made his discovery a decade later.

Today's *traineiras* vary between about 10–25 metres (32–80 ft) long, with small superstructures housing the bridge and berths. They are fitted with diesel engines in place of sails, and the further-venturing ones have radios and radar. The majority, however, stick to Portugal's coastal waters.

You may see the lights of the *traineiras* twinkling on the horizon as dusk falls, or you might be on the quayside as a boat returns with its catch. If you then delve into your pocket for a 50-escudo coin, minted with the emblem of a caravel, you might notice the similarity between the two vessels.

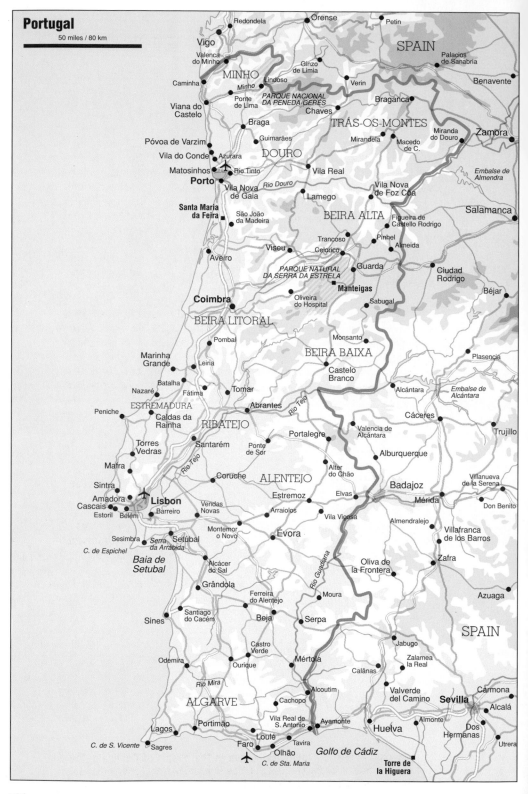

Portugal

50 miles / 80 km

SPAIN

Redondela
Orense
Petin
Vigo
Palacios
de Sanabria
Valenca
do Minho
Ginzo
de Limia
Benavente
MINHO
Caminha
Lindoso
Verin
Minho
Ponte
de Lima
PARQUE NACIONAL
DA PENEDA-GERÉS
Bragança
Viana do
Castelo
Chaves
Braga
Guimarães
TRÁS-OS-MONTES
Miranda
do Douro
Zamora
Póvoa de Varzim
DOURO
Mirandela
Macedo
de C.
Vila do Conde
Azurara
Rio Tinto
Vila Real
Vila Nova
de Foz Côa
Embalse de
Almendra
Matosinhos
Porto
Rio Douro
Salamanca
Vila Nova
de Gaia
Lamego
**Santa Maria
da Feira**
São João
da Madeira
BEIRA ALTA
Figueira de
Castello Rodrigo
Ciudad
Rodrigo
Aveiro
Viseu
Trancoso
Celorico
Pinhel
Almeida
Guarda
Béjar
Coimbra
PARQUE NATURAL
DA SERRA DA ESTRELA
Manteigas
Oliveira
do Hospital
Sabugal
BEIRA LITORAL
Pombal
Monsanto
Plasencia
Marinha
Grande
Leiria
BEIRA BAIXA
Castelo
Branco
Batalha
Alcántara
Embalse de
Alcántara
Nazaré
Fátima
Tomar
ESTREMADURA
Peniche
Caldas da
Rainha
Abrantes
Rio Tejo
Cáceres
Trujillo
RIBATEJO
Portalegre
Valencia de
Alcántara
Torres
Vedras
Santarém
Ponte
de Sor
Villanueva
de la Serena
Mafra
Rio Tejo
Coruche
ALENTEJO
Alter
do Chão
Badajoz
Sintra
Estremoz
Elvas
Mérida
Don Benito
Amadora
Lisbon
Vendas
Novas
Arraiolos
Cascais
Estoril
Belém
Barreiro
Vila Viçosa
Almendralejo
Villafranca
de los Barros
Sesimbra
*Serra
da Arrábida*
Setúbal
Montemor
o Novo
Évora
Zafra
C. de Espichel
*Baia de
Setubal*
Alcácer
do Sal
Rio Guadiana
Oliva de
la Frontera
Azuaga
Grândola
Ferreira
do Alentejo
Moura
Santiago
do Cacém
Beja
Serpa
SPAIN
Sines
Castro
Verde
Mértola
Jabugo
Zalamea
la Real
Odemira
Ourique
Calañas
Valverde
del Camino
Cármona
Rio Mira
Alcoutim
Alcalá
ALGARVE
Cachopo
Vila Real de
S. Antonio
Ayamonte
Sevilla
Dos
Hermanas
Lagos
Portimão
Almonte
Loulé
Tavira
Huelva
Utrera
C. de S. Vicente
Sagres
Faro
Olhão
Golfo de Cádiz
C. de Sta. Maria
**Torre de
la Higuera**

PLACES

There's no *wrong* way to explore Portugal – except to make too many plans in advance. A car is the handiest way to travel because, although the trains are good and the buses adequate, they won't allow you the freedom to go just over the next hill... and the next, and the next. Portugal is wonderfully seductive.

Roads have been enormously improved and extended in recent years. A motorway links Lisbon with Oporto in the north. The southward road from Lisbon bypasses several once tortuous towns. East–west expressways help you leap distances but north–south roads tend to be narrower, more winding, and less well maintained.

Lisbon and its environs are the best starting point for a first taste of Portugal. From there, if the weather is fine, you may want simply to head south, to the glorious beaches of the Algarve. After relaxing here for a few days, you might start meandering back up through the Portuguese countryside. Begin by exploring the expanse of the Alentejo, spectacular plains with the entrancing ancient town of Évora in their midst.

Cutting back toward the Atlantic, still heading north, you could visit the old university town of Coimbra and some of the surrounding sights. Look in on some of the traditional fishing communities along the coast here. To the north is the Douro river and the wine districts of Douro and Minho. Here, world-famous port, the delicious *vinhos verdes*, and other wines are produced – and shipped to the city of Oporto at the mouth of the Douro.

The far interior north of Portugal is called Trás-os-Montes, a marvellous, remote area that is hauntingly beautiful. And below Trás-os-Montes, still ruggedly hilly, is the Beira Alta; below that, the plains of the Alentejo creep up into the province of Beira Baixa.

Taste decides how you travel Portugal – the north cooler and damper, the south hot and crowded. You'll wander towns with a rich and ancient architecture – and discos and smart shops. Accommodation ranges from luxury hotels, *pousadas* and private manor houses to simple rooms above village restaurants. Portugal is small, but almost everywhere you can have the sensation of being lost in a magical landscape – yet knowing that Lisbon, or wherever you next want to go, is handily close.

Once upon a time, fleets of bold explorers sailed from Portugal. You might think discovery an out-dated notion – until you discover, for yourself, the pleasures of Portugal.

__Preceding pages__: a shaggy traffic jam in the streets of Carviçais; the cavalry parades in Belém, near Lisbon; a *cavaleiro* expertly plants the *farpa* in mid-gallop; a reluctant worker.

Lisbon

0.5 miles / 800 m

BENFICA

Estrada de Benfica

Avenida do Uruguai

COLEGIO
MILITAR

DAMAIA

Rua C.Michaelis de Vasconcelos

Avenida General Norton de Matos

ALTO D
MOINH

Sintra

CALHARIZ

Cruz da
Pedra

PARQUE

Palácio
Fronteira

Forte de
Monsanto

SETE RIOS

BAIRRO DA
BOA VISTA

FLORESTAL

Aqueduto das
Águas Livres

CARNAXIDE

DE MONSANTO

Auto Estrada do Oeste

Auto Estrada Viaduto Duarte Pacheco

Av. de Ceuta

Estrada dos Marcos

Cascais, Estoril

CASELAS

Estrada de Queluz

Estrada do Alvito

Avenida da Ponte

Avenida das Descobertas

CARAMAO

Av. de Ilha da Madeira

ALCÂNTARA

Rua Maria Pia

Rua Sampaio Bruno

Casalinho da Ajuda

Ajuda
Palace

Jardim
Botanico

Rua Cruzeiro

ESTREL

Calçada da Ajuda

Avenida de Ceuta

TAPADA DAS
NECISSIDADES

RESTELO

Igreja da
Memorial

Calçada da Tapada

L. de
Alcântara

C. das Necessidades

Avenida do Restelo

Avenida da Ponte

Avenida Infante S

Gulbenkian
Planetarium

Archeology &
Ethnology
Museum

Calçada do Galvão

BELÉM

Rua Jau

R. do P

Maritime
Museum

Jeronimos
Monas-
tery

R.V.Portuense

Coach
Museum

SANTO
AMARO

Rua de Cascais

Avenida Vinte e Q

Avenida da India

Centro
Cultural

Praça do
Império

Praça Alfonso
de Albuquerque

Rua da Junqueira

Torre de
Belém

Monument of the
Discoveries

Avenida da India

Ponte
25 Abril

Rio Tejo

TELHEIRAS

Aeroporto
Portela de
Sacavém

Av. Padre Cruz

Al. d.L. de Torres

CAMPO
GRANDE

Avenida Marechal Craveiro Lopes

CALVANAS

Avenida General Norton de Matos

CAMPO
GRANDE

Av. A.G. Coutinho

Av. Cidade do Porto

Rotunda
do
Aeroporto

Av. M.G. da Costa

da Luz Laranjeiras

Avenida dos Combatentes

CIDADE
UNIVERSITÁRIA

City
Museum

ALVALADE

Avenida do Brasil

Av. Rio de Janeiro

TERESINHAS

Campo Grande

LARANJEIRAS

Av. Prof. G.Pinto

Av. da Igreja

ALVALADE

Avenida de Roma

Av. das Teresinhas

Avenida das Forças Armadas

ENTRE
CAMPOS

Avenida Estados Unidos da América

Avenida Almirante Gago Coutinho

Av. Álvaro Pais

Av. dos Combatentes

ENTRE
CAMPOS

ROMA

SETE RÍOS

Av. José Malhoa

Avenida Calouste Gulbenkian

PALHAVÃ

Avenida de Berna

CAMPO
PEQUENO

CAMPO PEQUENO

Av. F.M. Contreiras

Avenida João XXI

AREEIRO

Areeiro

CHELAS

Pr. de
Espanha

Calouste
Gulbenkian
Museum

C. de Outubro

Avenida da República

Palácio
Galveias

Av. A.J.de Almeida

Av. Almir. Reis

Estrada da Chelas

S. SEBASTIÃO

Av. Antonio Augusto Aguiar

SALDANHA

ALAMEDA

Fonte
Monumental

CAMPOLIDE

R.Marquês da Fronteira

SALDANHA

Av. Duque de Ávila

R. B.de Sabrosa

ALTO DE
SÃO JOAO

Saldanha

Rua Castilho

Rua de Campolide

Estufa
Fria

Estufa
Quente

PARQUE

PARQUE
EDUARDO VII

PICOAS

ARROIOS

R. P.de Melo

Rua Morais Soares

Av. Mouzinho de Albuquerque

Rua Guadim Pais

E.D.Pacheco

Shopping
Centre
Amoreiras

Av. R.J.A.D.Aguiar

Marquês
de Pombal

ESTEFÂNIA

R. Gomes Freire

Av. Almirante Reis

Avenida General Roçadas

R.Dom João V

Pr. Marquês
de Pombal

ROTUNDA

R. Jacinta Marto

ANJOS

Rua da Penha

MOREIRAS

Largo do
Rato

Rua Alex. Herculano

Avenida da Liberdade

Rua Luciano Cordeiro

INTENDENTE

R. dos Sapadores

De Azulejos
(Museum)

Saraiva

RATO

Rua do Salitre

Jardim da
Estrêla

Rua de S.Bento

Jardim
Botânico

Rua Escola Politécnica

R.da Palma

B.LOPES

Madre de
Deus (Church)

XABREGAS

silica
strêla

Calç. da Estrêla

GRAÇA

CAMINHOS
DE FERRO

Rua da Lapa

AVENIDA

Restaura-
dores

SOCORRO

R.D.V.d Operário

Santa
Engrácia

Avenida Infante D. Henrique

LAPA

Av. D.Carlos I

RESTAURADORES

Estação
do Rossio

BAIRRO
ALTO

Calç. do Combro

ROSSIO

S.Jorge
Castle

São
Vicente

R. de Santa Apolónia

Estação
Santa Apolónia

Rua do Conde

Rua D. Luis I

Rua Aurea

BAIXA

ALFAMA

Artillery
Museum

Antique Art
Museum

Avenida Vinte e Quatro de Julho

Rua do Alecrim

Sé
Cathedral

Julho

Praça do
Comércio

Av. Ribeira das Naus

Rio Tejo

Estação
Cais do Sodre

Terminal
Fluvial

Ferry to Cacilhas ↙

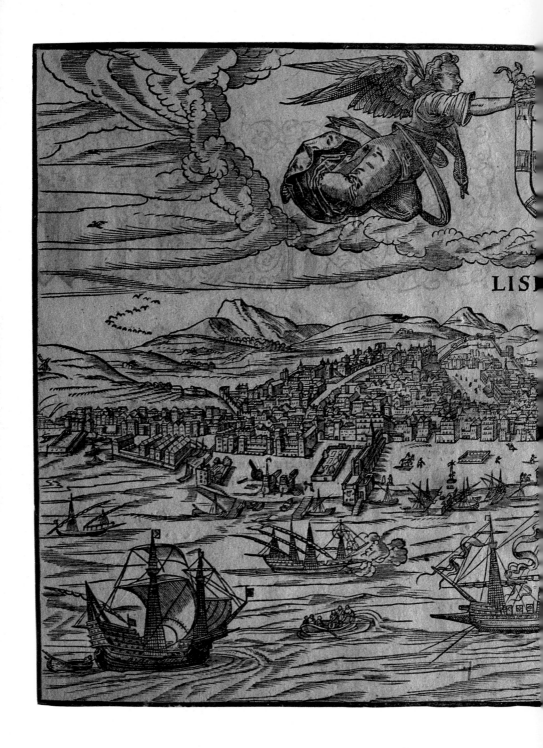

LISI

A.

LISBON

Lisbon, once the centre of the world's last great colonial empire, nostalgically holds on to the past as it comes to terms with Portugal's role as a member of the European Community (EC).

A sense of history and tradition permeates central Lisbon, giving it a leisurely, old-world quality. The Portuguese still celebrate the achievements of Vasco da Gama and Prince Henry the Navigator. They still gather in the evenings in small wineshops in the Alfama quarter to sing of lost glories and lost loves. They browse for poetry in the dusty bookstores of Bairro Alto and pause for flowers and coffee on Rossio Square. They buy fresh fish at the Ribeira Market. They bask in the shade of tropical gardens, stroll along the palm-lined mosaic pavements of Avenida da Liberdade and while away the time dreaming by the great olive-green Tagus (or Tejo) river.

The Portuguese seem better able than most people to relax. Food is a pleasure, wine a joy – when the talk is good. Shops tend to open at 9am, take a lunch break from 1–3pm and close at 6 or 7pm. Dining hours are around 7.30pm or 8pm, unlike the later hours of their Spanish neighbours. Weekends are sacred, as much for sport as church. The shops that do open on Saturday generally close at 1pm.

Lisboetans retain a certain formality that has long since disappeared from other European capitals. In business relations and even between friends and relatives, there is still much use of the third person. Titles of respect, such as *Senhor Doutor* or *Senhor Engenheiro*, *Excêlentissimo Senhor* and *Vossa Excêlencia* are often heard.

Appearances are very important. There's a popular expression, "*para Inglês ver,*" – which, loosely translated, means "putting up a good front for the foreigners."

Contemporary heroes still tour the world, not as seafarers but as soccer players, cyclists and runners. The Por-tuguese characteristics of persistence and agility, which served the ancient explorers well, have made their descendants winners.

Lisbon has felt the winds of change. Many dilapidated palaces and mansions have been tastefully renovated and turned into elegant restaurants and bars, fashionable boutiques, art galleries and discotheques. Crumbling houses in the old quarters are beginning to be restored. In outlying neighbourhoods, there are new hotels, vast and popular shopping malls, office complexes, cinemas and museums. Beyond lies the monotony of satellite dormitories.

The first view of Portugal's capital should come from the great suspension bridge on the Tagus, one and-a-half miles long and clearly inspired by San Francisco's Golden Gate. Originally called the Salazar Bridge after the late dictator António de Oliveira Salazar, under whose auspices it was completed in 1966, it was rebaptised the **25th of April Bridge**, in honour of the bloodless 1974 revolution which restored democracy to Portugal.

Lisbon possesses relatively few architectural wonders, yet is a pleasing city to tour. The ensemble of buildings, with their faded elegance and harmonious arrangement on the hills and valleys along the northern shore of the Tagus, make it one of the loveliest capitals in the world. Located a short drive from the Atlantic Ocean, Lisbon is really a Mediterranean city: pastel and white buildings, red tiled roofs, luminous sea and sky, mild winters and hot summers. But from time to time the Atlantic prevails, bringing a dark opaque mist, chill rains and threatening waves.

With a population of about a million, Greater Lisbon has absorbed many Portuguese from rural areas, and many refugees from Portugal's former colonies, the last of which, with the exception of Macau and East Timor, gained independence in 1975 as a result of the Revolution. Portuguese-Africans and Portuguese-Asians make Lisbon a cosmopolitan city.

History: According to Portuguese tradition, it was Ulysses who founded the city and gave it its original name, Olisipo. The Phoenicians, who occupied the area around 1200 BC, are said to have called it Alis Ubbo, or "delightful shore". The Romans named the site Felicitas Julia. Remains of their rule are seen in the Castelo de São Jorge, the castle that still overlooks the city, but the ramparts are essentially Visigothic, dating from the 5th century AD.

The city became increasingly important under Moorish rule, from the 8th to the 12th centuries, when it was called Al-Ushbuna. The period of the Moslem-Christian wars of the 12th and 13th centuries was a time of great building, evident in many residential palaces.

It was only after 1249, when Afonso III drove the Moors out of the southernmost region of Portugal, that Lisbon became capital of the kingdom. Under the long reign of King Dinis (1279–1325), urban life flourished. But the Black Death, which is thought to have invaded Lisbon from the sea in 1348, decimated the capital.

In the 15th century, Lisbon became an important trading centre and seat of a vast empire, rivalling Italy's Genoa and Venice. In 1497–98 Vasco da Gama opened the sea route to India, and Portuguese navigators began to establish trading posts around the world. By 1499, King Manuel I assumed the new title "lord of the navigation, conquest and Commerce of Ethiopia, Arabia, Persia and India".

Lisbon's golden age was the 16th century. Countless ships sailed to the colonies and many, although certainly not all, returned – laden with riches to glorify the Portuguese court.

Although Portugal's fortunes declined due to the heavy cost of expansion, royal feuds and 60 years of Spanish rule, Lisbon's glory continued, reaching a new apogee during King João V's reign (1706–50), thanks to the gold and diamonds from Brazil.

Then came the terrible earthquake of 1755, followed by devastating fires. The total catastrophe took as many as 30,000 lives and left most of Lisbon in ruins. Voltaire's *Candide* is one witness to the

Praça do Comércio seen from the south-east.

devastation: "The sea boiled up in the harbour and broke the ships that lay at anchor. Whirlwinds of flame and ashes covered the streets and public squares, the houses crashed down, the roofs toppled upon the foundations, and the foundations crumbled." Philosophical arguments arose over his companion's profoundly satirical response: "*All this is a manifestation of the rightness... everything is for the best.*"

The Marquês de Pombal entirely rebuilt the lower (Baixa) area of Lisbon into the form you will see today: an imposing, cleanly designed 18th-century city. The grid design of the neighbourhood makes it relatively easy to find your way around.

City centre: Lisbon is a walking city of pleasant esplanades with kiosks, cafes, benches and belvederes (ornate viewpoints). Black-and-white mosaic cobbled squares and streets are decorative, if treacherous for high heels. To cope with the hills, there are plenty of reasonably priced, black-and-green taxis – except when it rains. City transport includes bright yellow *eléctricos* or street cars, buses (some double-decker) and a metro system.

The heart of the city is a vast square facing the Tagus river called **Praça do Comércio**. This gracious space, also called Terreiro do Paço (the Place of the Palace), has in the past been compared to Venice's Piazza di San Marco, but, unhappily, is now used as a parking lot. Along the other three sides of the square are stately 18th-century government buildings. Occasionally, English-speaking visitors refer to Praça do Comércio as "Black Horse Square" because of the large equestrian statue (confusingly now green because of its patina) in its centre. The figure astride the horse is King José, ruler during and after the 1755 earthquake.

It was on the northwest corner of this square, opposite the main Post Office, that King Carlos and his oldest son and heir, Luís Felipe, were assassinated in 1908, leading to the abolition of monarchy two years later.

Praça do Comércio is also a port: from

Moonrise over Castelo São Jorge.

a landing beside the square, orange ferry-boats briskly ply back and forth. All kinds of vessels may be seen going up and down the river: long flat river barges loaded with coal or steel, container ships, and the world's great cruise liners.

In this area, unfortunately, there are no great promenades along the quay, no attractive riverside restaurants or cafés. But from April to late October, there are daily afternoon boat excursions. These provide wonderful views of the city and the busy river life. Arrangements may be made at the main hotels or at the pier on the southeast corner of Praça do Comércio.

Northwest of this square lies the **Praça do Município**, where the imposing 19th-century **City Hall** stands. In the centre is a fine 18th-century pillory, once a symbol of authority. Atop the spiral is the Manueline sphere, a symbol from King Manuel I's reign seen frequently in Portuguese architecture (and on the country's flag). The banded globe recalls the glory days of Portugal's conquests around the world.

A little further west, the **Cais do Sodré railway station** is the starting point for the electric riverside train that goes to Estoril and other resorts. Here, too, is the **Ribeira**, the dock where fishing boats come in with their catch.

Across the road, the **Mercado da Ribeira**, with its attractive dome, has an overwhelming, lush display of fresh fish, fruits and vegetables. Local restaurants serve the market's fresh swordfish, fresh grilled sardines or steamed bass, depending on the season and the catch.

Returning to Praça do Comércio, the triumphal arch on the north side of the square leads to **Rua Augusta**, which, like a number of side streets, has been closed to traffic and turned over to cafés, street vendors and shoppers.

This area is the **Baixa** or lower town, forming part of Pombal's well-planned grid of streets. Pombaline architecture is classically graceful; the handsome colour-washed buildings have carved corners and broad, stone-framed windows. Now mainly an area of banks, offices and shops, the Baixa used to be **Roses in the Rossio.**

divided into crafts. **Rua d'Ouro** and **Rua da Prata**, the streets of gold and silver respectively, still exist, and still claim quite a few jewellery shops, but they are now joined by a variety of other stores, including an inexplicable proliferation of shoe shops. On the eastern side of the Baixa, **Rua dos Fanqueiros**, which means "street of haberdashers", is still a street of textiles, but also high-rent offices.

The Baixa leads into a square that everybody calls Rossio but is formally named the **Praça de Dom Pedro IV**. Once bullfights and executions were held here; today it's a cheerful scene where old men feed pigeons, flower sellers preside over an elaborate display of seasonal blooms, and people of all ages congregate at the pavement cafes. The two fountains in the centre were brought from Paris in 1890.

At the north end of the Rossio, the **National Theatre of Dona Maria II**, built in the middle of the 19th century and restored in 1964, is a handsome building with arched windows and classic columns. To its west is a notable mock-rococo structure, the **Rossio railway station**. Trains leave from here for Sintra and nearby towns.

Rossio is linked to another square called **Praça dos Restauradores**, with an obelisk in its centre honouring the leaders of the 1640 movement against Spanish domination. Under the square there's a convenient parking lot.

On the eastern side of the Restauradores square is the Post Office. The street running behind this large building is **Rua das Portas de Santo Antão**, where shoe-shine men practise their art with a flourish while their clients sit splendidly on throne-like chairs. It is an area of popular, cheap chicken-on-the-spit restaurants and some expensive seafood places.

Back across Restauradores, the **Ministry of Tourism** is located in the lovely rose-coloured **Palácio Foz**. An office on the ground floor is open to visitors with maps, brochures and counsel.

To the north lies Lisbon's Champs Élysées, the **Avenida da Liberdade**, a

The Rossio and the Dona Maria II Theatre.

broad boulevard lined with palm trees, pools and benches. This splendid thoroughfare was laid out in 1879. It terminates at the **Praça de Marquês de Pombal**, with a statue of the man who rebuilt Lisbon on a tall column.

About halfway up the avenue on the left, a secluded square called **Parque Mayer** has several pleasant, very Portuguese restaurants not aimed at tourists. Here, too, are several popular theatres that specialise in Portuguese musical comedy: known as *revista*, it is a kind of political burlesque show with girls, songs, comics and sharp satirical comments on current events, all, unfortunately, only in Portuguese. During the dictatorship and press censorship, the *revista* was the only place where the regime was openly criticised.

The eastern hills: The easiest way to approach Alfama, the oldest quarter of Lisbon, is to take a taxi to its highest point, the **Castelo de São Jorge** and then wend your way down on foot. On close view, the Moorish castle and medieval ramparts have been perhaps too

perfectly restored; but it is a pleasant place, with shady cobblestone terraces and peacocks. The view of Lisbon, the estuary and across the Tagus to the *"Outra Baude"* is spectacular.

Descending a little, you come to the **Largo das Portas do Sol**, with another terrace providing a splendid vista over Alfama's vividly-tiled rooftops, maze of television antennae and the river.

In a handsome 17th-century palace on the Largo is the **Museu Escola de Artes Decorativas**. Philanthropist and banker Ricardo Espírito Santo established a foundation in 1953 to preserve the skills of Portugal's master craftsmen. By arrangement (tel: 886-2183) you may visit the workshops and see artisans working in leather, ceramics, wood, iron, bookbinding, carpet restoration and other crafts.

The small church of **Santa Luzia** has some interesting old tiles, including a large panel outside depicting Martim Moniz, a soldier, in the process of helping to take Lisbon from the Moors. The *miradouro*, or lookout, located here is

The Marquês de Pombal surveys the Avenida da Liberdade.

especially charming, with benches and trellised flowers.

Continuing downwards, the **Rua do Limoeiro** leads past the palace prisons of Aljube and Limoeiro, where many of Salazar's political opponents sojourned. They are now for common criminals. You should stop at the **Sé** or **Cathedral**, with its handsome Romanesque doorway, two square towers and rose window. The cloisters date back to the 13th century. They contain a variety of remnants, including some particularly interesting column fragments. The Sé was badly damaged by earthquakes in the 14th century and has been largely restored since.

There are two other churches on the way down: **Santo António da Sé**, built in 1812 on the birthplace of Lisbon's unofficial patron saint, St Anthony of Padua; and the **Church of Madalena**, built in 1783, with a fine Manueline doorway.

Another way to visit Alfama is to begin at the bottom, starting from the main square near the Tagus, **Largo do Chafariz de Dentro**. There's no particular way to go, just up: along the narrow winding alleys and stairs, past peeling facades and lines of well-scrubbed laundry, pausing in the shady cobblestone squares. **Rua de São Pedro** is a quintessential Alfama street, and it will lead you to the **Beco do Mexias**, a tiny alley with an inner court where women come to do their washing.

In summer, particularly June, every night seems to be a festival in Alfama. The streets and squares are decorated with coloured lights and streamers, and the air sparkles with fireworks. It seems that the whole city converges on Alfama to eat grilled sardines and sausages, drink wine and declaim poetry for sheer fun. The liveliest festival is on the night of St Anthony, 12 or 13 June, when neighbourhood groups parade down Avenida da Liberdade with colourful costumes and floats and end up singing and dancing in the squares of Alfama. If you are planning to wander these streets at night, be wary of youthful muggers.

To the north of Alfama rises the hill of

Shoeshine after a rough day on the cobbles.

Graça, well worth the taxi ride. The *miradouro* gives yet another magnificent view. The baroque church **Nossa Senhora da Graça** has very fine tiles.

There are three other remarkable churches on the eastern heights, outside of what was, in the Middle Ages, the city wall of Lisbon. The churches are visible from the Alfama lookouts, but it is wise to take a taxi – the labyrinth of the ancient streets can muddle your sense of direction. The 16th-century **São Vicente de Fora**, whose huge dome was restored after the 1755 earthquake, now serves as the Pantheon of the royal house of Bragança. Most of the members of Portugal's last royal family are buried here, including Dom Manuel II, who found exile in England in 1910 when the Portuguese monarchy was overthrown. King Carol of Rumania, who spent his last years in exile in Portugal, is also temporarily buried here, as is his wife, Madame Lupescu.

The National Pantheon is located in **Santa Engrácia**, nearby, and contains representative tombs of national heroes: Prince Henry the Navigator, Afonso de Albuquerque, Nuno Alvares Pereira, and Pedro Alvares Cabral, among others. The church was begun in the 16th century. According to popular legend, a merchant was wrongly accused of stealing the host from Santa Engrácia and put to death around 1630. It was said that he cast a spell whereby the construction of the church would never be completed – which it wasn't. Thus the Portuguese expression: "*obras de Santa Engrácia,*" meaning a task never done.

Salazar, however, took up the challenge and had the church completed in 1966. Some people wish he had not bothered, as it is not one of Lisbon's loveliest monuments.

On the eastern outskirts of Lisbon beyond the Santa Apolónia railroad station, the old monastery of Madre de Deus is now the **Museu dos Azulejos**, the Tile Museum. Founded in 1509 by Queen Leonor, the monastery boasts one of the best collections of Portuguese tiles of the 16th to 18th centuries. Among the most outstanding tile scenes

The ruined cloisters at Lisbon cathedral.

are a panorama of Lisbon from 1730 and the life of St Anthony, about 1780. The church, connected to the museum, is decorated with rich gilded woodwork, huge panels of fine paintings, and, of course, tiles. Close by in the waterside area of the docks, Lisbon is changing again – for Expo 98.

The western hills: The quickest way to get to **Bairro Alto**, or the high neighbourhood, from the city centre, is by using the **Santa Justa Lift**. This mini-Eiffel Tower on Rua Santa Justa, just off Rua d'Ouro, was designed by the noted French engineer. For a small fee, you can ride to the top of the hill to the ruins of the 14th-century **Carmo Monastery**. The roof and other sections of this building were destroyed by the 1755 earthquake; what remains provides a dramatic setting for summertime concerts. The monastery serves as an archaeological museum as well, with marble bas reliefs, tombs from the 13th century and prehistoric pottery.

Then there's the slow approach, strolling up the **Chiado**, Lisbon's most fash-ionable shopping area. From Rossio, head for **Rua do Carmo**, a pedestrian mall, which leads past areas recovering from a 1988 fire into **Rua Garrett**. Here are the best boutiques, shoe shops, silver and porcelain shops and bookstores. Here, too, is the **Brasileira**, the favourite café of Lisbon's artists and politicians.

On the south side of the Chiado is another great view of the city, the river and São Jorge, from the **Largo da Biblioteca Nacional**. Nearby, the opulent **Teatro São Carlos**, built in 1792 and inspired by La Scala of Milan, has a season of international and Portuguese opera, ballet and concerts. Around the corner, the less ornate municipal theatre of **São Luiz** also presents good concerts and the National Ballet Company.

At the top of the **Rua do Alecrim** is a small square with a romantic statue of 19th-century novelist Eça de Queiroz embracing his scarcely clad muse.

Rua Garrett leads into the **Largo de Chiado**, with two churches of interest: 17th-century **Nossa Senhora de Loreto**,

Fashionable shopping in the Chiado.

with some good marble and wood sculptures, and **Nossa Senhora de Encarnação**, rebuilt in the 18th century with a lovely painted ceiling and an entire wall of blue tiles.

Adjoining the Chiado is the large **Praça de Camões** with shady elms and a monument to the great epic poet Luís de Camões, who died in obscure poverty in Lisbon in 1580. John Dos Passos compares Camões's monumental poem, *Os Lusíadas*, which glorifies the discoveries, to the *Odyssey*: "An epic of the sea, full of the smell of pitch and creaking timbers and the spray screaming off the caps of the ocean waves."

Nearby is another 16th-century church, **São Roque**. The facade, however, was largely destroyed in 1755 and has been very plainly restored. The interior is notable for its fine tiles, painted wood ceilings and beautiful marbles. One of its side chapels is the fabulous **Chapel of St John the Baptist**, with columns made of lapis lazuli. Adjacent to this is the **Museum of Sacred Art** with a very small collection of fine 17th- and 18th-century silver, paintings and embroidered altarpieces.

Moving up **Rua São Pedro de Alcântara**, noted mainly for its antique shops, you arrive at another shady terrace with an admirable view of the city and the São Jorge castle. Just across the street is the **Port Wine Institute** (*Sólar do Instituto do Vinho do Porto*) located in an 18th-century palace. Its cosy bar offers a vast selection.

Here on the left is Bairro Alto proper, a picturesque maze of cobblestone alleys and old tenements. This quarter was built on solid rock and generally withstood the great earthquake. Some of the buildings have peeling facades or worn blue tiles but are decorated with fine wrought-iron balconies, flowerpots and birdcages.

In the old days, Bairro Alto was known for its good *fado* houses. There are basically two kinds of *fado*: the epic song born in the former African colonies of hardship, full of *saudade* or bittersweet nostalgia; and *fado vadio* – amateur singing off the cuff. *Fado* is still a rite and you should remain silent during a performance. Most Portuguese go to *fado* houses after dinner (the food in *fado* houses is generally not outstanding), drink wine and lose themselves in nostalgic reflections. Today, many have become blatantly commercial, offering foreign guests songs like "The Yellow Rose of Texas".

Some mansions in the Bairro Alto have been restored and turned into fashionable restaurants, discotheques and art galleries. Avant-garde Portuguese art can be seen and purchased in several elegant galleries, among them: **Os Cómicos** and **Emi-Valentim Carvalho**. Another fine gallery is located in **São Mamede**, on Rua da Escola Politécnica.

The Portuguese delight in gardens, so naturally Lisbon is laced with green spaces. Perhaps the finest of them all is the **Jardim Botánico**, one of the richest botanical gardens in Europe. Created in 1873, just off the Rua da Escola Politécnica, the garden has a magnificent wall of 100-year-old palm trees, banana trees, bamboo and water lilies and many exotic tropical plants.

Mass at São Roque.

Northwest of Bairro Alto is another hill with the charming **Estrêla Gardens** and splendid 18th-century **Basilica of Estrêla** with its great dome and pink, yellow and blue marble interior. Here can be found the remarkable room-sized crib carved by Machado de Castro. This neighbourhood is in some ways an Anglo-Saxon oasis. Close by is the British hospital, the little English **Church of St George**, and the adjacent English cemetery where Henry Fielding, the author of *Tom Jones,* is buried. Descending the hill on Rua São Domingos á Lapa, and turning to the right, you will see the **American Ambassador's Residence**, a splendid old-rose palace and garden with a marvellous view of the river. Further down the hill is another rose palace housing the **British Embassy** and, just beyond, the **British Ambassador's Residence** in a 17th-century convent.

There are a number of ways to get to the **Palácio de São Bento**, where the National Assembly is located. You may take the Calçada de Estrêla downhill, or climb the Avenida Dom Carlos I, which begins on the riverfront road just west of the central market. Special permission must be obtained to enter São Bento. Originally built as a monastery, the palace was transformed into the parliament at the end of the 19th century. It was renovated in 1935 and decorated with rich sculptures and paintings.

Former dictator António de Oliveira Salazar lived and worked in a small house behind the palace, hidden by a high wall. It was here in 1975 that Portugal's new leaders drafted their revolutionary constitution, which has since been amended.

Going back to the river road and continuing westward, you will reach the **National Museum of Ancient Art**, (*Museu Nacional de Arte Antiga*), located in a fine 17th-century palace with a tasteful modern extension. On display are many pieces of 16th-century porcelain brought back by Portuguese sailors from India, Japan and Macau. Don't miss the masterpiece attributed to the 15th-century painter Nuno Gonçalves,

__Left__, wedding music at São Roque. __Right__, the Estrêla Basilica.

a polyptych depicting St Vincent, Lisbon's patron saint, and a select group of admirers including a figure presumed to be Prince Henry the Navigator, who wears a large black hat.

There are also fine wood and terracotta figures by the great 18th-century sculptor, Machado de Castro. Foreign works include Pierro Della Francesca's *St Augustine*, Hans Memling's *Virgin And Child*, Raphael's *St Eusebius*, Bosch's dizzying *The Temptation of St Anthony* and Dürer's *St Jerome*.

Leaving the museum you can head a short distance westward, and climb the Avenida do Infante Santo. There, on the left is a pre-earthquake royal palace called the **Palácio das Necessidades**, which was originally a monastery. This fine building in Lisbon's ubiquitous rose-coloured stone has a magnificent view and gardens. It is now the Portuguese Ministry of Foreign Affairs, and is not open to the public.

The northern hills: Newer Lisbon rises on the hills to the north of the city like a many-tiered fan. The Praça de Marquês de Pombal can be used as a point of reference for various tours.

Directly north of this circle rises the **Parque de Eduardo VII**, commemorating a visit by the British king to Lisbon in 1902. At the top of this grassy sloping lawn with box hedges in geometrical design is one of the finest views directly down to the city and the river. On the northwestern corner of is the **Estufa Fria**, or Cold Greenhouse, a kind of tropical jungle, protected by bamboo slats. Overlooking the park on the west are several of the city's best and most elegant hotels.

Heading in a northwesterly direction from Praça Marquês de Pombal on Rua Joaquim António de Aguiar (towards Sintra) you will suddenly come upon a group of startling pink and blue box-like towers. Called **Amoreiras**, the vast complex of hotels, offices, apartments and shopping centre looks like some futuristic toy made from building bricks. Architect Tomás Taveira's other multi-coloured edifices are increasingly disrupting the rows of conformist struc-

Two views of Parque de Eduardo VII.

tures that characterise much of Lisbon's modern architecture.

On the hill at the northern end of Eduardo VII park stand the picturesque old penitentiary and the sleek new court building. Beyond lies the neighbourhood of **Benfica**, known mainly for its stadium and as the home of one of Portugal's favourite soccer teams.

Here, too, is found the **Jardim Zoológico** which is not an ordinary zoo but rather a garden with animals. Founded in 1905 in the Quinta das Laranjeiras, the zoo is constantly trying to improve its inmates' conditions.

One area changing fast is the **Praça de Espanha**, slightly to the northeast of Pombal and the park. Here is the **American Embassy** in a renovated old palace.

Nearby in a well-designed modern complex is the **Calouste Gulbenkian Foundation and Museum** and the **Centre of Modern Art**. Gulbenkian, an Armenian oil magnate from Turkey who personally owned five percent of Iraq Petroleum Company, spent the last 13 years of his life in Lisbon. He died in 1955. Besides supporting artists around the world, the Gulbenkian Foundation sponsors a comprehensive year-round programme of music, ballet and modern dance at its headquarters in Lisbon.

The Gulbenkian Museum contains one of the richest private collections in the world. Outstanding is the section of Middle Eastern and Islamic Art, which includes an alabaster bowl from Egypt's Old Kingdom (about 2,700 BC) and an Assyrian bas-relief representing the *Genius of Spring* in alabaster dating back to the 9th century BC. There are Syrian mosque lamps and glass items from the 14th century, and many richly illuminated Armenian manuscripts from the 12th to the 14th centuries.

There's an outstanding collection of Greek gold and silver coins from the 6th century BC to the 1st century AD. Among the Oriental pieces are fine Chinese porcelains of the 17th century, jades of the 18th century and Japanese prints and lacquers of the 18th and 19th centuries.

In the European collection are paint-

Amoreiras shopping and office complex.

ings by masters such as Carpaccio, Van Dyck, Ruysdael, Colbert, Rubens and Rembrandt. There are splendid 16th-century Italian tapestries and furniture by the finest French *ébénistes* (ebony craftsmen) of the 18th century. There's also an unusual display of the flamboyant jewellery and glass by the dean of Art Nouveau, René Lalique.

A well-tended park with ponds, paths with modern sculpture and an outdoor auditorium connect the Gulbenkian Museum with the more recent **Centre of Modern Art**. Here are the works of many of Portugal's finest contemporary artists, including Maria Helena Vieira da Silva, who made her reputation in Paris. Others include the powerful first generation of modernists – José de Almada Negreiros, Eduardo Viana and Jorge Barradas – and the talented painters that followed, including Julio Pomar, Maria Ines Menez, Paula Rego.

Carlos Botelho prints the soul of Lisbon; and sculptor João Cutileiro creates statues of the slender frolicking women with big breasts and bushy hair that are increasingly visible in the city's parks and gardens.

The easiest way to get to northeastern Lisbon and the "new avenues" is by taking Avenida Fontes Pereira de Melo, again from Pombal circle. On the left, the tall yellow-tile Sheraton Hotel looks like the office building that it was originally meant to be. Across the way, the large modern convention hall called **Picoas**, with a cafeteria, bookstore and bank, also has exhibition facilities.

Along Avenida da República you cannot miss the large red bull ring, **Campo Pequeno**, built in 1892. More sensitive visitors may enjoy Portuguese bullfights, called *touradas*, because unlike the Spanish, the Portuguese don't kill their bulls – at least not in public.

Across the street, the **Feira Popular** is essentially an amusement park, but it's a good place to get snails in butter and grilled sardines when they are in season (from June to October).

The avenue runs through **Campo Grande**, a shady promenade with a small lake. On the left stands **Cidade**

Lisbon's bullfights are in the Campo Pequeno.

178

Universitária, a group of pleasant if not spectacular modern buildings. The university campus is generally orderly these days although there was a time, just after the 1974 revolution, when the students took the law into their own hands.

Attached to the campus is the **Biblioteca Nacional**. The National Library was founded in 1796, but moved to this building in 1969. Its collection is extensive; you can get a glimpse of exhibitions that change monthly. Nearby, and architecturally much more striking, is the fort-like **Torre de Touto**, which holds the national archives.

At the end of Campo Grande you may turn right to the airport, or visit two museums. In an 18th-century palace, the **Museu da Cidade**, or Municipal Museum, has an interesting collection of archaeological pieces and old engravings relating to Lisbon's past. About a mile down the road to Lumiar, the **Museu do Traje**, or Costume Museum, is located in an old manor with delightful gardens.

Belém: In a green, spacious zone by the river, on the western side of Lisbon, a number of monumental buildings stand as a reminder of Portugal's maritime and colonial past. **Belém** actually means Bethlehem in Portuguese, reflecting the involvement of the Portuguese rulers with the Crusades.

Lisbon's most glorious monument is the **Monastery of Jerónimos**, built to honour Vasco da Gama and his successful journey to India in 1499. King Manuel personally laid the cornerstone of the Hieronymite monastery in 1502 at Belém, on the site of a chapel founded by Prince Henry the Navigator.

It was here, too, in the cloisters of Jerónimos, that the formal ceremony was held on 1 January 1986 marking Portugal's long-awaited entry into the European Community.

This vast opulent limestone building is a masterpiece of Manueline (or late Gothic) architecture. Notable are: the two tiered cloisters completed in 1517, the southern door with multiple carved statues and the Templar cross, and two windows with carved rope, anchors and

Left, the Monument to the Discoveries; **right**, Christ in Majesty.

other seafaring symbols. The grand interior has six great octagonal stone columns with ornate decoration which have withstood time and the earthquake of 1755. Also of special interest are the finely chiselled modern altars, brilliant stained glass windows and monumental carved tombs. Vasco da Gama and Camões lie here. Today the church is a favourite place for weddings and is open to all.

Some critics complain that Jerónimos has been too thoroughly cleaned, because its golden patina is gone. Others also lament the recent construction of a wing in rather poor Manueline imitation, obscuring a fine door. Built on the western side of the church in the latter part of the 19th century, this wing houses the **National Museum of Archaeology and Ethnology** with an interesting collection of folk art dating to the Stone and Bronze Ages.

On the other end of this wing, the **Museu da Marinha** (Navy Museum), tells the story of Portugal's seafaring discoveries with paintings, models, sculpture and maps from the empire.

Close by – too close, some say – is the huge squat **Centro Cultural de Belém**, opened in 1992 when Portugal, for six months, assumed the EC presidency. With facilities for conventions as well as culture, it has not been warmly received in Lisbon.

Across the park and to the west on the river stands the **Torre de Belém**, where Vasco da Gama and other navigators set forth on their explorations. This exquisite little 16th-century fortress is another fine example of the unique Manueline style with its richly carved niches, towers and shields bearing the Templar cross.

A short distance east stands the **Monument to the Discoveries**, built in 1960. It is a stylised caravel with figures representing the Portuguese who took part in the great adventure standing on the prow, Prince Henry the Navigator at the fore, looking out to sea.

Across the railway rises the ornate rose-coloured **Palácio de Belém**, which once served as a royal retreat and is now the Presidential palace. Decorated with lavish Oriental and European furnishings, this is where the President of the Republic has his offices and gives official receptions.

Adjacent, in what was once the royal riding-school, is the **National Coach Museum**, housing one of the finest collections of its kind in Europe. The museum contains a 16th-century coach that once belonged to King Philip II of Spain and a number of well preserved gilt carriages of the 17th and 18th centuries, royal litters and sedan chairs and an ecclesiastical throne.

Behind the palace is a wonderful but rather neglected **Botanical Garden**, with all kinds of exotic plants and shady walkways.

On the eastern side of Belém Palace, up the Calçada da Ajuda hill is the imposing **Palácio da Ajuda**, built after the earthquake as a royal palace but never completed. The palace is used for exhibitions and concerts, and some rooms with unusual ceilings, fine tapestries and lavish furnishings are open to the public.

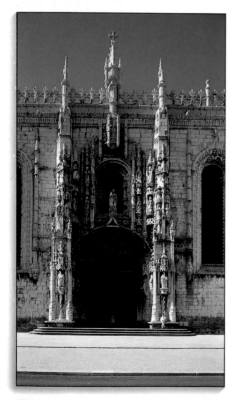

Left, Jerónimos Monastery. Right, Torre de Belém.

CASCAIS AND ESTORIL

In the tourist trade this strip is known as the Costa do Sol. At its heart is the *Marginal*, a delightful 29-km (18-mile) drive along the northern bank of the Tagus, or Tejo, river to the Atlantic.

There are several ways of getting there. A good way is by the electric train that leaves from Lisbon's Cais do Sodré station and wends its way along the coast as far as Cascais. It's about a half-hour ride, with stops. Particularly in the spring the bank along the train track is filled with colourful wildflowers. A leisurely yellow tramway also runs from the Praça do Comércio as far out as the resort of Cruz Quebrada.

If you're driving, the inland *autostrada* or super highway starts at Marquês de Pombal Circle, runs past the Amoreiras shopping complex, through the valley of Alcântara, and parallel to the grandiose **Aqueduto das Aguas Livres**. The 17.5-km (11-mile) aqueduct was built in the 18th century as the main source of water for the capital, and it still supplies public parks and fountains. The highway goes through the park of **Monsanto**, a vast area of eucalyptus trees and umbrella pines, pleasant winding roads and belvederes with magnificent views over Lisbon. Beyond the park, the highway (with a branch right to Sintra) will take you past Oeiras to Estoril and Cascais.

The river road starts out at the Praça do Comércio as the Avenida de 24 de Julho, changes its name to the Avenida da India and becomes the *Marginal* at the 25th of April Bridge.

As the road passes by the working quarter of **Alcântara**, some dramatic political art is visible. These murals are mostly the work of the Portuguese Communist Party and Marxist-Leninist groups, dating mainly to the early days of Portugal's 1974 Revolution.

Further on is the **International Fair Building**, which frequently hosts trade fairs and exhibitions. Then comes Belém with its historical monuments and parks.

Preceding pages: Cabo Espichel. Below, the beach at Estoril.

Just beyond lies the elegant hillside neighbourhood of **Restelo**, where many embassies and diplomatic residences are located. **Algés** is the first town outside the city limits, and it is here that taxi drivers turn off their meters and start counting the fare by kilometres.

A string of small riverside towns follow. **Dáfundo** has several fine old mansions standing in sad contrast alongside dilapidated rent-controlled housing. It also boasts the **Vasco da Gama Aquarium**, with its fascinating world of sea turtles, eels, barnacles and all kinds of fish.

Cruz Quebrada is the site of a stone-seated stadium built for soccer matches. **Caxias** is known for its flowering villas, 18th-century gazebos and an infamous hillside prison-fort. **Oeiras** has a fine 18th-century baroque church, lovely park, modern apartment blocks and an austere 16th-century fort.

Just beyond lies the 17th-century fortress of **São Julião da Barra**, marking the point where the Tagus river meets the Atlantic. **Carcavelos** has several moderate hotels and a broad sandy beach.

You've arrived: Finally, **Estoril** is the first point of what has often been called the Golden Triangle and includes Cascais and Sintra. A flowering, palm-lined, pastel resort, it first gained fame at the turn of the century for its therapeutic spring waters. During World War II, Estoril became known as a hunting ground for international spies. Later, this corner of the Atlantic, with its mild weather and gracious lifestyle, became a home-away-from-home for European royalty and other refugees fleeing the political upheavals after World War II. Among the Triangle's illustrious residents were former King Simeon of Bulgaria, former King Umberto of Italy, and Antenor Patiño of Bolivia.

With changing times, local aristocrats are beginning to sell or rent their villas. More and more Portuguese and foreigners come to the Triangle either to live, retire or keep summer homes. Estoril has now become a cosmopolitan playground with its celebrated casino, first-rate hotels, restaurants and a range of

The gardens at Estoril Casino.

popular international tennis and golf tournaments.

The **Casino** is a low white modern building with immaculately kept gardens. A passport or identity card is necessary, and the minimum age limit is 18. Some people come to the casino to see the show, usually a colourful international extravaganza. There is also an elegant dining room, an art gallery, a cinema and a bar.

The **Estoril Music Festival** takes place from mid-July to mid-August. Concerts and recitals are held in the **Estoril Cathedral,** the **Cascais Cidadela** (fort) and other impressive settings.

The **Handicrafts Fair** has become a major production, lasting throughout the months of July and August. Located near the railway station, the fair features arts, crafts, food, wine and folk music from all over the country.

Unfortunately **Estoril Beach** and most other beaches along the Costa do Sol are polluted and crowded.

There is a lot to do in the way of sports in the Triangle. The **Estoril Golf Club**'s course, on the outskirts of town, is one of the loveliest in Europe. It was laid out by McKenzie Ross on a hillside dotted with pine and eucalyptus groves. The smaller **Estoril-Sol Golf Course** is located in a pine wood at **Linhó** near Sintra. Overlooking the Atlantic coast just beyond Cascais is the **Marinha Golf Club**, with swimming pools, tennis and riding facilities and a course designed by Robert Trent Jones. The **Estoril Autódromo** or automobile race track, located inland on the road to Sintra, draws large crowds for the Grand Prix Formula One races. It is also the site for the start and finish of the annual international Port Wine Rally.

Cascais has its own bull ring – the largest in the country – but not many fights are scheduled. The main problem is that it is very windy: it would have made a better place for a windmill. There's horseback riding at the **Escola da Equitação de Birre**, on the road to Sintra and at the **Centro Hípico da Marinha**, inland from the Guincho Beach. The Marinha Club also has mini-cruises of Cascais Bay. The **Cascais**

Naval Club has facilities for water skiing, wind-surfing and sailing, and holds the Star Class Sailing World Championship.

Although it was once a royal resort, Cascais doesn't have the glitter of Estoril. In 1870, King Luís I established his summer residence in the 17th-century **Citadel** on the Bay of Cascais. Before that, it was known only as a fishing port. Locals claim that a fisherman from Cascais, Afonso Sanches, actually discovered America in 1482, and Christopher Columbus merely repeated the trip 10 years later and got all the glory.

In 1580, the Duke of Alba attacked the village as part of Spain's claim to Portugal. And in 1589, the English arrived here as retaliation for the Spanish Armada's 1588 foray. But for the most part, Cascais has been as quiet as it is today, with the main attractions of the little town being the comings and goings of the colourful fishing boats in the bay, the noisy nightly auction at the central fish market, and good shopping and restaurants.

There are several lovely old churches and chapels in Cascais, including the 17th-century **Nossa Senhora da Assunção** with its plain facade, lovely tiles and marble nave. It contains several paintings by Josefa de Óbidos. A weekly market displays handicrafts as well as fresh fruits and vegetables.

On the outskirts of town in an exotic garden, is the **Castro Guimarães Museum** with displays of 17th-century Portuguese silver, tiles and furniture, and good 19th-century paintings.

Beyond Cascais lies the rocky Atlantic coast. Lisboetans flock here on weekends to several popular seafood restaurants. Some swim at the broad clean beach of Guincho, where the waves can be wild and the undertow fierce. Windsurfers love it.

Others come to shop in this unlikely spot where apart from a cluster of stalls at **Boca do Inferno** (Mouth of Hell), vendors sell colourful woven rugs, sheepskin carpets and craftwork. And some people simply like to take the road to Sintra, through the pines and along the open coast.

Right, windsurfing at Praia do Guincho.

SINTRA

With its lush forests and gentle surrounding plain, Sintra has long been a favourite summer resort for Portuguese and foreign aristocrats and vacationers. People delight in the area because of its sheer natural beauty, in spite of man playing a few of his tasteless tricks.

Lord Byron, who could find little good to say about the Portuguese, was enamoured of Sintra and likened it to "Elysium's gates". In *Childe Harold*, he wrote: "Lo! Cintra's glorious Eden intervenes in variegated maze of mount and glen."

Byron, Southey, Beckford and others who have written eloquently of the charms of Sintra would probably be horrified by some recent signs of development. The most conspicuous mistake is the Tivoli Hotel, a large graceless block, incongruously placed beside the imposing National Palace. The romantics would be dismayed by the recent growth of small, new, rainbow-coloured houses below Sintra where there used to be large estates or wooded countryside.

Some 32 km (20 miles) to the northwest of Lisbon, Sintra is another world with its own special climate and almost bucolic way of life. The most practical way to go is by train from Rossio. If you drive, rush hour traffic should be avoided if at all possible. It seems that most of the inhabitants of Sintra commute to Lisbon on weekdays and vice-versa on weekends.

The road to Sintra from Lisbon starts at the Pombal Circle and is well marked. Avenida Duarte Pacheco runs into the *autostrada* or super highway that leads out of town, past the Aqueduto das Aguas Livres, up the hill through Monsanto Park, turning right to join the highway to Sintra.

A slight detour to visit **Queluz** is well worthwhile. The town has become a rather drab Lisbon dormitory; the **Palace**, however, is a marvellous rose-coloured edifice with a magnificent facade. It was first built as a simple manor for King Pedro in the mid-17th century and enlarged when the court moved there. Most of the palace is baroque, but the courtyard and formal gardens were modelled after Versailles.

In summer, concerts are sometimes held in the **Music Room**. At other times, the public may visit the lavishly decorated **Throne Room** with its fine painted wood ceiling, the **Hall of Mirrors**, **Ambassador's Room**, and others. The great kitchen, with its stone chimney and copperware, has been turned into a luxury restaurant called Cozinha Velha. Palace and gardens are a spectacular stage during August and September for **Noites de Queluz** (Nights at Queluz), enchanting musical recreations of 18th-century court life.

Back on the main road continue along rolling hills, past modest whitewashed villages and rich *quintas*, or manors, to arrive at the **Serra de Sintra**. At the base of the mountain lies the village of **São Pedro de Sintra**, where on the second and fourth Sunday of each month, a wonderful country fair takes place. On display are all kinds of crafts from primi-

Left, the eccentric Castelo da Pena. Right, Sintra's Palácio Nacional.

tive wood carvings and ceramics to fine antique furniture, as well as the latest plastic utensils and polyester tablecloths. São Pedro is also known for its popular tavernas, with spicy sausages, hearty codfish and heady wines.

The road climbs slightly and curves around the mountain to reach the centre of town. Here is the office of *Turismo* with maps, information and exhibition halls. Also nearby, the **Estalagem dos Cavaleiros**, formerly called the Hotel Lawrence, where Lord Byron stayed in 1809. New owners hope to turn semi-ruin to restored inn.

Two 12th-century churches in town, **Santa Maria** and **São Martinho**, have both been much altered over time. There is also a Municipal Museum, which offers a pleasant way of getting acquainted with Sintra's history.

The centrepiece of Sintra is the former royal palace, now called the **Palácio Nacional**, parts of which date back to the 14th century. Broad stairs lead up to the stately building with Gothic arches, Moorish windows and two extraordi-nary chimney cones. Of special interest on the guided tour of the palace are: the **Sala dos Brasões**, with its remarkable ceiling panels painted in 1515, which show the coat-of arms of 72 Portuguese noble families (note that actually only 71 exist; that of the Távoras was removed after the conspiracy against King José in 1758); the **Sala dos Arabes**, with marble fountain and 15th-century Moorish tiles; the **Sala dos Cisnes**, an enormous reception hall with swans painted on the panelled ceiling; the **Sala das Pegas**, whose ceiling is covered with magpies brandishing banners reading "Por Bem". It is said that when Queen Philippa caught King João I courting a lady-in-waiting, he claimed it was an innocent kiss. "Por Bem," he said, which loosely translated means: "All for the good."

Sintra's other palace-museum, the **Castelo da Pena**, dominates the town from the top of the mountain. You can drive up, take a taxi, or even walk. The road winds up steep rocky slopes through thick woods to the castle, built on the **Queluz, Portugal's Versailles.**

site of a 16th-century monastery. For many visitors, Pena is better viewed from afar, where it gives the impression of some medieval stronghold.

Close at hand, the castle is an architectural monstrosity, a potpourri of various styles and influences. Arabic minarets, Gothic towers, Renaissance cupolas, Manueline windows. It was commissioned by Prince Ferdinand of Saxe-Coburg-Gotha, husband of Queen Maria II, and built by German architect Baron von Eschwege around 1840.

At the entrance of the castle, a tunnel leads to the ruins of the original monastery. The old chapel walls are decorated with fine 17th-century tiles and there is a splendid altar of alabaster and black marble by 16th-century French sculptor Nicolas Chanterène. But the best thing about the castle is the view. Below lies **Pena Park**, with lakes and black swans, tangled forest and tile fountains. When Richard Strauss visited the park, he supposedly said: "I know Italy, Sicily, Greece, Egypt, but I have never seen anything equal to Pena."

Across the way, another mountain-top castle, the **Castelo dos Mouros**, is now the only ruins of a Moorish fortress, dating to perhaps the 11th century. The fortifications visible along the mountain ridge were restored in the middle of the 19th century. To the southwest rises the highest peak called **Cruz Alta**, 540 metres (1,772 ft) high and marked by a stone cross.

The mountainside is a luxuriant mass of vegetation – subtropical plants, boulders covered with moss, giant ferns, walnut, chestnut and pine trees, and rhododendron bushes.

One of the strangest sights on the mountain is the **Convento dos Capuchos**, a 16th-century monastery built entirely out of rocks and cork. Some say the monks lined their cells with cork to obtain absolute silence – but there is little noise in the forest other than bird sounds. More likely, the cork helped insulate the monks from the long and bitter winters.

On the outskirts of town stands the **Palácio de Seteais**, an obscure name

The Throne Room at Queluz.

said to mean "The palace of the seven sighs", perhaps relating to the beauty of the surroundings. Built by a Dutch diamond merchant in the 18th century, Seteais is remembered as the site where Generals Junot and Dalrymple signed the Convention of Sintra in 1809, after the defeat of Napoleon by British and Portuguese forces.

The palace was restored and turned into a luxury hotel and restaurant in 1955 and should be seen, if only for tea or a drink. The elegant rooms are decorated with crystal chandeliers, wall-hangings, murals and antique furnishings. From the gardens, with their sculpted hedges and lemon trees, you have a magnificent view of the surrounding countryside.

At the **Quinta de Penha Verde**, not far from here, João de Castro planted the first orange trees in Portugal after retiring as viceroy of India in 1542.

Nearby is the **Quinta da Monserrate**, a strange Moorish-type villa built in the 19th century by Sir Francis Cook. The property is now owned by the State but poorly maintained. The villa is closed but the exotic garden and greenhouse are worth seeing for their trees and plants from all over the world: palm trees, bamboo, cedars, magnolia trees, cork-oaks, pines and giant ferns.

Once part of the Monserrate gardens, the **Quinta de São Thiago** is a 16th-century manor with a fine chapel, majestic kitchen, cell-like bedrooms, garden and its own swimming pool. Like other gentry, the owners found taxes and utilities prohibitive and, in 1979, opened the *quinta* to paying guests. Nearby, an extremely attractive option is the **Quinta da Capole**.

The main cultural event of the area is the annual **Festival of Sintra**, generally running for three weeks in July. First-class recitals, concerts and ballet are presented in the National Palace, Queluz Palace and some of the great *quintas* of the region. And all summer long, the "Sound and Light" programme is presented on weekend evenings at the National Palace.

For a delightful excursion, the **Colares Road** leads through vineyards, white-washed hamlets and stone walls to the sea. En route, it is possible to visit the **Adega Regional**, a traditional winery. Colares grapes grow in sandy soil with humid maritime climate. The wines are dark ruby and very smooth.

Cabo da Roca is a wild desolate cape, known as the westernmost point of continental Europe. Visitors receive a certificate to mark their visit. Heading north, there are several beaches frequented mainly by Portuguese: broad, sandy **Praia Grande** and **Praia das Maçãs**. The fishing village of **Azenhas do Mar** has a natural rock seashore swimming pool.

Huge palaces: Another excursion could be to **Mafra**, the immense palace-convent which is almost as large as Spain's Escorial. To get there follow the road for **Ericeira**, a beach resort and fishing village, and then drive inland for 10 km (6 miles). (From Lisbon there is now a good fast road.)

Mafra rises just like some dark mirage across the plain from the modest low-lying houses that make up the vil-

Palácio de Seteais.

lage of the same name. Originally, a Capuchin monastery stood on the site, but João V erected the new collection of buildings, on quite a different scale, in fulfilment of a vow he made in hopes of begetting an heir. Work began on the palace in 1717 and ended 18 years later. Estimates of the enormous cost of the project vary, but more than 50,000 workers and 1,000 oxen were employed. Planned to house a mere 13 friars, it has room for hundreds – and many novices as well.

Mafra's construction drew so many artists from so many countries that João decided to found the School of Mafra, utilising these talented artisans as masters to local apprentices. The most famous teacher was probably Joaquim Machado de Castro.

The limestone facade is massive at 220 metres (720 ft) long. At its centre is the **church**, with two tall towers and an Italianate portico. The interior of the church is decorated with the finest Portuguese marbles of different colours. The 14 large statues of saints, located in the vestibule, are carved from Carrara marble – they were made by Italian sculptors. The church contains a generous supply of organs – six.

Part of the monastery is off-limits to the general public, being used by the military, but many sections can be visited. The most impressive room is the **library**, full of baroque magnificence and light. Among its 35,000 volumes are first editions of *Os Lusíadas* by Camões and the earliest edition of Homer in Greek.

Other areas open to the public include the **hospital**, with original decorations and fittings, the **pharmacy**, the **audience room**, painted with a trompe l'oeil, and the oval **chapterhouse**. There are three **cloisters**. The north tower can be climbed, and the two **towers** together contain more than 100 bells, some of which were cast in Belgium.

The town of Mafra is also the site of the church of **Santo André**, which contains the tomb of Diogo de Sousa. Pedro Hispano was priest here before he was elected Pope John XXI in 1276.

The library at Mafra.

SETÚBAL AND THE ARRÁBIDA PENINSULA

Lisboetans call it *Outra Banda*, the other shore, meaning the southern bank of the Tagus river, long neglected because of the sheer inconvenience of getting there. This all changed after 1966 with the completion of what was then Europe's longest suspension bridge, the 25th of April Bridge. The region, known as the **Arrábida Peninsula**, has developed rapidly and not always wisely.

Directly across the river is the unassuming ferryboat port of **Cacilhas**. Its main charm is a string of riverfront fish restaurants with a grand view of Lisbon. About 5 km (3 miles) west of the bridge is **Trafaria**; the whole town, since rebuilt, was burned to the ground on the harsh orders of Pombal in 1777 as punishment for resisting press gangs. Most visitors tend to drive through the neighbouring industrial town of **Almada**, except those who want to examine the **Christ the King** monument close at hand. Christ seems dwarfed by his pedestal – irreverent Portuguese say some priest must have dipped into the till before the statue was completed. Visitors may go up to the top of the pedestal by elevator and stairs for a magnificent view of Lisbon. Almada also contains the monastery of **São Paulo**, founded in 1568.

Most people avoid the *Outra Banda* dormitory district by taking the super highway leading directly from the bridge. After a few kilometres, a turnoff leads to **Costa da Caparica**, a series of broad Atlantic beaches with moderately priced hotels and restaurants. This popular resort is cleaner than the Costa do Sol, and the currents are safer than those of the Atlantic north of the Tagus.

Continuing south on the highway, you pass new factories. The road marked **Palmela** leads to a small town with a great **medieval castle**. This has been restored and converted into a luxury *pousada*, with a lounge in the cloisters, elegant dining-room in the old refectory, and antique furnishings. The at-

The Igreja de Jesus.

tached **church** is a beautiful, simple Romanesque structure. The walls are covered with 16th- and 18th-century tiles. The church contains the tomb of Jorge de Lencastre (1431–1550), natural son of João II.

Built by the Moors, the castle was reconstructed in 1147 as a monastery and the seat of the Knights of the Order of Saint James. In 1484, the bishop of Évora, Garcia de Meneses, was imprisoned in the dungeon here for his role in conspiring against the king, João II. He died a few days later, probably of poison. Palmela castle was badly damaged by the 1755 earthquake, but the monks rebuilt and remained until the abolition of religious orders in 1834.

Just outside Setúbal rises another great castle-turned-*pousada*, **São Filipe**, with a magnificent view of the Sado river estuary. Philip II of Spain ordered the construction of the strategic castle in 1590 to keep a watch over the area – Portugal was under Spanish rule at the time. The **chapel** is decorated with tiles that recount the life of Saint Philip (not Philip of Spain), signed by the master painter Policarpo de Oliveira Bernardes and dated 1736.

According to local legend, **Setúbal** was founded by Tubal, the son of Cain. It is said that Phoenicians and Greeks, finding the climate and soil of Arrábida similar to their Mediterranean homelands, started vineyards.

Setúbal is known to have been an important fishing port since Roman times. Today it is an industrial town, a centre of ship-building, fish-canning, and the production of fertilisers, cement, salt and moscatel wine. Nevertheless, there are also a number of interesting sights.

Setúbal's pride is the **Church of Jesus**, a spectacular monument dating back to 1491. The church was designed by Diogo Boytac, known as the founding master of the Manueline style of architecture. The narrow building has a high arched ceiling supported by six great stone pillars that look like coils of rope; its apse is etched with stone and lined with tiles. Arrábida marble was used, and the pebbled, multi-coloured stone

gives the whole a distinct appearance. There are also lovely tile panels along the walls. The **cloister** has been turned into a museum.

Nearby is the **Praça do Bocage**, with palm trees and a statue honouring one of the town's illustrious sons, 18th-century sonneteer, Manuel Barbosa du Bocage. Off the square stands the church of **São Julião** with a handsome Manueline doorway built in 1513. The inside walls are decorated with 18th-century tiles showing the life of the saint and popular fishing scenes. Also of interest is the **Ethnographical Museum**, with models depicting the city's main industries: fishing, farming and textiles.

One of the best locations is **Setúbal Harbour**, particularly in the morning with the arrival of brightly painted trawlers loaded with fish. Then there's the continual show of fishermen mending nets and working on their boats. Best of all is the lively fish auction.

Setúbal is the main point of departure for the peninsula of **Tróia**. Ferryboats make the 20-minute crossing frequently in season. Tróia, a long narrow spit jutting out into the Sado estuary, is said to be the site of the Roman town of **Cetóbriga**, buried by a tidal wave in the 5th century. Substantial ruins have been found but little has been excavated besides a temple and tombs. Underwater, you may see the walls of Roman houses.

On the northern end of the peninsula, there is a rather unattractive modern beach resort. The **Tróia Golf Club** has an 18-hole course designed by Robert Trent Jones. On the southern end of the peninsula, however, there are still miles of pine forest and fine empty beaches and dunes.

At the mouth of the Sado, about 5 km (3 miles) southwest of Setúbal, is the **Torre de Outão**, originally a Roman temple to Neptune, which offers a great view. Another delightful excursion from Setúbal goes along the ridge of the **Serra da Arrábida** which rises to 606 metres (2,000 ft). As you leave the city, the only sight that mars the natural beauty of the coast is the cement factory, usually spitting out black smoke.

A road descends to **Portinho da**

Arrábida, a popular bathing beach with transparent waters, white sand and the splendid **Grotto of Santa Margarida**. Hans Christian Andersen, who visited the region in 1834, marvelled in his diaries at this cave with its imposing stalactites. Scuba diving is popular here.

But it was Robert Southey, a young traveller who was very difficult to please, who consecrated Arrábida for English readers, calling it "a glorious spot". He tells of going swimming at the base of the mountain and writes: "I have no idea of sublimity exceeding it."

Regaining the ridge, continue along the skyline drive. The next turnoff leads to **Sesimbra**, a lovely fishing village and resort with several notable sights. The castle above the village, although known as Moorish, has been entirely rebuilt since that time. Afonso Henriques captured it in 1165, but the Moors utterly razed the structure in 1191. King Dinis almost certainly helped with the rebuilding, and King João IV again added and repaired in the 17th century. Inside the walls are ruins of a Roman-esque church, Santa Maria, and the old town hall. King João IV also ordered the fort of São Teodosio built, to protect the port from pirates.

But the most fascinating sight is the port with its fishermen, which is always busy. There are several simple bistros near the port – swordfish is the local speciality.

Going westward about 11 km (7 miles), the road ends at **Cabo Espichel**. This promontory with the shrine of **Nossa Senhora do Cabo** used to be an important pilgrimage site, as shown by the long rows of dilapidated pilgrims' quarters on either side of the church. There is still a fishermen's festival here each October. On the edge of the high cliff is the small fishermen's **Chapel of Senhor de Bomfim**, in a rather desolate state but with a breathtaking view.

The road back to Lisbon goes through **Vila Nogueira de Azeitão**, sometimes simply called Azeitão, which means large olive tree. In the centre of this charming village is the stately **Távora Palace**, where the Duke of Aveiro and

The endless beach of Tróia Peninsula.

his friends are said to have plotted to overthrow King José. The Duke, and his friends, were burned at the stake in Belém in 1759. Lovely baroque fountains border the town's main street. The **Church of São Lourenço** has been restored and boasts beautiful 18th-century altars, paintings and tile panels.

The **Azeitão fair**, held in the central square on the first Sunday of the month, became so popular that it caused havoc and had to be moved to the outskirts of town. Less picturesque now, it is still a major attraction offering everything from shoes and pottery to furniture. There is also a large section devoted to livestock and poultry.

In the village, is the original **José Maria da Fonseca winery**, founded in 1834. The old family residence, which now houses a small museum, stands nearby. The winery still produces one of Portugal's best red table wines, the soft rich Periquita, as well as Setúbal's popular moscatel wines. Visitors are welcome to tour the factory and see its assembly-line production.

Not far from town stands one of the oldest inhabited manors in the country, the **Quinta da Bacalhoa**, built in 1480. It had fallen into ruins and was saved by an American woman from Connecticut, Mrs Herbert Scoville, who bought it in 1936. The gardens, which are open to the public, are admirable with their clipped boxwood in geometric design, orange and lemon groves, and pavilion with beautiful tile panels. One of these scenes, showing Susanna and the Elders, is dated 1565, and said to be the earliest known dated panel in Portugal.

Another attractive manor, the **Quinta das Torres**, stands just outside the neighbouring village of **Vila Fresca de Azeitão**. This 16th-century *quinta*, decorated with tile panels and set in a romantic garden, has been converted into a cosy inn and restaurant.

In the village, there is yet another charming church, **São Simão**, with more ancient tile walls and polychrome panels.

The easiest route back to Lisbon is to take the old national highway, N10, which runs into the super highway.

Cabo Espichel sweeps into the Atlantic.

ALGARVE

Separated from the rest of Portugal by rolling hills, the Algarve, the southernmost province, seduced the ancient Phoenicians with its abundance of sardines and tuna, which they salt-cured for export almost 3,000 years ago. Four centuries later, around 600 BC, the Carthaginians and Celts arrived, followed in turn by the Romans.

It was the Romans who adopted the Phoenician practice of curing and exporting fish – the precursor to Portugal's large tinned sardine industry. They built roads, bridges and spas, such as that in Milreu. They also enjoyed the springs of Monchique.

But the Algarve really blossomed under Moorish rule, which began in the early 8th century. The province's name comes from the Moorish *Al-Gharb* meaning "The West".

The Moorish period was one of vivacious culture and great strides forward in science. Moorish poets sang of the beauty of Silves, while the more practical settlers introduced orange crops, and perfected the technique of extracting olive oil, still very much an important Portuguese product. The blossoming almond trees in February are one of the most beautiful sights of the Algarve thanks, according to folklore, to the passion a Moorish king once held for a northern princess.

Legend has it that the princess, pining for the snows of her homeland, slowly began to waste away. Distraught, the king ordered thousands of almond trees to be planted across the region, then one February morning carried her to the window where she saw swirling white "snow flakes" carpeting the ground – the white almond blossoms. She quickly recuperated, and the two lived happily ever after.

King Afonso Henriques led the Portuguese conquest southward in the 12th century, and later his son Sancho I was to lead the siege against Silves and its estimated population of 20,000 people with the help of the crusaders. It took 49 days before the Moors of Silves surrendered. But in 1192 they came back and reconquered the city and remained there for another 47 years. It was Sancho II who, supported by military religious orders headed by Paio Peres Correia, finally crushed them. The last major city to fall was Faro in January 1249.

But the Arabic influence is visible even today: town names, words beginning with the "al" prefix, the "north African" blue used in trimming the whitewashed homes, terraces atop houses used for the drying of fruit, and the white-domed buildings still popular in many towns. The Algarvian sweets made of figs, almonds, eggs and sugar called *morgados* or *Dom Rodrigos* are yet another reminder of the area's ancient heritage.

For centuries almond, fig, olive and carob trees represented a major part of the Algarve's agriculture, as they are suited to the dry inland areas. Recently, citrus fruit has taken on greater importance, and there are residents who actually *pick* a fresh lime for their gin.

Thanks to the area's gentle climate the Algarve also produces pears, apples, quince, loquats, damask plums, pomegranates, tomatoes, melons, strawberries, watermelon, avocados and grapes.

Specialities: Unfortunately Algarve wine is rarely of any quality, though it's cheerful, cheap and often strong, the high alcoholic content due mainly to heat. The Algarve does have four "demarcated" areas – Lagoa, Portimão, Lagos and Tavira. All the wine produced sells locally. You will find Algarve wines in *mini-mercados* – quite acceptable if your taste is undemanding. Wine critics regard all Algarve wines as undistinguished, and even in quite modest restaurants the mandatory house wine is usually from the far better Alentejo range, or perhaps from even further to the north.

An agreeable way to decide for yourself the merits of a few worthy Algarve wines is to taste them – for free – in the Artisans' Village beside the main Estrada Nacional 125, 4 km (2½ miles) east of Lagoa. The proprietor, Klaus Schoon (despite the name he is an Eng-

lishman and an enthusiastic collector of port) offers visitors two or three of the Lagoa wines, including a pleasant dry *rosé* (*rosado seco*) and a full-bodied dry red (*tinto*). Much, much sweeter is the exotic-sounding local liqueur, Amendôa Amarga, made from almonds.

You'll find good beer, the preference of most young *algarvios*, widely available. Older men passing the time in *tabernas* and *tascas* drink *medronho*, a clear firewater with the kick of a mule distilled from the arbutus, a kind of wild strawberry.

The best *medronho* is homemade in the village of Cachopo in the inland eastern part of the Algarve, where a tiny pixie-like old widow soberly dressed in the obligatory black will be happy to usher you into the back of her house (if you can find her) and tip herself almost upside down into her huge *medronho* barrels to fill your empty bottles with her own special make. Another individual drink in the Algarve is *Brandy-mel*, a type of honey brandy.

The pleasant market town of Loulé, with its central tree-shaded walkway, is the craft centre of the Algarve, but local handicrafts are widely sold everywhere. Among them, *esparto* or straw baskets, hats, mats and hampers – made by women who pick and dry the *esparto* in spring, then shred it into thin strips before they weave and plait it.

You will see mats of grass, and of cotton and wool (some from the Alentejo). Cane basketry is almost always the work of men in the eastern towns of Odeleite, Alcoutim and Castro Marim. Despite a modern prevalence of cardboard boxes, baskets are still used to carry eggs, to display golden smoked sardines, and as fish traps.

Lagos, Loulé and Tavira – as well as numerous stores along the main N125 highway – are good places to find pottery, from big pitchers, plant pots big and small, hand-painted plates and tiles, to the distinctive, lace-like chimney tops that embellish the Algarve skyline. You'll find a considerable range of copper pots and bowls – one shop is on a street corner beside the market in Loulé. If you walk down the avenue you'll see

– and hear – coppersmiths at work in tiny workshops.

Attractive as well as entirely functional is the copper (sometimes stainless steel) *cataplana*, grandmother of the pressure cooker. Like a wok with a hinged lid, the *cataplana* is used for such delicious steamed dishes as *Amêijoas na cataplana*, made with fresh clams, onion, parsley, green peppers, olive oil, and sometimes chunks of tender pork. (Shellfish are carefully monitored now but anyway don't try to eat one that hasn't opened.)

Woodwork is also a regional craft, from spoons made in Aljezur to the brightly-coloured mule-drawn carts you'll still see on the roads. Hand-made lace is a skill that's being kept alive in such places as Azinhal. Up in the hills of Monchique (where a small crafts shop has grown to an extensive display) you'll find wooden furniture and woollen weaves. Even cobblestones, of the kind you see in splendidly-patterned squares and pavements, are still cut by hand in Algarve quarries.

Key routes and places: Travellers to the Algarve can fly directly in to Faro International Airport. By road Lisbon is an easy four-hour drive. Access from Spain is via several small entry roads or across the striking bridge now spanning the Guadiana river and a new highway, the IPl, that slices through the eastern hills to take you quickly to coastal towns as far as Guia, near Albufeira (with Lagos and Sagres in the west as the ultimate road-building target).

Faro is the Algarve capital, its roots ancient but not well documented. Certainly it was used by Greeks and Romans as a trading post before it became a flourishing Moorish town. Largely devastated by the 1755 Great Earthquake, the city, set around a small boat basin, now has an architectural hodge-podge of styles and eras.

To one side of the little harbour, through the 18th-century **Arco da Vila**, lies a peaceful and historic inner town dominated by the Renaissance **cathedral** with its 13th-century tower. (The cathedral is usually open only in the mornings until noon on weekdays.)

A late 20th-century ideal of beauty on the Algarve coast.

Eighteenth-century polychrome tiles are an impressive feature in its chapels as well as in the body of the church. The red chinoiserie organ is also 18th-century, the choir stalls a notable trophy from Silves cathedral when the seat of the diocese was moved to Faro in the 16th century.

In the square behind the cathedral a former convent with strikingly beautiful Renaissance cloisters is now an **Archaeological Museum**, with a selection of Roman mosaics and stonework from Faro and the important Roman site at Milreu some 12 km (7½ miles) to the north. The **Ethnographic Museum** in the district assembly building in Praça Alexandre Herculano (at the top end of the main pedestrian street) has replicas of traditional Algarve homes, costumes and handicrafts. Beside the harbour, in the Port Authority building, the Maritime Museum is worth a visit to see the broad range of Algarve fishing methods, complete with model boats and a vivid depiction of the old way of trapping tuna in the bloody "bullfight of the sea".

Faro's most bizarre and macabre sight is a **Chapel of Bones**, reached through the baroque **Carmo** church with its impressive facade and twin towers. The little chapel was built in 1816, its walls entirely covered with bones and skulls (allegedly 1,245 of them) from the church cemetery. This rather grim display of mortality is less depressing to some than the high-rises that contrast with the church's fine facade.

The centre of Faro is walkable, its character changing as you step through streets of tiny houses, 19th-century mansions, modern villas and shops. As a bustling capital (with too much traffic), it still has considerable charm. To the north especially are stretches of attractive countryside dotted with picturesque villages.

Estói, 12 km (7½ miles) north of Faro, is a pleasant village with a fine parish church, but it's best known for its 18th-century **Palace of the Counts of Carvalhal**. With 28 rooms under restoration by Faro municipality, the palace may not be open if you go, but just the

Cruising the coast.

highly ornamental gardens of this "Queluz of the south" are worth seeing. And **Milreu**, Roman ruins with some very lovely mosaics, is close by – the largest structure you will see there, a temple, became a Visigothic basilica in the 3rd century.

North of Estói, São Bras de Alportel – or rather a high hill on its outskirts with a grand view – is the setting of one of the Algarve's two *pousadas*. (The other is at Sagres.) See the chapter *Pousadas and Manor Houses*.

Some 13 km (8 miles) west is **Loulé**, a charming town whose old quarter, like the *medinas* or *casbahs* of north Africa, is a maze of narrow streets. The old **parish church** overlooks a little garden. Three different Portuguese kings slept in the **castle** between 1359 and 1573. Worth a visit is the *Mae Sobevana* or **Sovereign Mother Chapel** which was built in the early 16th century – today overshadowed by an incomplete dome-shaped structure once intended as a modern shrine – whose interior is covered in 17th-century tiles and frescoes.

North again and off the beaten track is the **Serra do Caldeirão**. This range of hills, reaching 545 metres (1,800 ft), has been left largely untouched by the tourist explosion; areas of it are still home to some not very friendly wild boars. Walks through these mountains can be wonderfully peaceful after the summer bustle of the coastal resorts, and it is a great place for picnics under the cork trees, holm oaks and pink and white blossoming oleanders. Sheep, goats and their shepherds are the only inhabitants. The plain white houses with their small windows and simple tiled roofs reveal the hardworking character – and poverty – of the shepherds.

If you drive to the Algarve from Lisbon, through the Alentejo, the main road passes beside the mountain village of **São Marcos da Serra**. There are several roadside restaurants here – ignore the dusty appearance and go inside and taste their fresh fish, chicken and meat grilled on a wood fire.

A turnoff then leads to **São Bartolomeu de Messines**, whose small

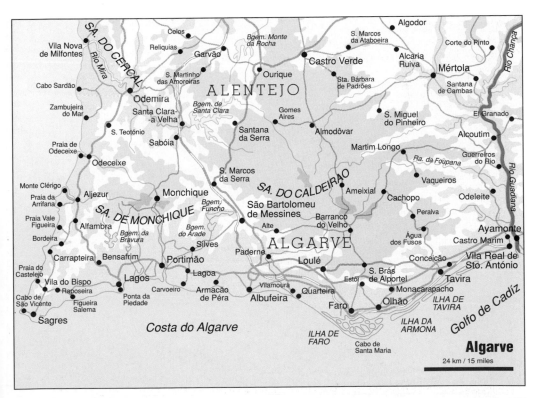

15th-century red sandstone **church** is filled with 17th-century tiles. Drive on then to the coastal resort town of **Albufeira**. Once a small fishing village favoured by the Romans and Moors, Albufeira today is a populous and popular tourist spot with an active nightlife, hundreds of bars with a taste for rock music, plenty of restaurants ranging from La Pizza to more typical regional fare, and late-night discos.

The old part of town is still very attractive, as are the rock-protected beaches where the fishermen keep their boats, gaily painted with large eyes (to ward off evil), as well as stars and animals. There is a bustling fish market near the fishermen's beach and a fruit, meat and vegetable market in the main town square.

The distance between towns east or west of Albufeira is small. Roads vary from brand new to pot-holed. A relentless tourist industry has built so much in between that it is hard to tell when you have left one town and entered another. Much of the area has been ruined by massive billboard advertising and bad urban planning.

Yet, veering off to the shore you can still find uncrowded beaches. An alternative is to hire a boat (and a fisherman) for the day, fill the boat up with food and drink (not too heavily: small boats are not equipped with life jackets) and explore the coast's deserted beaches and grottoes that can only be reached by sea. (Some are favoured by quite legal nudists.)

All the well-known golf courses, more than 15 now, lie east of Faro, among them **Quinta do Lago**, a 27-hole course, **Vale do Lobo**, and **Vilamoura**, which was originally designed by Frank Pennink and is part of a 1,600-hectare (4,000-acre) tourist development. **Penina**, designed by three-time British Open champion Henry Cotton, is west of Albufeira, closer to Portimão. More than 120,000 golfers visit the Algarve's courses every year.

Northeast of Albufeira is **Alte**, a naturally elegant village lying at the foot of hills and huddled around its parish **The beach of Albufeira.**

church. **Nossa Senhora da Assunção** dates from the 16th century and has magnificent 18th-century tile panels. The tiles in the **Our Lady of Lurdes Chapel**, among the best in the Algarve, are of 16th-century Sevillian origin. Alte is one of the most typical villages of the province with its delicate laced white chimneys, simple houses and timeless serenity.

A nearby stream (to which people come from miles around) has transformed the area into an oasis amid the region's arid landscape. It's a lush garden of oleanders, fig and loquat trees and rose bushes. The blue and white tile panels at **Fonte Santa** or fountain contain poems by Cândido Guerreiro. This area is perfect for picnics, or a walk up the Pena hill where you can visit the **Moors' Cave** (*Buraco dos Mouros*). Further up the mountain is **Rocha dos Soidos**, a cave filled with stalactite and stalagmite formations.

Northwest of Albufeira is **Silves**, a town populated as long ago as the 4th century BC. Although it was important in Roman times, it reached its greatest splendour under the Moors, who made it the capital of the Algarve.

In its glory days Silves was the home of some of the greatest Arab poets. They recorded its ruin when the city fell to Portugal's King Sancho I in 1189: "Silves, my Silves, once you were a paradise. But tyrants turned you into the blaze of hell. They were wrong not to fear God's punishment. But Allah leaves no deed unheeded, " wrote one. His call may have been heard because in 1191 the Moors occupied Silves once more before it was finally re-conquered by the Portuguese.

Yemenite Arabs built the walled city, but the **castle** (on top of a Roman citadel, itself on top of neolithic foundations) and the defensive towers were rebuilt in the later Almohad period of the 12th and 13th centuries and heavily restored in modern times. The Moorish castle and Christian **Sé** (cathedral) dominate the city, the dark-red sandstone contrasting with the soft pinks and faded blues of the older surrounding houses.

The cathedral in Silves.

A sense of ancient history and poetry still permeates Silves and the castle – except in June when a beer festival held within its walls considerably changes the atmosphere.

The Moorish cistern to the north once supplied the city's water, and is architecturally similar to 13th-century cisterns found in Palestine and in Cáceres, Spain. Built both by Romans and Moors, the advanced irrigation system transformed the Algarve into the garden of Portugal.

The Sé is originally 13th-century Gothic, restored in the 14th century and almost destroyed by the earthquake of 1755. Its apse is decorated with square arches, pyramid-shaped battlements and fanciful gargoyles. The inner chapel of **João de Rego** dates from the 15th century. Various tombs here are said to be of crusaders who helped capture Silves from the Moors in 1244. Here, too, for four years lay the remains of D. João II, who died in nearby Alvor in 1495, aged only 40, from dropsy, said doctors. Poison, thought others.

Still with a cork factory, and surrounded by citrus plantations, today Silves depends more on tourism.

South of Silves is **Lagoa**, where growers from around the area take their grapes to the central cooperative wine cellar. East of here is **Porches**, famous for its painted pottery, and 13 km (8 miles) to the south, past almond groves and new developments is **Carvoeiro**, a craggy coastline of isolated beaches, like that of Algar Seco. Praia de Carvoeiro itself is a lively tourist spot, a little beach framed by villa-studded cliffs.

Portimão lies west of Carvoeiro. An important fishing port, it is also a pleasant shopping town built on the west bank of the Arade river estuary (and facing the pretty village of Feragando), with a number of sidewalk cafes and a good fish market. Portimão is famous for its grilled sardines – have lunch beside the river – and pastry shops. Close by is the ocean-front **Praia da Rocha**, a superb and much-photographed beach with rock formations standing in the blue-green sea.

Silves has a long pedigree.

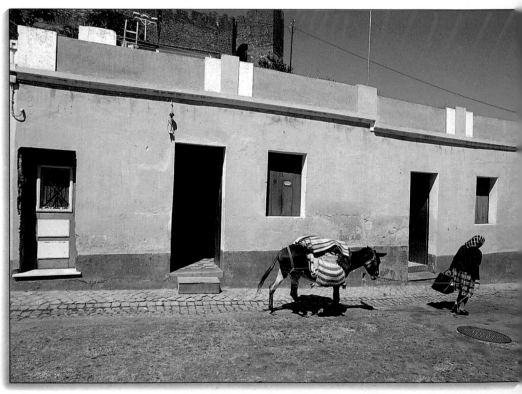

Driving west you will come to **Lagos**, which some believe was founded by a Carthaginian chieftain, and later taken by the Romans in the 5th century BC, when it was called *Lacobriga* or "fortified lake". The Moors took it over in the 8th century and renamed it *Zawaia*, or "lake". The city finally fell to the Portuguese during the reign of Afonso III.

In 1434 Gil Eanes left Lagos and was the first sea captain to round Cape Bojador of northwest Africa, south of the Canary Islands – then the limit of the known world. Most of the city was rebuilt in the 18th century. Some evidence of the town's darker past still stands in the columns and semicircular arches of Portugal's first slave market in the **Praça da Republica** (Portugal brought slaves in from Guinea and Senegal). Note, too, the modern **monument** by Portuguese artist João Cutileiro recording King Sebastião's departure to the disastrous battle of Alcacer-Quibir.

A walk through the city's winding streets will lead you to the **Church of Santo António**, a sober-looking church on the outside. Inside, however, is an extraordinary and beautiful example of gilded carving. The nave has an impressive painted wood barrel-vault with an 18th-century shield in the middle, and baroque paintings on the walls.

Lagos has several pretty coves and beaches. Don't miss the rock formations called **Ponte da Piedade**. From the cliffs you might also hire a boat from local fishermen to explore the grottoes with their cathedral-like natural skylights.

The countryside changes drastically towards the west, particularly after **Salema** and **Figueira**, to a rockier and more undulating landscape. The trees, usually the hardier carob, fig and almond, look smaller and squatter, permanently bent from the unrelenting wind.

To the west: The western Algarve is divided into two parts: the Atlantic coast and the Monchique mountains. In spring Monchique is covered in flowering mimosa and wildflowers bloom in the deep valleys between the **Fóia** and **Picota** peaks. Fóia is the highest point of the Algarve reaching 900 metres (2,950 ft)

Fortifications at Lagos.

above sea level. It is easily accessible by a winding road lined with cheerful chicken restaurants. The town of **Monchique** is rather disappointing if you merely drive through, but park the car and walk about the steep streets to get a better feel for the place.

The Monchique spas (*caldas*) are off to the right heading south, and are surrounded by chestnut, cork, pine, orange and eucalyptus trees. The spa has been in use since Roman times and the waters are believed to cure a number of ailments ranging from convulsions to rheumatism. The springs pour out an estimated 20 million litres (about 4 million gallons) of water a year.

The Algarve's western coastline begins at **Odeceixe** and sweeps dramatically down to Cape St Vincent and Sagres, and is still largely unexploited. Odeceixe is a small Moorish-style village that reaches out to long sandy beaches and looming high cliffs. Further south is **Aljezur**, sprawled over the hills – and the last town to be taken from the Moors.

Directly west are the **Monte Clérigo** and **Arrifana** beaches. South of these are other beaches including Penedo, Bordeira and the vast, dune-backed Carrapateira. Once the hideout of pirates, this wild and lovely coast is now the refuge of more adventurous tourists and for many species of marine birds.

From Aljezur the road leads down to the wild and windswept forked promontory of **Sagres** and **Cape St Vincent**, known to ancient mariners as *O Fim do Mundo*, the End of the World. From within the walls enclosing the lighthouse you can look down upon St Vincent's rocky "throne".

Sacred ravens: Legend has it that in medieval times Christian followers of the martyred St Vincent defied the Moors and buried his body on the cape, with a shrine to honour him. Sacred ravens were said to have maintained vigil over the spot and over the ship that carried the bones of the saint to Lisbon. Here, even on a calm day, waves crash against the cliffs with spray-tossing violence. In spring, the smell of the sea competes

A house in Sagres.

with the scent of cistus, the rock-rose bush whose perfumed leaves were once supposedly used by the Egyptians for embalming.

Early in the 15th century Prince Henry the Navigator invited the most renowned cartographers, astronomers and mariners of his day, to **Sagres,** forming a fund of knowledge though not exactly, so modern historians believe, founding a formal School of Navigation. Nothing that Prince Henry built is left so it is hard to be sure. But you can see clues – discovered only in the 20th century – notably a huge, 43-metre (141-ft) compass rose on the stone ground of the fortress. Less pleasing to many is the entirely modern construction of tourist and education facilities. Sagres itself is a small fishing town, with Baleeira bay as its port.

North and inland is **Vila do Bispo**, an unspoiled town where oxen still have right of way and chattering women gather at the communal washing place to do the family laundry. While you are here, you might like to see the Torre de Aspa, a rock formation some 150 metres (500 ft) high, the area's highest point. A road from Vila do Bispo takes you just north to the grand beach of Castelejo. From just above it, another road leads to Cordama, yet another beach that receives the full force of the Atlantic between tall, white-veined cliffs.

Just east of Vila do Bispo, close to Raposeira on the road to Lagos is a chapel to Our Lady of Guadalupe, probably built by the Templars.

Among the least travelled routes in the Algarve is the hearteningly peaceful road along the **Guadiana river** which, in the south, divides Portugal from Spain. It is a soothing meander through golden, furze-covered hills dotted with corks, olive and fig trees. (Road numbers are N122 and 1063 for the riverside drive.) **Alcoutim** is the northernmost Algarve town, and here it often seems as if time has stopped still. Sunning dogs in the only square in town have priority, so you'll have to park around them.

From the promenade built on the edge

The clear waters of Sagres.

of the Guadiana river you can see the nearby Spanish town of **San Lucar de Guadiana** reflected in the slow-moving water. San Lucar's **village church**, also by the riverside, has interesting bas-relief carving on the baptismal font dating from the 16th century. Signs to the "**castle**" lead to an empty shell of walls – but the view from here is worth the short walk.

Castro Marim, 34 km (21 miles) to the south near the mouth of the Guadiana river, is architecturally appealing. The little town is also one of the oldest and historically most important areas of the Algarve. Once a major Phoenician settlement, it was also host to the Greeks and Carthaginians before the Moors and Romans invaded. Portugal's kings later used it as a natural point from which to fight the Moors to the east. The huge **castle** built by King Afonso III is still standing, overlooking the surrounding valley. In 1319, it was the first headquarters of the Order of Christ. The fort on the hill opposite dates to 1641.

Surrounding the town is the **Castro Marim** fen or marsh, wetland home of many migratory birds including storks and flamingoes, and a hundred different species of plant life. Ask the local *Serviço de Parques e Reservas* (located just inside the castle) for a guided tour and information.

Further south, facing Spain, is **Vila Real de Santo António**, its grid of geometric streets the mark of the Marquês de Pombal – the same man who was responsible for redesigning old Lisbon. Pombal intended this town as an administrative, industrial and fishing model and he founded the Royal Fisheries Company here. But he lost favour with the court, and his plans never really took off. Fishing, all the same, is an important activity.

Travelling west past the popular beach resort towns of **Monte Gordo, Praia Verde, Alagoas** and **Cacela** you will come to **Tavira**, a graceful little town which has avoided the excesses of development. It elegantly borders both sides of the Sequa river, which becomes the Gilão as it slides under the seven-

Left, a Tavira belltower. **Right**, **Fortaleza in Sagres**.

arched Roman-style bridge towards the sea. With its estuary and outlying island, Tavira flourished in the 16th century. But trade dwindled as the fish disappeared, and this lovely town composed of narrow streets, palatial houses, miniature towers, domes, unusual four-sided roofs and minarets today leads a quieter life.

There are 23 churches and chapels (many of them closed) in Tavira, of which the most interesting are perhaps the **Igreja da Misericórdia** and the church of **Santa Maria** rebuilt on the site of the town's old mosque. Information and maps are available from the tourist office, to be found up the steps from the town hall.

From Tavira it is a brief drive past Fuzeta to **Olhão**, a 17th-century town built in the Moorish style, with a big fish market. Get there early and be prepared to use your elbows to get to the slithery hills of fish which the women hawk at the top of their voices, poking them to prove their freshness. The best buys are gilt-head bream (*dourada*), bass (*robalo*)

A typical church, this one at Boliqueime.

and sole (*linguado*). Nearby there is a fruit, vegetable and live fowl market.

With a basket of fresh food, head back towards Tavira but veer off at the little fishing port of Fuzeta. There, you can get a ferry to **Fuzeta Island** with its long strip of beach, and have a barbecue. Or alternatively, you can get a simple lunch from a local *tasca*.

Fuzeta lies practically in the middle of the **Parque Natural Ria Formosa**, an 18,400-hectare (45,000-acre) wild life area that stretches some 50 km (30 miles) from Ancão in the west to Cacela in the east, its width some 6 km (4 miles) around Faro.

This natural lagoon system, protected from the sea by a network of sand bars, is crucial, as it provides for 90 percent of Portugal's total harvest of clams and oysters. The Ria is also an important bird sanctuary, especially for waders like egrets, black-winged stilts, oyster catchers, and rare species like the purple gallinule. Although the park is normally protected, the heavy influx of people threatens the entire area.

ÉVORA AND THE ALENTEJO

Alentejo, literally "beyond the Tejo" (the Tagus river), has a distinctive character and beauty unlike that of any other Portuguese province. Its vast plains, coloured burnt ochre in summer, are freckled with cork oaks and olive trees which are the only shade for the small flocks of sheep and herds of black pigs.

Nicknamed *terra do pão* (land of bread) because of field upon field of wheat, oats and rice, the Alentejo supports acres of grapevines, tomatoes, sunflowers and other plantations.

The Alentejo is the largest and flattest of the Portuguese provinces; about the size of Belgium, it occupies one-third of Portugal's total land area yet has only 6 percent of its population. It stretches from the west coast eastward to the Spanish border and separates Ribatejo and Beira Baixa in the central regions from the Algarve in the south. The open countryside is punctuated by picturesque whitewashed towns and villages, many of which were built on the low hills which dot the horizon.

The Alentejo is rich in handicrafts. Rustic pottery with naive, colourful designs can be found everywhere. In addition, certain towns specialise in particular crafts or products: handstitched rugs from Arraiolos, loom-woven carpets from Reguengos; cheese from Serpa; tapestries from Portalegre; sugar plums from Elvas. All can be purchased, of course, elsewhere in the Alentejo, or in Lisbon or Oporto, but for price, selection, freshness and adventure, isn't it more satisfying to go to the source?

By Portuguese standards, the roads which connect the towns are excellent. Most of the traffic is local and slow moving. You will need to equip yourself with a reliable road map; signposting is limited, and without a map you could drive miles before discovering you've taken a wrong turn.

The Portuguese in general are not renowned for their tidiness but the *Alentejanos* are the exception. The towns are litter-free and there is always a *dona de casa* in view whitewashing her already pristine home. Cool and simple is the theme for the Alentejo architecture; low, single-storey buildings are painted white to deflect the sun's glare, with a traditional blue skirting to reflect the sky. Large domed chimneys indicate chilly winters. This practical style is followed from the humblest cottage to the large hacienda-style homes of the wealthy landowners; ornate and impressive architecture is reserved for cathedrals and churches.

Inland from the coastline, the Alentejo's temperature in the summer can reach inferno level: what little wind there is blows hot and dry from the continental land mass – no cooling sea breezes here. Temperatures can drop dramatically in winter, resulting in some bitterly cold nights.

Geographically the province is split into two regions, Upper (*Alto*) and Lower (*Baixo*) Alentejo. Portalegre is the capital of the former and Beja of the latter. To the east are two low mountain ranges, the Serras of **São Mamede** and **Ossa**. Some of the towns in these ranges, particularly Marvão, have breathtaking, even precipitous settings. Portugal's third longest river, the Guadiana, flows through the province and in places provides the border between Portugal and Spain. This is by no means the only waterway. The region is crisscrossed by a network of small rivers and dams.

The Alentejo is steeped in history which goes back to the days of Roman colonisation. Later, it was the seat of the great landed estates of the Portuguese nobility and home to former kings. Even as late as 1828 Évora – the capital of the Alentejo – was considered as the second major Portuguese city, an honour which was first bestowed on it by King João I (1385–1433).

Estremoz, whose ancient castle has been converted into a comfortable *pousada* (state-run hotel) was a nerve centre in medieval Portugal. Vila Viçosa has a history which began in the Middle Ages and continued up to the early 20th century. It was the seat of the dukes of Bragança, whose royal dynasty began in 1640 with the coronation of João IV and ended in 1910 with the fall of the monarchy.

Political change: Modern Alentejo is a far cry from the days of aristocratic domination, although farming techniques in the smallholdings have changed little. The greatest change is political: after the restoration of democracy in 1974 the Alentejo became the heartland of Portuguese communism.

Many of the great estates – so vast that they included villages, a school and even small hospitals – were taken over by the farmworkers during the Revolution. Some of the land-owning families were forcibly ejected, but the majority lived away from the farms for most of the year anyway, in other properties nearer Lisbon or Oporto. Unfortunately, lack of management skills has led many of the cooperative-run farms to near-bankruptcy, but others flourish. Government legislation is attempting to ensure that the former owners have their lands – or parts of them – reinstated and/ or that they receive compensation for their losses. There is also a new land-owning generation that has a modern approach to agriculture and is skilled at effective farm management.

Farming is the pulse of Alentejo, and the lives of its people revolve around the seasons. Aside from Évora the towns are small and the rest of the population is scattered in hamlets linked to farms. Secondary schools are restricted to the larger towns; in the more remote areas the general practice among young people is to leave school early to work in the fields, or head to the cities.

Throughout the year, but particularly at harvest time, you will see the fieldworkers making their way to and from work on foot, by bicycle or crammed into open-topped trucks. Most rural *Alentejanos* adopt the traditional dress: black wide-brimmed hats for both men and women, black trousers, waistcoats, jackets and white collarless shirts for men, black shawls and thick black skirts for women or trousers for field work. Neckerchiefs for extra protection against sun and dust are loosely knotted around the men's necks, while women favour head-squares worn under their hats. The faces of the old *Alentejanos* are extraordinary – leathery skins baked a deep brown, furrowed like tree bark and coloured like walnuts.

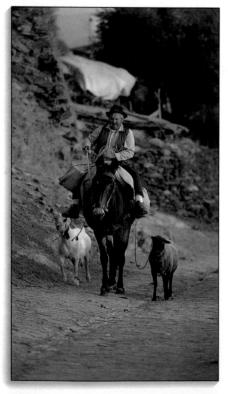

One of the traditional pastimes for the menfolk is a wild boar hunt near the Spanish border. It really is a case of out of the frying pan and into the fire for the poor creatures. They cross the border from Spain to flee the Spanish hunters, only to find themselves hunted here, although to a lesser extent. During the season (October–February), you will inevitably see men out with their shotguns, pouches and a gaggle of dogs.

Singing and dancing are popular across the length and breadth of Portugal, and the Alentejo does its share. Here, the folk songs are the domain of the men. The songs are slow, rather melancholic, but of a completely different style from the haunting *fado* which is heard elsewhere. A slow tempo is set by the stamping of the men's feet as they sing in chorus, swaying to the rhythm by the time they reach the end of the song. A performance is well worth listening **On the road in Monsaraz.**

to; ask at an Alentejo tourist office about where to hear the *ceifeiros*.

Évora is the largest and most important of all the Alentejo towns. It is a superb city, full of fascinating sights, all of which are in a good state of preservation. They are likely to remain so as the entire city has been proclaimed a world heritage site by UNESCO, therefore qualifying for its financial aid.

It takes about two and a half hours to drive from Lisbon to Évora, and a tour could be comfortably managed as a day trip. But that would not leave time to see the lovely towns and villages along the way. To base yourself in Évora is easy; there are plenty of small guest houses and hotels.

To reach Évora leave Lisbon via the April 25th Bridge and head down towards the *autostrada* for Setúbal, and then turn eastwards on the IP7 past Montemor-o-Novo for Évora. You will not need a welcome billboard to tell you that you have just reached the Alentejo; suddenly the road is broad and less potholed, and you will find yourself at the edge of the rolling plains. Look for the jumbles of twigs on top of the high walls and buildings – homes to the storks that flourish in the province. As you drive further inland you will also notice the waning breeze and the increase in temperature.

Pegóes is the first small Alentejo town on the route. It's a rather dry, dusty and deserted town nowadays, especially as it is by passed by the new highway. A little further along is **Vendas Novas,** also off the new road. Shady, neat and with an air of affluence, it is typical of modest Alentejo towns.

Montemor-o-Novo can be seen from quite a distant approach, its ruined medieval castle crowning its low *monte* (hill). The castle ramparts are thought to date back to Roman times. The town is divided into the upper old town and lower new town. As you might expect the old town is more interesting to stroll through. It was here that St John of God (São João de Deus) was born in 1495. He was baptised in the ruined parish church, the only part of which still intact

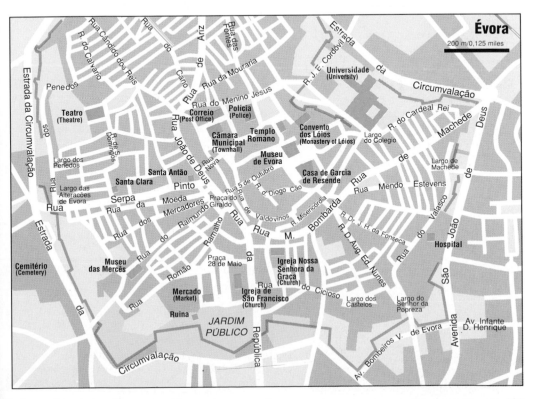

is the granite Manueline portal. In the square outside the church is a statue commemorating the saint, a Franciscan monk of great charity and humility. According to legend, he carried a beggar to the hospital one stormy night. Although it can hardly boast the population to support them all, the town, because of its religious significance, has five churches, three convents and two monasteries.

Alentejo's city: As you enter **Évora** on the main Lisbon road, there is a small tourist office just before the town's Roman walls. There is a larger tourist office in the centre, but at this one you can pick up a street map with suggested walks marked to take in the most important sights. The best place to park is the centre of the city at the **Praça do Giraldo**, a large square with arcades on two sides and a 16th-century **church** and fountain at the top end. From this central area you can explore the inner city with ease.

The history of Évora can be traced back to the earliest civilisations on the Iberian peninsula. It derives its name from *Ebora Cerealis*, as it was called during the Luso-Celtic colonisation. The Romans later fortified the city and renamed it *Liberalitas Julia*. It thrived under the Romans, who elevated it to the status of *municipium*, which gave it the right to mint its own currency. Its prosperity declined somewhat when it was conquered by the Visigoths, but rekindled under the long Moorish rule (early 8th century to 1165). Much of the architecture reflects the Moorish presence with arched, twisting alleyways, tiled patios and potted plants.

Évora was liberated from the Moors by a Christian knight, Geraldo Sem-Pavor (Gerald the Fearless), in 1165. He did so in the name of King Afonso Henriques I, the first king of Portugal.

For the next 400 years Évora enjoyed great importance and wealth. It was the preferred residence of the kings of the Burgundy and Avis dynasties. During these centuries the courts attracted famed artists, dramatists, humanists and academics to Évora. Great churches, mon-

A prospect of Évora.

asteries, houses and convents were built. The splendour culminated in 1559 when the last of the Avis kings, Henrique – who was also the Archbishop of Évora – founded a Jesuit university there. In 1580, following the annexation of Portugal by Spain, Évora's glory waned. The Castilians paid little attention to it, except as an agricultural and trading centre. Even after Portuguese independence was restored in 1640, Évora did not regain its former brilliance.

The oldest sight in Évora is the so-called **Temple of Diana**, which dates back to the 2nd or 3rd century AD. To reach it walk down Rua 5 de Outubro, off Praça do Giraldo. The temple is presumed to have been built as a place of imperial worship, dedicated, perhaps, to the goddess Diana. The Corinthian columns are granite, their bases and capitals hewn from local marble. The facade and mosaic floor have disappeared completely, but the six rear columns and those at either side are still intact. The temple was converted into a fortress during the Middle Ages and then used as a slaughterhouse until 1870. Although not an elegant role, this use saved the temple from being torn down; its brick walls helped preserve the columns as well.

There is a good viewpoint just across from the rear of the temple in the shady garden. From here you can look down over the lower town and across the plains: the tiny village of Évoramonte is just visible to the northeast.

To the right of the temple is the **Monastery of Lóios** (also known as the church of John the Evangelist). The convent buildings have been converted into an elegant *pousada* but the church is still a public one. Founded in 1485, its style is Romano-Gothic, although all but the doorway in the facade was remodelled after the earthquake in 1755. The nave has an ornate vaulted ceiling and walls lined with beautiful tiles depicting the life of St Laurence Justinian, dated 1771 and signed by António de Oliveira Bernardes. Guided tours of the church, cloisters and chapterhouse can be taken.

Nearby the temple is the **cathedral** (*Sé*), dedicated to the Virgin Mary. An imposing, austere building, its granite facade was built in the 12th century, also in Romano-Gothic style. Its main portal is flanked by two grand conical towers. These towers are unusual in that they are asymmetric the glittering blue tiled one is particularly lovely. Both were added in the 16th century.

Before going into the cathedral, take a close look at the main entrance. It is decorated with magnificent 14th-century sculptures of the apostles. The vast broken barrel vaulted ceiling inside is quite stunning; suspended from it are huge chandeliers, their supports appearing to be of interminable length. The cathedral has the most capacious interior in Portugal: its three naves stretch for 70 metres.

Once you've seen the cathedral, it really is worth paying the nominal sum to see its cloisters, choir stalls and **Museum of Sacred Art** lodged in the treasury. They are open at the usual visiting times (9 am–midday and 2–5pm, closed Monday and public holidays). A short

Temple of Diana.

climb up a staircase will take you to the museum, which contains a beautiful collection of ecclesiastical gold, silver and bejewelled plate, ornaments, chalices and crosses. The Renaissance-style choir stalls, tucked high in the gallery, are fashioned with a delightful series of wooden carvings whose motifs are of both sacred and secular design. Particularly charming are those of day-to-day life: wine pressing, wheat threshing, singing and feasting. From the choir stalls you get a good bird's-eye view of the cathedral.

The **cloisters** are 14th-century Gothic, large and imposing in their granite plainness, more awe-inspiring than encouraging of meditative contemplation.

Next door to the cathedral is the **Regional Museum**, formerly the Bishop's Palace and now home to a fine collection of paintings, both Portuguese Primitives and Flemish. There is also interesting sculpture, furniture and decoration from local buildings.

More elegant and graceful cloisters are visible at the old **Jesuit University** .

You have to follow a short road down to the east of the city to reach it. The marble of the broad **students' cloisters** seems to have aged not at all since the 16th century. The cloisters still maintain the peaceful atmosphere of the serious academic: it's the sort of place that makes you involuntarily drop your voice to a hushed whisper.

The classroom entrances at the far end of the cloister gallery are decorated with *azulejos* representing each of the subjects taught. If you take a slow walk back up the hill and head for the church of St Francis (São Francisco), you'll pass by another church, the **Misericórdia**, noted for its 18th-century tiled panels and baroque relief work. Behind it is the **Soure Mansion**, a 15th-century Manueline house formerly part of the Palace of Infante D. Luís.

As you walk, take notice of the houses. Nearly all have attractive, narrow, wrought-iron balconies at the base of tall rectangular windows. An odd tradition in Évora as elsewhere in Portugal, is that visiting dignitaries are welcomed

14th-century Apostles on Évora's cathedral.

by a display of brightly coloured bedspreads hung from the balconies.

When you reach the Misericórdia church, take a brief detour of the **Portas de Moura Square**. The gates mark the fortified northern entrance to the city, the limit of construction and safety as it was in medieval times. This picturesque square is dominated by a Renaissance fountain, built in 1556.

Back on the road again, keep an eye out for the church of **Nossa Senhora da Graça** (Our Lady of Grace), just off the Rua Miguel Bombarda. Built in granite, it is a far cry from the austerity of the cathedral. A later church (16th-century), its influence is strongly Italian Renaissance. Note the four huge figures supporting globes which represent the children of grace.

A mother's curse: The church of **São Francisco**, from the late 15th or early 16th century, has a remarkable chapel, the **Capela dos Ossos**. This bizarre and macabre room is entirely lined and decorated with bones of some 5,000 people. It was "created" in the 16th century by a Franciscan monk. At the entrance lies the inviting Latin inscription: "We bones lie here waiting for yours."

The skulls and bones have not merely been placed in a random fashion; a lot of creative thought has gone into their placement! Hung at the far end of the chapel are the corpses of a man and a small child. These centuries-old bodies are said to be the victims of a dying wife and mother's curse. Father and son were supposed to have made her life a misery and their ill treatment killed her. On her death bed she cursed them, swearing that their flesh would never fall from their bones. The corpses are far from fleshy, but there is plenty of leathery substance attached to their bones.

Braids of human hair dating to the last century are hung at the entrance of the chapel, *ex-votos* put there by young brides. The **chapterhouse** that links the chapel to the church is lined with *azulejos* depicting scenes from the Passion and contains an *altar dos promessas* (altar of promises) on which are laid wax effigies of parts of the body, particularly

The macabre Capela dos Ossos.

arms, legs, and feet. The ailing, or their friends and relatives, go to the altar and pray for a cure. If it comes, then an effigy of the cured part is placed in thanks on the altar.

Évora's **public gardens** near the church provide a very pleasant walk; if you're lucky you may catch the band playing on the park's old-fashioned wrought-iron bandstand. A delightful **palace** stands in the park, that of King Manuel (1495–1521). Luso-Moorish in style, it has typical paired windows in horseshoe arches. Exhibitions are held in the long Ladies' Gallery.

During the last week of June, Évora is filled with visitors who come to enjoy the annual **Feira de São João**. This huge fair fills the grounds opposite the public gardens. If you don't mind the crowd then you'll enjoy what is offered: a local handicraft market, an agricultural hall, a display of local light industry, the general hodge-podge of open-air stalls selling everything, folk singing and dancing, and special restaurants serving typical cuisine.

If you're visiting Évora during the summer and want to cool off, go to one of the local swimming pools on the edge of town. Although well-patronised because they are inexpensive, they are spotlessly clean, with plenty of lawn on which to stretch out and dry.

If you're not intent on going inside Évora's monuments, a night stroll reveals its exterior architecture admirably. Nearly all the monuments are flood-lit until midnight, and the winding narrow streets are very inviting on a balmy evening.

The Alentejo has a number of megalithic monuments scattered across its plains, and some of the most important are just outside Évora. (Turismo will give you a map.) The best preserved and most significant stone circle, or *cromlech*, on the Iberian peninsula is 12 km (7 miles) west of the city, close to the hill of Herdade dos Almendres. **Cromleque de Almendres** has 95 standing stones.

Near to the Agricultural Department of the University of Évora in Valverde,

One of the indignities of being a statue in Évora's public gardens.

which neighbours Évora, is the largest dolmen on the peninsula. The **Zambujeiro Dolmen** stands some 5 metres (17 ft) high with a 3-metre (10-ft) diameter and is dated about 3,000 BC.

Estremoz is a lovely town steeped in a history which goes back to the Middle Ages. Although much smaller than Évora, it has fascinating monuments.

The old part of this town, crowned by a castle now converted into a *pousada*, was founded by King Afonso III in 1258. The monument was a residence of King Dinis in the 1300s and it is with him that it is most often associated. His wife, the sainted Queen Isabel of Aragon is honoured by a statue in the main square, and a **chapel** dedicated to her can be seen in one of the castle towers. (To view it ask either at the *pousada* or at the museum on the main square.)

The chapel is at the top of a narrow staircase; small, and highly decorated, it is where she is said to have died. Mind you, she is said to have died in the nearby **King's Audience Chamber** as well. The chapel walls are adorned with 18th-century *azulejos* and paintings depicting scenes from the Queen's life. The most famous incident, represented here, is the "miracle of the roses". Isabel was a very charitable woman, sometimes more so than her husband might have wished. Once when Isabel was distributing alms to the poor, King Dinis came upon her. She hastily hid the coins in the folds of her skirts, but the king demanded to see what the gown held. When Isabel spread her skirt, the gold miraculously had turned to roses. Behind the altar is a tiny, plain room bearing a smaller altar on which the Estremoz faithful have placed their *ex votos* or offerings.

The most impressive part of the castle is the wonderful 13th-century **keep** which is entered via the *pousada*. To get to the top you need to be fairly fit – or make a slow and steady ascent. The second floor has an octagonal room with trefoil windows. From the top platform there is a breathtaking view. The red rooftops contrast beautifully with the whitewashed houses and the green

Estremoz.

plains beyond, much of which are planted with rows of olive trees.

Across the square from the *pousada* is the **Royal Palace of D. Dinis**. It must have been a beautiful palace, but all that remains standing after a gun-powder explosion in the palace arsenal in 1698 is the Gothic colonnade and star-vaulted chamber (D. Dinis' audience chamber). It is used nowadays for exhibitions by local artists.

Having survived the narrow roads and hairpin bends on the drive up to the castle, the descent should seem easier. The upper town is connected to the lower town by 14th-century ramparts and fairly modern buildings: the wrought-iron balconies here are decorated with coloured tiles.

Estremoz is famed for its pottery jugs and figurines, which can be bought throughout the town, but they are perhaps most attractively displayed at the Saturday market in the **main square** of the lower town. If you're a lover of Portuguese wines then you're likely to be familiar with the name **Borba**, where

a cooperative wine company produces a good red wine. The ancient village of Borba, which is said to date back to the Gauls and Celts, does not have much to show except for a splendid fountain, **Fonte das Bicas**, built in 1781 from local white marble.

Bragança's base: Just down the road from Borba is **Vila Viçosa**, the previously-mentioned seat of the dukes of Bragança. Vila Viçosa comes as quite a surprise after the Moorish-influenced towns perched on the top of hills. The town is cool and shady, its large main square (**Praça da República**) is filled with orange trees, and elsewhere there are lemon trees and lots of flowers. *Viçosa* means lush, and its luxuriant boulevards are a pleasure to walk.

A lovely, if rather overgrown, medieval **castle** overlooks the town square. It is very peaceful there, the only sound being the cooing of the white fan-tail doves which nest in the ramparts. The drawbridge is lowered across the moat (now dry), and the first floor has been converted into a modest archaeological **museum**.

Vila Viçosa is best known for the **Ducal Palace**, a three-floor building with a monumentally long facade open to the public for guided tours. Its furniture, painting and tapestries are very fine, and worth an hour or so. The palace also contains an excellent collection of 17th- to 19th-century coaches.

The palace overlooks a square in which stands a bronze statue of João IV, the first king of the Bragança dynasty. To the north of the square is a striking gateway, the **Knot Gate**, part of the 16th-century town walls. It is so called after its design: the stone archway appears to be roped together.

Between Évora and Estremoz stands **Évoramonte**, a village at the foot of a recently renovated **castle**. It was in this village that the convention ending the civil war was signed on 26 May 1834. A plaque commemorating the event is placed over the house where the historic signing took place.

Évoramonte castle perches on a high hill and the views from there are remarkable: well worth the detour and the

The 16th-century Porta dos Nós at Vila Viçosa.

clamber up to the top of the castle which, despite its refurbished look and Manueline knots, dates to 1306.

Close to the Spanish border, about 50 km (30 miles) from Estremoz, is the strongly fortified town of **Elvas**. Founded by the Romans, it was long occupied by the Moors and finally liberated from them in 1230 – nearly 100 years later than Lisbon.

The town was of great strategic importance during the wars of independence with Spain in the mid-17th century. The fortress of **Santa Luzia**, south of town, was built by a German, Count Lippe, for the purpose of repelling the Spanish. The older **castle**, above the town, was originally a Roman fortress, rebuilt by the Moors and enlarged in the 15th century.

If you walk around the ramparts you cannot fail to be impressed by the effective engineering which completely encircled the town. The town itself is particularly attractive, from the triangular "square" of Santa Clara, with its 16th-century marble pillory, to the main square, **Praça da República**, with its geometrically patterned mosaic paving.

Elvas has a country-house style *pousada* whose restaurant is well frequented by Spanish visitors. One of its specialties is a *Bacalhau Dourado* – slivers of salted cod fried with thinly-chipped potatoes, onions, olives and scrambled egg. (If you stay overnight, ask for a quiet room; the *pousada* is close beside the main IP7 highway.)

An interesting history surrounds the **Amoreira Aqueduct**, designed by a great 15th-century architect, Francisco de Arruda. It took nearly 200 years to complete, all 8 km (5 miles) and 843 arches of it. Its cost was borne by the people of Elvas under a special tax named the *Real de Agua*.

Handwoven rugs (different from the stitched patterns of Arraiolos) used to be manufactured throughout the Alentejo, but nowadays the small town of **Reguengos** is the only place where they are still made, in a factory that has been using the same looms for the past 150 years. Reguengos is another nu-

Sleepy afternoon in Vila Viçosa.

cleus of megalithic stones and dolmens, found in several sites near the town.

About 15 km (9 miles) distant from Reguengos is the delightful walled town of **Monsaraz**, so small it can easily be seen on foot – leave the car at the fortified gate. Its proximity to the Spanish border combined with its height made it of strategic importance. Once the threat from Spain had gone, however, Reguengos became gradually more influential and Monsaraz relaxed into a charming, peaceful village. Its main street, **Rua Direita**, is all 16th- and 17th-century architecture, yet, the town maintains a distinctly medieval feel.

The countryside surrounding the capital of the Upper Alentejo, **Portalegre**, is rather different from that in the lower lands. This area is in foothills of the Serra de São Mamede, and the cooler and slightly more humid climate makes it much greener.

Quite a large town by Alentejo standards, Portalegre is unusual in that it is not built on top of a hill, but on the site of an ancient ruined settlement called Amaya. In the mid-13th century, King Afonso III instructed that a new city was to be built and called it Portus Alacer: Portus for the customs gate which was to process Spanish trade and Alacer (*álacre* means merry) because of its pleasing setting.

King Dinis ensured that the town was fortified in 1290 (although only a few of those ruins can be seen today) and João III gave it the status of a city in 1550.

The lofty 16th-century interior of the **cathedral** (*Sé*) is late-Renaissance style. The side altars have fine wooden *retábulos* and 16th- and 17th-century paintings of Italian style. The sacristy contains lovely blue-and-white *azulejo* panels from the 18th century depicting the life of the Virgin Mary and the flight to Egypt. The cathedral's facade is 18th-century, and is dominated by marble columns, granite pilasters and wrought-iron balconies.

Portalegre's affluence began in the 16th century, when its tapestries were in great demand. Continued prosperity followed in the next century with the estab-

Silhouettes in Monsaraz.

lishment of silk mills. Don't miss the opportunity to see the tapestry workshops in the former Jesuit Monastery. The looms are still worked by hand.

Portalegre was home to one of Portugal's major writers: poet, dramatist and novelist José Régio (1901–69). His house has been opened as a museum. Of particular interest is his collection of regional folk and religious art.

Also of note is the 17th-century "Yellow Palace", where lived the 19th-century radical reformer, Mouzinho da Silveira. The ornate ironwork is remarkable.

Marvão must be one of the most spectacular sights of the Alentejo. About 25 km (15 miles) north of Portalegre, it is a medieval fortified town perched on one of the São Mamede peaks. Its altitude (862 metres/2,830 ft) affords it an uninterrupted view across the Spanish frontier. The precipitous drop on one side made it inaccessible to invaders and an ideal defensive situation.

At this height the land is barren and craggy. The seemingly impenetrable castle was built in the 13th century from the local grey granite. Clinging to the foot of the castle is the tiny village, a few twisting alleyways flanked by red-roofed whitewashed houses. Close by the church of **Espírito Santo**, on the street of the same name, is a baroque granite fountain. On the same street is the sober-looking **Governor's House**: its only decoration is two magnificent 17th-century wrought-iron balconies.

On the road to Castelo de Vide are the ruins of the Roman settlement of **Medóbriga**. Many artefacts have been found here, although most were removed to Lisbon. Completing the triangle of noteworthy upper Alentejo towns is **Castelo de Vide**, a delightful town built under the shade of an elongated medieval castle situated on the summit of a foothill on the northern *serra*.

Castelo de Vide is a spa town. You can drink its curative waters from plastic bottles which are sold in the supermarkets, or sip from one of the numerous fountains located in the town and environs. Perhaps its prettiest outlet is

The rooftops of Marvão.

the quadrangled, covered fountain (**Fonte da Vila**) set in the small square below the Jewish Quarter. The baroque fountain has a pyramid roof supported by six marble columns. The central urn is carved with figures of boys and the water spills from four spouts.

Near Castelo de Vide you will find still more megalithic stones: these *Pedras Talhas* seem everywhere, standing in fields, open scrubland or in local villages. The town itself was first a Roman settlement. Alongside it ran the major Roman road which traversed the Iberian peninsula. The settlement was sacked by the Vandals at the beginning of the 4th century, occupied by the Moors during their domination of the southern part of the peninsula, and fortified by the Portuguese in 1180.

As in nearly all fortified Alentejo towns, Castelo de Vide has two very distinct faces. The first is the older one, situated next to the castle. The most interesting and picturesque is the medieval **Jewish Quarter** (Judiaria). This host of back alleys, cobbled streets and whitewashed houses is splashed with green, as potted plants sprout their tendrils from every available niche, windowsill and step. Notice the doors: this section of Castelo de Vide has the best-preserved stone Gothic doorways in Portugal. The majority of the inhabitants in this part appear to be old people who sit in the doorways of their homes calmly watching the world go by.

Further down the hill is the newer part of town: essentially 17th- and 18th-century buildings with wider, less steep streets, more space, more order and more elegance. On the main square (**Praça D. Pedro V**) stands the grandiose 18th-century **parish church** and the old town hall (**Paços de Concelho**), remarkable for the huge 18th-century wrought-iron gate securing the main entrance.

Nisa is a small, rather rambling town northwest of Castelo de Vide. It has the mandatory medieval castle, walls and an unusual squat, round-towered chapel. Homemade cheese is Nisa's speciality.

Some 26 km (15 miles) south of Nisa on the road to Estremoz is **Crato**, once

The Santa Maria church in Castelo de Vide.

the seat of the Order of Hospitallers of St John. Its most notable building is the convent and church of Flor da Rosa dating to 1356 (and its fortune linked to the *pousada* network.) The main square is dominated by a splendid 15th-century stone veranda (**Varanda do Grão-Prior**), which is all that survives of the former priors' residence.

Two royal marriages took place in this town. The first was that of Manuel I, who married Leonor of Spain in 1518 (his third marriage). The second was seven years later when King João III married Catarina of Spain.

Further south, in countryside filled with olive groves is **Alter do Chão**, a medieval town interesting for its equine traditions. It is from here that the Alter Real horse takes its name. Based on Andalusian stock, the Alter stud was founded in 1748 by José who became king in 1750. The horse thrived until the Napoleonic Wars when the best animals were stolen and the royal stables abolished. Happily, the breed has been revived to a highly respected standard.

Unspoiled beaches: If you like unspoiled cliffs and beaches, quiet roads and villages, then you will delight in the Alentejo coast, although more and more tourists are retreating here. It borders on the open Atlantic and the ocean is therefore much rougher than on the south coast. But there are plenty of sheltered bays for swimming, although the water is chilly.

The Alentejo coast is not renowned for its nightlife. Bars, discos, and fancy restaurants hardly exist; nor do large hotels, except at Vila Nova de Milfontes. There are campsites, however, and all the villages have at least one *pensão*. You'd better bring along your phrase book. Where tourists are relatively rare, so are natives who speak English.

Access to the coast is easy; ICA, the coastal highway, was a well-used north–south route until the faster inland road was built. From Lisbon, heading south, the IP8 branches southwest just before Grândola to **Santiago do Cacém**, which is crowned by a castle built by the Knights Templar. From

Cork trees on the Alentejo plain.

there it's just a short hop to the Alentejo's largest coastal town, **Sines**.

Sines is not what you'd call a beauty spot, but you may find it interesting as an exercise in misguided expansionist idealism. For centuries it was a pretty fishing village, the birthplace of Vasco da Gama. The old part is still picturesque; but what surrounds it is visually horrible. During the Caetano regime it was decided to build a massive oil refinery to process the oil from the hundreds of tankers which were expected to port there. They didn't. Sines was left with an ugly white elephant which dominates the town. It functions, as does a large power station on the northbound approach, but between them they produce pervasive smells of gas and chemicals and make the area look like some futuristic industrial forest.

To forget the ugliness of Sines, clear your lungs at the village of **Porto Corvo**. The road which takes you there is tree-lined and virtually traffic-free. Several tracks lead from the main road down to shingly beaches. Porto Corvo is a tiny little village, with cobbled streets swept scrupulously clean. The main square, grandly named **Largo Marquês de Pombal**, is very small, bordered by homes and the tiny parish church. A few small trees and plentiful benches surround the square. Down by the sea you can find shops, cafes and a restaurant.

Just off the coast of Porto Corvo is the fortified **Ilha do Pessageiro** (Peach Tree Island), which in bygone days provided protection from raids by Dutch and Algerian pirates.

Some 15 km (9 miles) down the road from Porto Corvo is the small town of Cercal, and from here the main road goes to **Vila Nova de Milfontes**, the busiest of the coast's resorts and very pleasing it is, too. The only time it gets really busy is in high summer when many *Alentejanos* and *Lisboetas* come for their annual holiday at the large campsite there.

Again, there is little nightlife but there are a few more seafood restaurants and a range of accommodation that includes the pricey Castle Hotel which overlooks

Left, Gothic castle in Beja. **Right**, refinery pipelines at Sines.

the sea, converted from an ivy-clad fortress – drawbridge and all.

Vila Nova de Milfontes is set at the mouth of the Mira river, whose estuary provides long golden beaches and a calm sea. Park out at the headland overlooking the ocean, and you can turn back to see the town to your left, the winding river and the hills beyond – all very idyllic. If you are planning a day or two on this coast, then here is the place to stay.

Almograve and **Zambujeira** offer more stunning, deserted beaches and some fine clifftop viewpoints across the basalt cliffs to the sea. Between these two beaches is another one, **Cabo do Girão**. But it is naval property and access is prohibited.

If you have extra time and feel like looking inland from here, in the lower Alentejo is the pretty town of **Odemira**, set on the banks of the Mira river after which it's named. It is full of flowers and trees, so green that you are apt to forget that it is in the Alentejo. Water, water everywhere can also be found up at the nearby **Barragem de Santa Clara**, a huge dam on the Mira. You can indulge in water sports here.

Ourique is an agricultural town north of the dam. In its surrounding fields (**Campo do Ourique**) are grown fruit, olive and cork trees. These fields, however, have seen far more than just farming. In the hamlet of **Atalaia**, archaeologists excavated an extraordinary Bronze Age burial mound, and it was on a battleground called Ourique (maybe here, maybe not) thousands of years later in 1139, that a fateful encounter was fought between the Portuguese and the Moors. Afonso Henriques had just become the first king of Portugal. The victory on this battlefield strengthened his determination to rout the Moors from Portuguese soil, and gave a tremendous boost to his army's morale.

The capital of lower Alentejo, **Beja**, is the hottest town (in air temperature terms) in Portugal during the height of summer. It is a three-hour drive from Lisbon and an hour or so from Évora. A town existed on the present-day site as

Local colour.

early as 48 BC and when Julius Caesar made peace with the Lusitanians the settlement was named after this event, *Pax Julia*. During the 400-year Moorish occupation the name was adulterated to Baju, then Baja, until it finally became known as Beja.

Beja is now a fairly prosperous town, its income derived from olive oil and wheat. A long-time German Air Force base has been turned over to the Portuguese Air Force. Beja is not a beautiful town, but it does have interesting sights.

The 15th-century **Convento da Conceição** is a fine example of the transition between Gothic and Manueline architecture. The baroque chapel is lined with carved, gilded woodwork. The chapterhouse which leads to the cloisters is tiled with superb Hispanic-Arabic *azulejos* dating back to the 1500s. Their quality is rivalled only by those to be found in the Royal Palace at Sintra. The convent also houses the **regional museum**.

The small and modest **Santo Amaro** is the oldest church in Beja. It is thought to date back to the 7th century and is a rare example of Visigothic architecture. Beja's 13th-century castle keep still stands, and its castellated walls run around the town perimeter. The tall keep contains a **military museum**, and a narrow balcony on each side from which you can enjoy a remarkable view across the plains.

Driving in to **Serpa** is – as with so many small Alentejo towns – like driving into a time warp. The **castle** and fortified walls were built at the command of King Dinis. A difference here from other 13th-century walls is that these have an aqueduct built into them.

A well-preserved gateway is the **Portas de Beja**, which, along with the rest of the walls, were almost sold by the town council in the latter half of the 19th century. Cooler heads prevailed and the walls were saved, though a great part of them had been destroyed in 1707 when the Duke of Ossuna and his army occupied the town during the War of the Spanish Succession.

There are several churches worth seeing, as well as the delightfully cool and elegant palace belonging to the Count of Ficalho. The **Paço dos Condes de Ficalho** was built in the 16th century. It has a majestic staircase and lovely tiles. The present Marquise, incidentally, is the granddaughter of Portugal's great 19th-century novelist Eça de Queiroz.

The **Guadiana** is considered the most peaceful of Portugal's three big rivers (the others being the Tagus and Douro), but an exception is at Pulo do Lobo near **Mértola**. This is a stretch of high and wild rapids, which can be reached by road and is worth a visit if you're in the area. Mértola, an ancient fortified town set in the confluence between the Guadiana and the Oeiras rivers, is also worth a stop to see the **parish church**, originally a mosque and one of the few mosques in Portugal to have survived virtually intact.

Food and drink: The Alentejo's culinary specialities should not be missed. Try *sopa alentejana* – a filling soup of bread, lots of coriander (a herb used a great deal in Alentejo cooking), garlic and poached eggs. One of the classic meat dishes is *carne de porco à alentejana* – chunks of pork seasoned in wine, coriander and onions and served with clams. Two much heavier but delicious stewed dishes are *ensopada de cabrito* – kid boiled with potatoes and bread until the meat is just about falling off the bone, and *favada de caça*, a game stew of hare, rabbit, partridge or pigeon with broad beans. The best Alentejo cheese comes from Serpa. Made from sheep's and goat's milk it has a creamy texture and a strong, slightly piquant flavour. Évora has its own goat cheese which is hard, salty and slightly acid. It is preserved in jars filled with olive oil.

Alentejo is a demarcated wine region. Its reds are full-bodied and mature well in the bottle. Most towns have their own cooperative winery from which you can buy stocks at rock-bottom prices. Most restaurants have a modestly priced cooperative house wine. To appreciate really good Alentejo wines, try the reds from the Reguengos cooperative or those from Borba. White wines from the Vidigueira cooperative are far superior to any other Alentejo whites.

Right, Capela de São Gens in Serpa.

COIMBRA

Perched on a hill overlooking the Mondego river, Coimbra is surrounded by breathtakingly beautiful countryside. The city itself is a mixture of ancient and new, rural and urban. The tourist office in the centre of the lower town in **Largo de Portagem** will provide you with a good map of the city.

While there are few traces of the Roman occupation, vestiges of the Middle Ages still abound.

The University is the most stalwart guardian of the past. Students clad in black capes, the traditional academic dress, resemble oversized bats as they flit around town. The hems of the capes are often ripped, a declaration – at times – of romantic conquest. These capes, by the way, have only recently come back into style, since for a time they were associated with Salazar's New State, and therefore not worn in the years after the Revolution.

In May each year, the University celebrates the *Queima das Fitas*, the "burning of the ribbons", when graduating students burn the ribbons they have been wearing, the colour of the ribbons signifying a student's faculty – yellow for medicine, and so on. The celebrations last a week, their grand finale a large, drunken parade.

Another Coimbra tradition is *fado*, its music a more serious cousin of Lisbon *fado*. The sombre Coimbra *fado* theoretically requires you to clear your throat in approval after a rendition, and not applaud. This type of *fado* is performed only by men, often cloak-wrapped graduates of the University.

The country's third-largest city, Coimbra is the centre of an agricultural region and has a large market. The students are not the only ones in black: it is the traditional dress of many of the rural women who come to town as well. Coimbra also has a considerable manufacturing industry.

Roman roots: Coimbra traces its roots to the Roman municipality of *Aeminium*. The city gained in importance because the city of Conímbriga, a few miles south, proved vulnerable to invasion. Convulsions in the empire and various invasions brought an end to Roman rule in the city. The Moors took over in 711, ushering in 300 years of Islamic rule, with a few interruptions. One such interruption occurred in 878 when Afonso III of Asturias and León captured the city. But Coimbra was not permanently taken by Christians until 1064.

Coimbra then became a base for the reconquest of other parts of Portugal from the Moors. It was about this time – the 11th century – that the city was originally walled. From 1139 to 1385, Coimbra was the capital of Portugal.

The 12th century was an age of great progress for Coimbra, including construction of the city's most important monastery, Santa Cruz, which still stands; building began in 1131. The city was a lively commercial centre and included Jewish and Moorish quarters. Division was not only by religion, but by class as well. Nobles and clergy lived inside the walls; merchants and craft

Preceding pages: a Lusitanian stallion; a mural in Moita. Left, a Coimbra University student. Right, from Coimbra's library.

workers lived outside in what is today called the Baixa, the lower area.

The University was founded in 1290 – not in Coimbra, however, but in Lisbon. In 1308 it moved to Coimbra, only to return to Lisbon in 1377. These shifts were the result of continual political conflict between the monarchy and the academic leaders. It was not until 1537 that the University settled permanently in Coimbra. A few years later, it moved to its present site at the top of the hill.

Most areas of interest are easily reached on foot – that is, if you're willing to do some uphill walking. There is an extensive bus system, although the bus maps are difficult to read. Don't try to drive within the city. The old city and the University crown Coimbra's central hill. The Baixa, which is the main shopping district, lies at the foot of the hill along the Mondego river. Santa Clara lies across the river, while Turismo is handily located at the northern end of the bridge.

Old city: Once enclosed within walls, the old city is a tangle of narrow streets and alleys, lined by ancient buildings and filled with squares and patios – and cars. The University buildings are a compelling mix of styles, from the odd baroque **Torre**, a clocktower known to the students as *a cabra* (the goat), to bleakly Salazarist faculty blocks. The passage of centuries is evident. The modern centre of the University is the statue of Dom Dinis, its founder. Near it are the buildings that house the **Faculties** of **Science and Technology, Medicine and Letters** and the **New Library**.

Of more historical interest than these rather stolidly functional buildings is the **Pátio das Escolas**, Patio of the Schools. To enter the patio, pass through the 17th-century **Porta Férrea**, a large portal decorated in the Mannerist style, to a large, rather dusty courtyard, which unfortunately is used as a parking lot. Here are some of the oldest and stateliest buildings of the University. The figure of João III, who installed the University in Coimbra, still reigns from the centre of the patio. Behind him, there is a magnificent view of the river.

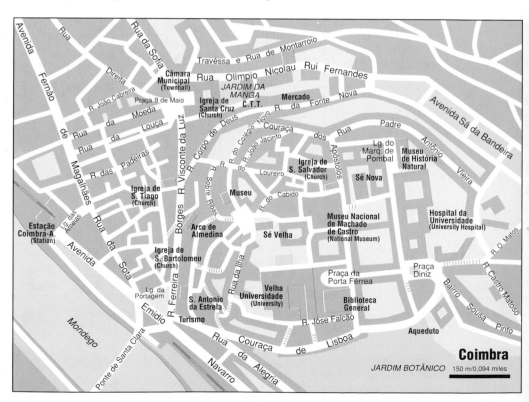

Coimbra

JARDIM BOTÂNICO   150 m/0,094 miles

The building in the farthest corner from the Porta Férrea is the Biblioteca Joanina, among the world's most resplendent baroque libraries. To enter, ring and wait for the caretaker to open the door (closed for lunch, noon –2 pm). The three sumptuous 18th-century rooms were built during the reign of João V, whose portrait hangs at the far end. Bookcases, decorated in gilded wood and oriental motifs, reach gracefully to an upper galleried level; even the ladders are intricately decorated. Note the frescoes on the ceilings. More than 30,000 books fill the cases and are still consulted by scholars.

Next door is **St Michael's Chapel**, begun in 1517, and remodelled in both the 17th and 18th centuries. The chapel is notable for its "carpet" style tiles, the painted ceilings, the altar, and the baroque organ. Beside the chapel is a **museum of sacred art**.

The arcaded building to the right of the Porta Férrea on the Via Latuna houses the **Sala dos Capelos**, where many academic ceremonies take place. Portraits of the kings of Portugal hang from its walls. Other rooms which you may enter are the **Rectory** and right by the bell tower, the **Private Exam Room**.

A short walk down from the University grounds is the **Sé Nova** (new cathedral) whose sand-coloured facade presides over an uninteresting square. Built for the Jesuits in 1554, it became a cathedral in 1772. Inside, the altar and much else is of lavish gilded wood. Many of the paintings around the altar are copies of Italian masters.

The **Machado de Castro Museum**, open 10am–1pm and 2–4.30pm, is housed in the old episcopal palace and the neighbouring 12th-century church of **São João de Almedina**. Built over the city's Roman forum, the palace was the residence of Coimbra's early bishops. The museum is named after Portugal's greatest sculptor, and medieval sculpture as well as later work is on display. It has an excellent collection, both extensive and varied. Unfortunately, much of it is unlabelled. Still, the museum is certainly worth a visit to see

Coimbra at night.

also Roman artefacts, a large collection of Portuguese painting from the 15th century onward, gold work, ceramics, tapestries, furniture, and even two coaches. There is also a grand view of the Romanesque **Sé Velha** (old cathedral) and the roofs of the old city from the courtyard.

The Sé Velha, renovated this century, was built between 1162 and 1184. It served as cathedral until 1772, when the episcopal see was moved to the Sé Nova. The fortress-like exterior is relieved by an arched door and an arched window directly above. The intricate Gothic altar within is of gilded wood, created by two Flemish masters in the 15th and 16th centuries. Sanches I was crowned king here in 1185, and João I in 1385. There are several **tombs** in the church, including those of 13th-century Bishop Dom Egas Faíes (left of the altar) and Dona Vetaca, a Byzantine princess who lived in the Coimbra court in the 14th century. The **cloister** is early Gothic; construction began in 1218.

Construction on the **Colégio de Santo Agostino**, on Rua Colégio Novo, began in 1593. The ecclesiastical scholars and monks who first occupied it would be shocked by the goings-on here today, for this pleasant building, lined with pretty *azulejos*, is now home to the University's Psychology Department.

Nearby, on Rua Sobre-Ripas (confusingly, also Sub-Ripas), the medieval **Torre** (Tower) **de Anto** was once part of the 12th-century walls of the city. Much later it was the home of poet António Nobre during his undergraduate days. Today it displays and sells traditional crafts from the Coimbra area, sponsored by the city council.

The **Casa de Sobre-Ripas**, also on Rua Sobre-Ripas, is an aristocratic mansion from the 16th century. Note the archetypal Manueline door and window, but don't bother knocking, it's still a private residence. Here, according to tradition, Maria Teles was murdered by her husband João, eldest son of the tragic Inês de Castro. João had been convinced by Queen Leonor Teles, who was jealous of Maria, that his wife – the queen's sister – was unfaithful.

The **Arco de Almedina**, an entrance to the old city just off Rua Ferreira Borges (the main downtown street) was also part of the Coimbra walls.

The Baixa is the busy shopping district. **Rua Ferreira Borges**, with many fashionable shops, is the principal street. Although this district lay outside the walls of the old city, it dates back to nearly the same time. The **Santa Cruz Monastery**, in Praça 8 de Maio, a continuation of Rua Ferreira Borges, was founded in 1131 by Portugal's first king, Afonso Henriques. The facade and portal date from the 16th century, when the church was restored. Inside, although the church is small, it is light and spacious. Eighteenth-century *azulejos* adorn either wall: the right side depicts the life of Saint Augustine, the left scenes relate to the Holy Cross.

Another striking work by a major 16th-century artist is the exquisite **pulpit** on the left wall, by sculptor Nicolau Chanterène. The sacristy is open from 9–noon and from 2–5pm, and contains several paintings including *The Pentecost* by the notable Beira painter Frão Vasco, a silverwork collection, and some vestments. You can visit the **tombs** of the first two kings of Portugal, Afonso Henriques and Sancho I, who are ensconced in truly regal monuments. You may also see the **Chapterhouse** and the lovely **Cloister of Silence**.

The **Rua da Sofia**, off Praça 8 de Maio, a 16th-century street, was extraordinarily wide for its time. It was the original home of several colleges of the University before they were moved.

Praça do Comércio, off Rua Ferreira Borges, is an oddly shaped square lined with 17th- and 18th-century buildings. At the north end stands the sturdy **Santiago Church**, dating from the end of the 12th century. The capitals are decorated with animal and bird motifs. At the south end is the church of **São Bartolomeu**, built in the 18th century.

The Santa Clara section of town lies across the river. **Santa Clara-a-Nova** (New Santa Clara) **Monastery** is worth a visit if only for the view of Coimbra. Inside, in a wildly baroque setting, is the **tomb of the Queen Saint Isabel**, the patron saint of Coimbra. Closer to the river, too close for its own comfort in fact, is **Santa Clara-a-Velha**, the old Santa Clara Monastery. This 12th-century edifice is simpler and lovelier than its replacement, for which it was abandoned in 1677. Damaged by frequent floods, it is now partially restored.

Nearby, **Portugal dos Pequenitos** is an outdoor museum of small-scale reproductions of traditional Portuguese houses and famous monuments. To the east of the city, the **Celas Monastery** is notable for its cloister and the pretty church of **Santo António dos Olivais** was an old Franciscan convent.

Shops and parks: If you are interested in traditional Coimbra ceramics and handicrafts, the city's showcase shop is the **Torre de Anto**, in the old city. For a different shopping experience, go to the **covered market** on Rua Olimpio Nicolau, not far from the Baixa, which is open every morning but best on Saturday. The market vendors hawk fish, bread, fruit, vegetables, flowers and live animals (chickens and rabbits). You'll get an authentic taste of Coimbra life.

Coimbra's many parks are agreeable resting places. The **Botanical Garden**, on Alameda Dr Júlio Henriques, next to the aqueduct, is a lovely garden filled with plant life. Unfortunately, not all the grounds are open to the public. Other parks are **Santa Cruz**, off the Praça da República, and **Choupal**, west of the city – a larger park good for walks and bike rides. The very small **Penedo da Saudade** has a nice view.

Canoeing in Coimbra: For physical exercise, rent a canoe from the municipal boat club near the **Santa Clara Bridge**, on the far side of the river.

Outlying districts accessible by bus or by car include **Penacova**, an upriver village with a striking view – try lunch there at the Panorâmico Restaurant. The drive/bus ride to Penacova runs along the lovely Mondego river valley. There are windmills on hilltops in the surrounding countryside. Or visit **Penela**, a village south of Conímbriga with a Moorish castle overlooking the area; or **Lousã**, a mountain town.

Alumni of the Medical School gather at the Old University.

SIDE TRIPS FROM COIMBRA

The largest excavated Roman ruins in Portugal, complemented by one of the country's finest museums, lies not far from Coimbra, near the town of Condeixa. **Conímbriga** is a fascinating site that includes the remains of a Roman wall, several public buildings and private houses, and beautifully preserved mosaics which alone would be worth the visit.

Conímbriga lies about 15 km (9 miles) south of Coimbra. The drive is easy; there is also a bus service. The site and museum are open daily 10am–1pm and 2–6pm; the museum is closed on Monday (tel: 039-941177).

Of an estimated 13-hectare (32-acre) site, only a few hundred metres have been excavated. A glance out on to the hot, dusty field that is still off-limits to tourists reveals signs of further ruins, and, happily, the beginnings of more excavation. Archaeologists believe remains may be found as far away as the main highway and even under the homes of people in the nearby village of Condeixa-a-Velha.

Conímbriga was probably settled as early as the Iron Age (800–500 BC). It was not until the last part of the 2nd century BC that Romans came. Conímbriga profited from its location along the Roman road between *Olisipo* (present-day Lisbon) and *Bracara Augusta* (now Braga). Some time around AD 70, the Roman Empire designated Conímbriga a *municipium*.

Great wall: Conímbriga's prosperity was not to last. Crises in the empire and Barbarian incursions into Iberia prompted the construction of the defensive wall which is still prominent today on the site. To take advantage of the natural defensive position of the area, the inhabited area of Conímbriga had to be reduced.

Despite the new wall, in 464 Suevi successfully attacked the city. Conímbriga continued to be inhabited, but it lost its status as an important

Batalha Monastery.

centre to its neighbour, the more easily defensible *Aeminium* (Coimbra).

As you enter the site, you are walking down the very road that gave Conímbriga its original importance – the highway between *Olisipo* and *Bracara Augusta*. In front of you is the enormous wall.

Passing through the main entrance in the wall, and continuing along the path through to the right, you'll come to the arch of the aqueduct (rebuilt), parts of the aqueduct itself, and the remains of several buildings which might have been small shops.

Cantaber's house stretches to the south (left, with your back to the entrance). The house is full of ornamental pools, but perhaps the most interesting part are the baths, which lie at the extreme south end. They are easily recognisable by their hexagonal and round shapes, and by the heating system (of pipes) which is visible through the stone grid covering the floors.

Back around the other side of the wall, you can see more baths: public ones. For Romans, bathing was an im-portant daily ritual, and the bathroom was also a place to discuss politics. They covered themselves with olive oil after their baths and then scraped their skins clean with a curved blade.

Beyond the baths is an area of marvel-lously-patterned mosaics. The colours were once much brighter than the pleasing pastels to which they have mellowed today.

The **museum** is small but thoughtfully designed. A long case displays artefacts relating to ceramics, weaving, agriculture, lighting, writing, health and hygiene, jewellery, and other areas. There is also statuary and a very good model of the forum and temple.

The Silver Coast: Coimbra is the largest city in the province of Beira Litoral, which lies above the provinces of Estremadura and Ribatejo. All three are lush, green and laced with waterways. The Beira Litoral has a very ragged coastline, as the Atlantic constantly pushes in with greedy fingers, both at the Ria de Aveiro and to the south. Ricefields are planted in this low coastal area, which is often called "Costa da Prata", or the Silver Coast. Patches of pine trees have been planted in some spots in an effort to stabilise the sand dunes. Inland, the ground begins to rise very gradually, and fruit trees and grain fields flourish.

Estremadura stretches below the coastal part of Beira Litoral like an arm reaching down to touch Lisbon and Setúbal. This was once the southern extremity of Portugal, a fact confirmed by its name, which means "farthest land on the Douro". It is an alluvial plain, planted with grains. Wherever flooding allows, ricefields are sown. But most important are the large meadows on which graze the horses and bulls which are bred for bullfighting. These beautiful animals are used all over Portugal, and the Festival of the Red Waistcoats, which is held each July in **Vila Franca de Xira**, is five days of bull running and celebration.

There are many other colourful festivals in these provinces, but the most important celebration – indeed, one of the most populous Catholic events in

The Silver Coast
40 km / 25 miles

the world, is the pilgrimage at **Fátima**. On 13 May 1917, three shepherd children had a vision of the Virgin here. Thereafter, she appeared before the children and once, as a shining light, to the townspeople that gathered with them on the 13th of every month until October. The processions that now take place each year draw thousands from around the world.

The two younger children died shortly after the apparitions, but one, Lucia, lived well into her eighties, a forthright nun in a convent near Coimbra. Today, Fátima has capitalised on its massive appeal with ubiquitous merchandising of religious souvenirs. Many thousands of pilgrims still walk for days suffering penitential hardship.

The Venice of Portugal: The largest town in the local provinces, apart from Coimbra, is **Aveiro**. It has been described as "the Venice of Portugal", but in truth is nothing like the Italian city.

The comparison stems from the canals that traverse the city and the boats that ply them. The canal system is modest: only one main canal with two smaller ones along the edges of town. But they are linked with the **Ria**, the lagoon that extends 47 km (29 miles) just inland of the Atlantic ocean, with dunes and long sand beaches.

The Ria plays a large part in Aveiro's economy as an expanding port for fishing fleets and industrial cargoes. But still brightly conspicuous are the boats with large, graceful prows, the *moliceiros*, once widely used to gather *moliço*, seaweed, for fertiliser. Next to the canals are large saltpans, another local industry. Other important industries are wood, cork, and ceramics from nearby Vista Alegre.

Aveiro, known to the Romans as Talabriga, once lay directly on the ocean. However, over the centuries a strip of sediment has built up, creating the Ria but blocking ships and trade.

Aveiro was a small settlement during the Middle Ages. In the 13th century it became a town, later encircled by fortified walls (1418) at the suggestion of Infante Prince Pedro (after whom the

A boat moored in Aveiro.

city park is named). Shortly after this, the king granted Aveiro the concession of a town fair, and the March Fair still goes on to this day. In 1472, the king's daughter, Joana, entered the convent of Jesus in Aveiro against her father's will. Today the convent is a museum, and the princess has become Santa Joana Princesa, with several miracles attributed to her .

The 16th century was a time of growth and expansion for the town. With dredged access to the sea and to the interior, Aveiro became a mercantile and trade centre from which products of the entire Beira region were exported.

A fluke of nature cut short Aveiro's prosperity. In 1575 a violent storm shifted the sandbanks in the lagoon, blocking the canal to the sea. A dramatic decrease in population by emigration (to about one-third) accompanied the inevitable decline in Aveiro's importance. In 1808, another storm reopened the sea passage, but it was not until the last half of the 19th century that Aveiro's fortunes picked up.

An agreeable base for a trip on the Ria or nearby beaches, Aveiro itself is worth exploring. The city is divided into two parts by the principal canal. The southern part of the city is where the aristocracy once lived; the northern half is the old fishermen's section.

The southern half centres around the Praça da República. In the simple square, the nicest building is the solid and rather prim **town hall**. On the east side of the square, the 16th- and 17th-century **Misericórdia** church boasts a lovely Renaissance portal and 19th-century tiles on its facade.

In a square further south the 17th-century **Carmelite Convent** housed the barefoot Carmelite order. Note the paintings on the ceiling which depict the life of Saint Teresa.

Although the **museum** of Aveiro is not well-labelled, guides will take you through and answer questions. The museum is housed in the 15th-century **Convento de Jesus**. The church of the convent is a riot of gilded wood. Arching over the choir are lovely hand-

Aveiro's canal.

painted ceilings, and off the choir is a chapel with beautiful tiles. Just outside is Santa Joana Princesa's **tomb**, done in intricately carved coloured marble with statues supporting and crowning it. The tomb took 12 years to construct. The walls are also of marble.

The rest of the convent holds pieces of varying interest: many ornate altars, painted biblical scenes, a gruesome Christ covered in graphic sores. Perhaps the most interesting pieces are those that illuminate the life of the convent: the choir music stands, the Mother Superior's chair, the old convent pharmacy, where a bookcase holds containers for opium, belladonna, and cocaine extracts; drawers labelled for various herbs, scales to weigh the medicine, and books on pharmacology.

The **São Domingos Cathedral** is near the museum. Its baroque facade has twisted columns and sculpted figures of Faith, Hope and Charity. Inside, an enormous skylight over the altar lends the church an airiness that many baroque churches lack. The enormous blue altar

rises strikingly in the all-white interior. The **tomb of Catarina de Atalide** is here, a woman honoured, under the name Natércia, by the poet Camões in his sonnets. The church was founded in 1423 and remodelled during the 16th and 17th centuries.

Several blocks away is the refreshing **Dom Infante Pedro Park**, on the grounds of the old **Franciscan Monastery**. Colourful flowers, lush trees, fountains, and a small lake where you can rent paddle boats make this a nice spot for a break.

North of the canal lies the fishermen's section, where narrow one- and two-storey houses support facades that sometimes rise beyond roof levels. The arches and curves on the tops of these false fronts are reminiscent of the fishing boats themselves and their curved prows. The **fish market**, where the catch is sold each morning, is in this area. There is also the bright white, oddly shaped chapel of **São Gonçalinho** and the church of **São Gonçalo**. Inside this 17th- and 18th-century church gleam a gilt altar and newly placed tiles.

The beautiful **Ria** is a prime reason for coming to Aveiro. You can tour its length by boat, car, or bus, although boat is by far the most rewarding. It and its subsidiary canals extend as far south as Mira and as far north as Ovar. There is a fair range of hotels in the area and many camping sites. You will see the traditional *moliceiros,* shorelines dotted with saltpans, forests and villages, glorious sea fowl plummeting into the water after fish, and the sandbar which blocks the city's access to the sea.

The tourist office runs a boat tour to the area daily between 15 June and 15 September. Trips last from 10am to 5pm. Boat or drive, and you will see why this region also bears the name of *Rota da Luz*, the Route of Light.

Tomar, to the south – some 180 km (111 miles) from Aveiro, 120 km (74 miles) from Coimbra, or just a little more from Lisbon – is a delightful town with a host of charms: a setting on the banks of the Nabão river, a splendid historical monument in the **Convento de Cristo** – the monastery within the

Detail of the Convento de Cristo.

castle of the Knights Templar and the Order of Christ – fine art, and medieval streets paved with stone and fancifully patterned with exuberant flowers. With its pleasing ambience, rich culture, its ancient legends and appealing daily life, Tomar is a town to linger in and explore for a couple of days.

Tomar was the headquarters of the Knights Templar in Portugal, an order which was formed in 1119, during the crusades. The order spread quickly through Europe, gaining extraordinary wealth. It also made powerful enemies, and in the early 1300s, with accusations of heresy and foul practices, and finally the suppression of the order altogether, the Knights took refuge in Tomar where Grand Master Gualdim Pais had built a strong castle back in 1162. They re-emerged in 1320, reincarnated as the Order of Christ, whose proud symbol, the Cross of Christ, became the banner of the age of discoveries.

In Tomar they left behind the marvellous ruins of the old Templar castle and within its walls the still intact

church and cloisters. The castle is set on a hill above the city, a 10-minute walk up, and commands a view of the roofs of the old town.

The monastery – Convento de Cristo – is a maze of staircases, passages, nooks and crannies. The seven cloisters (only four are open to the public) have been added at irregular angles and several centuries. Even the beautiful main entrance is oddly tucked into a corner.

Inside the entrance, the original **Templar church** lies to the right. Begun in 1162, the octagonal temple was modelled on the Church of the Holy Sepulchre in Jerusalem. Here the knights would hear services while seated on their horses and pray for victory in battle, surrounded by gilt painting.

The **Chapterhouse** and **Coro Alto**, added much later, provide a sharp contrast to the original temple as again does the adjoining 16th-century cloister with 17th-century tiles. Some of the tombs of the Knights are found here. From here there is access to the upper level and then into the other cloisters. From the

Collecting weed in the Ria.

terrace of the small **Claustro de Santa Bárbara**, there is a view of the amazing ornate Manueline window, structured around two deep relief carvings of ships' masts and knots, cork, coral, and seaweed. The whole is topped by a shield, crown and cross, symbol of the union of church and king.

From the opposite side of the building there is a view of the surrounding forest and the castle yard where the Knights trained their horses and spent their off-duty hours. Also on this side lies an unfinished chapel, which was to be a copy of the entrance. Bad luck during construction persuaded the superstitious Knights to abandon it.

Tomar's **synagogue** is at Rua Joaquim Jacinto, 73. Although up to 70 percent of Portuguese have Jewish ancestry and Tomar was once the home of a thriving Jewish community, there are very few Jews left. When in 1497 the Portuguese king married Isabella of Castile, a condition of the marriage contract was their expulsion. Instead, Jews were allowed to remain, and convert, although prac-

tices were not closely monitored. Later, the Inquisition would brutally enforce these laws. The synagogue/museum is simple and moving, decorated with gifts from all over the world.

The church of **São João Baptista** has a dark wood ceiling and sombre atmosphere. Sixteenth-century wood panel paintings on the walls depict scenes including the Last Supper and Salome with the head of John the Baptist. On the left is a delicately carved pulpit.

Standing alone on the edges of town, **Santa Maria dos Olivais** is a simple church dating to the 12th century and containing many Templar tombs.

Tourist offices are located on Avenida Dr Cándido Madureira, near the road to the castle, and at 1 Rua Serpa Pinto.

Santarém, the central town of Ribatejo, lies some 80 km (50 miles) up the Tagus river from Lisbon. It was named after Santa Iria, a young nun who was accused of being unchaste and martyred in 653 near Tomar. Her body, thrown into the river, washed ashore here. A riverbank shrine has a statue

A sultry day in Tomar.

whose feet act as a sacred gauge to water level – if they are touched by floods, even Lisbon is in danger.

Among several fine churches, the Romanesque Gothic church of **São João de Alporão** contains a fine archaeological museum, as well as the beautifully carved tomb of Duarte, a son of Pedro I who died in the Battle of Alcacer-Quiber in 1458. It contains only one of Duarte's teeth, the sole relic which was delivered to his wife.

In northeastern Santarém is the church of **Santa Clara**, originally part of a 13th-century convent, containing the elaborate tomb of Dona Leonor, daughter of Afonso III. The church of **Nossa Senhora da Graça**, a bold Gothic structure with a beautiful nave, contains several tombs, among them that of Pedro Alvares Cabral, discoverer of Brazil. In **Alpiarça**, across the river, look for the architectural 19th-century gem of the Casa dos Patudos, today a wonderfully eclectic museum.

Batalha's monastery appears magnificently, if incongruously, to one side of the Lisbon-Oporto main highway. It is one of Portugal's most beautiful monuments.

The **Santa Maria da Vitória Monastery**'s origins lie in Portugal's struggle for independence from Castile. One of the decisive battles for independence was fought at Aljubarrota, which was not far from Batalha.

The Castilian king, Juan, based his claim to the Portuguese throne on his marriage to a Portuguese princess; he invaded Portugal to force the claim in 1385. The 20-year-old Dom João, Master of the Order of Avis and illegitimate son of Pedro I, promised to raise a monastery to the Virgin Mary if the Portuguese won. With his young general, Nuno Álvares Pereira, João defeated Juan and became João I. The monastery was constructed between 1388 and 1533.

The front portal, though large, is smaller than most. The arches sweep upward to a sculpture of figures representing the hierarchy in the heavenly court – as it was perceived in the Middle

The Unfinished Chapels of Batalha.

Ages. In the centre is Christ surrounded by Matthew, Mark, Luke, and John. Though the outside of the monastery is ornate, the interior is endowed with a simple Gothic elegance and dignity. Vaulted ceilings arch above a slender nave which is illuminated through windows by stained glass.

To the right is the **Founder's Chapel** (Dom João's Pantheon), built around 1426 by João I. And here are the tombs of João and his English queen, Philippa; effigies eloquently holding hands. Other tombs, including that of Prince Henry the Navigator, are set into the walls under regal arches. The room is topped by a dome supported by star-shaped ribbing.

On the other side of the building you may enter **Dom João's Cloister**. Arches filled with Manueline ornamentation surround a pretty courtyard and are patterned with intricate designs.

The **chapterhouse** is the first room off the cloister. It has an unusual and beautiful ceiling, which has no support other than the walls. The impression is of precarious balance. The window is filled with a stained-glass Christ on the cross, remarkably rich in colour. This chamber holds the tombs of two unknown soldiers, whose remains were returned to Portugal from France and Africa after World War I. The sculpture of "Christ of the Trenches" was given by the French government. An armed honour guard seems out of place in this peaceful place.

To reach the *Capelas Imperfeitas* (**Unfinished Chapels**), walk outside the monastery. This octagonal structure is attached to the outside wall and its abrupt rooflessness is a shock. Ordered by Dom Duarte to house the tombs of himself and his family, the chapel was begun in the 1430s but construction was never finished. No one is quite certain why. (A national trend toward unfinished projects is called by the Portuguese in self-mockery the "*síndrome das Capelas Imperfeitas*" or even "*obras de Santa Engrácia*", after a similar unfinished project in Lisbon.)

The shell contains simple chapels in

Left, the beautiful lines of Alcobaça. **Right**, inside Batalha.

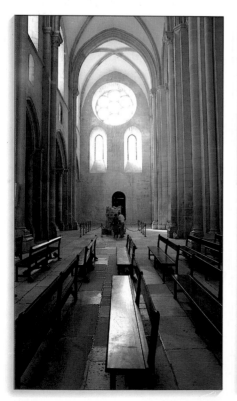

each of seven walls. The chapel opposite the door holds the tomb of the king and Leonor, his wife. The eighth wall is a massive door of limestone, with endless layers of beautifully detailed ornamentation in carved Manueline style.

There is little else to see in the village of Batalha. A shopping mall next to the monastery has tourist-oriented "handicraft" shops and a tourist office.

About 12 km (8 miles) south of Batalha lies the town of **Alcobaça**, named after two small rivers the Alcoa and the Baça. At its heart is the huge, magnificent **Cistercian Abbey**. The first king of Portugal, Afonso Henriques, founded it to commemorate the capture of Santarém from the Moors. Afonso laid the foundation stone himself, in 1148.

The Cistercian monks were energetically productive. Numbering, it is said 999 ("one less than a thousand"), they diligently tilled the land around the abbey, planting vegetables and fruit. In Sebastião I's reign, the exceedingly wealthy and powerful Santa Maria Abbey, as it is also known, was declared by the Pope the seat of the entire Cistercian order. The monks here were particularly known for their lively spirits and lavish hospitality. They ran a school, perhaps the first public school in Portugal, and a sanctuary and hospice as well. In 1810, however, the abbey was sacked by French troops. In the Liberal Revolution of 1834, when all religious orders were expelled from Portugal, the abbey was again pillaged.

The long baroque facade, added in the 18th century, has twin towers in the centre, below which are a Gothic doorway and rose window, surviving from the original facade. Directly inside the serene and austere **church** – the largest church in Portugal – are three tall aisles and plain walls emphasise the clean lines. In the transepts are the two famous, richly carved **tombs** of Pedro I and Inês de Castro.

Off the south transept are several additional royal tombs, including those of Afonso II and Afonso III, and a sadly mutilated 17th-century terracotta of the Death of St Bernard. To the east of the ambulatory there are two fine Manueline doorways that were designed by João de Castilho.

An entrance in the north wall of the church leads to the 14th-century **Cloister of Silence**. Several rooms branch off the cloister, including the chapterhouse and, upstairs, a dormitory. There is a large but narrow **kitchen**, with an enormous centre chimney and a remarkable basin – a rivulet runs through it which supposedly once provided the monks with a constant supply of fresh fish. Next door to the kitchen is the **refectory**, with steps built into one wall leading to a pulpit.

At left of the entrance is the **Sala dos Reis**, with statues, probably carved by monks themselves, of many of the kings of Portugal. The panel in the same room, which tells the history of the Alcobaça abbey, is a rare example of a manuscript *azulejo* panel.

Alcobaça today is at the centre of a porcelain and pottery industry. There are many shops in and around the central square. Some of the factories welcome visitors.

The Cistercian Abbey in Alcobaça.

COASTAL COMMUNITIES

Women still gaze out over the sea along Portugal's Atlantic coast as they have since this rocky edge of Europe was first settled by Phoenician sailors 3,000 years ago. Some wait anxiously for the fishing boats to return with their husbands, brothers, fathers and sons. Others, dressed in black, stare into waters that have claimed their menfolk for ever.

Fishing remains the trade most emblematic of the Portuguese soul. Skill in handling tides and winds, pioneering ship-building and navigational techniques, and the courage to explore the unknown took Portuguese navigators around the uncharted globe.

Similar prowess and bravery is shown today by the hardy Portuguese fishermen who trawl for cod in the North Atlantic, for tuna off the Azores islands, or set sail in small boats into the treacherous Atlantic swell from the fishing communities that stand on the edge of westernmost Europe.

A 90-minute journey northwest of Lisbon takes you to the port of **Peniche** and into the heart of the age-old Portuguese fishing industry. Like most of Portugal's coastal towns, Peniche has no natural harbour, only a bay sheltered by the rocky promontory of Cabo Carvoeiro, the second most westerly point in Europe. The town has built a seawall to protect the bay.

Peniche is an uncompromising town of around 18,000 people. Here, the spare white houses cling to the slopes for shelter from the sweeping northwesterly winds. Too stark and exposed for tourism to have taken hold, the town typifies life in Portuguese fishing communities.

The **Fortaleza Prison** physically dominates the town. The veteran leader of Portugal's Communist Party, Alvaro Cunhal, escaped in 1960 by climbing down the cliffs to a waiting boat that reportedly took him to a Soviet-bloc submarine. Today, the building serves as a local museum.

Most of the boats that work out of Peniche are small trawlers, or *traineiras*, about 24 metres (80 ft) long, powered by diesel engines with a cabin enclosing the wheel and equipped with a basic VHF radio of limited range. They are wooden-hulled with high, broad bows and, characteristic of all Portuguese fishing boats, painted in bright colours and designs to encourage visibility.

Traineiras stand in the front rank of Portuguese fishing. Of the country's 11,900 working boats, only some 1,480 are more than 12 metres (40 ft) long and two-thirds are powered by small outboard, oar, or sail. Most vessels are 20 years old or more, and barely 100 are designed to fish in deep waters.

Peniche bustles with activity when the boats return, usually early in the morning, the sea birds wheeling hungrily behind. The men hurl plastic crates packed with gleaming fish from the decks high up on to the quay where the women sort the catch before it is taken to the auction building.

The bulk of it is usually sardines, the fish that account for more than a third of the 210,000 metric tons of seafood harvested by Portugal each year. The other main catches are cod from Newfoundland and Greenland and tuna from around the islands of Madeira and the Azores. Much of the sardine and tuna is canned for both export and domestic use, in factories such as the one in Peniche.

Some 40,000 men are employed in the fishing industry. A good night's fishing could land a catch worth $5,000. The owner's share is usually a little more than half, out of which he has to meet high running and maintenance costs, particularly fuel. The remainder is divided between the crew of around 25 in decreasing sums depending on position. These would be high earnings in Portugal if they were consistent. But many nights at sea yield catches of very little value; often the weather prevents boats leaving harbour for days on end.

You can get a sense of the Atlantic swell that is the fisherman's constant companion by taking the ferry from Peniche to **Berlenga Island**, 7 km (4

Preceding pages: Mira beach. **Left**, dawn at Nazaré.

miles) offshore. The ferry runs from June to September; the trip takes one hour. Once out of the shelter of the peninsula, the powerful current rocks the boat with unexpected force. The trip is nevertheless well worth taking. A 17th-century **fortress**, now converted to an inn, the **lighthouse** and a few fishermen's cottages are the only buildings. The entire island has been demarcated a national bird sanctuary, and seagulls and eider are everywhere. Officials patrol the makeshift paths to ensure that visitors don't disturb the birds. The greatest excitement lies in taking a boat trip around the reefs, caves and smaller islands, past a breathtaking sea tunnel called the **Furado Grande**.

Sport fishermen often choose the Berlengas as a home base. With a little expertise and experience you can land a 45 kg (100 lb) swordfish. Most offshore fishing does not require a licence. Complete fishing trips – including bait, tackle, and a professional craft – are available on the west coast at Peniche, Ericeira and Nazaré, and in the Algarve from Vilamoura, Portimáo and Lagos.

The hazards faced by Portuguese fishermen are reflected in their strong Roman Catholic faith and the many religious festivals along the coast dedicated to blessing their vessels and praying for their safety. On the first Sunday in August the people of Peniche hold the festival of Our Lady of Safe Voyages (**A Nossa Senhora da Boa Viagem**). The image of the Virgin, the fishermen's patroness, is carried by night from its shrine on the rocky cape to the harbour in a procession of boats gaily decorated with coloured paper and lit by lanterns. The townspeople gather on the quay as a priest, in a fishing boat moored alongside, blesses the small fleet.

For several days after this stirring convocation ceremony Peniche gives itself over to the *festa*. A fair fills the streets, brass bands play, fireworks burst over the harbour and the town dances into the early hours.

Forty-eight kilometres (30 miles) north, the fishing port of **Nazaré** nestles along a sweeping mile-long bay, a

Mending nets at Nazaré.

brightly-coloured, gay and bustling town in striking contrast to the severity of Peniche. In summer, thousands of holiday-makers pack the beach in rows of peaked, striped canvas tents that create the rather romantic atmosphere of a Moorish battle camp.

The abundance of tourists vitiates some of Nazaré's charm, but it also assures that all the visitor's desires will be catered to. Pleasant seafood restaurants and small hotels line the sandy bay; esplanade cafes, bars and souvenir shops abound. But the life of the hardy fishermen goes on.

Because they had no natural harbour, the fishermen used to launch their boats from the beach. They managed this by pushing their craft down log rollers into the sea then clambering aboard and rowing furiously till they overrode the incoming breakers. When they arrived home again, the boats were winched ashore by oxen and later by tractors. The building of a modern anchorage at the south of the beach has relieved the Nazaré fishermen of this arduous labour, though there are still stretches of west coast beach where man and ox do the hauling.

The traditional dress for which the Nazaré fisherfolk are famed is today seen more in souvenir shops than on the townspeople. But some women still wear the seven coloured petticoats under a wide black skirt and cover their head with a black scarf or shawl; the men still favour woollen shirts in traditional plaids, but few wear the distinctive black stocking bonnets.

The Nazaré fishing boat is traditionally about 5 metres (18 ft) long with a flat-bottomed hull and high bow rising in a spiked crescent. But motorised *traineiras* today account for the bulk of the catch. The yield is mainly sardines along with whiting, blue mackerel, sole and perch, and is sold at the *lota* (auction-house) or canned in a local factory.

Nazaré, named after a statue of the Virgin that a 4th-century monk brought to the town from Nazareth, lives literally on two levels. In the lower part of town, small, white-walled fishermen's

Festival at Viana do Castelo.

cottages line the narrow alleyways. High above on the cliff that towers 109 metres (360 ft) above the old town is the quarter known as **Sítio**. Reached by a funicular that climbs the tallest cliffside in Portugal, Sítio is dominated by a large square and on its edge the tiny chapel built to commemorate a miracle in 1182 when Our Lady of Nazaré saved the local lord by stopping his horse from plunging off the cliff as he pursued a deer.

The 17th-century **Church of Our Lady of Nazaré** on the other side of the square is the focus for the annual religious festivities during the second week of September that include processions and bullfights in the Sítio ring. The steep, narrow pathway and steps from the **lighthouse** west of the church afford stirring views of Atlantic breakers.

One of the most enjoyable aspects of Portugal's fishing communities is sampling the freshest of fish. West coast or south coast, you'll find markets piled high with fish from the mighty tuna to the – surprisingly large – sardine, as well as the thousand restaurants which know how to cook them to succulent perfection.

For excellent grilled fish, usually served with boiled potatoes, vegetables and a butter sauce, choose between *robalo* (bass), *cherne* (turbot), *salmonetes* (red mullet), *garoupa* or *mérou*, and *peixe espada* (scabbard fish). *Espadarte* (sword fish) is a delicacy worth paying a little extra for. Other delights include *tamboril* (monkfish) with a texture similar to shellfish, *lulas* (cuttlefish), *chocos* (squid), *polvo* (octopus) and *safio* (conger eels).

Shellfish has grown expensive in Portugal, principally because much of it is now imported. But if you can splash out a little on a local crayfish (*lagosta*) or lobster (*lavagante*) you will be unlikely to regret your decision. A good place to find them at reasonable prices is the picturesque fishing village of **Ericeira**, 48 km (30 miles) outside Lisbon and south of Peniche.

The village, which takes its name from the abundance of sea hedgehogs, or *ouriços,* found there, is on the clifftops looking down onto the rocky beaches. A small fishing beach is protected by a jetty and concrete boulders piled into the sea to break the Atlantic current. From the wall high up above the small harbour you can watch the fishermen unload their catch, mend their nets and repaint their boats.

The tiny chapel of **Santo António** above the harbour is the centre of the village's summer *festa*. The chapel, and a replica of a fishing boat holding a statue of the Virgin, are filled with hundreds of candles lit by the townspeople as a prayer for the safety of the local fishermen. The Virgin is carried at night in a procession down to the harbour where the priest blesses the brightly decorated boats.

A tiled plaque on the side of the chapel records the flight of King Manuel II and his family from the beach here in October 1910, after the monarchy was overthrown and Portugal became a republic. The king sailed via Gibraltar to Britain where he lived the rest of his life in exile, devoting himself to amassing an important collection of early Portuguese books. Documents including British newspaper reports on the escape can be seen in Ericeira's small but interesting **municipal museum**. Ericeira becomes a bustling resort in the summer, known for its seafood, much of it raised in tanks on the rocky shore.

Ericeira, Nazaré and Peniche are similar in spirit to the many other fishing communities that have struggled for centuries to earn a living from the sea on the frontier where Europe meets the Atlantic. Each is unique; others along the coast include **Sesimbra** nestled beneath the beautiful Arrábida hills south of Lisbon; the beautiful bay of **São Martinho do Porto;** and **São Pedro de Moel** surrounded by pine forest close to Nazaré.

In the north, **Vila do Conde** at the mouth of the Ave river is renowned for its lacemakers' procession in the third week of June, with an unforgettable folk fair in August. **Viana do Castelo** has prospered since the 16th century as the home of fishermen who brave the distant and icy Atlantic waters to fish for cod off Newfoundland.

A day's catch of sardines.

THE WINE DISTRICTS

Northern Portugal is wine country par excellence. Fine vineyards flourish throughout the land, but the best known wines, dating back to Roman times, come from the districts of Minho and Douro. These two provinces make up an area shaped like a large L – from the Minho river on the northern border with Spain, south to the Douro, then along the river valley eastward to Spain again. Grapes are grown everywhere. They hang from trees, pergolas and porches, and climb along slopes and terraces. They grow in rocky, poor soil where little else flourishes.

There are still great old grape-growing estates but most grapes are produced on small farms and then sold either to co-operatives or to large companies. The *vindimia,* or grape harvest, is still done by hand and is a wonderful sight to behold. Harvesting takes place in September and October and lasts until early November. It is often a hazardous task, requiring towering 30-rung ladders to get at the elusive treetop grapes, though most vines now are trained at lower levels. In the hilly country, men still carry huge baskets of grapes weighing as much as 50 kg (100 lb) on their backs. On some back roads, squeaky oxcarts transport the grapes to wine-presses. In these modern times, however, the fruit is generally transported in trucks.

While harvest is a festive occasion, it is no longer quite the unbridled merry-making of yore. In the old days, workers used to perform a kind of bacchanal dance, their arms linked and stamping on the grapes with their bare feet. It was said that this was the only way to crush the fruit without smashing the pips and spoiling the flavour of the wine. This was often accompanied by music and clapping, glasses of spirits and a good deal of sweat. Nowadays, mechanical extractors often remove the pips and presses are generally used to crush the

Preceding pages: the Rio Tâmega near Amarante; cards in Gerês. **Right**, local fair.

grapes, although treading still takes place on some vineyards.

The Douro: The name means "of gold" and the river, on certain glowing days, does resemble a twisting golden chain as it winds through the narrow valley between the steep hills and terraced vineyards. The countryside is exceptionally beautiful, particularly in spring and autumn. The base to explore the Douro Valley is the city of Oporto.

The river wends its way for about 210 km (130 miles) in Portugal and then another 120 km (75 miles) along the border with Spain. One option is a bus tour to the port wine estates, offered by several travel agencies in Oporto. The N108 road winds along the northern bank as far as Régua (the fast IP4 a speedier parallel to the north) and the N222 follows the southern shores of the river, sometimes high above, sometimes along the water's edge. There is also a train that runs along the northern bank of the river, crossing at **São João da Pesqueiro** and continuing along the southern bank as far as Pocinho. It might go further: the villagers of Barca de Alva have been campaigning fiercely for the restoration of a train service to their station close to the Spanish border. The ride takes about six hours.

The **Lower Douro** is technically *vinho verde* country although the Minho farther north, is more closely associated with the "green" or young wines. The main town is **Penafiel**, between the Sousa and the Tâmega rivers. There are some lovely old granite houses with gargoyles and wooden balconies and a 16th-century **parish church.**

A few miles to the northeast lies the charming town of **Amarante**, on the bank of the Rio Tâmega. The three-arched **bridge** was built in 1790. It leads to the convent of **São Gonçalo**, named after the local patron saint, protector of marriages. The festival held in the saint's honour every June is a particularly raucous one – and distinctly phallic cakes are served during it.

The convent, however, is much more sombre. It was begun in 1540 but not completed until 1620. Inside is the tomb

Sandeman port cellars.

of São Gonçalo, who died about 1260, and some lush gilded carved woodwork. There are two cloisters; above the rear one is the **Museu de Albano Sardoeira**, which includes some modern Portuguese painting – Sardoeira was a Cubist artist from Amarante.

Nearby is the **Quinta da Aveleda**, seat of one of Portugal's main wine empires and leading exporter of *vinho verde*. The Quinta is included on some wine-tasting tours. Individual visitors are welcome but advised to make prior arrangements at the company's office in **Oporto**. A tour of the 200-hectare (500-acre) Aveleda estate includes a visit to the **family chapel**, which was built in 1671. The luxuriant gardens contain a ruined window said to be from the palace of Prince Henry the Navigator in Oporto. You can also observe contemporary *vinho verde* production: miles upon miles of grapes; climbing poles, trellises and crosses; and mechanical crushers, modern concrete storage vats and mechanised bottling and labelling.

At the wine lodge you may taste different types of *vinho verde* and buy a bottle or a case from the old distillery, now converted to a store.

Beyond, the road turns abruptly south, running parallel to the Douro. From **Mesão Frio**, on a steep hillside, there is a sweeping view of the Upper Douro twisting through the gorges and port wine country.

Port wine region: Portugal's authoritarian Marquês de Pombal staked out the Douro in 1756, making it the first officially designated wine-producing region in the world. Subsequent legislation designated the Upper Douro as the Port Wine Region. The area stretches along the Douro river valley from **Barqueiros**, south of Mesão Frio, to **Barca de Alva** on the Spanish border. It includes the valleys of tributaries.

The port wine vineyards grow on neatly terraced hillside farms along the Douro. Seignorial manors and white-washed cottages perch among the vineyards and olive groves. The climate is cold, wet and foggy in winter. Summers are hot, and made hotter by the direct

Terraced vineyards and a port house on the Douro.

rays of the sun reflected on the schist, or crystalline rock.

Régua (its full name Pesoda Régua) is a busy river port and headquarters of the Casa do Douro, an organisation which has much power in the regulation of port wine production. In the area lie some of the oldest British and Portuguese estates. Here the road crosses the Douro and runs along the southern bank, recrossing the river at **Pinhão**, another wine centre.

Nearby lies the **Quinta do Infantado**, an ancient wine estate that once belonged to Prince Pedro. The Roseira family, which has owned the property since the turn of the century, recently began selling a drier "Estate Bottled" port with a label bearing the Quinta name, directly, without going through the normal channels of shippers of Vila Nova da Gaia. Other locally bottled wines to challenge the Gaia monopoly are Quinta do Cotto and Roma Nera. A grape growers' association has been established to stand up to the shippers.

At Pinhão, the traveller should make a side trip north to **Sabrosa,** the birthplace of Fernão de Magalhães, better known as Magellan, the man who led the first tour around the world in 1522 – under the Spanish flag.

A couple of miles northwest is the village of **Mateus**, with its celebrated **palace** and **gardens**. It was built by Nicolau Nasoni in 1739-43 for António José Botelho Mourão. Today, an illustration of the palace graces the distinctive label of the less-than-distinctive *rosé* wine from this area. The exquisite building with its striking baroque facade, double stairway, and huge coat of arms is open for visits.

To the southeast is the valley of the **Tua** with its orange groves, and across the Douro, along terraced hills, São João da Pesqueira, on a plateau. Winding southeastwards along the contours of the hills, past quaint churches and the ruins of a castle, you will come to **Vila Nova de Fozcôa** and the valley of the **Côa**. The Douro roads are often tortuous. Go with a good map. The views make every moment worthwhile.

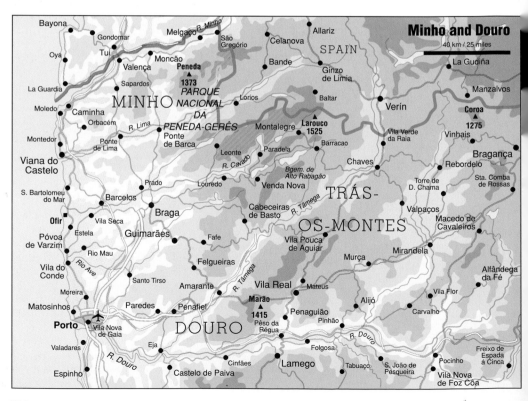

The Minho: The Minho is often described as Costa Verde, or the Green Coast, a reference to the vineyards and lush green of its well-watered landscape. It is beautiful countryside, with joyous fairs, festivals and pilgrimages. The *Minhotos* are good-tempered, hard-working, and seem to enjoy life.

With Oporto as a starting point again, a good way to visit the Minho is to drive up the coast and return by an inland route. The Atlantic beaches are generally broad with fine sand, but the sea is cold and rough. A fishing town and resort, **Vila do Conde** is the site of the vast **Convent of Santa Clara**, which was founded in 1318, the 16th-century parish church of **São João Baptista** and a lovely 17th-century **fortress**. Travellers are welcome to watch how fishing boats are made and to visit the lace-making school. Nearby, **Póvoa de Varzim** is another popular fishing port-resort, with an 18th-century fort and a parish church. There's also a casino and a modern luxury hotel, the Vermar, with heated pools and tennis courts. Further

Vila do Conde's aqueduct peers above the rooftops.

north, **Ofir** is a delightful sea and pine forest resort. Just across the **Cávado river** is the town of **Esposende** with the remains of an 18th-century **fortress**. There are many new, often garishly-painted houses in towns and villages along the way; these have very often been built by emigrants returned from France, Germany and elsewhere.

A lively fishing and ship-building port, **Viana do Castelo** was called *Diana* by the Romans. This was the centre of Portugal's wine trade until the port declined in the 18th century and Oporto took preeminence. There is a good deal to see in Viana, starting with the 18th-century **Palace of the Távoras**, now the main Tourist Office. On the central **Praça da República** there's a beautiful 16th-century fountain and the remarkable **Misericórdia Hospital**, with its three-tiered facade supported by caryatids. Nearby stands the handsome 15th-century **parish church** with a Gothic portal and Romanesque towers. The town is dominated by **Monte Santa Luzia** with a large and inappropriate modern basilica. To the west of the town, the baroque **Nossa Senhora da Agonia** church is the site of a popular pilgrimage every August. Dancers, musicians, and other celebrants, wearing vivid embroidered traditional costumes, come from all over the Minho to take part in the three-day *festa*, among Portugal's most spectacular.

Continuing north, the road leads to **Caminha**, an attractive town with echoes of its past as a busy trading port. The church, dating from the 15th century, has a beautiful carved-wood ceiling. There are several lovely 15th- and 16th-century buildings near the main square.

At the estuary of the **Minho river**, the road turns inland and follows the water, which forms the border with Spain. **Valença do Minho** is a bustling border town with shops and markets. Spaniards come here regularly to purchase items that include table linen and crystal chandeliers. The Portuguese, on the other hand, cross the border to Tuy or Vigo to buy canned goods such as asparagus and artichokes, and ready-made clothing. The old town of Valença is still

fairly intact with cobbled streets and stone houses with iron balconies, surrounded by 17th-century granite ramparts. Outside them, near the station, is a train museum. The ancient **convent**, with a splendid view of the Minho river and Spain, is now a *pousada*.

From **Monção**, a fortified town known for its spring water and classy *vinho verde*, take the road south through the heart of the Minho. You'll see lush green countryside, crisscrossed by rivers with medieval stone bridges; simple white churches with elaborate granite doorways and windows; and, of course, unending vineyards. Because of the high population density, the land has been divided and sub-divided for generations, so the average property is an acre or two. To get the most out of the land, the *Minhotos* train their vines to grow upwards, on trees, houses and hedges, leaving ground-space for cabbages, onions and potatoes. This free-wheeling system has made it difficult to modernise grape production, but in recent years the larger farms have begun to use a system of wire-supporting crosses which are called *cruzetas*.

The road passes **Arcos de Valdevez**, a charming hillside town built on the two banks of the **Vez river**, with a magnificent view of the valley. Just to the south, **Ponte de Barca** on the left bank of the **Lima river** has a lovely 15th-century **parish church** and an old **town square**, but the principal attraction is the fine stone **bridge** with arches, built in 1543 and often restored.

Here you might turn westward, along the beautiful valley of the Lima river, which the Romans believed was the Lethe, the mythological river of oblivion. The area has numerous great estates or *solares*, a tangible reminder of the glories of the old empire. Some are now guesthouses, and arrangements to visit or stay in these manors should be made beforehand, if possible, with Turismo in Ponte de Lima, Viana or Lisbon (see *Travel Tips*).

Generally the owners or family members live in the *solares* and welcome visitors to share their way of life. This **Ponte de Lima.**

might mean hunting and fishing, taking part in the grape harvest, or simply holding long conversations by the fireplace. Each *solar* has its own history and charm. On the outskirts of **Ponte de Lima**, the **Paço de Calheiros**, dating to the 16th century, belongs to a youthful modern-minded count. His *casa antiga* is one of the loveliest in the region.

Ponte de Lima is one of the loveliest towns in Portugal, mainly because of its location on the south bank of the Lima river. Its market, every other Monday, is a splendidly colourful "tent city" on the riverbank. The town faces a magnificent long **Roman Bridge** with low arches. Remains from the old city wall still stand. A 15th-century **palace** with crenellated facade is now the town hall. Across the river, the 15th-century **Santo António convent** has beautiful woodwork, including two baroque shrines.

Continuing towards Viana do Castelo there are more manor houses, such as the **Solar de Cortegaça**, with its great stone tower dating back to the 15th century. This is a working manor, with wine cellars, flour mill and stable. Guests are welcome to take part in the farm life.

South of Viana, another inland road leads to the charming market town of **Barcelos**, on the northern bank of the **Cávado river**. Barcelos boasts 15th-century **fortifications**, a 13th-century **church** and a 16th-century **palace**, but more than that, it has one of the best handicraft markets in the country. Every Thursday, merchants and artisans display their folk art and other wares at the fairgrounds in the centre of town. It was here that the late Rosa Ramalho, Portugal's most famous folk art sculptress, created her world of fanciful ceramic animals and people, a style continued by her grand-daughter. There is a good crafts exhibition (and shop) in the medieval keep next to Turismo in the Largo da Porta Nova. It includes copperware, hand-made rugs, wooden toys, bright cotton tableware, and of course the Barcelos cock, now a national emblem.

According to legend, a pilgrim from Galicia was suspected of committing murder and condemned to death. Protesting his innocence, the Galician pointed to a roast chicken on the magistrate's table, and declared, "As surely as I stand innocent, so will that cock crow." The cock obligingly crowed; the prisoner was set free and a monument built to mark the miracle.

Birthplace of a nation: A busy manufacturing town noted mainly for textiles, shoes and cutlery, **Guimarães** still possesses many reminders of its past glory as birthplace of the Portuguese nation.

Around the year 1128, an 18-year-old boy named Afonso Henriques proclaimed independence for the county of Portucale from the kingdom of León and Castile. In the field of **São Mamede**, near Guimarães, the young Afonso Henriques defeated his mother's army, which was battling on behalf of Alfonso VII, king of León and Castile.

The city's Festival of Saint Walter, the *Festas Gualterianas,* dates from the middle of the 15th century. This three-day celebration, held on the first weekend in August, includes a torchlight procession, a fair with traditional dances and a medieval parade.

Guimarães has long been the centre of the Portuguese linen industry. It still produces high quality, coarse linen from home-grown flax naturally bleached by the sun. The region is also known for its hand embroidery. This, unfortunately, is gradually being replaced by machine.

A visit could begin at the 10th-century **castelo** on the northern side of town. It is believed that Afonso Henriques was born here in 1110, the son of Henri of Burgundy, Count of Portucale, and his wife Teresa. The castle is a large mass of walls and towers on a rocky hill with a magnificent view of the mountains. The dungeon and fortifications were restored many times. Early in the 19th century, the castle was used as a debtors' prison; it was restored again in 1940. At the entrance stands the small Romanesque chapel of **São Miguel do Castelo** with the original font where Afonso Henriques was baptised in 1111.

Heading into town, you pass the 15th-century Gothic **Palace of the Dukes of Bragança**, now occasionally used as an official residence by the President of the Republic. Otherwise, it is a museum.

This massive granite construction consists of four buildings around a courtyard and has been completely restored. Outside is a fine statue of Afonso Henriques by Soares dos Reis. Visitors may also view the splendid chestnut ceiling of the Banquet Hall, the Persian carpets, French tapestries, ancient portraits and documents.

The **Rua de Santa Maria**, with its cobblestones and 14th- and 15th-century houses with wrought-iron balconies leads to the centre of town. On the left lies the **Convento de Santa Clara**, built in the 17th century and now used as the Town Hall.

The church of **Nossa Senhora de Oliveira**, dating to the 10th century, was rebuilt by Count Henri in the 12th century and has undergone several restorations. Still visible are the 16th-century watchtower and 14th-century western portal and window.

According to a 7th-century legend, an old Visigoth warrior named Wamba was tilling his field near Guimarães when a delegation came to tell him he had been elected king. He refused to take the office. Driving his staff into the ground, Wamba declared that not until it bore leaves would he become king. As these things happen, the staff turned into an olive tree. The church was named in honour of the miracle.

Adjacent to the church of Oliveira, the convent has been converted into the **Museu de Alberto Sampaio**. This includes the church's rich treasury of 12th-century silver chalices and Gothic and Renaissance silver crucifixes as well as 15th- and 16th-century statues, paintings and ceramics.

The busiest square in Guimarães is the **Largo do Toural**. Just beyond, the church of **São Domingoes** was built in the 14th century and still has the original transept, rose window over the portal, and lovely Gothic cloister. The **Museu Martins Sarmento** is located in the cloister, built in 1271 and enlarged early in the 20th century. Here are artefacts and objects from Briteiros and other *citânias* – ancient Iberian fortified villages – of northern Portugal; great

Douro man ready to party...

statues and granite slabs, Roman votives, inscriptions, ceramics and coins.

Continuing along the broad garden called the **Alameda da Resistência ao Fascismo**, you reach the church of **São Francisco**, founded in the 13th century. There is little left of the original Gothic structure. However, the sacristy is very fine with its 17th-century gilt wood-work and ceiling.

High on the outskirts of the city stands **Santa Marinha da Costa**, founded as a monastery in the 12th century and re-built in the 18th century. The church functions regularly and may be visited. The cells of the monastery, which were badly damaged by fire in 1951, have recently been restored with great care and turned into a luxury *pousada*. Visible in the **cloisters** are a 10th-century Mozarabic arch and vestiges of a 7th-century Visigothic structure. The ve-randa is decorated with magnificent 18th-century tile scenes and a fountain.

After seeing the Briteiros exhibit at the Martins Sarmento museum, you might like to visit the original site, some

11 km (7 miles) north toward Braga. At first, the **Citânia de Briteiros** appears to be nothing more than piles of stones on a hillside, but it is in fact one of Portugal's most important archaeologi-cal sites. Here are the remains of a prehistoric fortified village said to have been inhabited by Celts. It was discov-ered in 1874 by archaeologist Francisco Martins Sarmento.

Near the summit, two round houses have been reconstructed. Also visible are the remains of triple defensive walls, ancient flagstones and foundation walls of over 150 houses. Most houses were circular with stone benches running around the wall. A large rock in the centre supported a pole that in turn held up a thatched roof. Several houses are larger, with two or more rectangular rooms. The town was evidently well organised with a water system: spring water flowed from the top of the hill down gutters carved in the paving stones to a cistern and a public fountain.

Braga: Some people still refer to Braga somewhat wistfully as "the Portuguese

…and to work.

ESTAÇÃO VITI-VINÍCOLA
DO DOURO RIO TORTO

Rome". In Roman times, as *Bracara Augusta*, it was the centre of communications in north Lusitania. In the 6th century two synods were held here. Under Moorish occupation, Braga was sacked and the cathedral badly damaged. But in the 11th century, the city was largely restored to its former eminence by Bishop Dom Pedro and Archbishop São Geraldo. The Archbishop claimed authority over all the churches of the Iberian Peninsula, and his successors retained the title of Primate of the Spains for six centuries. Like a Renaissance prince, Archbishop Dom Diogo de Sousa in the 16th century encouraged the construction of many handsome Italian-style churches, fountains and palaces. Zealous prelates restored many of these works in the 17th and 18th centuries, but often with unfortunate results. Braga lost its title as ecclesiastical capital in 1716, when the Patriarchate went to Lisbon. Even so, it is still an important religious centre, the site of the most elaborate Holy Week procession in the country.

Any visit to Braga begins at the **Sé**, the cathedral built in the 11th century on the site of an earlier structure destroyed by the Moors. Of the original Romanesque building, there remains only the southern portal and the sculpted cornice of the transept. Although it has been greatly modified by various restorations, the cathedral is still an imposing edifice. The interior contains some fine tombs, including those of the founders, Count Henri and his wife Teresa, a fine granite sculpture of the Virgin, an 18th-century choirloft and organ case and richly decorated chapels and cloister. The cathedral treasury is now a **Museum of Religious Art** with a fine collection of vestments going back to the 15th century, and silver chalices and crucifixes of the 10th and 12th centuries.

Nearby, with plain west walls set off by an 18th-century fountain, is the **Palace of the Archbishop**, built in the 14th century. It, too, has been reconstructed several times. The palace now houses the **Public Library**, with city archives dating back to the 9th century, 300,000

The garden at Bom Jesus do Monte.

volumes and some 10,000 manuscripts.

On the western side of the Agrolongo Square stands one of the Rome-inspired churches, **Nossa Senhora do Pópulo**, built in the 17th century and remodelled at the end of the 18th century. It is decorated with tiles showing the life of St Augustine.

The **Casa dos Biscainhos**, across the way, is a 17th-century mansion with lovely garden and fountains. Now a museum, the collection includes 18th-century tiles, ceramics, jewellery and furniture. Part of the museum has been set aside for artefacts from recent excavations on the site of a protected zone established in 1977 – after some damage from modern construction. The University of Minho is directing the excavations, which have uncovered **Roman Baths**, a sanctuary called **Fonte do Idolo** and the remains of a house called **Domus de Santiago**. These may be visited.

On the northern side of the city, the church of **São João de Souto** was completely rebuilt in the late 18th century. But here is the superb **Chapel of Conceição**, built in 1525, with crenellated walls, lovely windows and splendid statues of St Anthony and St Paul.

There are many other churches and chapels of interest in the religious centre, but the best known is **Bom Jesus**, which is conspicuously set on the wooded **Monte Espinho**, just outside the city. This popular pilgrimage centre is remarkable, not so much for the building but for its grandiose stairway and the view from its terrace of the Cávado river valley and mountains in the distance. The double flight of stairs is flanked by chapels, fountains and often startlingly bizarre figures at each level, representing the Stations of the Cross. If you don't wish to climb the steps, there's a funicular, and a winding road to the top. There, in a park of oak trees, eucalyptus, camelias and mimosa, stands the 15th-century church, rebuilt in the 18th century. In its **Chapel of Miracles** are many votives and pictures left by past pilgrims. Several hotels, souvenir shops and restaurants are also located in the vicinity of the sanctuary.

Thousands gather at Bom Jesus do Monte on holy days.

OPORTO

As its name implies, Oporto is the commercial centre of northern Portugal and is the hub of the lucrative port wine trade. (The Portuguese spelling, by the way, is simply *Porto*.) Like Lisbon, Oporto is clustered on hills overlooking a river. But unlike the pastel walls and Mediterranean light of Lisbon. Oporto is a northern European city with granite church towers, stolid dark buildings, narrow streets and hidden baroque treasures.

Posed majestically on the rocky cliffs overlooking the Douro river, Oporto is linked by four bridges to Vila Nova de Gaia, an industrial area where most of the wine lodges are located. These days large ships often dock at the seaport of Leixões because of frequent silting of the Douro estuary; but coal barges, fishing trawlers and other small vessels still sail up the river.

The climate in town is temperate and the *Portuenses,* as the inhabitants are called, are traditionally industrious. The population of Greater Oporto is about one million.

In Roman times, the twin cities at the mouth of the Douro were known as Portus on the right bank and Cale on the left bank. During the Moorish occupation, the entire region between the Minho and Douro rivers was called Portucale. When Afonso Henriques founded the new kingdom in the 12th century, he took the name of his home province and called it Portucalia.

Closely linked to Portugal's golden epoch of the discoveries, Oporto prospered from the seafaring exploits. Its shipyards, adapting Douro river *caravelas*, produced caravels that sailed around the world. Prince Henry, who initiated and inspired exploration, was born in Oporto. Also proudly numbered among the *Portuenses* are the poet Almeida Garrett and novelist Júlio Dinis.

The city's close English connections developed with the wine trade. According to some accounts, it was actually the English who discovered port wine. It is said that in 1678, two sons of a wealthy English merchant stayed for a while in a monastery on the Upper Douro. They discovered that by adding a little brandy to the sweet wine of the Douro, it was sufficiently fortified to withstand temperature changes and long sea voyages. When the brothers returned to England, they reportedly took back large quantities of this fortified wine, which came to be known as port.

Inevitably, there are different versions of this story: in the 17th and 18th centuries, the wines of the Upper Douro were robust table reds. Then in 1820, a "climatic accident" occurred, with very warm weather producing unusually sweet grapes and a wine appreciated by the British. In the following years, amid much controversy, the wine companies added *aguardente,* or brandy, to stop the fermentation and fix the sugar content. This was the beginning of the sweet fortified nectar as it is known today.

In any event, the Methuen Treaty of 1703 opened English markets to Portuguese wines, and the British shippers of

Left, by the Douro in Oporto. **Right**, making port barrels at Vila Nova de Gaia.

Oporto became increasingly rich and powerful. In 1727 they established a Shippers Association, which regulated the trade and controlled prices paid to Portuguese growers. To combat the English monopoly, the Marquês de Pombal founded the Alto Douro Wine Company in 1757, which provided a measure of Portuguese control.

Rose Macaulay describes whimsically how British port wine shippers virtually "captured and occupied" Oporto in her delightful book, *They Went to Portugal*. She notes that the "Oporto families, some of them established in Oporto or Viana do Castelo since the 17th century, have the air of owning the city, so Britannically, so unconsciously arrogantly." The British presence can still be felt, although no longer is it overbearing.

Portugal's liberal revolution began in 1820 at Oporto. The severest fighting took place against absolutist King Miguel in 1832–33, leading to his exile and the restoration of liberalism.

In modern times, the city was a centre of liberal opposition to Salazar's right-wing dictatorship. After the 1974 Revolution, the city served as a bastion against the spread of communism to the north.

Oporto today is an energetic and lively commercial city with an individual taste in food and drink. Regional specialities include roast pork, fresh salmon, lamprey, trout and tripe.

Generally Oporto is a sober city. Apart from dining, there's not much nightlife. You may hear *fado* at some restaurants such as Mal Cozinhado or Taverna de São Jorge. The younger set frequents discotheques around Ribeira or in such suburbs as **Foz do Douro**. Their elders prefer to relax at the nearby coastal resort of **Espinho** with its casino and night club.

The city's main festival is around the *Dia de São João*, John the Baptist, on 23 and 24 June. It coincides with the ancient celebration of the summer solstice, so the Christian feast is laced with pagan traditions. People take to the streets and slap one another teasingly with bundles of leeks and, nowadays, plastic hammers. The most popular fes-

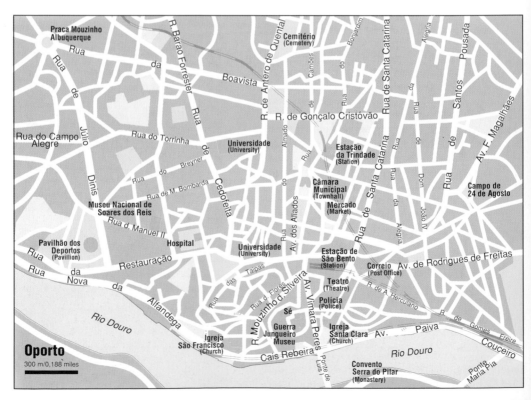

tivities take place at the **Alameda das Fontainhas**, a square overlooking the **Dom Luís I Bridge**, where people sing and dance around bonfires, drink *vinho verde* and feast on roast kid and delicious grilled sardines.

The heart of the city is the **Praça da Liberdade**, with an equestrian statue of Pedro IV in the centre. On the north side of the square is the broad **Avenida dos Aliados**, with bright flowerbeds and mosaic walks, leading uphill to the **Town Hall**. Here stands the modern stone statue of native son Almeida Garrett, liberal poet and novelist.

"From here, where it got its name, Old Portugal, the name will again rise up with distinction," Garrett wrote in 1819. "The brilliance, the honour, the healthy customs, pure love of native land, the sincere frankness, the noble independence of other epochs will resurge once more from here…"

To the southeast of Praça da Liberdade lies the **Praça de Almeida Garrett**, where the **São Bento** railway station has a fine entrance hall, decorated with traditional *azulejos* or tiles showing historical scenes.

Heading south up the hill, you arrive at the **Sé**, or cathedral, dating to the 12th century, with its square towers and small domes. Here King João I wed the English Philippa of Lancaster in 1387. The Gothic **cloister** is decorated with fine tiles. Nearby on **Pena Ventosa**, the site of an ancient citadel, stands the impressive 18th-century **Bishop's Palace**. Just beyond, the **House of Guerra Junqueiro**, a poet who died in 1923, is a museum with his memorabilia and furnishings.

Across the avenue stands the 15th-century church of **Santa Clara**, next to one of the best preserved parts of the old city wall. Santa Clara has been rebuilt several times but is noted for its splendid gilt-wood choirstalls and altars. Sacheverell Sitwell wrote: "After it, every other building in Porto, even São Francisco, is drab and dull."

To the west, the church of **São Lourenço** better known as **Grilos** (for the crickets that lodge there), is one of

The Douro snakes through Oporto.

the earliest examples of Portuguese baroque, built in 1570.

At the end of Rua dos Ingleses stands the bastion of English life, the **Feitoria Inglesa** or the Factory House. Here the old British port wine shippers do their business, play billiards or cards, read English newspapers and enjoy English cuisine, as they have for the past 200 years. Outsiders must obtain special authorisation from the British Port Wine Shippers Association to visit.

Around the corner, on Rua da Alfândega, stands the much restored **palace** where Prince Henry the Navigator was born in 1394. For a time it served as the customs house; it is now a museum.

Going by the **Praça do Infante Dom Henrique**, you reach the **Church of São Francisco**, founded by King Sancho II in 1233 and rebuilt in the 14th century. The interior glitters in baroque splendour with gilded columns, arches and statues. On the site of the convent, which burnt down in 1832, is the **Palácio de Bolsa**, the Stock Exchange. The building is noted for its opulent neo-Moorish reception hall. Up the hill is the **Port Wine Institute**, a government agency established in 1932 to control the quality of port. The Institute closely regulates virtually every aspect of port production.

Following the Rua Belmonte past old homes with balconies and tiled walls, you arrive at the church of **São João Novo**, built in 1592. Across the way stands the 18th-century **Palace of São João Novo**, a whitewash and granite building that houses the **Museum of Ethnography and History**. The collection includes archaeological finds going back to the Paleolithic Age, old wine presses and wine boats, fishing equipment, pharmacy, vases, ceramics, costumes, jewellery and folk art.

The road leads to the singular **Torre dos Clérigos**, a granite tower, the tallest in Portugal, designed – with its church – by Nicolau Nasoni, architect of the brilliant, baroque Solar de Mateus near Vila Real. It is worth climbing the 225 or so steps for the view.

To the east lies the busy **Praça da**

Left, portrait of King Carlos in the Bolsa (Stock Exchange). Right, gilded woodwork at São Francisco.

Batalha, with a statue of Pedro V in the middle and the imposing 18th-century church of **São Idelfonso** with a façade with bright blue-and-white tiles.

The main shopping street is **Rua Santa Catarina**, where you may find good buys in a variety of local products from shoes and clothing to pottery. **Rua das Flores** has the best gold and silver shops.

Northwest of the centre lies the main **University** building, a handsome granite structure built in 1807 as the Polytechnical Academy. Further north, stands the 12th-century **São Martinho de Cedofeita** church. "Cedofeita" means "done too soon"; the church was hastily built to honour St Martin of Tours.

On the western side of the city, in the old royal **Palácio dos Carrancas** is the **Soares dos Reis Museum**, named after the important 19th-century sculptor. It has a fine collection of archaeological articles, religious art, regional costumes, ceramics and contemporary paintings, as well as sculpture. Paintings by Grão Vasco are on display, among them *St Catherine* and *St Lucy*.

Past the modern **Sports Pavilion** is the **Solar do Vinho do Porto**, where you may taste a wide variety of port wines. It is located in the old wine cellar and stable of the Quinta da Macierinha (the Solar's entry is at Rua Entre Quintas, 220, Monday–Friday 10 am–11.30 pm, Saturday 11 am–10.30 pm. Closed Sunday and holidays. Tel: (02) 694749.) The **Quinta da Macierinha** is where the former King Charles Albert died in 1849, after abdicating the throne of Sardinia. Now an intriguing **Museu Romântico**, this mansion is set in a rose garden and contains most of its original furnishings. Further west, in Boavista, is the 1930s mansion **Casa dos Servalves**. As the **National Museum of Modern Art** it is Oporto's newest and most congenial focus of culture.

Returning to the river, you might spend some time strolling along the river bank, the **Cais da Ribeira**, the liveliest part of the city. Many small shops and restaurants are built right into what remains of the old city wall.

The splendid steel arch farther up-

The Bolsa's Moorish hall.

river is a railway bridge, **Ponte de Dona Maria Pia**, built in 1876 to a plan by the ubiquitous Alexandre Gustave Eiffel and only recently put out of use by the new São João Bridge. On the Western side of the city, the modern concrete span, **Ponte da Arrábida**, is a link in the north-south motorway.

In the centre of Oporto is the handsome **Ponte de Dom Luís I**, built in 1886, which provides splendid views. This two-storey iron bridge leads directly to **Vila Nova de Gaia**, an industrial zone with ceramic, glass, soap and other factories. But above all, Gaia is the true seat of the port wine industry, where most warehouses or lodges are to be found.

In spring, the new wine is brought down from the Upper Douro by truck, less picturesque but considerably more practical than the *barcos rabelos*, the flat-bottomed sailboats that used to sail the Douro. In the Gaia lodges, the wine is left to mature in 534-litre (139-gallon) oak casks, or pipes. Here the blending takes place for most ports, with wines from different vineyards and years blended to produce a distinctive aroma, taste and colour. Then the wine is bottled and again left to mature, the time allowed – in years – depending on the type of wine.

Like museum pieces, a few *barcos rabelos* are kept docked at Gaia near the Dom Luís I Bridge. Once a year, during the feast of São João on 24 June, the boats participate in a colourful regatta on the Douro.

You may also take a launch cruise on the Douro, with fine views of Oporto and the three bridges. A short excursion lasts 50 minutes and leaves from a dock near the **Ferreira Lodge** but cruise boats can also take you in comfort up the gloriously beautiful Douro river valley; the river is now navigable all the way to Barca de Alva.

There are about 60 port wine lodges in Gaia. Many of them welcome visitors who would like to tour the installations and to taste their wines. The **Sandeman**, **Ferreira** and **Ramos Pinto** companies have full-time guides.

Oporto's
best-known
product.

PORT DYNASTIES

In a technological age there are few trades where heritage and family ties are a matter of pride. Port is one of them, a commerce with its roots in the wild upper reaches of northern Portugal's Douro river valley, a wine region that has had virtually the same frontiers since the Marquês de Pombal defined them in 1756.

At the time, the reforming Pombal, who had a hearty dislike of the English and their dominant role in Portuguese trade, determined to restrict their hold on the area. Since then port has improved immeasurably in quality, the profits are more evenly spread and, though snobbish exclusivity is long gone, the English are still there.

The English association with port is long and eventful – although these days the French buy more. English buyers enthusiastically explored the Douro river valley back in the 17th century. A pioneer, Joseph James Forrester, who fought for high port standards and mapped every inch of the river, was made a baron in 1855 for his efforts. It was a national, not English, tragedy when, on a May day in 1862, Forrester's boat overturned and he drowned in the Douro. A survivor of the tragedy was another outstanding personality in the saga of port: Dona Antonia Adelaide Ferreira, whose vineyards covered huge areas of the Douro.

These and other colourful characters are familiar to everyone in the business. The founders of the port wine trade are ever-present, their faces and names on port wine labels, their blood in the veins of several generations. Many rival companies have family links. Their names, however, can be deceptive: for all its English ring, Cockburn Smithes has had a Portuguese managing director for years.

But at Taylor, Fladgate & Yeatman (founded 1692), managing director Alistair Robertson is descended from a Yeatman, and the company's characterful taster Bruce Guimaraens from a Fladgate. In 1983, 18-year-old Nicholas Delaforce, seventh-generation Delaforce home from school, was experiencing his first *vindima* or harvest; in 1993 he was involved in the company run by his father, David, in which grandfather John had been an eminent personality.

At Ferreira, too, the sense of dynasty remains strong. In the firm founded by the remarkable Dona Antonia Adelaide Ferreira, eighth generation Francisco ("Vito") de Olazabal is the managing director. In the early 1990s, his son, Francisco, was completing a degree in oenology. Even as a boy Francisco had made up his mind what he wanted to be – and he didn't even like wine.

Inescapable across port since the 1800s is the name of Symington. The family owns and manages a distinguished list of companies: Warre's (founded in the 1670s), Silva & Cosens (whose brand is Dow), Quarles Harris, Smith Woodhouse, and Graham's.

In the 1990s eight members of the Symington family, Paul and Dominic, Ian, Amyas, Peter and John, James and Rupert – two generations – are involved in management, production, sales and marketing of the fine ports made by these independent companies. In today's world, technology meets tradition. Even the Symingtons' Gaia offices hold echoes of port's memorable past: they are in Travessa do Barão Forrester, in the very house where Baron Forrester, who gave his life to port, once lived. ∎

Bruce Guimaraens, of Taylor, Fladgate and Yeatman.

TRÁS-OS-MONTES

To most Portuguese the remote north-eastern province of Trás-os-Montes ("behind the mountains") could be on the other side of the moon. Most *Lisboetas* are inclined to look at it as from a vast distance – albeit with fierce affection. It is a province for the more adventurous traveller who will not miss modern comforts.

The word "trás" – "back" or "behind" – fits the region like a glove, for it is backward in almost every aspect: cut off from the rest of the country by mountains, poor road and rail systems, and a grinding poverty which has driven the workforce of almost every village into migration to urban areas, or emigration up into the more advanced economies of northern Europe, or overseas. It's quite possible that this ancient historic area is the single most backward pocket of civilised Europe – on a par, perhaps, with the remoter areas and islands of Greece, and the hinterlands of Sardinia, Sicily or the eastern states.

The Portuguese, however, are proud of Trás-os-Montes, whether or not they have family connections. "You think we are poor?" queried a village priest from a tiny village in the Serra do Barroso. He was seated on a stone slab inside the stone structure of the communal bake oven, the broiling sun outside the open doorway cooking the dust and dung that paved the village street. Against a far wall stood an ox-cart with wooden wheels, a design used in the Middle Ages. A hand-held wooden plough, a type used in pre-Roman times, leant against the ox-cart, its metal tip freshly hammered into place by a local smith readying it for work the next day.

"Well, we are poor up here," the priest said with a broad smile, "but if you look around you – anywhere you go in Trás-os-Montes – you will not see people begging as in the streets of Lisbon or Oporto. We grow enough food up here to feed everybody. We eat well. Our wine is the best. Others should come and learn from our example…"

There has been higher emigration from the north of Portugal than from the south, and one of the principal reasons is due to the division of lands. The south is an area of *latifundios* – large landholdings – while the north has *minifundios* – small holdings. A farmer's land in the north is often not sufficient to provide him and his family with a living. The northern people are conservative, and resist cooperative farming such as operates in the southern province of Alentejo. Another reason for the *minifundios* is the terrain – high mountains and steep-sided valleys have made it difficult to organise farming on a large scale.

A more subtle factor affecting Portugal's conservative north is the church. While all of Portugal might be viewed as Roman Catholic, the sheer remoteness of the northeast corner of the country has meant that national government has little impact, while tradition and religion predominate. This has affected education, particularly; until recent years, often the only educated man in a village was the priest, whose wisdom and opinion would be sought on every matter ranging from the spirit to advice on crop harvesting.

You may enter the region, which includes the Alto Douro, the upper valley of the Douro river, from a number of directions. Northern border crossings from Spain are at Vila Verde da Raia, on the road leading south to Chaves (this is a historical invasion route – employed by the armies of Napoleon in the early 1800s); at Portelo, in the Parque Natural de Montesinho; from the east at Quintanilha, east of Bragança; and at Miranda do Douro and Bemposta, where the River Douro forms the frontier. From inside Portugal, the main routes into the region would be from Oporto via Vila Real; and from the south, from Lamego via Vila Real; or from Guarda via either Torre de Moncorvo or Freixo de Espada à Cinta. The region is split into two administrative districts, with capitals at Vila Real in the southwest and Bragança in the northeast.

Heading north, you are still in port wine country when you cross the Douro from the direction of Lamego and enter

Régua. There are two bridges crossing the river here – one a road bridge, the other a railway bridge that has never been used, but some 50 years ago was intended for a spur line connecting Régua with Lamego. Of greater curiosity is the tiny rail-link between Régua, Vila Real and Chaves, a south-north route built in 1890 which still at times uses original rolling stock – toy-sized carriages with wood-slat seats and a primitive toilet system.

Retired engines rest on a track behind the station. In the last few years the original steam engine has been replaced by a diesel locomotive, but in every station beautiful blue-and-white tile panels illustrate traditional rural ways. (For another scenic route, check with the railways on the Tua line from Tua to Mirandela.)

Driving north out of Régua, you will find refreshment, and a good port, in **São João de Lobrigos**. The trip to **Vila Real** gives you a first glimpse of the terraced vineyards of this province, where more than half of the working population is employed in agriculture.

Vila Real: An ancient settlement in the Terra de Panóias, Vila Real was founded and renamed by Dom Dinis, the sixth king of Portugal, in 1289. Its name literally means "royal town" – fittingly, as Vila Real once boasted more noble families than any city other than the capital. Ignoring the modern city, and walking in ancient streets, you will see many residences marked, often above the main entrance, with the original owners' coat of arms. Like as not, the same family is still living there. The famous 19th-century writer Camilo Castelo Branco lived in Vila Real, and wrote many of his most enduring works using the town as a backdrop.

"In what century are we on this mountain?" asks one of his characters.

"In what century?" comes the reply. "Why, it is the same 18th century here as it is in Lisbon."

"Oh!" says the first. "I thought time here had stopped in the 12th century."

Vila Real became a city proper only in 1925, but the importance of the region

The Corgo railway runs from Chaves to Régua.

dates from 1768 when the vineyards were first developed commercially: the area has good red and white wines, but it is the *rosé* that is best known – especially Mateus, which is exported to more than 150 countries. The famous **Solar de Mateus** itself, its baroque facade known worldwide from the wine label, is a kilometre to the east of town. Much of the building, a small museum and formal gardens are open to visitors.

Panóias, the original name given to the pre-King Dinis settlement, is also the name of a strange pagan sanctuary about 6 km (4 miles) out of town in the **Vale de Nogueiras**, where a series of enormous carved stones are believed to have been used as altars for human sacrifice. Inscriptions in Latin invoke the ancient god Serapis, known to both Greek and Egyptian mythology.

The **Sé**, or cathedral, was originally the church of a Dominican convent. Although much of the present building dates from the 14th century, still remaining are Romanesque columns from an earlier structure.

Vila Real's oldest church is the ancient **Capela de São Nicolau** on a promontory of high land behind the municipal hall, overlooking the valley of the **Rio Corgo**. Another church of note is **São Pedro**, its baroque touches by the architect at Mateus, Nicolau Nasoni.

Among fine houses dating from the 15th to the 18th centuries is the **Casa de Diogo Cão**, an Italian Renaissance-style house that was the birthplace of the navigator who discovered the mouth of the Congo River.

In the area of handicrafts, the Vila Real region is particularly noted for the black pottery of Bisalhães and the woollen goods of Caldas do Alvão and Marão.

International motorcycle races are held in Vila Real in June and July.

Serra de Alvão: Two scenic routes lead north out of this city, one on each side of the high Serra da Padrela – to Chaves in the north, and Bragança in the northeast. But the adventurous traveller may strike northwest into the rugged Serra de Alvão, and be treated to one of the most lavish vistas the country has to offer. The road leads through a small natural park and across the Rio Olo to **Mondim de Basto** on the banks of the Rio Tâmega. There it forms the border between Trás-os-Montes and the Minho.

Granite gives way to slate – many of the houses are roofed by it – and in the high passes, you can hear the rushing of mountain waters, the tinkle of goat bells, or the calling of a herder to his dogs. In the winter there is snow here, but at other times of the year you are likely to encounter a profusion of wild flowers and pine forests. Pine resin, used in making paints and turpentine, is a major product of this area.

A side trip of some 12 km (8 miles) from Mondim de Basto will take you to **Atei**, a delightful little village containing numerous archaeological remnants of Roman occupation. From here a curious subterranean passage of either Roman or Arab construction leads down to Furaco on the banks of the Tâmega.

Leaving Mondim de Basto, the road winds northwards to **Cabeceiras de Basto**, which is actually in the Minho province, at the head of a small "penin-

A stork near Bragança.

sula" that juts up into Trás-os-Montes. Stop at the imposing baroque **Refójos Monastery** before heading into the high Serra de Cabeceira and back into Trás-os-Montes at **Póvoa**.

Barroso district: You soon join the main Braga–Chaves road that runs beside **Barragem do Alto Rabagão**, a gigantic expanse of lake formed behind a dam, but here again another side trip could take you north – to Montalegre, the towering Serra do Larouco, and the primitive villages of the Barroso district.

As the largest town in the area, **Montalegre** might be considered the "capital" of Barroso. Given a charter in 1273 by King Afonso III, and restored and expanded in turn by King Dinis and King Manuel I, Montalegre (*monte* meaning hill, *alegre* meaning happy or cheerful) is thought to have enjoyed its status from a much earlier time, for the pillory in the centre of town carries the coat-of-arms of King Sancho I, who reigned from 1185 until 1211.

The hill on which the town stands commands a view over a wide area, so it is hardly surprising that it has been a military centre for some dozens of centuries. Montalegre is rich in archaeological finds. Ancient Lusitanians, the Romans, Suevi and Visigoths were here. At **Outeiro Lesenho**, near Montalegre, in the 18th century were found two gigantic granite statues of warriors. They are thought to be from the Iron Age, and have been attributed to Celtic influence. (Today they are in the Ethnology Museum of Belém in Lisbon.)

A magnificent four-towered **castle** stands at Montalegre, much used during the many wars that Portugal fought against Spain. North of the region rises the **Serra do Larouco**, the second highest range of mountains in the country (after the Serra da Estrêla), with a number of passes leading into Spanish Galicia.

The district of Barroso stretches from the foothills of the Serra do Larouco to some 9 or 15 or 20 km (12 miles) northwest of the city of Chaves. There is no absolute boundary, but it would include such villages as Meixido, Padornelos and Tourém, to name a few. If you can

Archaic building methods in Barroso.

shut out the "emigrant architecture" – uncontrolled modern housing that is built with money saved by the Portuguese who work abroad – you will find in these settlements a sense of history utterly remote in time.

The ancient houses are built of enormous granite or slate blocks. Doors, windows, and balconies are of weathered antique wood. Until recently, many houses were thatched. Streets are dirt, or simply bare rock. In many villages, electricity was installed only within the past decade. Almost every church is in Romanesque style – early Middle Ages – with the typical facade rising to a twin-columned peak to house the church bell.

For centuries the people of Barroso lived out their lives cut off from the outside world. They developed their own customs, songs, festivals and habits. In many corners of the world under similar circumstances, local people may treat outsiders with suspicion or alarm. This is certainly not the case in Barroso. It is hard to imagine a more warm-hearted, hospitable people, willing to share the peculiarities of their daily lives with others who come to visit them. By tradition, the bread oven, which is fired up once a week, is both meeting place for each village, and local hostel for travellers seeking shelter for a night or two. Winter or summer, the bread ovens are never cold – but they are housing at its most primitive – and overnight lodgers should have their own sleeping bags!

One of the region's most colourful festivals is the annual *Chega dos Toiros*, an intervillage competition which means "The Arrival of the Bulls". Each village takes enormous pride in its bull, a communal animal bred especially for the purpose of covering the various cows owned by the individual farmers. This bull, by both tradition and breeding, is the biggest and fiercest animal imaginable – intended, perhaps, as much to gain the honours at the annual competition as it is for stock purposes.

Held in June, July and August, the *Chega* is essentially a bullfight, where the bull of one village is pitted against another in a duel. Each animal is deco-

Wooden-wheeled cart in Rio de Onor.

rated and feted by his villagers, and paraded with bands and crowds.

The fight itself is deadly earnest, with the champions of each bull goading their animal into battle. The fight continues until one animal is injured, or turns and runs. The victor is led away by his villagers with much celebration.

At the end of the season there will be a regional champion – and this is the lucky animal who'll be put out to pasture with the region's cows. He is a source of great pride to the residents of the village from which he comes.

Chaves: Chaves, just a few kilometres down the road from Barroso, seems a world away. An ancient city, the fortified Lusitanian village of the present site was captured by the Romans in the year AD 78. The Emperor Flavius founded the city of *Aqua Flaviae* there, inaugurating the still popular hot springs and baths. Chaves is now a bustling town with a population of about 15,000. An agricultural and textile centre, it is famous for its *presunto*, smoked ham; you could taste it, with a glass of wine, at Faustino's which claims to be the largest *taverna* or *tasca* in Portugal.

Situated on the Rio Tâmega, Chaves commands a strategic position in a wide valley that extends from the Spanish frontier into the heart of Trás-os-Montes. Just about every invader who set his heart on Portugal, or chunks of it, routed his armies through this channel. Thus, at one time or another, Chaves has hosted Celts, Lusitanians, Romans, Vandals, Suevi, Moors, Spanish and French.

Here the Romans built one of the largest of their bridges in the Iberian peninsula. Completed in AD 104, it has 20 arches, is 140 metres (150 yards) in length – and is still very much in daily use. In the middle of the bridge are two inscribed Roman milestones.

Chaves means "keys" in Portuguese, but this is probably not the derivation of the name of the city. The ancient *Aqua Flaviae* was much later shortened to *Flavias*, and local mispronunciation eventually produced the current name.

Sights include the **parish church**, originally rebuilt in the 16th century;

Traditional tool near Aldeia Santo Andre in Barroso.

and the former Bragança ducal palace, now a museum, in the Praça de Camões.

Prior to the formation of Portugal, the fortified city was a part of the original County of Portucale. Various of Portugal's early kings added significantly to its **castle**, one of the most important in the land. A second castle, in its day also an integral part of the defences of this strategic valley, still stands at **Monforte**, about 12 km (8 miles) northeast.

Heading eastwards towards Bragança you will pass the old town of **Vinhais** high in the **Serra de Montesinho**, on the south flank of the natural park of the same name. Its castle is barely more than a ruin, though there was a significant population here. The wildly rugged park, habitat of wolves, boars and foxes, is worth a visit. The area survives on agriculture, particularly vines, woodwork, weaving and basket-making.

A mountain, **Cidadella**, rises behind Vinhais. Over it passed the Roman road that led from Braga to Astorga; today this ancient route is rich in archaeological discoveries.

In the 11th and 12th centuries there was a general movement of the population of this area towards the more fertile farm lands of the south. To prevent this, various monasteries were founded and encouraged by the early rulers of the region to develop their own agriculture and cottage industries. One of the most important of these was the **Mosteiro de Castro de Avelãs**, a few miles west of Bragança. Parts of the church of the Benedictine abbey have been incorporated into the present-day parish church.

To explore the region, first stop at the tourist office in Bragança and ask specifically for the book available on the Parque Natural de Montesinho. It contains a detailed map of the park area. Not all of the roads are paved. Whichever direction you take, you will have a journey through spectacular country.

Fascinating city: With a population of some 30,000, **Bragança** is the administrative capital, a university town, and also an agricultural trade centre (livestock, vineyards, olive oil, grains). It has a thriving textile industry, and has

been famous for its ceramics since pre-historic times (in a nearby cave at **Dine**, archaeologists have found pottery dating well into the Paleolithic Period).

Known as *Brigantia* to the Celts and *Juliobriga* to the Romans, Bragança received its first *foral* (royal charter) from King Sancho I in 1187 – when the family from which the dukes of Bragança are descended started building their feudal castle there.

The Braganças – still pretenders to the throne of Portugal – provided the land's kings and queens consistently from 1640 until the formation of the Republic in 1910, and the emperors of Brazil from 1822 to 1889. In 1662, Catherine of Bragança, daughter of the first Bragança king João IV, became Queen to Charles II of England, thus renewing the long alliance between the two nations. Since the fall of the monarchy, a foundation, the *Fundação da Casa de Bragança* has managed all royal properties including the family's 16th-century ducal palace in Vila Viçosa.

Bragança's ancient **castle** still stands, – with a **Princess's Tower** full of tragic ghosts. The keep of the castle houses a **military museum**. You can also see an unusual medieval *pedovrinho* (or pillory), its shaft piercing a granite boar. Nearby, still within the castle walls, you will find the 12th-century five-sided **Domus Municipalis**, the oldest municipal hall in the land. The town walls with their 18 watchtowers are still largely intact, and the city boasts a fine **cathedral** and fascinating **museum**.

Basing yourself in this historic city, it is relatively easy to make short day trips out into the surrounding region.

First, to the north through the Montesinho park in the farthest corner of Portugal, there is **Rio de Onor**, a tiny village that actually straddles the border. Only recently after a rare presidential visit did the village acquire its first bus. The people of Rio de Onor developed their own dialect and intricate communal social system. In their music and folk dances a common instrument is the *gaiteiro* – a bagpipe, which although commonly associated with Scotland and

Bragança's medieval skyline.

Ireland, is more accurately associated with the Celts.

A good time to visit the villages that extend in an arc from Vinhais, across Bragança, and down as far as Miranda do Douro and Freixo de Espada-à-Cinta, would be between Christmas Day and Epiphany (6 January), when the local population celebrate a number of feasts connected with the Christian calendar, but incorporating ferocious masks and unearthly costumes.

These celebrations date back to the dawn of time when the agrarian people of these pastoral regions practised fertility rites and paid more than passing attentions to strange magic. Carnival is another good time to visit. Forty days before Easter the masks come out again, and you cannot be sure if it is the Christian spirit or the bogeyman that dominates the season.

Fernando, the Duke of Bragança, in a 20th-century statue.

South of Bragança you may head towards the Spanish frontier at **Miranda do Douro** where the Douro river has cut a deep rocky gorge. This charming town is the site of a former **cathedral**, a 16th-century granite building with a sequence of gilded wood altarpieces.

The river flows southwesterly towards **Freixo de Espada-à-Cinta**. There are five dams along the Douro here, jointly operated by Spain and Portugal. This route will lead you through the area inhabited by the *Mirandês* – a word that denotes both the people living in the villages of this district and the language a few still speak. In fact, this language, close to Vulgar Latin, is such a valued relic of Portugal's cultural past that it is currently being revived.

Freixo is one of the oldest towns in the province, and was initially fortified by Lusitanians, then Romans, Visigoths and Moors – though nothing remains of their works. However, an important **castle** was built there when Dom Afonso Henriques granted the town its charter. The castle's beautiful seven-sided **Cock's Tower** and remnants of its walls remain. To promote settlement in a town lying so near – only 4 km (2½ miles) – to Spain, Freixo was once granted the status of sanctuary for fugitives.

Freixo's partly Manueline **parish church** was built over a long period and concluded only in the 17th century. It has a fine Gothic doorway, and, inside, a notable carved chancel.

Taking a more interior route south from Bragança, you could visit such beautiful villages as **Chacim**, in the **Serra de Bornes**, or **Vila Flor**, a little farther south.

If you like castles, you will want to see the impressive ruins at **Algoso**, south of Vimioso. Since the 12th century, this fortress has guarded the area surrounding its lofty perch – a hill called **Cabeça da Penenciada** – while 500 metres (1,650 ft) below, the **Rio Angueira** flows westward until it joins the **Rio Maçãs**.

And in the south centre of the province the castle ruins of **Carregade de Ansiães**, lonely atop a craggy hill, deserves special mention. As a fortification, the castle and its village grew in importance during the reign of Dom João I. In the 18th century most of the families living there drifted away; now these imposing stones guard only a modest town – and a realm of silence.

BEIRA ALTA AND BEIRA BAIXA

The provinces of Beira Alta and Beira Baixa, the Upper and Lower Beiras, constitute a large rural section of eastern Portugal – a modest and hardy geographical region in a country already among the poorest of western Europe. But it is rich historically, marked over centuries by the invasion routes of both the Spanish and Moors, defensive castles and remnants of fortresses. The area has its natural attractions as well: the dramatic mountains of the Alta or the stark plains and plateaus of the Baixa are some of the most beautiful natural landmarks in Portugal.

The region is bounded by the Spanish frontier in the east, the Douro river in the north, and the Tagus river in the south. The western boundary is a ragged line 60 km (38 miles) east of Oporto.

Guarda is the principal city and administrative capital of the Beira Alta's eastern district. The charter of Guarda was granted by Sancho I, Portugal's second king, in 1199. However, the city had already been established by 80 BC, when it had a role in the attempted secession from Rome.

Roman gates: There are still traces of Roman occupation. Ruins of the period can be found just outside town, near the Romanesque chapel of **Póvoa de Mileu**, notable itself for a small rose window and nicely carved capitals. Three town gates, the **Torre de Ferreiros** (Blacksmith's Tower), the **Porta da Estrela** (Star Gate), and the **Porta do Rei** (King's Gate), still stand from the 12th- and 13th-century castle and town walls, along with the castle **keep**. From the top there is a magnificent view of the mountains, and the broad plains to the north.

The **Sé** (cathedral) was built of granite cut from the surrounding area. An earlier cathedral, close to the city's original walls, was destroyed before this one was begun; it was believed to be in an unsafe position. Work on this "new" edifice started in 1390 and was not completed until 1540, so that there were many Renaissance and baroque elements added to the original Gothic architecture. The renowned builder Boytac worked on the cathedral, which bears some resemblance to Batalha. The exterior has flying buttresses and fanciful gargoyles. Inside, the 16th-century stone *retábulo*, later highlighted with gilt, represents scenes in the life of Christ, the stone carvings the work of João de Ruão (or Jean de Rouen). A beautiful Renaissance doorway, off the north aisle, leads to the **Capela dos Pinas**, which contains a late Gothic bishop's tomb.

Guarda has been dubbed the city of four F's – *fria, farta, forte e feia*, which means: cold, plentiful, strong and ugly. Perhaps the predominance of heavy grey granite is ugly to some, but the old parts of the city are charming. Strong alludes to Guarda's history as a defence point against the Moors and Castile. Plentiful refers, no doubt, to the rich land surrounding the town, noted particularly for its sheep farming. Cold it certainly is, in winter. Situated some 1,066 metres (3,500 ft) above sea level, Guarda is Portugal's highest city – high enough

for frost and snow during winter months, a rarity in this southern country.

South of Guarda, between two handsome castle-towns, Belmonte (birthplace of Brazil discoverer, Alvares Cabral) and Sabugal, is the oddly enchanting **Sortelha**, castle, crags and tiny village within a "magic ring" of stone. Ancient civilisations may have shaped some of the rocks, and they certainly mined in the area – there are entrances that have been closed for centuries.

Stretching southwest is the **Serra da Estrela**, the highest mountain range in Portugal and the source of Portugal's most highly-rated cheese. The highest point is at the (over-commercialised) Torre, 1,993 metres (6,537 ft). Near Torre is a pilgrimage site, a statue of the Virgin carved into the rock, to which the faithful journey on the second Sunday of August. The Serra offers skiing in winter, pleasant walking – or driving – with grand views in all directions.

Covilhã, on the eastern side of the range, is the prime winter resort. Low enough so that it seldom receives snow itself, it is a short drive to the ski area at **Penhas da Saúde**.

West of the Serra, in Beira Litoral province, is the darkly haunting **Buçaco Forest**. For centuries this area has been protected, and 700 varieties of native and exotic trees have flourished.

Benedictine monks established a hermitage here in the 6th century. In 1622 women were forbidden by Pope Gregory to enter. The Carmelites, who built a monastery in 1628, began cultivation, planting species brought back from the Portuguese voyages. These included Himalayan pines, monkey-puzzles, Japanese camphor trees, huge Lebanese cedars, and ginkgoes. In 1643 the Pope threatened to excommunicate anyone harming the trees.

In September 1810, Wellington routed Napoleon's army at Buçaco, as the French attempted for the third time to conquer Portugal. A military museum is among a host of sights.

A royal hunting lodge was built in Neo-Manueline style at the end of the 19th-century next to what remained of **Buçaco Forest.**

the convent. After the fall of the monarchy in 1910, it became the spectacular Palace Hotel (where you may still, at a price, lodge in the suite of the last king, Manuel II.) There is a small **church**, the **cloister**, and several **monks' cells** remaining from the monastery. In one of these small cells, Wellington spent the night before the Battle of Buçaco.

Downhill from Buçaco is the village of **Luso**, famed for its water which flows freely here from fountains and is available bottled throughout Portugal.

The eastern district of Beira Alta is governed by the city of **Viseu**. In the 2nd century BC the Romans built a fortified settlement here – some of their road system can still be seen, along with a number of Latin-inscribed stones.

A thorn in the side of the Romans was a rebel Lusitanian named Viriathus, who harassed local Roman legions until he was finally betrayed and killed. A monument to this hero is at the edge of a park – the **Cova de Viriato** – on the site of a Lusitanian and Roman military encampment. Here you can still see the old

earthworks once used by the Romans.

Viseu was made a bishopric during the Suevian-Visigothic kingdom, and a record still exists: a signature of the Bishop of Viseu, dated 569 AD.

The city suffered alternating invasions of Moors and Christians from the 8th until the 11th century. Fernando the Great of Castile and León captured it for the Christians in 1057. Teresa, mother of the first king of Portugal, granted the city its first charter in 1123.

From the 14th to the 16th century, building in Viseu seems to have been concentrated in the upper part of town. About this time also an active Jewish colony evolved here. In 1411 the Infante Dom Henrique (Prince Henry the Navigator) became Duke of Viseu, and toward the end of that century the town walls were completed. But the area was becoming a centre for the vigorous agricultural activity in the surrounding area, and by the 16th century the walled area was emptying.

Perhaps this was fortunate, because over the next two centuries, much of

Church of the Misericórdia in Viseu.

this space was filled with a lavish assortment of baroque churches, chapels, mansions and fountains. Today the architectural richness lends a dignified air to the enclosed city.

Pure baroque: You should see the 13th-century **Cathedral**. The ribbed vaulting is beautifully carved to look like knotted cables, and the ceiling of the **sacristy** is extravagantly painted with illustrations of animals and plants. The twin-towered **Misericórdia church** across the square is whitewashed granite and pure baroque.

You might also keep time for the **Grão Vasco Museum** in the old Bishop's palace in the same square. Many of the works represent the fine school of Portuguese Primitive painting that flourished here in the 16th century.

The São Mateus Fair, held annually in August and September, is a major event; the Festival of St John the Baptist is another, held each 24 June. A Tuesday market is held throughout the year, with plenty of fresh produce, bolts of cloth, pots and pans, and handicrafts. Viseu is well known for its lace, carpets, and black pottery. Some 30 km (19 miles) west of Viseu, on the IP5 highway toward Aveiro on the coast, you enter the valley of the Vouga river, which divides the mountain ranges of the **Serra de Arada** and the **Serra do Caramulo**.

North of the IP5 is the small town of **São Pedro do Sul** and, some 4 km (2½ miles) on the **Termas de São Pedro do Sul** – possibly the best known and most frequented hot springs in the country. Sinus, rheumatism, hangover or foul temper, the springs are said to cure all ailments.

The town of **Caramulo** south of the IP5 has a **museum**, with medieval decorative arts, and 19th- and 20th-century European paintings, but is best known for its more than 50 antique cars and motorcycles, including an 1899 Peugeot and several Bugattis.

To the south is the **Barragem de Aquieira**, a gorgeous man-made lake popular with campers and boat enthusiasts. A few kilometres away is the charming village of **Mortágua**.

Azulejos in Viseu.

From here it is about 5 km (3 miles) to the town of **Santa Comba Dão**, known principally for being the birthplace of Portugal's former dictator, António de Oliveira Salazar. Political divisions within the old town are still marked.

There are several other delightful villages to visit in this region. Just south of São Pedro do Sul is **Vouzela**, in the valley of the Vouga river, with a lovely 13th-century **parish church**. Close by is the village of **Cambra**, clustered around the remnants of its **castle**. Just to the south is a Celtiberian site called **Cova de Lobishomem** (Werewolf's Cave). And near Caramulo is the pretty village of **Tondela**.

South of Viseu, just off the IC12 to Nelas is the village of **Santar**, a gem once known as the "court of the Beiras". Due south (and west of the Serra de Estrela) is **Oliveira do Hospital**, which once belonged to the Hospitallers. Tombs of the Ferreiros, in the **parish church**, are crowned by a carving of an equestrian knight on the wall above. To the southwest, in the village of **Lourosa**

is the extremely old church of **São Pedro**. In 911, Ordoño II ordered building begun; it has a central nave, horseshoe arches, Moorish windows, and Visigothic decoration.

If you return to the Vouga river and journey northeast from São Pedro do Sul, you will find a particularly lovely stretch of road between the **Serra de Montemuro** and the **Serra De Leomil** toward Lamego. This road (228) passes through the high town of **Castro Daire**. The Romans used this site as a garrison and built an important bridge here, the **Ponte Pedrinha**, over the **Paiva river**.

Lamego itself is a city of historical importance. Although the Lusitanians had finally been subjugated by the Romans, the tribespeople of this area arose in revolt, refusing to pay the heavy taxation. In retaliation, the Romans burned the town to the ground. But it was an important defensive location, so Emperor Trajan ordered it rebuilt.

By the 4th century AD, the town had turned to Christianity, and was granted the status *civitas*, the Roman equivalent

The daily news in Viseu.

of city franchise. Then came the invasions of the Suevi and Visigoths – and then the Moors. Finally, in the same sweep that won him Viseu, Fernando of León and Castile took the city, aided by the legendary El Cid. Fernando allowed the Moslem *wali* to continue to govern Lamego – as long as he converted, and paid tribute to the king.

Perhaps the city's most significant moment in Portugal's history was in 1143, when the *cortes* met for the very first time. At this meeting, the nobles declared Afonso Henriques to be Afonso I, first king of Portugal.

Lamego's 12th-century **castle**, on one of the city's two hills, preserves a fine 13th-century **keep**, with windows that were added later, and an unusual vaulted **cistern**, very old, possibly Moorish, with monograms of master masons.

Atop Lamego's other hill is its most visually striking building, the pilgrimage church of **Nossa Senhora dos Remédios** crowning a vast stairway reminiscent of Braga's Bom Jesus. The first chapel of the sanctuary was founded by the Bishop of Lamego in 1361, and dedicated to Saint Stephen. In 1564, it was pulled down, and a new one built. From that time, there has been a steady stream of the faithful seeking cures. The present sanctuary was started in 1750, and was consecrated 11 years later – but the magnificent baroque-style **staircase** leading up to it, started in the 19th century, was completed in the 1960s. Fountains, statues and pavilions decorate each level of the 600 or so steps.

The **Cathedral**, a Gothic structure, was built by Afonso Henriques in 1129. Only the Romanesque **tower** is left from the original building. The city **museum**, housed in the 18th-century Bishop's Palace, has a collection which includes 16th-century Flemish tapestries and works by Grão Vasco.

Some 16 km (10 miles) southeast of Lamego the village of **São João de Tarouca** (not Tarouca, which you come to first) has the ruins of the first Cistercian monastery to be built in Portugal. The church beside it contains fine paintings, Dutch tiles, lovely **choir stalls** and the impressive **tomb** of Conde Pedro de Barcelos, illegitimate son of King Dinis, and author of *O Livro das Linhagens*, an early register of the country's nobility.

Just outside Lamego (start on the Tarouca road) in the valley of the **Balsemão river**, is the tiny **São Pedro de Balsemão**, a Visigothic church believed to be the oldest in Portugal and second oldest in Europe.

To the east of Lamego, there is a fine **castle** at **Penedono**, a graceful structure with two lovely detailed towers and an arch between them. The castle, which is known to have existed before 960, is thought to be the birthplace of Alvaro Gonçalves Coutinho, immortalised for his bravery and gallantry by Portugal's national poet, Luís Vaz de Camões, in Canto VI of *The Lusiads*.

Some 20 km (12½ miles) southeast of Penedono is **Sernancelhe** with a ruined castle built by the Knights of Malta.

Among villages of special interest – there are many – might be **Ermida do Paiva**, just northwest of Castro Daire, where there is a 12th-century **church** built by the Augustinians. **Vila Nova de**

Fountain of the church of Nossa Senhora dos Remédios.

Paiva to the east of Castro Daire, and villages near by, have been dubbed the **Terras do Demo**, Lands of the Devil, made famous by a number of Portuguese literary figures – notably Aquilino Ribeiro in his 19th-century romance *Malhadinhas*.

Aguiar da Beira lies east of Vila Nova de Paiva and south of Sernancelhe. A well-preserved example of a medieval town, it has a **town square** with an ancient **keep** and pillory and an unusual **council chamber**, atop a squat structure and open to the sky.

Travelling now south toward the Beira Baixa, you come to the **Zêzere river**, which roughly divides Beira Alta from Beira Baixa. The river flows most swiftly from early April through June. A good place for water sports is the **Barragem de Castelo do Bode**, a long, many-armed lake that runs south into the province of Ribatejo. Both the river and the lake have rather fine fishing. There's canoeing in places.

The **Tagus** (or **Tejo**) **river** at **Fretel** marks the southern limit of Beira Baixa.

Upstream the Tagus reaches and crosses into Spain. Here, on both the Portuguese and Spanish sides, is desolate scrub country. The gorge formed by the river is steep-sided and virtually inaccessible to vehicles other than four-wheel-drive jeeps. Along much of the Portuguese side of the river here runs an **ancient road** built by the Romans. Originally it was the route from **Vila Velha de Rodão** to the Spanish town of Santiago de Alcántara. Water now conceals large chunks of the work, but where the road rises above the surface, you will that instead of building the road with flat stones, the entire way is paved with local slate stood on edge, its upper surface rutted by centuries of cart traffic.

Both Beira Alta and Beira Baixa have numerous castles. Among the most intriguing is in the village of **Monsanto** in Beira Baixa, once declared "the most typical Portuguese village". Built around and atop a steep rocky mass in a broad valley some 50 km (30 miles) northeast of the city of Castelo Branco, Monsanto is located in the middle of a major invasion route. The castle, above a granite village whose houses are often tucked between giant boulders, commands a superlative view in every direction.

It is thought that this *monte* has been fortified since neolithic times, and the castle is so well integrated into the natural rock it looks almost as if it grew here.

Rice-filled calf: Some say it was during the Roman invasion in the 2nd century BC, others claim it was some 1400 years later during a Moorish invasion, that the people of Monsanto, under a long siege and nearly out of food, fooled their attackers by killing a calf, filling its belly with rice, and hurling it off the ramparts to the soldiers below. The attackers were so impressed with the evidence of ample supplies that they packed up and left. Today one of the biggest feast days is 3 May, when young villagers toss down pitchers filled with flowers from the battlements.

Much of the castle was destroyed at the beginning of the 19th century. One Christmas Eve, there was a tremendous thunderstorm, and a bolt of lightning hit the gunpowder magazine. Divine retri-

Vineyards near the village of Carapito, Lamego.

bution, the people of the village believed, for that year the unpopular governor had forbidden the traditional burning of a tree trunk in front of the parish church. The gunpowder exploded, and the irons flew from the hearth and struck the governor dead.

The folk music of the Monsanto area is charming if strange. Half chanted, half sung, there is nothing quite like it elsewhere in the country. Its rhythm is beaten out with the assistance of a square tambourine known as an *adufe*.

The great **Idanha Plain** stretches all the way south to Castelo Branco and beyond – a vast area of cattle-raising country, bitterly cold in winter, scorching in the summer. Near Castelo Branco are large areas of pine and eucalyptus.

Castelo Branco itself, with 25,000 inhabitants, is an ancient city the origins of which, like so many communities in Portugal, are lost in time. It dates its "modern" history back to 1182 when it and the surrounding area – then called Vila Franca de Cardosa – were given as a gift to the Knights Templar by Dom Fernão Sanches. It received a charter in 1213, and became a city in 1771, in the reign of José I.

The battlements of the old Templar **castle** – the "white castle" of the city's name – provide a fine view, though the castle itself is not noteworthy. The old town is delightful, with narrow winding streets. Points of interest include two churches, **São Miguel** and **Misericórdia Velha**, a 16th-century structure with a notable doorway; and the **Praça Velha**, also known as the Praça de Camões – a fine medieval square off which you can find the ancient **municipal library**.

The most important thing to see in Castelo Branco is the splendid **Episcopal Palace**, built on the order of the Bishop of Guarda, in 1596. It served as the winter residence of the bishops of the diocese. It now houses the **Museu de Francisco Tavares Proença Júnior**, with prehistoric pieces from the area and Portuguese art.

In 1725 Bishop João de Mendonça commissioned the building of a garden at the side of the palace – the **Bishop's**

The ruined fortifications at Monsanto.

316

Garden, today considered one of Portugal's finest formal gardens. It is not particularly large, you can walk around it in a matter of minutes. But it is an extraordinary sight, if only for the multitude of statues.

These statues are all named, and have been placed in homage to just about everybody and everything the bishops thought important: the kings of Portugal, of course (the two hated Spanish rulers of Portugal, Felipe I and II, are represented, but by smaller figures); the saints, apostles and evangelists, along with the virtues; but also the seasons of the year, the signs of the zodiac, the elements of the firmament. There once were even *more* statues, but the invading French armies of 1807 carted off the best. The plinths of the stolen statues have been left standing in their places, in many cases with the name of the missing item clearly engraved.

If you are looking for your own spoils to cart off, you might consider a bedspread made in Castelo Branco. Since the 17th century it has been the custom for brides-to-be painstakingly to hand-embroider their wedding bedspreads. From this practice, and skill, a cottage industry was born. Traditionally, the spreads were white, but in recent years, they have become available in interwoven colours. Earlier patterns were geometric, echoing Persian carpets, but other decorative themes have since become popular as well.

Northeast of the city, **Idanha-a-Velha** was an episcopal See until 1199, when the See was moved to Guarda. There remains here a strange, ancient **basilica** with dozens of Roman inscriptions inside. It is said that Wamba, the legendary king of the Goths, was born here. There is a Roman **bridge** in the village, still in use, and various coins, pottery and bones have been found.

Other appealing villages in the Beira Baixa include **Proenca-a-Velha**, **São Miguel de Acha**, **Bemposta**, and, west of Monsanto, **Peruha Garcia**. There is a tourist office in Castelo Branco, and it is worthwhile calling in to obtain literature about the district.

The garden of the Episcopal Palace, Castelo Branco.

MADEIRA

The discovery of the Madeiran archipelago, 608 km (380 miles) west of Morocco, was an early triumph for the ambitious seafaring inspired by Prince Henry the Navigator. In 1418, while sailing south to explore the West African coast, the caravels of João Gonçalves Zarco and Tristão Vaz Teixeira were blown west by storms – eventually finding shelter on a low-lying, uninhabited island they gratefully called Porto Santo (Holy Port). Two years later the navigators returned, discovering a large and mountainous island 37 km (23 miles) to the southwest which they named Ilha da Madeira – the Island of Wood.

Modern explorers, now arriving by jet and cruise ship, will find Madeira is still a wild and idyllic place to visit. Its great forests may have gone – burnt down by the first settlers with fires that are said to have raged for years – but man has contributed his own wonders to an Atlantic island whose natural splendour has earned it ecstatic subtitles such as "God's Botanical Gardens" and "The Floating Flower-pot".

The city: A statue of Zarco now stands as a central landmark in **Funchal**, the capital of Madeira and home to a third of its 280,000 islanders. The city squats in the centre of a wide bay on the sunnier south side of the island, its name inspired by the wild fennel (*funcho*) that the discoverers found growing on the surrounding plain. Behind it rises an amphitheatre of terraced hills and mountains that provides shelter from the northeasterly winds that frequently dowse the island – rain, storms and consolatory rainbows are the price you pay for Madeira's splendid verdancy.

New Year's Eve is the best time to appreciate Funchal's panoramic setting, and the climax in a busy calendar of island festivities. That night the bay is crowded with brightly-illuminated cruise liners and pleasure boats, and the city's buildings, churches and trees adorned with Christmas decorations and a haze of 300,000 coloured lights. At midnight Funchal erupts – as if sending some hedonistic signal to outer space – in a cacophony of fog-horns, sirens, fireworks and flashing lights. Up on hotel rooftops sunseeking Finns embrace overwintering English aristocrats, while in the streets below families celebrate the annual return of the prodigal emigrant from Venezuela or South Africa with dancing, wine and specially-made, two dozen-ingredient editions of the islanders' rich molasses-based cake, *bolo de mel*.

If you can't make this party, there are other memorable ways to appreciate Funchal. Cruise ship passengers and tourists with limited time usually settle for the two essential Madeiran experiences, the **Monte toboggan ride** and tea at **Reid's Hotel**. The first involves driving up to Monte, a cool and leafy hilltop resort with *quintas*, sanatoriums and chapels once frequented by the ailing rich, titled exiles and upper-class travellers. From here you can descend to Funchal by *carro de cesto*, a wicker sofa attached to wooden runners that is

guided down the steep lanes by a pair of drivers wearing boaters and white flannels. This unique form of transport was invented by an English resident looking for a speedy way to get down to his office from his *quinta*, and is similar to the toboggan runs once used around the island to slide farm produce grown on the terraces to the harbours below.

Tea at Reid's is far less strenuous, and simply involves climbing into a wicker armchair, ordering a pot of Earl Grey and some crustless cucumber sandwiches, then falling asleep with a copy of yesterday's *Times* over your face. A world-famous five-star hotel with a prestigious site overlooking Funchal harbour, Reid's was opened in 1891 to cater for the growing number of well-to-do visitors to the island – particularly the British who liked to stopover en route to and from their colonies.

Their presence on the island has proved influential in many ways – besides endorsing Madeira's reputation as a refined holiday destination famed for its civility and hospitality, the English taste for cane furniture, acquired in the Orient, stimulated the islands' wicker industry. Centred on the eastern town of Camacha, this now employs some 2,000 islanders. Another important cottage industry, the production of an intricate and understandably expensive embroidery (*bordados*), is also indebted to an Englishwoman, Elizabeth Phelps, who introduced it after disease devastated the island's vines in the 1850s.

Lomquats and scabbard fish: Funchal's true pleasures, however, are not its nostalgic tourist attractions, which can get crowded and histrionic, but the more modest sights woven into the everyday life of the city. A visit to its cornucopious **Mercado dos Lavradores** (Workers' Market) costs nothing – unless, of course, you are tempted to buy some lomquats, tomarillos, pittangas or any of the many other exotic fruits and vegetables now grown on or imported to the island.

Venture into the Mercado's inner halls and you can gaze in safety upon the gloriously ugly *espada* (scabbard fish) that frequently features on Madeiran **Mercado dos Lavradores, Funchal.**

menus (not to be confused with the equally common traditional dish called *espetada* – beef cooked on a skewer over a wood fire scented with laurel twigs). Despite its vicious teeth and eel-like appearance, *espada* tastes good and is something of a rarity as it is only caught here and off Japan. The most important catch in the archipelago, the fish lives at a depth of up to 762 metres (2,500 ft) and is hunted year-round by fishermen from Câmara de Lobos, who use lines with baited hooks and flies spaced at regular intervals that can be over 1.6 km (1 mile) in length.

For a rewarding insight into Madeira's past, pay a visit to the **Museu Photographia Vicentes** in Rua da Carreira, which houses a collection of old photographs of life on the island as recorded since 1865 by the Vicente family, and to the **Quinta das Cruzes** (Calada do Pico 1), a stately home once owned by a wine-shipping family and now packed with art treasures. The Quinta's gardens stay open through the lunch break and are one of several exotic oases around the city, the largest being the **Jardim Botânico** (Botanical Gardens) on Caminho de Meio.

Most of Madeira's hotels are located in a zone on the west side of the capital – only a short bus or taxi ride away from Funchal's main square, **Praça do Município**. Decorously paved with black and white stones, this is bordered by imposing buildings with white-washed facades and dark basalt outlines that remind visitors how church and state have lorded it over this Portuguese outpost. A Jesuit church and college, founded in 1569, fills its north side, while the 18th-century Câmara Municipal (Town Hall) to the east was once the palace of the Conde de Carvalhal. His country residence was at Quinta do Palheiro Ferreiro, 8 km (5 miles) east of Funchal, now a 320-hectare (800-acre) estate owned by the Blandy family, with magnificent gardens open to the public.

On the south side of Praça do Município, the former Bishop's Palace houses Madeira's principal art museum, the **Museu de Arte Sacra** (Museum of

Madeira has been described as a "floating flower-pot".

Sacred Art). Amongst its exhibits is a fine collection of 15th- and 16th-century Flemish paintings acquired during the island's profitable trade in sugar with Flanders. "White gold" was the spur that provoked Madeira's rapid colonisation – by the 1450s merchants from Lisbon had established lucrative plantations on the island, worked by slaves brought over from Africa and the nearby Canary Islands, 416 km (260 miles) to the south. By the 17th century most of Madeira's terraces had been given over to producing its eponymous fortified wine, originally derived from Cretan vines introduced to the island by Henry the Navigator. Amongst these was the sweet *malvoisie* grape, which gave rise to the malvasia or malmsey wines that so besotted Europe in the 16th century. In Shakespeare's *Henry IV*, Falstaff is accused of selling his soul for "a cup of Madeira and a cold capon's leg".

Wine routes: Madeira's fortunes have long been entwined with those of its famous sherry-like drink, and the names of English, Scottish and Irish immigrant families like Leacock, Cossart, Gordon and Blandy have become synonymous with its history. In the 18th century it was discovered that long sea voyages through the heat of the tropics improved the wine's quality, a lengthy process of maturation that has now been replaced by the *estafugem* system, where the young wine is stored in hot-houses (*estufas*) for several months. Four main types of Madeira are produced today: a dry Sercial and medium-dry Verdelho, both ideal as aperitifs, and the richer Bual and dark, sweet Malmsey, both often served with desserts.

Madeira wine travels well and keeps well, and few visitors leave for home without a bottle or two. Funchal has many invitingly fusty wine lodges and tasting bars where you can indulge in some serious research. **D'Oliveiras** and **Henriques & Henriques**, both in Rua dos Ferreiros, are two worth seeking out, though the best initiation into the history and production of Madeira wine is provided by the Adegas de São Francisco (Avenida Arriaga 28). **Madeira.**

Take any road out of Funchal, and the audacious work required to produce the island's wines, fruit and agricultural crops soon becomes apparent. The true heroes of Madeiran history are its farm labourers and their enslaved predecessors, who over the centuries have toiled to win cultivable land from the island's steep and irregular terrain. Unaided by beasts of burden, who cannot keep a steady foothold on the sheer cliffs and valley walls, workers have resolutely sculpted the island with staircases of tiny stone-walled fields – sometimes built by suspending men on ropes from above, with baskets of soil carried up from the river beds far below.

These *poisos*, or terraces, are fed by a phenomenal network of irrigation channels, known as *levadas*, that today run for some 2,136 km (1,335 miles), including 40 km (25 miles) through tunnels. Besides bringing water down from the mountains, the maintenance paths adjacent to the *levadas* provide long, **Into the** level walks into the silent heart of the **mountains.** island, with the stream of water serving as a faithful and unarguing companion.

Even without the terracing that has transformed the island's landscape into a precipitous work of art, Madeira would be staggeringly attractive. A range of volcanic mountains runs east-west across the island, rising to a central conference of peaks of which the highest is Pico Ruivo (1,862 metres/6,106 ft). The nearby summit of **Pico do Arieiro**, which can be comfortably scaled by car, provides a physical and spiritual high point. From here, providing you have prayed away the clouds, you can follow an exhilarating on-top-of-the-world path across the peaks to **Achada do Teixiera**.

From all sides of these central mountains deep ravines run seawards to boulder-strewn beaches where small villages have grown up – most spectacularly at **Ribeira Brava** and **São Vicente**. The ridges above them invariably culminate in sheer cliffs that are amongst the highest in the world – if you have the head for it, a viewing platform at Cabo Girão enables visitors to contemplate a verti-

cal drop of 580 metres (1,902 ft). Along Madeira's wild north coast, narrow roads have been stitched into the cliffsides, threading through tunnels, round hairpins and under waterfalls that provide a free and unexpected car wash. **Porto do Moniz**, a remote weatherbeaten town on the island's northwestern tip with a couple of small hotels and several fish restaurants, provides a welcome goal for adventurous motorists searching for the raw side of Madeira.

For all this natural drama, Madeira is a fundamentally benign and relaxing island. Blessed with fertile soil, abundant water and an equable subtropical climate, the countryside is graced by a profusion of native plants and flowers that have been supplemented by exotic imports. The island is a heaven for walkers and the botanically-inclined, with the mountain pass at Boca da Encumeada and the Parque das Queimadas popular starting points for hikers.

With the advent of new roads, footpaths, and purpose-built viewpoints, Madeira's appeal is widening. Driving along its intestinal roads can still be tiring and time-consuming, but two mountain *pousadas* and several small, modern hotels have recently been built around the coast. Popular points of call are the village of **Santana**, where the islanders' traditional A-shaped thatched cottages have been colourfully restored, the forest resort of **Ribeiro Frio** and the wicker-making centre of **Camacha**.

Off the beaten track: Like all good islands, Madeira has plenty of secrets. An easy and worthwhile trip from Funchal is up to **Curral das Freiras** (Corral of the Nuns), a secluded crater-like valley that until the late 1950s could only be reached by the narrow mountain paths that still snake down its sides. It gets its name from the nuns of Funchal's Santa Clara convent, who fled here in 1566 when French pirates sacked the capital. Another surprise lies to the west of Ribeira Brava – a plateau of austere and often misty moorland known as the Paúl da Serra, where an enormous white statue, Nossa Senhora da Montanha, supervises the grazing sheep and cows.

Traditional house in Santana.

The east side of Madeira is less mountainous and consequently the most developed part of the island. Here you can find the airport, golf course, stretches of intensive farmland and **Machico**, which can claim to be Madeira's second city even though it only has 13,000 inhabitants, one high-rise hotel and a seafront commandeered by a sandy football pitch. In the northeastern corner of the island the mood changes again as the land narrows to a low-lying, sandy peninsula called Ponta de São Lourenço, reached through a tunnel to the north of Machico. Here Canial was, until 1981, the island's principal whaling station.

Lonely islands: Continue to the end of the headland, which offers good views and blustery walks, and you will often meet old men selling souvenirs carved from redundant stocks of whalebone. The arid landscape of Ponta de São Lourenço provides a foretaste of that found on Madeira's neighbouring island, **Porto Santo**. In fact this peninsula is linked underwater to another separate group of islands, the three enigmatic

The beginnings of a wicker basket.

and barren **Ilhas Desertas**. Only 16 km (10 miles) southeast of Madeira, these rise as high as 479 metres (1,571 ft) and can easily be seen from the southern shores. Despite repeated attempts over the centuries, the islands have proved uninhabitable and are now a nature reserve where seabirds, wild goats, some poisonous black spiders and a colony of monk seals live in curious harmony.

Another set of islands, even more inhospitable, also belong to the Madeiran archipelago. Known as the **Ilhas Selvagens**, these lie 216 km (135 miles) to the south and, despite being closer to the Spanish Canaries, remain under Portuguese jurisdiction. The Ilhas Desertas can sometimes be visited by boat trips from Funchal. More accessible is the sleepy world of Porto Santo, connected daily by ferry and aeroplane. The island is a complete contrast to Madeira: while the former has a surplus of mountains, water and vegetation but no beaches to speak of, Porto Santo has just a few parched volcanic hills and a south coast that is one long, 7-km (4½-mile) stretch of unspoilt sand. It is as if God was planning to add beaches to Madeira but, like a builder who leaves a pile of sand outside your front door then disappears, He somehow forgot.

This divine oversight is a blessing for beach-potatoes and connoisseurs of small-island life. Plagued by rabbits and erosion, and vulnerable to attack by pirates, Porto Santo has always been ignored in favour of its lush and fertile neighbour. The capital, Vila Baleira, makes a virtue out of inertia, and has only recently made efforts to cash in on its most famous resident, Christopher Columbus. He was amongst the many sugar buyers who came to the islands in the 1470s, and later married the daughter of Porto Santo's first governor, Bartolomeu Perestrello.

During the summer months holiday-makers from Funchal and mainland Portugal flock to Porto Santo, giving it the semblance of a seaside resort. But even at the height of the season there is space enough to wander along its magnificent beach – following in Columbus's footsteps.

THE AZORES

All islands are inherently beguiling, and the nine islands of the Azores in the Atlantic ocean are gratifyingly rich in romantic history, cryptic legend, and astonishing natural beauty. You cannot ignore their volcanic origins – deep craters or *calderas* are their most outstanding feature. But greenery and trim, patchwork fields impose order and a surprising gentleness. With their tall cliffs and farm-quilted countryside, their tiny homesteads rooted in rock, they are a magical presence in a volatile ocean.

To Portuguese explorers, who first mapped them in the 15th century, the Azores became vital landmarks in an expanding empire. Christopher Columbus, returning from his momentous 1492 voyage to the New World, took on water at the eastern island of Santa Maria. For centuries of other mariners the Azores have offered a safe haven and restful stopover.

The island group is important strategically to Western powers and meteorologically to weather forecasters – an Azores High (high-pressure area) means fine weather for western Europe. This geographic region has an extra dimension if you share the view that the 650-km (400-mile) long archipelago's two tiny, westernmost islands, Flores and Corvo, more than a third of the way across the Atlantic, mark the true outermost limit of Europe. The islands' capital, Ponta Delgada, and international airport, are on the easternmost São Miguel island, 88 km (55 miles) north of Santa Maria and the largest island in the group.

Origins: The name Azores, or Açores, was bestowed on the islands by Gonçalo Velho Cabral who, with Diogo de Silves, landed at Santa Maria in 1427. The word means goshawks, which Cabral saw flying high above. But from myth, fable and fanciful charts, other names persist. Here, some believe, is the lost Atlantis, from Plato's account of a sunken empire lying beyond the Pillars of Hercules. Yet chroniclers wrote that all the islands were uninhabited when the Portuguese arrived.

By 1439, settlement had begun in São Miguel through the efforts of Prince Henry the Navigator, his colonisation policy so zealous that he offered – through his sister Isabel, married to the Duke of Burgundy and ruler of Flanders – land to Flemish farmers. Prince Henry not only foresaw the role of the islands in his larger purpose of African discovery but, in his businesslike way, organised the planting of grains, sugar cane and vines – you'll observe grapevines neatly terraced within grey lava walls.

In Portuguese history, the islanders have held themselves apart from Lisbon, and have often chosen an opposing path. In the 19th-century War of the Two Brothers between two sons of King João VI, islanders supported the liberal Dom Pedro IV against his absolutist brother, Dom Miguel, who had the support of most of Portugal.

Hardy islanders live by farming and fishing. There's a significant dairy industry. You'll see cows milked on steep

Preceding pages: São Miguel is the largest island. **Left,** the coastal approach. **Right,** windmill on Faial.

hillsides, their milk ferried in churns by farmers on horseback. But from the Azores, too, have emerged many of the finest poets, novelists and philosophers in Portuguese culture. One of several daily newspapers, *O Açoriano* is the third oldest in Europe. The islands' identity was established long ago; autonomous government came in 1976.

In recent years, the Azores (about 2 hours' flight from Lisbon, four hours from New York) have become a modestly expanding tourist destination. What they are not, though, are bland resorts for sophisticates or sun-worshippers. There are relatively few sand beaches, and these are mostly volcanic black. The weather outside June to September, though mild (the winter averages 14°C/57°F, summer 23°C/74°F) is often wet and windy. Accommodation ranges from adequate to very pleasant but is rarely classy, and entertainment is generally limited to discos and bars. Yet you'll drink well – local as well as Portuguese wines – and eat generously (island fish includes the tasty *arbrotea*,

or forkbeard). You'll find delicious breads and a superb island cheese – the *queijo da ilha* made on São Jorge island.

Attractions: Island pleasures are simple and relaxed. You will discover thrilling scenery, odd crater lakes and hot springs, great flat rocks called *lajes* or *lages*, solidified lava flows fatalistically called *mistérios*, splendid trees and, in summer, spectactular hydrangea hedges – also many other gorgeous flowers and ferns (50 of 850 species are endemic). There is also much to see in the daily spectacle of working life. Custom and religion are served by frequent *festas*, the striking baroque churches carved from basalt, and gaudy chapels (or *impérios*) that reflect the islanders' ardour for the Espirito Santo cult.

You can see the relics of a long tradition of whaling, and will encounter the sons and grandsons of whaling men – and, in summer, numerous emigrant families on annual trips home. The islands are worth a visit even if you only have time for São Miguel – hiring a car **No need for** is the easiest way to get around – but **petrol.**

government Turismo can provide information or the Ornelas Travel Agency (tel: 096-25379; fax: 096-24473), can help you work out a routing to other islands. SATA Air Açores flies to all the islands. (All three organisations have offices on Avenida Infante Dom Henrique, 9500 Ponta Delgada, São Miguel.) There are inter-island boats.

The islands are good for walking or cycling. With a guide, you have a relatively easy climb of Pico, Portugal's tallest mountain (2,351 metres/7,714 ft) on – what else? – Pico island, meaning peak. Additionally, fast-expanding sports facilities range from golf and tennis to deep-sea fishing and diving. In the growing capital of Ponta Delgada is the Azores's first hypermarket.

The islands divide naturally into three groups: São Miguel and Santa Maria in the east; Terceira, São Jorge, Graciosa, Faial and Pico in the centre; and Flores and Corvo to the west.

Island by island: São Miguel, the largest island (65 km/40 miles by 16 km/10 miles) is also the most populated, with nearly half the group's total population of 250,000. The capital, **Ponta Delgada**, main port and international airport are here, as is a choice of hotels.

On the island's south coast, Ponta Delgada sprawls behind the waterfront Avenida Dom Infante Henrique and 18th-century arched city gates, dramatically set off by patterned cobbles. City sights include a 1552 fort on the sea front and several fine churches, among them the 16th-century parish church, Igreja Matriz de São Sebastião. Architecturally pleasing are the Palácios da Conceição and Fonte Bela as well as the curious baroque Casa de Carlos Bicudo with its mermaid facade.

For a view that overlooks the city, head for the Reduto da Mãe de Deus, where in 1944 an ill-informed anti-aircraft battery shot at an aircraft carrying General Eisenhower on his way to the United States. There's a good museum, the Museu Carlos Machado, in Rua João Moreira, west of the redoubt. In the streets leading to the waterfront are shops selling island crafts, including pottery.

Ponta Delgada's city gates.

To the west of the island are the enchanting twin lakes within the Caldeira das Sete Cidades. In sunlight, one is blue, the other green – stemming from the tears, legend has it, of a princess forced to part from her shepherd lover. A half-day circuit might take you past pineapple plantations (visitors welcome) just north of the capital, on to Sete Cidades and the promontory of Ponta dos Mosteiras, eastwards to Capelas and its tobacco fields, and finally to the attractive town of Ribeira Grande (tea plantations, a good beach, several handsome churches). Just south, in the village of Santa Barbara, is the popular regional restaurant Cavalo Branco.

Heading west from Ponta Delgada, past sandy beaches, the potteries of Lagoa, the underwater diving centre (and hotel) at Caloura, is the attractive town of Vila Franca do Campo with three particularly lovely churches – São Miguel, São Pedro and Santo André. Just offshore, accessible from the pretty harbour, is the tiny island of Ilheu with a natural seawater swimming pool.

Northeast inland, past the crater lake of Lagoa das Furnas, is Furnas, meaning caverns. It still has the rich stink of volcanic sulphur. But here too is a lush botanical park, a mineral-heated lake you can swim in and a pleasant hotel and restaurant, the Terra Nostra. The dish of the house is *Cozido à Furnas* – meats and vegetables steamed in underground ovens. For a picnic, boil your own eggs in the hot springs beside the crater lake.

The island of **Santa Maria**, only 17 km by 9 km (10 miles by 5 miles), has peaceful fields, windmills, red-roofed whitewashed houses in an Algarve style (initial settlers came from the Algarve). Alone in the Azores group, the island is not volcanic, and its beaches therefore are a shining gold. Just north of the airport in Anjos is the (reconstructed) church, Igreja da Nossa Senhora dos Anjos, where Columbus once knelt in prayer. Today, the island has ambitious plans for a Free Trade Zone. The main town is **Vila do Porto**.

In the central group of islands, oval **Terceira**, 29 km by 17 km (18 miles by

Furnas, where the ground is hot enough to cook on.

10 miles), rich in history and culture, is distinguished by its notable capital, **Angra do Heroismo**, on UNESCO's world heritage list. Once the Azores capital, it won its heroic title from Queen Maria II, daughter of Dom Pedro IV, whose regency the island stoutly supported. Damaged by earthquake in 1980, the city is recovering. Its cathedral, several churches, castles and palaces are of considerable interest. A circuit of the island, which has a US military airbase, encompasses stunning views of sea, green patchwork fields, the vast Caldeira de Guilherme Moniz – with a 15 km (9 mile) perimeter the islands' largest crater – and wisps of steam from *furnas* far below. Terceira's loudest *festas* are around 24 June, day of São João (St John) and include *touradas à corda*, the running of rope-restrained bulls.

Beautiful and hardworking **São Jorge**, 56 km (35 miles) long by only 8 km (5 miles) wide, makes the solid and savoury *queijo da ilha* cheeses that are widely exported. Stunning scenery fills the eye in all directions – including,

Pico from Faial.

from the 1,053-metres (3,454-ft) high Pico da Esperança, views of all the central islands. Velas, with views across to Pico, is the place to stay.

Faial, facing Pico from the west, is possibly better known than any island: its harbour in **Horta** is port of call for virtually all trans-Atlantic sailors. The town is very pleasant, with good museums and churches. Dramatic contrast to island greenery and Horta's genial ambience is at Ponta dos Capelinhos where, in 1957-8, an undersea volcanic eruption rumbled and grumbled and left a vast, grim dune of black dust.

Graciosa is sweetly gracious with soft slopes, flowers and waterfalls. Yet it also has a volcanic heritage in its Caldeira do Enxofre where you may descend 182 stone steps to a cavern with a sulphurous lake. Shafts of light illuminate this *furna*, which is unique. The island surface, where you may see smiling farmers loading produce into cow-powered carts with solid wooden wheels, is infinitely more soothing.

Pico's peak is the main reason to visit **Pico** island, but a look round the island shows the flat rocks, the *mistérios*, the sturdy cottages carved from volcanic rock that are characteristic of the Azores and the sturdy people who live there. A small whaling museum, Museu dos Baleeiros, recalls the all-too-recent past. To climb the mountain (in summer only, and with a guide), contact the tourist office in Horta on Faial.

To the west, **Flores** (17 km by 12 km/ 10 miles by 7 miles) means flowers, and they flourish year-round. Among the sights: Fajãzinha village and waterfall, the basalt cliff of the Rocha das Bordões and Enxaréus grotto. And if you get to the islet of Monchique you have reached the westernmost point of Europe.

You can now fly to **Corvo** (6 km by 4 km/4 miles by 2 miles), although a fisherman might take you from Flores. The little island has some 400 inhabitants and a dozen or so cars, an *albergaria* where you can stay, a restaurant, O Caldeirão, even – in the quarters of the fire brigade – a bar-disco. The island's prime sight: a crater lake whose islets are like a map of the Azores.

INSIGHT GUIDES
Travel Tips

FOR THOSE WITH MORE THAN A PASSING INTEREST IN TIME...

Before you put your name down for a Patek Philippe watch *fig. 1*, there are a few basic things you might like to know, without knowing exactly whom to ask. In addressing such issues as accuracy, reliability and value for money, we would like to demonstrate why the watch we will make for you will be quite unlike any other watch currently produced.

"Punctuality", Louis XVIII was fond of saying, "is the politeness of kings."

We believe that in the matter of punctuality, we can rise to the occasion by making you a mechanical timepiece that will keep its rendezvous with the Gregorian calendar at the end of every century, omitting the leap-years in 2100, 2200 and 2300 and recording them in 2000 and 2400 *fig. 2*. Nevertheless, such a watch does need the occasional adjustment. Every 3333 years and 122 days you should remember to set it forward one day to the true time of the celestial clock. We suspect, however, that you are simply content to observe the politeness of kings. Be assured, therefore, that when you order your watch, we will be exploring for you the physical—if not the metaphysical—limits of precision.

Does everything have to depend on how much?

Consider, if you will, the motives of collectors who set record prices at auction to acquire a Patek Philippe. They may be paying for rarity, for looks or for micromechanical ingenuity. But we believe that behind each $500,000-plus

bid is the conviction that a Patek Philippe, even if 50 years old or older, can be expected to work perfectly for future generations.

In case your ambitions to own a Patek Philippe are somewhat discouraged by the scale of the sacrifice involved, may we hasten to point out that the watch we will make for you today will certainly be a technical improvement on the Pateks bought at auction? In keeping with our tradition of inventing new mechanical solutions for greater reliability and better time-keeping, we will bring to your watch innovations *fig. 3* inconceivable to our watchmakers who created the supreme wristwatches of 50 years ago *fig. 4*. At the same time, we will of course do our utmost to avoid placing undue strain on your financial resources.

Can it really be mine?

May we turn your thoughts to the day you take delivery of your watch? Sealed within its case is your watchmaker's tribute to the mysterious process of time. He has decorated each wheel with a chamfer carved into its hub and polished into a shining circle. Delicate ribbing flows over the plates and bridges of gold and rare alloys. Millimetric surfaces are bevelled and burnished to exactitudes measured in microns. Rubies are transformed into jewels that triumph over friction. And after many months—or even years—of work, your watchmaker stamps a small badge into the mainbridge of your watch. The Geneva Seal—the highest possible attestation of fine watchmaking *fig. 5*.

Looks that speak of inner grace *fig. 6*.

When you order your watch, you will no doubt like its outward appearance to reflect the harmony and elegance of the movement within. You may therefore find it helpful to know that we are uniquely able to cater for any special decorative needs you might like to express. For example, our engravers will delight in conjuring a subtle play of light and shadow on the gold case-back of one of our rare pocket-watches *fig. 7*. If you bring us your favourite picture, our enamellers will reproduce it in a brilliant miniature of hair-breadth detail *fig. 8*. The perfect execution of a double hobnail pattern on the bezel of a wristwatch is the pride of our casemakers and the satisfaction of our designers, while our chainsmiths will weave for you a rich brocade in gold *figs. 9 & 10*. May we also recommend the artistry of our goldsmiths and the experience of our lapidaries in the selection and setting of the finest gemstones? *figs. 11 & 12*.

How to enjoy your watch before you own it.

As you will appreciate, the very nature of our watches imposes a limit on the number we can make available. (The four Calibre 89 time-pieces we are now making will take up to nine years to complete). We cannot therefore promise instant gratification, but while you look forward to the day on which you take delivery of your Patek Philippe *fig. 13*, you will have the pleasure of reflecting that time is a universal and everlasting commodity, freely available to be enjoyed by all.

Should you require information on any particular Patek Philippe watch, or even on watchmaking in general, we would be delighted to reply to your letter of enquiry. And if you send us

fig. 1: *The classic face of Patek Philippe.*

fig. 4: *Complicated wristwatches circa 1930 (left) and 1990. The golden age of watchmaking will always be with us.*

fig. 6: *Your pleasure in owning a Patek Philippe is the purpose of those who made it for you.*

fig. 9: *Harmony of design is executed in a work of simplicity and perfection in a lady's Calatrava wristwatch.*

fig. 2: *One of the 33 complications of the Calibre 89 astronomical clock-watch is a satellite wheel that completes one revolution every 400 years.*

fig. 5: *The Geneva Seal is awarded only to watches which achieve the standards of horological purity laid down in the laws of Geneva. These rules define the supreme quality of watchmaking.*

fig. 7: *Arabesques come to life on a gold case-back.*

fig. 10: *The chainsmith's hands impart strength and delicacy to a tracery of gold.*

fig. 11: *Circles in gold: symbols of perfection in the making.*

fig. 3: *Recognized as the most advanced mechanical regulating device to date, Patek Philippe's Gyromax balance wheel demonstrates the equivalence of simplicity and precision.*

fig. 8: *An artist working six hours a day takes about four months to complete a miniature in enamel on the case of a pocket-watch.*

fig. 12: *The test of a master lapidary is his ability to express the splendour of precious gemstones.*

PATEK PHILIPPE
GENEVE

fig. 13: *The discreet sign of those who value their time.*

your card marked "book catalogue" we shall post you a catalogue of our publications. Patek Philippe, 41 rue du Rhône, 1204 Geneva, Switzerland. Tel. +41 22/310 03 66.

Reality check. Call home.

—— *AT&T USADirect® and World Connect®. The fast, easy way to call most anywhere.* ——

Take out AT&T Calling Card or your local calling card.** Lift phone. Dial AT&T Access Number for country you're calling from. Connect to English-speaking operator or voice prompt. Reach the States or over 200 countries. Talk. Say goodbye. Hang up. Resume vacation.

Austria*†††......................022-903-011	Luxembourg 0-800-0111	**Turkey*** 00-800-12277
Belgium* 0-800-100-10	**Netherlands***.................06-022-9111	**United Kingdom**..............0500-89-0011
Czech Republic* 00-420-00101	**Norway** 800-190-11	
Denmark 8001-0010	**Poland†◆¹** ....0◊010-480-0111	
Finland 9800-100-10	**Portugal†** 05017-1-288	
France...................................19-0011	**Romania*** 01-800-4288	
Germany............................0130-0010	**Russia*†(Moscow)**...............155-5042	
Greece*...........................00-800-1311	**Slovak Rep.*** 00-420-00101	
Hungary*.......................00◊-800-01111	**Spain●**............................900-99-00-11	
Ireland 1-800-550-000	**Sweden** 020-795-611	
Italy* 172-1011	**Switzerland*** 155-00-11	

AT&T
Your True Choice

**You can also call collect or use most U.S. local calling cards. Countries in bold face permit country-to-country calling in addition to calls to the U.S. World Connect® prices consist of USADirect® rates plus an additional charge based on the country you are calling from. Collect calling available to the U.S. only. *Public phones require deposit of coin or phone card. †May not be available from every phone. †††Public phones require local coin payment during call. ◆Not available from public phones. ◊Await second dial tone. ¹Dial 010-480-0111 from major Warsaw hotels. ●Calling available to most European countries. ©1995 AT&T.

For a free wallet sized card of all AT&T Access Numbers, call: 1-800-241-5555.

GETTING THERE

BY AIR

TAP Air Portugal is Portugal's national airline and it has wide international links. Moreover many major airlines make non-stop direct flights to Lisbon from capital cities in Europe and other continents. You may also, from some countries, fly directly to Oporto in the north and Faro in the south. Links with London are particularly good. There are several flights a week from New York, and from Boston. Between regular airlines and charter companies the choice is considerable – and ticket prices variable.

In Lisbon and Oporto, the international airports are on the outskirts of the city. Taxis can take you to the city centre. All have meters, and lists of charges for out-of-town journeys. In Lisbon, taxi drivers are entitled to charge an excess for luggage over 30 kg (66 lb). All three airports also have bus services to their city centres and good air links with each other. Across Portugal, too, are several small domestic airports.

BY RAIL

Nowhere in Portugal is yet linked to the superfast TGV system, but there's a busy international (and national) train service. A daily train makes the Paris–Lisbon run, and the Paris–Oporto route (from Paris to the Spanish border it's the same journey as Paris–Lisbon). Madrid–Lisbon (usually twice a day) takes around 10 hours. There are routes from northern Spain (Galicia) or southern Spain (Seville) into Portugal. These tend to be slow and time-consuming. Once *in* Portugal, you have a good fast north–south route (Oporto–Lisbon–Faro) as well as, if you care for them, slow, scenic rides, especially in the north. But you'll find on some routes trains have been replaced by bus services.

BY ROAD

Good roads link Portugal with its neighbour Spain at numerous border points. Main east–west routes to Lisbon are from Seville via Beja; from Badajos via Elvas; from Salamanca via Viseu. Journey time is two days from most of Europe. Driving from England, using the Channel ferries, allow three days; or, via Plymouth–Santander or Portsmouth–Bilbao, two.

There are drivers who boast of doing the journey faster, but don't try. Road accident figures are appallingly high.

TRAVEL ESSENTIALS

VISAS & PASSPORTS

European Community (EC) nationals may enter Portugal with a national identity card. Citizens of Great Britain (which issues no national card), Australians, Americans and Canadians need nothing more than a valid passport for a 3-month stay.

All non-EC visitors must show a valid passport to enter Portugal. On arrival, your passport will be stamped with a 60-day tourist visa. No one with a tourist visa is permitted to work in Portugal.

MONEY MATTERS

CURRENCY

The *escudo*, which is divided into 100 *centavos*, is the basic unit of currency. The coin with the smallest denomination is the 1 *escudo* piece; the largest is the 200 *escudo* coin (but this could change). 1,000 *escudos* is usually called a *conto*. Notes go from 500 to 10,000 *escudos*.

The symbol for the *escudo* is the same as for the dollar sign, but is written after the number of *escudos* (and before the number of *centavos*). Thus, 75$oo is 75 *escudos*; 75$5o is 75 *escudos* and 50 *centavos*.

CHANGING MONEY

There is neither a minimum nor a maximum for buying Portuguese currency. While you may want to buy a small amount of *escudos* before you leave home, you'll get a better exchange rate if you wait until you're in Portugal. Once you have bought *escudos*, however, it may be costly to re-exchange them for foreign currency. The best policy is to change money as you need it.

Money is best changed at banks (rather than hotels or travel agencies). Outside normal banking hours, there are currency exchanges at Lisbon's Santa Apolónia railway station as well as at the airports. Traveller's cheques entail paying a commission, but the rate is higher than for cash. You'll also see many cashpoints in cities and large towns. If you are driving out of town, you can use Visa cards (and sometimes charge cards) to buy fuel. A 100$oo tax is added to card purchases.

TRAVELLER'S CHEQUES AND CREDIT CARDS

Traveller's cheques are accepted in all banks; it is best not to spend them in stores, where, if they are accepted at all, you can be certain that they're being changed at a rate disadvantageous to you. Major credit cards can be used in the more expensive hotels, restaurants and shops.

WHAT TO BRING

Bring enough prescription medication to last through your stay, if only to avoid confusion with brand names and/or language. Toiletries and personal effects are all available locally, and are often much cheaper than in other countries. Common methods of contraception are available with the exception of contraceptive cream specifically for use with diaphragms.

Bring batteries with you: they'll be of better quality and longer lasting. Film and photographic equipment are probably cheaper outside the country.

What *not* to bring – drugs, which are illegal. Customs keep a close watch.

EXTENSION TO STAY

To obtain an extension, contact the *Serviço de Estrangeiros* (Foreigner's Service). In Lisbon this is located at Rua Conselheiro José Silvestre, 1°. Tel: (01) 7142328.

GETTING ACQUAINTED

GEOGRAPHY

Portugal is roughly the shape of a rectangle, bordered on the east and north by Spain and the west and south by the Atlantic Ocean. It is about 560km (360 miles) north–south and 220km (130 miles) east–west with a total area of 88,684 sq. km (34,216 sq. miles). A 840-km (522-mile) coastline borders the country.

The mountainous northern half of the country is more populated. The intense greens of the northern valleys, the winding riverbeds, and the mountain peaks (the highest of which is the Serra da Estrêla, at 2,000 metres (6,500 ft), make central and northern Portugal extraordinarily beautiful. But it's a matter of taste: there are those who prefer the great open spaces of the south.

Portugal is divided into eight principal regions: in the north and northwest are the rich wine lands of the Minho and the Douro valley; in the northeast the still remote Trás-os-Montes, (Behind the Mountains). The Beiras – the litoral, Alta and Baixa (upper and lower) – reach across north-central Portugal. In the middle area, Estramadura and the Ribatejo encompass the areas just above Lisbon. In the southern part of Portugal the dry, flat and and under-populated Alentejo (administratively divided into Alto and Baixo) occupies a third of all Portugal. The far south – the Algarve – is hilly, and boasts long stretches of beautiful beaches, most of which have been discovered by vacationers.

CLIMATE

Spring and summer are definitely the best times of year to visit Portugal. Especially in the north and central regions, including Lisbon, winters are rainy, and while not frigid, are surprisingly chilly. Furthermore, few homes, restaurants and inexpensive hotels are properly heated or insulated, so to keep warm you must have an adequate supply of sweaters. In the mountains it's even colder, and variable snow falls on the Serra da Estrêla between November and February (sometimes enough for ski enthusiasts, although conditions are far from ideal.) Winters are short, beginning November or December and ending in February or March, averaging 12°C/53°F. The weather starts getting warm in May and June and usually stays warm to very hot until September. The weather is changeable and difficult to predict from year to year: winters can be considerably shorter or longer; the rainy season heavy or light.

Nights can be cool even in summer, especially along the coast of north Lisbon. Along the western coast, the Atlantic tends to be cool until July (22°C/72°F). It warms up earlier along the southern coast. Summers in the Alentejo are extremely hot. The Algarve is moderate to baking hot in summer (31°C/88°F) and with a generous share of sun even in winter. It is far from hot, however, between November and April.

ETIQUETTE & TIPPING

The Portuguese are usually courteous. A few minutes to learn the basics, and liberal use of these thereafter, will serve you well. "*Obrigado*" (if you're a man) or "*obrigada*" (if you're a woman) is "thank you". "Please" is "*por favor*". To get someone's attention when you want service, say "*faz favor*" (pronounced "fash fuhVOOR"). Greet people with "*bon dia*" in the morning, "*boa tarde*" in the afternoon, and "*bom noite*" at night. Take leave in the same way.

Other hints: If you are invited to someone's house, it is polite to bring flowers for the hostess or a small toy if there are young children. Don't bring wine.

There are always orderly queues at bus stops. Be certain to respect them.

For some reason, stretching in public – on the street or at the table – is considered rude. Otherwise, use common sense and a smile.

A tip of 10 percent is sufficient in restaurants and for taxi drivers. Barbers and hairdressers receive the same or a little less. Theatre ushers get a tip of at least 20 *escudos*.

WEIGHTS & MEASURES

Portugal uses the metric system of weights and measures. While conversions are given below, here are a few tips:

- 100 grams of cheese or cold cuts is more than enough for a sandwich.
- Shellfish in restaurants is usually sold by the gram. About 300 grams is sufficient for one person.

To convert Celsius temperatures to Fahrenheit (roughly), multiply the Celsius temperature by 2 and add 32. Thus, 20°C x 2 + 32 = 72°F.

1 metre	=	1.09 yards
1 yard	=	0.92 metres
1 km	=	about 5/8 mile
1 mile	=	1.6 km
1 kilo	=	2.2 pounds
1 pound	=	about 0.46 kilo
1 litre	=	1.76 pints
1 pint	=	about 0.57 litre
1 cm	=	about 0.3 inch
1 inch	=	2.56 cm

ELECTRICITY

The electrical current in Portugal is 220 volts AC, with a Continental (round-prong) plug. If you plan to bring electrical appliances on you trip, bring a voltage converter as well.

BUSINESS HOURS

Most stores open for business Monday–Friday 9am–1pm, and from about 3–7pm. Stores are open on Saturday from 9am–1pm, and are closed Sunday and holidays. Major banks are open Monday–Friday 8.30am–3pm and are closed Saturday, Sunday and holidays.

HOLIDAYS

The following is a list of public holidays in Portugal. All banks and most stores are closed on these days.

1 January	New Year's Day
25 April	Anniversary of the Revolution
1 May	Labour Day
10 June	Portugal and Camões Day
13 June	Saint Anthony's Day (Lisbon only)
24 June	Saint John's Day (especially in Oporto)
15 August	Day of the Assumption
5 October	Republic Day
1 November	All Saints' Day
1 December	Restoration Day
8 December	Day of the Immaculate Conception
25 December	Christmas Day

Other holidays are Carnival (February or March), Good Friday (in April), Corpus Christi (in June), and local Saints' days.

COMMUNICATIONS

POSTAL SERVICES

Post offices open Monday–Friday 9am–6pm; smaller branches close for lunch from 12.30–2.30pm. In larger cities, the main branch may be open on weekends. Mail is delivered Monday to Friday; in the central business districts in the larger cities, it is delivered twice a day.

To buy stamps, stand in any line marked *selos*. To mail or receive packages, go to the line marked *encomendas*. Postage rates are currently (though they rise frequently) as follows:

- letters and postcards inside Portugal cost 42$oo for the first 20 grams, and usually take one to two days to arrive.
- letters for the first 20 grams and postcards cost 70$oo within the EC. These can take anywhere from two days to two weeks, depending on destination.
- letters and postcards to North America cost 130$oo for 20 grams. Letters take a week or so to the East Coast of the US and two country.

Be certain to write *Via Aerea* on all airmail items. To send large packages home when speed is not important, consider less expensive sea mail.

The Post Office also provides services such as

THOMAS COOK MASTERCARD TRAVELLERS CHEQUES...

...HOLIDAY ESSENTIALS

Travel money from the travel experts

THOMAS COOK MASTERCARD TRAVELLERS CHEQUES ARE
WIDELY AVAILABLE THROUGHOUT THE WORLD.

Don't be overcharged for overseas calls.

Save up to 70% on calls back to the U.S. with WorldPhone.®*

While traveling abroad, the last thing you need to worry about is being overcharged for international phone calls. Plan ahead and look into WorldPhone – the easy and affordable way for you to call the U.S. and country to country from a growing list of international locations.

Just dial 1-800-955-0925 to receive your free, handy, wallet-size WorldPhone Access Guide – your guide to saving as much as 70% on phone calls home.

When calling internationally, your WorldPhone Access Guide will allow you to:
- Avoid hotel surcharges and currency confusion
- Choose from four convenient billing options
- Talk with operators who speak your language
- Call from more than 90 countries
- Just dial and save – regardless of your long distance carrier back home

WorldPhone is easy. And there's nothing to join. So avoid overcharges when you're traveling overseas. Call for your free WorldPhone Access Guide today – before you travel.

Call 1-800-955-0925.

THE TOP 25 WORLDPHONE COUNTRY CODES.

COUNTRY	WORLDPHONE TOLL-FREE ACCESS #	COUNTRY	WORLDPHONE TOLL-FREE ACCESS #
Australia (CC)♦ To call using OPTUS■	008-5511-11	**Japan** (cont'd.) To call anywhere other than the U.S.	0055
To call using TELSTRA■	1-800-881-100	**Korea** (CC) To call using KT■	009-14
Belgium (CC)♦	0800-10012	To call using DACOM■	0039-12
China (CC)	108-12	Phone Booths+	Red button 03, then press*
(Available from most major cities) For a Mandarin-speaking Operator	108-17	Military Bases	550-2255
Dominican Republic	1-800-751-6624	**Mexico** ▲	95-800-674-7000
El Salvador♦	195	**Netherlands** (CC)♦	06-022-91-22
France (CC)♦	19▼-00-19	**Panama** Military Bases	108 2810-108
Germany (CC) (Limited availability in eastern Germany.)	0130-0012	**Philippines** (CC)♦ To call using PLDT■	105-14
Greece (CC)♦	00-800-1211	To call PHILCOM■	1026-12
Guatemala♦	189	For a Tagalog-speaking Operator	108-15
Haiti (CC)+	001-800-444-1234	**Saudi Arabia** (CC)+	1-800-11
Hong Kong (CC)	800-1121	**Singapore**	8000-112-112
India (CC) (Available from most major cities)	000-127	**Spain** (CC)	900-99-0014
Israel (CC)	177-150-2727	**Switzerland** (CC)♦	155-0222
Italy (CC)♦	172-1022	**United Kingdom** (CC) To call using BT ■	0800-89-0222
Japan♦ To call to the U.S. using KDD■	0039-121	To call using MERCURY■	0500-89-0222
To call to the U.S. using IDC■	0066-55-121		

(CC) Country-to-country calling available. May not be available to/from all international locations. Certain restrictions apply.

+ Limited availability.

▼ Wait for second dial tone.

▲ Rate depends on call origin in Mexico.

■ International communications carrier.

♦ Public phones may require deposit of coin or phone card for dial tone.

WORLDPHONE℠ From MCI

Let it take you around the world.

* Savings are based on typical hotel charges for calls back to the U.S. Your savings may vary depending upon originating country and hotel, time of day and length of call. All rates effective 7/94.

express mail (*Exprès: Correio Azul Internacional*), postal money orders (*vales*), general delivery (*posta restante*), registered mail (*registos*), insurance on packages (*seguro*), and telegraph, telephone and fax services (*see below*).

TELEPHONE

There are plenty of pay phones in most cities; the problem is finding newer phones, which are easiest to use. Newer phones equipped for international calls are located in city centres. Instructions are written in English and other major languages. The older phones are close to incomprehensible no matter what language you speak. You'll need patience and good luck, as well as a large supply of small coins.

If you lack the proper change, you can make calls – international and local – from the post offices. Go to the window for a cabin assignment and pay when the call is finished. In Lisbon there is also a phone office in the Rossio, open everyday from 9am–11pm; in Oporto, there is one in Praça da Liberdade (same hours).

Many village stores and bars have metered telephones. Phone first, pay later, but be prepared to pay more than the rate for pay phone or post office calls. Calls made from hotels are higher still.

To reach an English-speaking international operator, dial 098 (intercontinental service) or 099 (European service). To call direct to the US or Canada, dial 097–1, plus the area code and phone number. For the UK, dial 00–44 plus the full phone number. Dial slowly. For US phone credit card holders the major access numbers are as follows: AT&T Tel: 05017–1288. MCI Tel: 05017–1234, Sprint Tel: 05017–1877.

Telephone numbers in Portugal change with infuriating frequency. To get a current number, dial 118 – but, be warned. That could change, too.

TELEGRAMS

You may place telegrams by phone (tel: 10) or from the Post Office. The rates are high – for example: to the US: 1,404\$oo plus 73\$5o per word.

Another way to make fast contact outside Portugal is to use the fax/telecopy machines which operate in all major post offices. You can write (or draw) your message, which is charged per page, and if you wait to watch it go, it's there instantaneously. Fax costs to the EC: first page – 1,900\$oo; and 1,000\$oo for each following page; to the US and Canada: first page – 2,750\$oo, and 1,800\$oo per page thereafter. (If you make an arrangement with a private firm the cost is a great deal less.)

EMERGENCIES

SECURITY & CRIME

Police or ambulance emergency: Tel: 115 (freephone).
Fire brigade: tel: 3422222.
Police station: In the event of theft report it to the police within 24 hours in order to reclaim on insurance. The Lisbon station most used to dealing with foreigners' problems is in the Rua Capelo in the Bairro Alto, to the left of the São Carlos opera house as you face it.
Lost property: Anjos police station in Lisbon, Rua dos Anjos, 56 (Anjos Metro). For property left on buses, go to the Carris office at the top of the Santa Justa lift, from 3–7pm.

MEDICAL CARE & CHEMISTS

Emergency ambulance: tel: 115 (freephone).
Ambulance (Portuguese Red Cross): tel: 3017777.
Poisons unit: tel: 7950143.
Linha Aberta (for information of drug use and abuse): tel: 7267766.
Linha Sida (AIDS line): tel: 7599943.

There are half a dozen large **hospitals** in Lisbon and a central telephone number: 860131/873131. The following have casualty departments:
Hospital de la Cruz Vermelha: Rua Duarte Galvão 54 (behind the zoo). Tel: 783003/786171.
Hospital de Santa Maria, Avenida Prof Egas Moniz (in the Areeiro district to the northeast). Tel: 775171/775191.
The British Hospital, Rua Saraiva de Carvalho (notoriously overlooking the British cemetery near the Jardim de Estrêla). Tel: 602020/603785. It has no casualty department, but takes outpatients and may be able to help as all staff speak English.
Chemists: When closed, all chemists (*Farmácias*) have a list on their doors highlighting the nearest open chemist. Newspapers also publish a list of chemists open late each day.

GETTING AROUND

BY AIR

TAP Air Portugal is the national airline. There is daily service between Lisbon and Oporto, Faro and Covilhã. Flights run several times weekly between Lisbon and Bragança, and Lisbon and Portimão.

BY RAIL

Trains in Portugal range from the comfortable and speedy *rápidos* to the painfully slow *regionais*. Generally the most efficient routes are the Lisbon-Coimbra-Oporto and the Lisbon-Algarve lines.

Rápidos, which run only on the two routes mentioned above, are quick and punctual and cost more. Some *rápidos* have first-class carriages only; others have a very comfortable second-class as well. Next in line are the *directos*, which make more stops and travel more slowly. These have both first- and second-class compartments; second-class here is likely to be less comfortable than in the *rápidos*. Finally, the *semi-directos* and especially the *regionais* seem to stop every few feet and take longer than one could have believed possible. On *directos*, *semi-directos*, and *regionais*, second-class seats are not assigned, and CP (Caminhos de Ferro Portugueses, the train company) has no qualms about issuing more tickets than seats, if the need arises. If you want to be certain of a seat, board early.

On rural routes, trains are almost always regional. Furthermore, to reach more remote – or even not-so-remote – destinations, it may be necessary to change trains, and schedules are seldom coordinated. Except for the *rápidos*, which are punctual, leave yourself plenty of time between transfers, as trains are often late.

There are four train stations in Lisbon. Cais do Sodré and Rossio are commuter stations. International and long distance trains with northern and eastern destinations leave from Santa Apolónia Station, just to the east of Praça do Comércio. For trains to the Alentejo and the Algarve, take a ferry boat at the Terreiro do Paço station (the popular name of the Praça do Comércio). The price of the boat is included in the train ticket, which you can buy at the boat station. Just be certain to buy the right one; there are two boat stations next to each other. For the train link-up, use the eastern station, i.e. the one to the left as you face the river.

Oporto and Coimbra each have two train stations. Oporto's São Bento and Coimbra A are located in the respective town centres. Most long-distance trains, however, arrive and leave from Oporto's Campanhã station and Coimbra B station, outside the cities. There is a shuttle service between São Bento and Campanhã and between Coimbra A and B.

BY ROAD

Buses: Bus networks are private but many systems have adapted their name from the former Rodoviária Nacional so that, for example, the main bus company in the far north is now Rodoviária Entre Douro e Minho. Only the Algarve bus company dropped the word Rodoviária, calling itself Eva Transportes. Outside the routes between major cities, the bus is often faster than the train, and the bus system is certainly more extensive. This is particularly true in the north and between the smaller towns in the Algarve and Alentejo.

There are quite a few private bus lines which tend to specialise in particular routes or areas of the country. Often, they have more direct routes to smaller towns. Many travel agencies can book tickets on a private line, or may even run their own.

PUBLIC TRANSPORT

LISBON

Trains: There are four train stations in Lisbon. Commuter trains to Cascais (stopping in Oeiras, Carcavelos, Estoril and other towns along the western coast) depart from Cais do Sodré, west of the Praça do Comércio. Depending on the day of the week and the time of day, trains depart every 15 to 20 minutes; they arrive in Cascais (the end of the line) between 33–40 minutes later (again depending on the time of day).

Trains to the northwestern suburbs, including Sintra, leave from the Rossio station at 15-minute intervals. The trip to Sintra takes about 45 minutes. This station houses an information centre for national services. For more information about long distance trains, *see "Domestic Transport"*.

Buses/Trams: CARRIS, the city bus company, maintains an extensive system of buses, trams (*eléctricos*) and funiculars. Bus stops are clearly marked by signposts or shelters. All stops display a diagrammatical map of the bus route; many have a map of the entire city system.

The CARRIS information kiosks scattered throughout the city provide information about buses and trams and sell tickets and passes. If you're lucky, they may even have city bus maps in stock. Two of the most convenient kiosks are located in Praça da Figueira, near the Rossio, and near Eduardo VII park (the Marquês de Pombal statue).

An alternative for tourists is to buy a three-day or seven-day tourist pass, which gives unlimited access during the period of validity. If you have no pass, you may pay a flat rate when you board. Less expensive are the pre-paid *modules* that you can buy in packs of 20 from the kiosks. It is unwise to board the bus without paying, as ticket inspectors appear from time to time and the fine is steep.

Pre-World War I trams ply the smaller, steeper streets where buses are unable to navigate the narrow passages. Some of them are quite beautiful, inside and out; they are slower and cheaper than the buses and are a good way to see the city.

CARRIS also runs two funiculars and an elevator. The Santa Justa *elevador*, located near the Rossio, leads to the Bairro Alto. One funicular climbs and descends the steep Calçada da Gloria from Praça dos Restauradores; the other is in São Bento. Pay the driver only after boarding the funicular.

Metro: The Metro, with 25 stops, is principally useful for travel in the central zone of the city. The line is V-shaped, with the point of the "V" in the Rossio, and the two arms stretching up Avenida da Liberdade and Avenida Almirante Reis. Though limited, the system is easy to use.

A tourist pass is valid on the Metro. You can also buy books of 10 tickets or single tickets. You must validate your ticket at the machines next to the ticket booths. As with buses, it is inadvisable to try to ride for free.

OPORTO & COIMBRA

Buses/Trams: Oporto's public transportation is limited to buses and trams – the trams to be phased out – and Coimbra's to electric buses. Both these systems run on the same principal as Lisbon's system: you may either pay the driver a flat fee, or buy prepaid modules and validate the number required by the length of the journey. You may buy *modules* and get information from bus company kiosks in both Oporto and Coimbra.

Taxis: In all of Portugal's cities, taxis are plentiful and cheap. The great majority of them are black with green roofs. In the city, they charge a standard meter fare, with no additions for extra passengers. (They carry as many as four people.) Outside city limits, the driver may run on the meter or charge a flat rate, and he or she is entitled to charge for the return fare (even if you don't take it). Tip taxi drivers about 10 percent.

PRIVATE TRANSPORT

Car Rentals: Portugal is a trying place for drivers. In the cities, traffic is heavy, road construction hinders movement, parking is close to impossible, and cars and pedestrians regularly ignore both the rules of the road and plain common sense.

Outside cities, conditions vary enormously – from broad north–south and east–west highways (a network of mainly new roads numbered IP1 to IP8) – to smaller roads, all too often in poor condition.

Many of these are narrow, making it difficult to pass slow-moving rural trucks and tractors. On winding mountain roads, driving takes skill and concentration. Portugal's accident rate is high: drivers too often pass at the last minute on two-lane highways. And wherever you are, fuel is expensive.

If you're determined to drive, the Yellow Pages are full of car rental firms. The big two – Hertz and Avis – are there, along with many other smaller (and often cheaper) companies. With Hertz and Avis, you can book a car before leaving home and this, inexplicably, is often less expensive.

It's advisable to shop around, as costs vary and many agencies offer special packages from time to time. There are various options to choose from, including having a driver. The type of car you can hire ranges from the tiny Mini to much larger vehicles. For more information look up car rentals in the local Yellow Pages under *Automóveis – Aluguer com e sem Condutor*. Most companies employ staff that speak English.

To rent a car in Portugal, most agencies require you to be at least 21 years old and to have had a valid driver's license for a minimum of one year. An international license is not necessary.

WHERE TO STAY

Accommodation ranges from luxury hotels to private rooms. Recently, the middle range of reasonably-priced hotels has been considerably expanded with new Portuguese hotels and foreign investment – the French Ibis chain, for example, has opened hotels in several locations. The *pousadas*, state-run inns, remain stylish and comfortable accommodation, some in historic castles, usually with excellent regional food, across the country (*see* "*Pousadas and Manor Houses*", and for full contact details consult the listings below). *Turismo no espaço rural* – private accommodation that ranges from classically elegant manor houses to pretty converted mills – is coming into its own.

HOTELS

The Portuguese tourist office divides accommodation into several categories: hotels, residentials and pensions are the most popular.

Hotels offer amenities such as restaurants and room service. All rooms have bathrooms. Hotels are rated from 1–5-stars: 5-stars denote a luxury hotel;

4-stars, while not luxury, is pretty close; 3-star hotels are good value but sometimes slightly run-down; 1- and 2-star hotels are often depressing.

The list below includes a small sample of hotels in Portugal. Remember, however, that you'll have difficulty finding a decent room in July and August if you haven't made a reservation. The following are listed by area, beginning from the north and moving towards the south.

LISBON

☆☆☆☆☆
Hotel Alfa Lisboa, Avenida Columbano Bordalo Pinheiro, 1000 Lisboa. Tel: (01) 7262121, fax: (01) 72673031. Very modern; a bit out of the way.
Hotel Altis, Rua Castilho, 11, 1200 Lisboa. Tel: (01) 522496, fax: (01) 548696. Amenities include indoor pool and sauna.
Hotel Avenida Palace, Rua Primeiro de Dezembro, 123, 1200 Lisboa. Tel: (01) 3460151, fax: (01) 3422884. Smack in the old centre of town, between the Rossio and Praça dos Restauradores. Grandly 19th century.
Hotel da Lapa, Rue do Pan da Baudeira, 4, 1200 Lisboa. Tel: (01) 390005, fax: (01) 3950665. Glamorously restored 19th-century mansion in the best residential quarter.
Hotel Lisboa Sheraton, Rua Latino Coelho, 1, 1000 Lisboa. Tel: (01) 575757, fax: (01) 547164. Good for short stays and business trips, but there are better hotels for the price.
Hotel Meridien, Rua Castilho, 149, 1000 Lisboa. Tel: (01) 690900, fax: (01) 693231. Elegant. Overlooking the park.
Hotel Ritz, Rua Rodrigo Fonseca, 88, 1000 Lisboa. Tel: (01) 692020, fax: (01) 691783. High-quality rooms and service. Overlooking Eduardo VII Park. The top of the luxury hotels.
Hotel Tivoli, Avenida da Liberdade, 185, 1200 Lisboa. Tel: (01) 530181 or 521101, fax: (01) 579461. Big, handsome and handy to all parts of town. Friendly service.

☆☆☆☆
Hotel Diplomático, Rua Castilho, 74, 1200 Lisboa. Tel: (01) 3562041, fax: (01) 522155. Centrally located.
Hotel Lisboa Plaza, Travessa do Salitre, 7, 1200 Lisboa. Tel: (01) 3463922, fax: (01) 3471630. Just off Avenida da Liberdade. Interior very attractively decorated.
Hotel Principe Real, Rua da Alegria, 53, 1200 Lisboa. Tel: (01) 3460116, fax: (01) 3422104. Small and quiet; a few blocks from Avenida da Liberdade in an interesting area below the Bairro Alto.
Hotel Tivoli Jardim, Rua Julio C. Machado, 7, 1200 Lisboa. Tel: (01) 3539971, fax: (01) 3556566. Run by the same company, the 5-star Tivoli, right next door.

☆☆☆
Hotel Botânico, Rue Mãe d'Ague, 16–20, 1200 Lisboa. Tel: (01) 3420241, fax: (01) 3420125. Between the Bairro Alto and the Avenida da Liberdade; pleasant and comfortable.
Hotel Britania, Rua Rodrigues Sampaio, 17, 1100 Lisboa. Tel: (01) 3155016, fax: (01) 3155021. Clean, if slightly shabby, and on a nice street near Avenida da Liberdade but far from the noise.
Hotel Dom Carlos, Avenida Duque de Loulé, 121, 1000 Lisboa. Tel: (01) 539071, fax: (01) 3520721. On a busy, centrally located street.
Hotel Eduardo VII, Avenida Fontes Pereira de Melo, 5–C, 1000 Lisboa. Tel: (01) 530141, fax: (01) 533879. Next to the park of the same name. A good view from the restaurant and the front rooms. Slightly dark, but clean.
Hotel Flamingo, Rua Castilho, 41, 1200 Lisboa. Tel: (01) 3862191, fax: (01) 3521216. Near the Marquês de Pombal, but on a quieter street.
Hotel Miraparque, Avenida Sidónio Pais, 12, 1000 Lisboa. Tel: (01) 578087, fax: (01) 578920. Decent rooms; poor service; a good location on a quiet street overlooking the park.
Hotel Rex, Rua Castilho, 169, 1000 Lisboa. Tel: (01) 3882161, fax: (01) 687581. For those who can't afford the Ritz or the Meridian, the Rex is a nice place next door.

GUIMARÃES

☆☆☆☆
Estalagem São Pedro, Avenida Narciso Ferreira, Riba de Ave. Tel: (052) 931338, fax: (052) 932301.
Hotel Fundador Dom Pedro, Avenida Dom Afonso Henriques, 740. Tel: (053) 513781, fax: (053) 513786.

BRAGANÇA

☆☆☆☆
Albergaria Santa Isabel, Rua Alexandre Herculano, 67. Tel: (073) 22427.

☆☆☆
Hotel Bragança, Avenida Dr Sá Carneiro. Tel: (073) 331578, fax: (073) 331242.

OPORTO

☆☆☆☆☆
Hotel Infante de Sagres, Praça Filipa Lencastre, 62, 4000 Oporto. Tel: (02) 2008101, fax: (02) 314937. Near the central square.
Hotel Meridien, Avenida da Boavista, 1466, 4100 Oporto. Tel: (02) 6001913/6001921, fax: (02) 6002031. A little bit farther out than the above.
Hotel Porto Atlantico, Rua Afonso Lopes Viera, 66, 4100 Oporto. Tel: (02) 694941, fax: (02) 6067452.
Hotel Porto Sheraton, Avenida da Boavista, 1269, 4100 Oporto. Tel: (02) 6068822, fax: (02) 6006397.

☆☆☆☆
Grande Hotel da Batalha, Praça da Batalha, 116, 4000 Oporto. Tel: (02) 2000571, fax: (02) 2002468. Near the centre.
Hotel Castor, Rua Doze Casas, 17, 4000 Oporto. Tel: (02) 570014, fax: (02) 566076.
Hotel Dom Henrique, Rua Guedes Azevedo, 179, 4000 Oporto. Tel: (02) 2005755, fax: (02) 2019451.
Hotel Inca, Praça Coronel Pacheco, 50, 4000 Oporto. Tel: (02) 2084151.
Hotel Ipanema, Rua do Campo Alegre, 156/174, 4100 Oporto. Tel: (02) 6068061, fax: (02) 6063339.
Hotel Porto Boega, Rua do Amial, 607, 4200 Oporto. Tel: (02) 825045, fax: (02) 825220.
Residencial Castelo Santa Catarina, Rua Santa Catarina, 1347, 4000 Oporto. Tel: (02) 495599.
Residencial Rex, Praça da Republica, 117, 4000 Oporto. Tel: (02) 2004548, fax: (02) 2083002. In the centre of town.

☆☆☆
Grande Hotel do Porto, Rua Santa Catarina, 197, 4000 Oporto. Tel: (02) 2008176/2005741, fax: (02) 311061. A few blocks east of the central square.
Hotel Corcel, Rua de Camões, 135, 4000 Oporto. Tel: (02) 2080268, fax: (02) 7622784. Just north of the town centre.
Hotel do Império, Praça da Batalha, 127, 4000 Oporto. Tel: (02) 2006861, fax: (02) 2006009. In the centre of town.
Hotel Tuela, Arq. Marques da Silva, 200, 4100 Oporto. Tel: (02) 6004747, fax: (02) 25216.
Pensaõ-Residencial Pão de Açúcar, Rua do Almada, 262, 4000 Oporto. Tel: (02) 2002425. A large, clean, standard place right in the middle of town.

☆☆
Hotel Ibis, Afurada – 4400 V.N. Gaia, Vila Nova de Gaia. Tel: (02) 7720772, fax: (02) 7720788. Easy access from motorway; one of an international chain.

AVEIRO

☆☆☆
Hotel Afonso V, Rua Dr Manuel das Neves, 65, 3800 Aveiro. Tel: (034) 25191, fax: (034) 381111. A few blocks from the centre.
Hotel Imperial, Rua Dr Nascimento Leitão, 3800 Aveiro. Tel: (034) 22141, fax: (034) 24148. Very modern and central.
Hotel Pomba Branca, Rua Luís Gomes de Carvalho, 23, 3800 Aveiro. Tel: (034) 381992, fax: (034) 381844. Charming converted villa near town centre.
Pensão Residencial Estrêla, Rua José Estevão, 4, 3800 Aveiro. Tel: (034) 23818. Across from the Arcada Hotel.

☆☆
Hotel Arcada, Rua Viana do Castelo, 4, 3800 Aveiro. Tel: (034) 23001. A bit drab, but very centrally located along the canal.

COIMBRA

☆☆☆☆
Hotel Tivoli Coimbra, Rua João Machado, 4e5, 3000 Coimbra. Tel: (039) 26934, fax: (039) 26827. On the western outskirts, new and very comfortable.

☆☆☆
Hotel Astória, Avenida Emídio Navarro, 21, 3000 Coimbra. Tel: (039) 22055, fax: (039) 22057. Belle Epoque, river front, across from tourist office.
Hotel Bragança, Largo das Ameias, 10, 3000 Coimbra. Tel: (039) 22171/2/3, fax: (039) 36135. Near Coimbra A train station.
Hotel Dom Luís, Quinta da Várzea, Santa Clara, 3000 Coimbra. Tel: (039) 442510, fax: (039) 813196. Tall, modern, on southern bank of the Mondego River with grand view of Coimbra.
Hotel Oslo, Avenida Fernão de Magalhães, 23, 3000 Coimbra. Tel: (039) 29071. Behind the Bragança.

☆☆
Pensão Rivoli, Praça do Comércio, 27, 3000 Coimbra. Tel: (039) 25550. Centrally located. A beautiful courtyard, friendly management; slightly run-down.

RESIDENTIALS & PENSIONS

Residentials offer fewer amenities than hotels, and are rated from 1–4-stars. Pensions, usually smaller than residentials, are also rated from 1–4-stars. Despite being less expensive and "lower" on the scale than hotels, many residentials and pensions are lovely and clean and offer a more personal atmosphere than the larger hotels.

LISBON

☆☆☆☆
Albergaria Senhora do Monte, Calçada do Monte, 39, 1100 Lisboa. Tel: (01) 8866002, fax: (01) 877783. Beautiful views overlooking São Jorge castle, Alfama and down to and across the Tejo River.
Residencia Roma, Travessa da Gloria, 22–A, 1200 Lisboa. Telephone and fax: (01) 3460557. Many of the amenities of a hotel; private baths and TVs in every room. Don't let the shabby exterior faze you; the inside is well kept and very clean.
York House—Residencia Inglesa, Rua Janelas Verdes, 32, 1200 Lisboa. Tel: (01) 3962435 or 3968143, fax: (01) 3972791. In a class by itself: comfort and charm combined. The great favourite of, among others, Graham Greene. In an interesting neighbourhood, about 15 minutes by bus from the Rossio. Reserve well in advance. The annex is down the street at number 47.

Pensão Ninho das Aguias, Costa do Castelo, 74, 1100 Lisboa. Tel: (01) 8867008. One of the few pensions in the Alfama. Come for the charm, if not the comfort. Some rooms have great views; others none at all. Some people love it; others don't.
Residenciae Dom João, Rua José Estevão, 43, 1100 Lisboa. Tel: (01) 524171, fax: (01) 3524569. In quiet, residential neighbourhood, a bit off the beaten track, but only a 15-minute walk to the Praça Marquês de Pombal.

☆☆
Residenciae Florescente, Rua das Portas de Santo Antão, 99, 1100 Lisboa. Tel: (01) 3426609, fax: (01) 3427733. Simple and inexpensive. Tiled hallways and bright, clean rooms, some with full baths. Very centrally located, near Restauradores Square.

WEST COAST – ALENTEJO

Hotel Castelo de Milfontes, Largo Brito Pais, 7555 Vila Nova de Milfontes. Tel: (083) 96108.

ÉVORA

Évora is small enough so that nothing is far from the city centre. The *pousada* (*see following list*) has the best location, right between the Cathedral and the Temple of Diana.

☆☆☆☆
Albergaria Vitória, Rua Diana de Liz, 7000 Évora. Tel: (066) 27174, fax: (066) 20974.
Estalagem Monte das Flores, Monte das Flores, 7000 Évora. Tel: (066) 25490; 25018, fax: (066) 27564.
Hotel Convento de São Paulo, Aldeia da Serra, 7170 Redondo. Tel: (066) 999100, fax: (066) 999104. Gorgeous furnishings, beautiful gardens, in a national forest.
Residenciae Riviera, Rua 5 de Outubro, 49, 7000 Évora. Tel: (066) 23304, fax: (066) 20467.

☆☆☆
Hotel Planicie, Largo de Àlvaro Velho, 40, 7000 Évora. Tel: (066) 24026, fax: (066) 29880.
Residenciae Diana, Rua Diogo Cão, 2, 7000 Évora. Tel: (066) 22008, fax: (066) 743101. A nice little place near the Cathedral.
Residenciae O Eborense, Largo da Misericórdia, 1, 7000 Évora. Tel: (066) 22031, fax: (066) 742367. In a converted mansion.

☆☆
Hotel Santa Clara, Travessa da Milheira, 19, 7000 Évora. Tel: (066) 24141, fax: (066) 26544. Good value, very central.

THE ALGARVE

☆☆☆☆☆
Hotel Atlantis Vilamoura, Apartado 210, 8125 Vilamoura. Tel: (089) 389977, fax: (089) 389962.
Hotel Dona Filipa, Vale do Lobo, 8136 Almancil. Tel: (089) 394141, fax: (089) 394288.

☆☆☆☆
Estalagem Aeromar, Praia de Faro, 8000 Faro. Tel: (089) 823542. *Not* in Faro but nearer the airport and on the beach.
Hotel Dom Pedro Marina, 8125 Vilamoura. Tel: (089) 389802, fax: (089) 313270.
Hotel Eva, Avenida da República, 7000 Faro. Tel: (089) 803354, fax: (089) 802304. Make sure your room overlooks the harbour, *not* the street.
Residencial Samé, Rua do Bocage, 66, 8000 Faro. Tel: (89) 824375, fax: (089) 804166. In the centre of town.

☆☆☆
Hotel Faro, Praça Dom Francisco Gomes, 8000 Faro. Tel: (089) 803276, fax: (089) 803546.

Hotel Algarve, Avenida Tomás Cabreira, Praia da Rocha, 8500 Portimão. Tel: (082) 415001, fax: (082) 415999. Grand hotel on gorgeous beach.
Hotel Bela Vista, Avenida Tomás Cabreira, Praia da Rocha 8500 Portimão. Tel: (082) 24055, fax: (082) 415369. Small, stylish, on the beach.

LAGOS & WESTERN ALGARVE

☆☆☆☆
Albergaria Caza de São Gonçalo, Rua Cándido dos Reis, 73, 8600 Lagos. Tel: (082) 762171, fax: (082) 763927. On a street within old Lagos.
Hotel de Lagos, Rua Nova da Aldeia, 83, 8600 Lagos. Tel: (082) 769967, fax: (082) 769920. Short walk from town centre, with pool, beach club and tennis courts.
Hotel Golfinho, Praia Dona Ana, 8600 Lagos. Tel: (082) 769900, fax: (082) 769999. Somewhat dated, but well set among coves and beaches.

☆☆☆
Hotel da Meia Praia, Meia Praia, 8600 Lagos. Tel: (082) 76200. On the Meia Praia beach near Lagos.
Hotel Riomar, Rua Cándido dos Reis, 83, 8600 Lagos. Tel: (082) 76309. Centre of town.

Loulé Jardim Hotel, Largo Manuel Arriaga, 8100 Loulé. Tel: (089) 413092, fax: (089) 63177. Converted town house with swiming pool.

SAGRES

There are many private rooms to let in Sagres – just ask *Turismo* or look for signs in the windows. Aside from these and the *pousada*, there's the 3-star **Hotel**

da Baleeira, Baleeira, 8650 Sagres, Vila do Bispo. Tel: (082) 64212, fax: (082) 64425. It has ocean views, a seawater swimming pool and tennis court.

POUSADAS

The government-run network of *pousadas* provides first-class accommodation in historic castles, palaces and monasteries, in attractive country houses or lodges (the older, grander buildings are the most expensive) in specially built sites. The following is a list of *pousadas* by area. For reservations, contact the *pousadas* directly, a travel agent or ENATUR, Avenida Santa Joana Princesa, 10, 1700 Lisboa. Tel: (01) 8481221 or 8489078, fax: (01) 805846.

DOURO, MINHO & TRÁS-OS-MONTES

Pousada Barão Forrester, 5070 Alijó. Tel: (059) 959215, fax: (059) 959 304. Near Vila Real.
Pousada Dom Dinis, 4920 Vila Nova da Cerveira. Tel: (051) 795601, fax: (051) 795604. North of Viana do Castelo. Inside the walls of the village's old castle.
Pousada Santa Catarina, 5210 Miranda do Douro. Tel: (073) 42255, fax: (073) 42665. Overlooking the river.
Pousada Santa Maria de Oliveira, Apartado 101, 4800 Guimarães. Tel: (053) 514157, fax: (053) 514204.
Pousada Santa Marinha, 4800 Guimarães. Tel: (053) 514453, fax: (053) 514459. Area showcase *pousada*, in an exquisitely renovated monastery.
Pousada São Bartolomeu, 5300 Bragança. Tel: (073) 22493, fax: (073) 22453.
Pousada São Bento, 4850 Caniçada. Tel: (053) 647190, fax: (053) 647867.
Pousada São Gonçalo, 4600 Amarante. Tel: (055) 461113, fax: (055) 461353. East of Oporto.
Pousada São Teotónio, 4930 Valença do Minho. Tel: (051) 824242, fax: (051) 824397. North of Viana do Castelo, on the border with Galicia.p

NORTH-CENTRAL PORTUGAL

Pousada do Castelo, 2510 Obidos. Tel: (062) 959105, fax: (062) 959148. Small but lovely, part of the original castle.
Pousada Mestre Afonso Domingues, 2440 Batalha. Tel: (044) 96260. Right next to the famous abbey.
Pousada Ria, 3870 Murtosa. Tel: (034) 48332, fax: (034) 48333. Near Aveiro, right on the lagoon.
Pousada Santa Barbara, 3400 Oliveira do Hospital. Tel: (038) 52252, fax: (038) 50545. Between Coimbra and the Serra da Estrêla.
Pousada Santa Maria, 7330 Marvão. Tel: (045) 93201, fax: (045) 93202. Near Portalegre, within walled town with border fortress.
Pousada Santo António, Serém, 3750 Águeda. Tel: (034) 523230, fax: (034) 523192. Between Aveiro and Coimbra.

Pousada São Jeronimo, 3475 Caramulo. Tel: (032) 861291. Between Viseu and Aveiro. Small, a staging post with a swimming pool.
Pousada São Lourenço, 6260 Manteigas. Tel: (075) 982450, fax: (075) 981664. High in the Serra da Estrêla.
Pousada São Pedro, Castelo do Bode, 2300 Tomar. Tel: (049) 381175/381159, fax: (049) 381176. Overlooking dam near Tomar.
Pousada Senhora das Neves, 6350 Almeida. Tel: (071) 54283, fax: (071) 54320. East of the Serra da Estrêla, northwest of Guarda within small fortress town.

SOUTHERN PORTUGAL

Pousada de Palmela, 2950 Palmela. Tel: (01) 2351226, fax: (01) 2330440. Near Setúbal. Spectacularly set, inside castle walls.
Pousada de São Miguel, 7470 Sousel. Tel: (068) 52194. Small, country house style, aims for hunting parties.
Pousada do Infante, 8650 Sagres. Tel: (082) 64222, fax: (082) 64225. Each room has a balcony overlooking pool and the ocean.
Pousada dos Lóios, 7000 Évora. Tel: (066) 24051, fax: (066) 27248. Former monastery. Book early.
Pousada Rainha Santa Isabel, 7100 Estremoz. Tel: (068) 22618, fax: (068) 23982. Very dramatic, in former castle.
Pousada Santa Clara, Santa Clara-a-Velha. Tel: (083) 98250, fax: (083) 98402. On Algarve-Alentejo border, overlooking dam lake.
Pousada Santa Luzia, 7350 Elvas. Tel: (068) 622194, fax: (068) 622127. Close to main road; good restaurant.
Pousada São Bras, 8150 São Bras de Alportel. Tel: (089) 842305, fax: (089) 841726. North of Faro.
Pousada São Filipe, 2900 Setúbal. Tel: (065) 523844, fax: (065) 532538. In an old fortress, overlooking the harbour.
Pousada São Gens, 7830 Serpa. Tel: (084) 53724, fax: (084) 533337. East of Beja.
Pousada São Tiago, 7540 Santiago do Cacém. Tel: (069) 22459. Just east of Sines.
Pousada Vale do Gaio, Alcacer do Sal, 7595 Torrão. Tel: (065) 669610. Southeast of Setúbal, small, beside a lake.

MANOR HOUSES

An alternative to hotels, residentials, pensions or *pousadas* in the country are private properties adapted, or totally converted, to guest use. Government supervised, the network comes under an inclusive heading of *turismo de habitação*, or more lately *turismo no espaço rural* (tourism in the country). The range includes centuries-old manor houses – variously described as *paço*, palace, *quinta* or estate, *solar* a manor house in the north, *monte* an Alentejo property, *casa* – a house – modern lodging, farmhouses, mills. All have bathrooms. Some are owner-occupied; most are not. You can book directly or through owner-associations whom you can contact for lists and prices.

These are:

Solares de Portugal Turihab (Assoc. de Turismo de Habitação), Praça da República, 4990 Ponte de Lima. Tel: (058) 942729 or 741672, fax: (058) 741444. Strong on northern *Casas Antigas*, *Quintas* and *Casas Rústicas*.

PIT (Promoções e Ideias Turísticas), Rua Frederico Arouca, 72–2F, 2750 Cascais. Tel: (01) 4844464 or 4844207, fax: (01) 4842901. Country-wide representation.

PREVITUR (Assoc. Portuguesa de Turismo de Habitação), Rua João Penha,10, 1200 Lisboa. Tel: (01) 690549, fax: (01) 688115.

ANTER (Assoc. Nacional de Turismo no Espaço Rural), Quinta do Campo, Valado dos Frades, 2450 Nazar. Tel: (062) 47135 or 47126, fax: (062) 47555.

Manor houses which are mentioned in the chapter on "Pousadas and Manor Houses" are listed below, in alphabetical order:

Casa das Torres, Lugar de Arribão, 4990 Ponte de Lima. Tel: (058) 941369 or 823779.

Casa de Barreiro, Largo das Escolas, 6095 Alpedrinha. Tel: (075) 57120.

Casa de Crasto, Lugar de Crasto Ribeira, Ponte de Lima. Tel: (058) 941156.

Casa de Pedra, Rua das Pedras Negras, 16, 2000 Santarém. Tel: (043) 75754.

Casa de Peixinhos, 7160 Vila Viçosa. Tel: (068) 98472 or 98859.

Casa de Sezim, Apartado 410, 4800 Guimarães. Tel: (053) 523000 or 523196, fax: (053) 523196.

Casa de Terena, Rua Direita, 45, 7250 Alandroal. Tel: (068) 45188 or 45132, fax: (068) 45155.

Casa do Adro, Eiro-Soajo, 4970 Arcos de Valdevez. Tel: (058) 67327 or (053) 973477.

Casa do Antepaço, Lugar do Antepaço, 4990 Ponte de Lima. Tel: (058) 941702.

Casa do Outeiro, Lugar do Outeiro, 4990 Ponte de Lima. Tel: (058) 941206.

Casa dos Cedros, Azoia de Cima, 2025 Alcanade. Tel: (01) 800986.

Casas de Cruzeiro, 6270 Sabugeiro. Tel: (038) 22825, fax: (038) 23243.

Herdade Dom Pedro, Terena, 7250 Alandroal. Tel: (068) 45137.

Moinho de Estorãos (contact Solares de Portugal–*see above*).

Paço de Calheiros, Calheiros, 4990 Ponte de Lima. Tel: (058) 947164.

Pátio do Salóio, Rua Padre Amaro Teixeira, Azevedo, 14, Várzea, 2710 Sintra. Tel: (01) 9241520.

Quinta da Capela, Estrada de Monserrate, 2710 Sintra. Tel: (01) 9290170.

Quinta da Sobreira, Vale de Figueira, 2000 Santarém. Tel: (043) 420221 or (01) 3424733.

Quinta de Benatrite, PO Box 17, Santa Bárbara da Nexe, 8000 Faro. Telephone and fax: (089) 90450.

Quinta de São Thiago, Estrada de Monserrate, 2710 Sintra. Tel: (01) 9232923.

Quinta do Caracol, São Pedro, 8800 Tavira. Tel: (081) 22475, fax: (081) 23175.

Quinta do Paço d'Anha, Lugar de Penedos, 4900 Viana do Castelo. Tel: (058) 322459, fax: (058) 323904.

Quinta do Rio Alcaide, 2480 Porto de Mós. Tel: (044) 402124.

Vila Hostilina, 5100 Lamego. Telephone and fax: (054) 62394.

FOOD DIGEST

WHAT TO EAT

Portuguese food is simple and fresh, abundant and filling. Portuguese rely on hearty basics; few complicated sauces, but broad flavours and lots of garlic, olive oil and herbs. Canned and frozen foods are scorned. Portions are more than filling, and you'll often have to work hard to clean your plate.

Soup is made especially well in Portugal. Perhaps the best – certainly the most famous – is the traditional *caldo verde*, a kale and potato purée with a piece of *chouriço* (sausage) in every bowl. For garlic lovers, there's *açorda à alentejana*, a bread-thickened garlic broth with egg. *Canja* is chicken soup; *sopa de mariscos* is a seafood chowder; both are mouth-watering.

Fish, of course, is abundant. *Bacalhau* (codfish) is a national obsession. There are, supposedly, 365 ways to prepare it, and almost every restaurant features at least one of the ways. Shellfish ranges from the miniature clam-like *conquilhas*, to lobster and everything in between including snails, squid and octopus.

Carne de porco à alentejana (clams and pork with coriander) is a favourite meat dish. So is *cozida à portuguesa*, a stew. Other popular meats are goat, rabbit, suckling pig and chicken.

The Portuguese make wonderful regional cheese. Try *queijo da serra*, from Serra da Estrêla, in northern Portugal. While the real stuff is difficult to get in Lisbon, there is no shortage of *queijo tipo serra*, its imitation.

Desserts are at times excessively sweet. They include *arroz doce* (rice pudding), flan (custard), mousse (at its best when it is homemade and thicker than the French variety), and a wide selection of pastries and cakes.

Portuguese meal times are relaxed: lunch is anywhere between 1 and 3pm; dinner is usually between 8 and 9.30pm. The following is a short list of regional specialities.

IN THE NORTH

COIMBRA & AVEIRO

Chanfana (kid stew); *leitão* (roast suckling pig); *pasteis de Tentugal* and *pasteis de Santa Clara* (pastries).

DOURO & MINHO

Port and *vinho verde* (white and red); *Tripas a moda do porto* (tripe with butter beans).

SERRA DA ESTRÉLA

Queijo da serra (serra cheese); roasted kid; varieties of sausage.

TRÁS-OS-MONTES

Alheiras (flour sausage); *chouriços de sangue* (blood sausage); *feijoada* (bean stew); veal; goat; rabbit; trout; lamprey.

IN THE SOUTH

ALENTEJO

Açorda de alhos and/or *de coentros* (a bread soaked in broth heavily spiced with garlic and/or coriander); *carne de porco à alentejana* (clams and pork with coriander); lamb dishes.

ALGARVE

Ameijoas na cataplana(clams with ham and sausage, spiced with parsley and pepper); fried sardines; snails; seafood in general.

WHERE TO EAT

Restaurants are rated on a scale of one to four, depending on expense, decor and service. The quality of food does not necessarily relate to the rating; there are plenty of great 1- and 2-star neighbourhood places. Here are a few recommended restaurants (some in hotels). There are, of course, many more. The *pousada* dining rooms are of consistently high quality (and are usually expensive).

LISBON

It is wise to reserve at the more expensive restaurants, especially at weekends.

EXPENSIVE

Avis, Rua Serpa Pinto, 12b. Tel: (01) 342 atmosphere, international menu.

Casa da Comida, Travessa das Amorei (01) 3885376.

Casa do Leão (in St Jorge castle). Tel: (01) 875962. Lunch – and tea – only, but a grand view.

Conventual, Praça das Flores, 45. Tel: (01) 609106. Pleasant decor, good food with interesting sweets.

Escorial, Rua das Portas de Santo Antão, 47. Tel: (01) 3464429. Shellfish specialities.

Gambrinus, Rua das Portas de Santo Antão, 25. Tel: (01) 3421466. Favourite of old families, famous for its seafood.

Tágide, Largo Academia das Belas Artes. Tel: (01) 3460570. Blue-and-white tiled setting, and a view. Food is international and Portuguese.

Tavares Rico, Rua da Misericórdia, 37. Tel: (01) 3470906. Lisbon's oldest and most sumptuous restaurant.

MODERATE

Adega do Tia Matilde, Rua do Beneficência, 77. Tel: (01) 7972172.

Casa Transmontana, Calçada do Duque, 39. Tel: (01) 2073270.

Pap' Açorda, Rua da Atalaia, 57 (in the Bairro Alto). Tel: (01) 3464811.

Pile ou Face, Rua Barroca, 17 (in the Bairro Alto). Tel: (01) 3422345. Smart, soothing; international food.

Porto de Abrigo, Rua dos Remolares, 18. Tel: (01) 3460873.

Xele Bananas, Praça das Flores, 29. Tel: (01) 3952515.

INEXPENSIVE

Bota Alta, Travessa da Queimada. Tel: (01) 3427959. Popular restaurant in the Bairro Alto.

Bomjardin, Travessa de Santo Antão. Tel: (01) 3424389. To some tastes, the best roast chicken in town.

Casa do Alentejo, Rua das Portas de Santo Antão, 58. Tel: (01) 3428011. Huge Alentejo meals in lavishly tiled dining rooms.

Cervejaria da Trindade, Rua Nova da Trindade, 20c. Tel: (01) 3423506. Classical wall-to-wall tiles – a large and very popular restaurant. Go early at weekends.

Malmequer Bemmequer, Largo de São Miguel. Tel: (01) 876535. In the heart of the Alfama.

O Bichano, Rua Atalaia, 78. Tiny place in the Bairro Alto.

Solar dos Presuntos, Portas de Santo Antão, 150. Tel: (01) 3424253. Hearty Minho food in the street-of-many-restaurants.

Sol Dourado, Rua Jardim do Regador, 19–25 (off Restauradores). Tel: (01) 3472570. Cheerful setting, tasty food.

Tasca do Manel, Rua da Barroca, 24. Another Bairro Alto favourite.

BRAGA

A Narcisa, Largo 1º de Maio, 2. Tel: (053) 22948. Charming, moderately priced.
Hotel do Elevador, Bom Jesus do Monte. Tel: (053) 676548 or 676607, fax: (053) 676679. Up at the sanctuary, excellent regional cuisine. Stay in comfort, too.
Inacio, Campo das Hortas, 4. Tel: (053) 613235. Regional, very pleasant.

BRAGANÇA

Hotel Bragança, Avenida Sá Carneiro. Tel: (073) 22578. Classy and varied.
Lá em Casa, Rua Marquês de Pombal. Tel: (073) 22111. Regional cooking.
Solar Bragançano, Praça da Fé, 34. Tel: (073) 23875. Small and popular.

SOUTH OF BRAGANÇA

A Lareira, Avenida Nossa Senhora do Caminho, Mogadouro. A large restaurant in a small town, it's owned by a French-trained chef. Excellent value.
Estalagem do Caçador, Largo Manuel Pinto de Azevedo, Macedo de Cavaleiras. Tel: (078) 421356, fax: (078) 421381. Good food in delightful Trás-os-Montes inn.
Hotel Aquae Flavia, Praça do Brasil, 5400 Chaves. Tel: (076) 26711, fax: (076) 26497. Modern, on the riverfront, this is *presunto* country.

OPORTO

Gambamar, Rua Campo Alegre, 110. Tel: (02) 6067604. Informal, very pleasant, excellent seafood.
Green's, Rua Padre Luis Cabral, 1086, Foz de Douro. Tel: (02) 6815704. Smart restaurant (a disco is here, too) in smart suburb.
João Ratão, Rua Tomás Ribeiro, 171, Matosinhos. Tel: (02) 9378941. Good atmosphere and food, moderate prices.
Portucale, Rua da Alegria, 598. Tel: (02) 570717. High class restaurant with a panoramic view.
Bébobos, Cais da Ribeira, 24. Tel: (02) 313565. Moderately priced.

NORTH OF OPORTO

Estalagem da Boega, Quinta do Outeiro, Gondarem, near Vila Nova da Cerveira. Tel: (051) 795248 or 795231. Distinguished Minho cuisine. Best to book.

VIANA DO CASTELO

Os Três Potes, Rua Beco dos Fornos, 9. Tel: (058) 829928. Traditional ambience, regional food, reasonable price.
The hilltop **Hotel de Santa Luzia** has international food and a grand view.

VISEU

Trave Negra, Rua dos Loureiros. Tel: (032) 26138. Roast kid and trout on a regional menu.

AVEIRO

A Cozinho do Rei, Hotel Afonso V, Rua Dr Manuel das Neves, 65. Tel: (034) 26802. Expensive, but the freshest of fish, and eels, from the lagoon.
Centenário, Praça do Mercado. Tel: (034) 22798. Portuguese cooking, moderate.
Imperial, Rua Dr Nascimento Leitão (in hotel of the same name). Tel: (034) 22141. Very good, but expensive.
The old district bounded by the canals has several small restaurants.

COIMBRA

O Alfredo, Avenida João das Regras (south of the river). Tel: (039) 441522. Seafood, regional cooking. Moderate .
Marquês de Marialva, Cantanhede (about 21 km northwest of Coimbra). Tel: (039) 420010. Varied cuisine, expensive.
Panorâmica, Penacova (about 23 km/14 miles northeast of Coimbra). Tel: (039) 477333.
Real das Canas, Vila Mendes, 7 Santa Clara. Tel: (039) 814877. South of the river, good food and view, very popular.

SERRA DA ESTÉLA

Estrela, Santa Cruz, Gouveia. Tel: (038) 42171. Modest and moderate in pleasant mountain town.
Hotel de Turismo, Guarda. Tel: (071) 212202, fax: (071) 212204. Well-maintained old hotel with good cooking and service.
O Camelo, Seia. On the main street. Large, with a pleasant atmosphere and good food. Moderate.
Solneve, (downstairs in the central Residencial of the same name), Rua Visconde de Coriscada, 126, Covilhã. Telephone and fax: (075) 323001. Large and cheerful regional restaurant; inexpensive.

NEAR TOMAR

Estalagem Vale da Ursa Cernache do Bonjardim (overlooking the Castelo do Bode dam lake). Tel: (074) 90981, fax: (074) 90982. Good regional cooking, and a grand view of the lake.

SINTRA

Hotel Palácio de Seteais, Estrada de Monserrate. Tel: (01) 9233200. Marvellous style, frescoed walls, a good meal, moderate to expensive.
Solar de São Pedro, Praça Dom Fernando II (in the village of São Pedro). Tel: (01) 9231860. Very popular regional food. Packed during fairs.

ÉVORA

The Portuguese favourite for classical regional food is **Fialho's** in Travessa das Mascarenhas, 14 (tel: 066-23079) although it's not cheap. Other restaurants include: **Lagoa**, Rua Cândido dos Reis (tel: 066-26882); and, especially good value, the robust **Típico Guião**, Rua da República, 81. Tour groups eat here, but in a large separate room.

THE ALGARVE

Almost the entire coast caters to holiday-makers so there are many, many restaurants. The best is a few minutes' drive inland from Faro: the **Hotel and Restaurant La Réserve**, the only Relais & Chateaux establishment in all Portugal – so it's not cheap, nor does it accept credit cards (tel: 089-90234). Near to Estói, a few kilometres away, is the attractive country hotel, **Monte do Casal** (its English owner is Savoy-trained), with terraces and swimming pool (tel: 089-91503). In Faro you could dine in the old town in the intimate **Cidade Velha**, small and stylish (tel: 089-27145) or enjoy good rustic cooking in the large and cheerful town-centre **Duas Irmãos**, the oldest restaurant in Faro.

Going west, you'll find many restaurants in the Almancil neighbourhood (near the big Vale do Lobo and Quinta do Lago resorts). Plenty of international menus everywhere. A popular Portuguese restaurant is **Duas Sentinelas** at Cascalheira, near Quatro Estradas (tel: 089-389522). If after a while you yearn for French cooking, **Les Lauriers** is just off the bypass-road in Almancil (tel: 089-397211) and, in nearby Loulé, there's the smaller, cheaper **Aux Bons Enfants** on Rua Engenheiro Duarte Pacheco, which is around the corner from the post office (tel: 089-62096).

Still going west, Albufeira's many restaurants include the always-popular **Ruina's**, for sea food beside the fishermen's beach (walk in and choose, though watch the prices, which are becoming steep); or **O Dias** and the neighbouring **O Cabaz da Praia** looking down on the sea.

If you're staying near Portimão, the nicest place to dine (no lunch) is **A Lanterna** to the east of the old bridge (tel: 082-23948). The duck is home-grown, the seafood excellent.

In Lagos, pleasant restaurants are **O Galeão**, at Rua da Laranjeira, 1 (tel: 082-763909) or the dark-beamed **Alpendre**, Rua Antonio Barbosa Viana, 17 (tel: 082-762705). Or you can get fresh fish in the simpler Gilberto's, right next to the market.

Sagres has a large and popular restaurant right above the fishermen's bay: **A Tasca**. Its shellfish is still at reasonable prices. Good value, too, is the **O Telheiro** beach restaurant right beside the lovely Praia da Mareta.

East of Faro, the choice is much less varied. In Olhão, delightful in the centre, there is **O Escondidinho** on Rua José Leonardo (tel: 089-702674). In Tavira, two restaurants with good Portuguese cooking are the **Avenida**, up the Rua da Liberdade on the left (tel: 081-81113); and the **O Canecão**, near the market and the river (tel: 081-81921). For dinner, on the river's east bank, you have the **Beira Rio** (tel: 081-23165).

Further east in Monte Gordo, **Jopel** is a pleasant seashore restaurant, right beside the casino. And in Vila Real de Santo António, on the banks of the Guadiana, is **Mendonça**, with all kinds of fresh fish at very reasonable prices.

DRINKING NOTES

Portuguese wine, at its best, is superb, and even cheaply-priced wines can be delicious. (You will find restaurants' house wines perfectly acceptable.) There are basically three types of table wine: red (often described as *maduro*, mature), white and *vinho verde*, light and slightly sparkling. (It's usually white; red is much rougher.) Port comes in a complexity of varieties and colours: white is a good *apéritif*, dark red aged ports a grand *digestif*, tawny a pleasure at any time. Local brandies are widely available. Wine is drunk at lunch as well as dinner.

Beer (*cerveja*) is very popular and well made in several varieties. You can order it by the bottle (*garafa*), or the glass (*imperial*) or even a mug (*caneca*).

A small, strong cup of coffee is *bica*; this same portion in a large glass filled with milk is a *galão*. If you want less milk and more coffee, order a *meia de leite*.

THINGS TO DO

COUNTRY

Peneda-Gerês National Park: The national park of Peneda-Gerês extends over some 70,000 hectares (270 sq. miles) and is located in the far north of the country. The park is bordered by Spain, and encompasses parts of the Peneda and Gerês mountain ranges, the Lima River, a branch of the Cavado river, and countless streams and dams. The highest peak on the Peneda-Gerês measures 1,544 metres (5,095 ft) with a view of the Minho, Trás-os-Montes, and across the border into Galicia.

The lush plant life is fed by heavy rainfall. The park is the home of 17 species of plants to be found nowhere else, as well as extensive forests of oak and pine. Wild ponies, deer, wolf, golden eagles, wild boars and badgers, as well as many other animals, live within the boundaries.

You may fish, ride horseback, hike and mountain climb amid the breathtaking scenery in the park. You can also visit picturesque villages including Castro Laboreiro, which are probably of prehistoric origin; Soajo, probably Roman; and Lindoso, medieval. There are also dolmens perhaps 5,000 years old, and milestones that once marked the old Roman road to Braga.

Entrance to the Peneda half of the park – the northern section – is from Melgaço, just at the Galician border. To Gerês, there are entrances from Ponte da Barca and from the Braga-Chaves road (follow the turn off to Caniçada). There is a *pousada* at the edge of the park, in Caniçada.

Tourist offices in the Minho, especially Braga, can provide information about the park.

Montesinho Park: In the far northeastern corner of Portugal, Montesinho lies between Bragança, Vinhais, and the Spanish border. Like Peneda-Gerês, varieties of flora and fauna abound. There is not only wild, heath-like scenery but ancient villages preserving their age-old customs. Access is from Bragança or Vinhais.

Serra da Estrêla: Granite peaks, glacial valleys, and streams and lakes and boulders lie within the natural park of the Serra da Estrêla. The highest peaks in Portugal are also quite accessible by car (though in wintertime roads may be briefly blocked). In winter, this is the place for the little that Portugal has to offer in the way of winter sports. Visitors ski here, despite poor facilities, but mostly they *scu*. (*Scu* is a combination of the words ski and *cu*, which means rear end in Portuguese. To *scu*, grab a plastic bag, sit on it, and slide downhill.) The prettiest season, with wild flowers everywhere, is spring.

There are places to stay in the larger towns in or near the Serra, which include Gouveia, Seia, Covilhã and Guarda. There is a *pousada* in Manteigas. The Serra is about two hours by car from Coimbra.

Serra da Arrábida: Just south of Lisbon, the Serra da Arrábida's natural beauty is accessible to anyone with a car. The steep hills, with a wide variety of flowers and trees, and the blue ocean for contrast, are beautiful. The Serra da Arrábida provides wonderful views all along road 379–1, west from Setúbal.

A good map will show you Portugal's several other protected areas. These include the Algarve's southwestern coast, and a coastal wetland, the Parque Natural de Ria Formosa, important to migrating birds. Rural areas outside parks are also still astonishingly beautiful and rich in birdlife.

CULTURE PLUS

MUSEUMS

Lisbon overflows with museums, Oporto has several, and any self-respecting town in Portugal has at least one. You won't be overwhelmed by the size of any museum in Portugal; they are all small enough to be manageable. Some of the most interesting are the local handicrafts museums, which are not museums in the purest sense, but rather showcases where works on display are sold. Most museums are open from 10am–noon and 2–5pm, and closed Monday. Generally, a small admission fee is charged.

The following is a list of museums in several cities and regions in Portugal. In Lisbon, try and check the times – they can change.

LISBON

Archaeological Museum, Largo do Carmo, at the top of the Santa Justa Elevador. In the ruins of the old Carmo Convent. Roman and medieval artifacts. Open 10am–1pm; 2–5pm.

National Museum of Archaeology and Ethnology, (next to the Jerónimos monastery at Belém). Tel: 3620022. Pre- and medieval history.

Calouste Gulbenkian Museum, Avenida de Berna, 45. Tel: 7934309. Among the world's best private collections of Egyptian, Oriental, Greek/Roman and European art. The museum's Modern Art Centre is in the landscaped gardens. Usually one or two excellent special exhibitions in addition to the regular collection. Open Tuesday, Thursday, Friday and Sunday, 10am–5pm (both museums). The Gulbenkian opens Wednesday and Saturday, 2–7pm. The Modern Art Centre, 10am–7pm.

City Museum, Campo Grande 245, in Pimenta Palace. Tel: 7591617. Traces Lisbon's past and present. Open 10am–1pm and 2–6pm.

Costume Museum, Parque de Monteiro-Mar, Lumiar, 2. Tel: 7590318. A delightful museum of antique dress and toys. A section detailing spinning and weaving processes. Restaurant and park gardens. Open 10am–1pm and 2.30–5pm.

Decorative Art Museum, Largo das Portas do Sol, in the Alfama. Tel: 862183. In an 18th century palace. Furniture, tapestries, and an interesting mix of other articles. Open Monday through Saturday between 10am–1pm and 2.30–5pm; opening hours on Sunday are 1–5pm.

Ethnological Museum, Avenida Ilha da Madeira. Tel: 3015264. Artifacts from all over the world, principally from former Portuguese colonies in Africa. Open 10am–12.30pm and 2–5pm.

Maritime Museum, Praça do Império, Belém, next to Jerónimos Monastery. Tel: 3620019. Maps, instruments and detailed models of ships. Open 10am–5pm.

Military Museum, Largo do Museu de Artilharia, near Santa Apolónia station. Tel: 8882131. Weapons and armour from the 15th century to the present. Open 10am–5pm; 11am–4pm on Sunday.

Museum of Sacred Art, Largo da Trindade, in the Bairro Alto. Tel: 3460361. A small museum in São Roque church. Open 10am–5pm.

National Art Gallery (Museu Nacional de Arte Antiga), Rua das Janelas Verdes, 95. Tel: 3964151. The most important national collection of European painting. Cafeteria and garden on the premises. Open Tuesday–Saturday 10am–5pm *except* Thursday: 2–10pm, Sunday 10am–7pm.

National Coach Museum, Praça Afonso de Albuquerque, in Belém. Tel: 3638022. A collection of antique carriages, one of the most complete of its kind. The oldest is from 1619. Open 10am–5pm.

National Museum of Contemporary Art, Rua Serpa Pinto, 6. Tel: 3468028. Open 10am–12.30pm and 2–5pm.

National Tile Museum, In the Convento de Madre de Deus in Xabregas to the east. Tel: 8147747. Lovely museum of antique and modern tiles. Open 10am–12.30pm and 2–5pm.

Popular Art Museum, Avenida de Brasilia on the docks in Belém. Tel: 3011282. Folk and popular art: filigree, porcelain, embroidery. Open 10am–12.30pm and 2–5pm.

Rafael Bordalo Pinheiro Museum, Campo Grande 382. Tel: 7590816. Pottery and drawings by the 19th-century artist. Open 10am–1pm; 2–6pm.

Water Museum, (St Manuel de Maia). In Calçada dos Barbadinhos east of the Military Museum. Tel: 8135522. Small, with a working steam room. Fascinating on the subject of the Aqueduct. Winner of the Council of Europe Museum Prize in 1990. Tuesday–Saturday 10am–12.30pm; 2–5pm.

THE ALGARVE

Infante Dom Henrique Archaeological Museum, Faro (in the old town's former Convento de Nossa Senhora da Assunção). Exhibits Roman and Moorish artifacts, tiles and ceramics.

Municipal Museum of Lagos, (beside the Santo António Church in Lagos). Archaeology, religious art and handicrafts.

Regional Ethnographic Museum, Faro. Models of Algarvian life, as well as handicrafts and photographs.

THE ALENTEJO

Elves City Museum and Library, (in 17th-century Jesuit *convento*).

Handicrafts Museum, Rua da República, Évora, across from São Francisco Church. Display and sale of local crafts.

Queen Leonor Museum, Beja (in the Convento da Conceição). Archaeology, ceramics and religious art.

Regional Museum, Évora (between the Cathedral and the Temple of Diana). Archaeology, Roman sculpture, good Portuguese Primitives.

Sacred Art Museum, Évora (in the Cathedral). Old costumes, intricate embroidery, silver pieces, sculpture.

COIMBRA & SURROUNDINGS

Abraham Zacuto Luso-Hebraic Museum, Tomar (in the old synagogue).

Grão Vasco Museum, Viseu (next to the Cathedral). A collection of mainly 16th-century paintings.

Machado de Castro National Museum, Largo de Dr José Rodrigues, Coimbra. Important collection of sculpture; Roman galleries.

Museum of Aveiro, Convento de Jesus, Rua Santa Joana Princesa.

Museum of Conímbriga Archaeological Site. Pieces from and explanation of the Roman ruins.

Regional Museum of Avade de Baçal, Rua Conselheiro Abilio Beça, Bragança. A stimulating collection started by a scholarly abbot.

Regional Museum, Guarda (in the old Paço Episcopal). Archaeology, painting, sculpture.

MINHO & DOURO

Alberto Sampaio Regional Museum, Guimarães (in the annex to the Church of Nossa Senhora da Oliveira). 14th-19th century art.

Braga City Museum, Regional art and history in the Palácio dos Biscainhos.

Dom Diogo de Sousa Museum, Braga. Roman Archaeology.

Martins Sarmento Museum, Guimarães (in a former convent). Archaeology; modern and contemporary art.

Sacred Art Museum, Braga (in the Cathedral). Beautiful tiles, sculpture, religious costume, jewellery and other objects in rather musty rooms.

OPORTO

Guerra Junqueira Museum, Rua D Hugo, 32. Collection of art objects and furniture from the 16th-19th century.

Municipal Museum, Viana do Castelo (in the 18th-century Maceias Barbosa palace). Holds exhibits of pottery, furniture, archaeology, anthropology.

Museum of Ethnography and History, Largo São João Novo, 11. Includes old customs of the Douro.

...seum of Modern Art, (in the Casa dos ...st of the city).
...useum (in the Quinta da Macieirinha; ...e Solar is here, too).
...Museum, (in the old College of São

Soares dos Reis Museum, Rua D Manuel II, in the Palácio das Carrancas. Art from prehistory to the 19th century, including the sculptures of Soares dos Reis.

CINEMA

Movies in Portugal are subtitled, not dubbed, so they're accessible to non-Portuguese speakers. Seats are assigned, and the usher should be tipped 5 or 10 *escudos*.

NIGHTLIFE

Nightlife in Portugal is different things to different people. For some, it's a jug of wine and a night of *fado*. For others, it's a flashy disco, or a night at the neighbourhood cafe.

Portugal's nightlife is liveliest in Lisbon, and Lisbon's nightlife – from *fado* to disco – throbs in the Bairro Alto, an odd mix of the historical and the trendy and in a small, smart area behind the Avenida 24 de Julho. Towns and smaller cities – anything smaller than Oporto, tend to go to sleep at about 10pm or 11pm, and you'll find very little to do besides a long, slow dinner or going to a disco. There are two exceptions: the tourist towns and resorts in the Algarve, where summer visitors like to stay up late; and any town, village, or city on the night of a festival.

For a list of just about everything going on and everywhere it's happening, consult the weekly newspaper *Sete*. Even if you can't read Portuguese, the listings are comprehensible.

MUSIC

The Portuguese musical tradition is much broader than simply *fado*. Folk music, very different from *fado*, is a surprisingly vibrant current. Portuguese rock music, born after the Revolution, ranges from the mediocre to the superb. Below are some of the better musicians that play in Lisbon or whose albums are available.

FADO

Amália Rodrigues, of course. Her two-volume *Greatest Hits* was released in 1986, and covers a wide range of her work. Other well-known *fadistas* include Carlos do Carmo, João Braga, Manuel de Almeida and António Pinto Basto.

FOLK/POPULAR

Carlos Paredes. Traditional Portuguese guitar. Beautiful instrumentals.
Vitorino. Folksy, traditional ballads, many from the Alentejo.
Janita Salome. Vitorino's brother sings folk music with an Arabic influence.
Julio Pereira. Portugal's best *cavaquinho* player; the *cavaquinho* looks like a baby guitar and is the ancestor of the ukelele.
Popular balladeers include **Fausto** and **Paulo de Carvalho**.

ROCK

Rui Veloso. The "father" of Portuguese rock music, influenced by soul and blues. His first album, from 1980, is *Ar de Rock* and he has cut many since – all of them good to excellent.
GNR. An energetic band whose name, by no coincidence, are the initials of the National Republican Guard.
Other bands include: **Xutos and Pontapés**, **Radio Macau** and **Trouvante**.

DISCOTHEQUES

Music – in *fado* houses, concert halls, and nightclubs alike – tends to start fairly late, perhaps around 10pm. Bars with live music – and often dancing – are called "boites" or "dancings". Discos occasionally have live music as well. "In" places can be "out" very quickly. Fashions change. Try to check.

LISBON
In or near the Bairro Alto, Rato and São Bento – areas west and up from the Avenida da Liberdade – or in a cluster off the Avenida de 24 de Julho.
Ad-Lib, Rua Barata Salgueira, 28. Tel: 3561717. Sleek, chic and pricy.
Alcântara-Mar, Rua da Cozinha Económica, 11. Tel: 3636432. Lisbon's largest disco, space for 2,000, and often bursting.
A Lontra, Rua São Bento, 157. Tel: 3961083. A bar with small dance floor; people usually end up dancing all over the place, anyway. Live African music.
Bairro Alto, Travessa dos Inglesinhos, 48–50. Tel: 3420238. Large, cheerful, tasteful Lisbon decor: a disco plus.
Copo do Três, Rua Marcos Portugal, 1 (in Praça das Flores). Tel: 3952230. Live music ranging from string quartets to jazz to Brazilian bands.
Frágil, Rua da Atalaia, 128. Tel: 369528. Among the trendiest discos in town. Right in the Bairro Alto. Good music.
Inda a Noite É Uma Crianca, Praça das Flores, 8. Tel: 3963945. Portuguese, Brazilian and Latin American folk music, live. Cosy, but it gets crowded.

Kremlin, Rua das Escadinhas da Praia, 5. Tel: 608768. Same Alcântara area, lively.

Longas Noites, Largo do Conde Baráo, 50 (in Casa Pia Athletic Club). Tel: 3964331. Open on Friday, just about all night. The name means "long nights", and if you've made it to this place, you've probably had one – it's the place to be at about 4am, after everything else has closed. Unpretentious; lots of room, lots of people.

The Plateau, Rua das Escadinhas da Praia, ll. Tel: 3965116. A neighbour, costly and exclusive.

Elsewhere in Lisbon

Jamaica, Rua Nova do Carvalho, 6 (near Cais do Sodré train station). Tel: 3421859. DJ'd American music and dancing. In the city's red-light district.

Primorosa de Alvalade, Avenida dos Estados, Unidos da America, 128–D. Tel: 7971913. Disco, mainly teens.

Rock RendezVous, Rua Beneficencia, 175. Tel: 7944402. Live rock music in a nice setting.

FADO HOUSES

Fado is a nostalgic – though not necessarily woeful – music, a popular art with a long and mysterious history. Once associated with working-class neighbourhoods, it is now of mixed appeal, tourists often a primary commercial target. (Sometimes more charming, if less skillful, is *fado vadio*, spontaneous amateur singing). The *fadista*, a powerfully-voiced singer, is usually backed by *guitarras* – the twelve-stringed Portuguese version, and *violas* – what we would call a guitar. The Portuguese say it takes more than a good voice to become a *fadista* – it takes soul as well.

Many *fado* houses are located in the Bairro Alto. There are others in the older neighbourhoods – the Alfama, Alcântara and Lapa. The houses usually serve dinner (optional) and often charge a fairly steep entrance or minimum consumption charge. Singing starts around 10pm. It's best to reserve in advance.

Arcadas do Faia, Rua da Barroza 54–56. Tel: 3421923.

A Sévera, Rua das Gáveas, 51–61. Tel: 3428314.

Adega Machado, Rua do Norte, 91. Tel: 3428713.

Senhor Vinho, Rue do Meio, 18 (in Lapa). Tel: 3972681.

Lisboa À Noite, Rua das Gáveas, 69. Tel: 3464006.

A Mascote de Atalaia, Rua da Atalaia. Traditional *fado*, for the neighbourhood, not the tourists. The local *fadistas* come to sing the night away in a small tavern. No food, no fancy decor – only wine and *fado*.

OPORTO

The Ribeira's handy and fun: the **Postigo do Carvão** (at Rua Fonte Taurina, 26–34) is a restaurant and piano bar. **Aniki-Bobo** – no food, but good music – is next door. Nearby, at Rua dos Mercadores, l32,

is live music. In the Boavista area, the Centro Comercial Dallas has a couple of *boîtes*, **Splash** and **Flying Dutchman**. In the Centro Comércial Brasilia, Rua Júlio Dinis, is **Griffon's** with a disco on one level and quieter bar on another. The smart set goes to **Swing** (Praceta Engenheiro Amaro Costa), another two-level disco/pub. Out at Foz do Douro, to the west, **Twins** (at Rua do Passeio Alegre, 1000) is the place to be.

COIMBRA

A city of young people so there are discos. But, best of all, is the enthusiasm for their own brand of *fado*. Among the best places: the **Trovador**, a good restaurant in the Largo da Sé Velha, the **Boémia** bar at Rua do Cabido, 6, the **Diligência**, a bar off Rua do Sofia, and the late-night **Agora**.

The **Gil Vicente theatre** usually has a bright weekly programme of concerts and other events. The tourist office can also tell you what's on.

SHOPPING

WHAT TO BUY

Portuguese handicrafts range from hand-carved toothpicks to wicker furniture to blankets and rugs. The most famous items are ceramic tiles (*azulejos*) and pottery, Arraiolos rugs, and embroidery and lace work. Different varieties of ceramic work are produced all over the country; in the Alentejo, for example, you'll find examples of *barro* pottery, a simple brown clay, sometimes decorated, sometimes glazed. Decorations on ceramics tend to be paintings of fruit or flowers, or sometimes scenes of rural life. Fine pottery from around Coimbra often carries animal motifs, and looks quite intricate in comparison with the simple *Alentejano* decorations. Farther north, blue-and-white glazed pottery appears.

Arraiolos rugs, by contrast, come from only one place: Arraiolos, in the Alentejo. (They are, however, sold in other parts of the country, especially Lisbon.) The art of designing and stitching these rugs probably goes back to the Middle Ages.

Additionally, the Vista Alegre porcelain and Atlantis glass crystal bears comparison with the best in the world.

SHOPPING AREAS

Lisbon, as capital, has several good shopping areas – in the central Baixa and around Rua Garrett – the burned Chiado coming back to vigorous life – and in the Avenida da Roma. Two large shopping malls are Amoreiras (uphill from the Praça Marques de Pombal) and Cascai shopping, off the new expressway near Cascais.

While many regional crafts are sold in Lisbon, there is usually a wider and more authentic selection in the provinces.

The following is a list of traditional crafts by area:

ALENTEJO

Cane and wicker work, cork products (baskets, coasters, sculpture), wool blankets, Arraiolos rugs, ceramics (*barro*), traditional hand-painted furniture, copper goods and lace.

ALGARVE

Palm and wicker work, copper and brass articles, candles, earthware pottery.

COIMBRA & THE BEIRAS
(including AVEIRO)

Ceramics (colourful animal motifs from near Coimbra; elegant Vista Alegre porcelain from the Aveiro region; black clay pottery from the Viseu region); woven rag quilts (from the Serra da Estrêla); as well as lace and embroidery.

DOURO & MINHO

Ceramics, wickerwork, straw baskets and hats; embroidery, crochet, and regional costumes (especially from the Viana do Castelo area), religious art (from Braga). The Thursday market in Barcelos, north of Oporto, has lots of handicrafts for sale.

TRÁS-OS-MONTES

Blankets; weaving and tapestries; crocheted bedspreads; black pottery from Bisalhões (near Vila Real).

SPORTS

PARTICIPANT

GOLF

LISBON

All golf facilities are located outside the city.
Clube de Campo de Lisboa, Quinta da Aroeira, Monte de Caparica (south of the Tagus River). Tel: 4869301.
Estoril Golf Club, Avenida da República, Estoril. Tel: 4680176.
Estoril-Sol Golf Club, Estrada da Lagoa Azul, 3, Linho, near Sintra. Tel: 9232461.
Lisbon Sports Club, Casal da Carregueira, Belas, near Queluz. Tel: 4310077.
Penha Longa Club, near Sintra. Tel: 9240420.
Quinta da Marinha Golf Club, near Cascais. Tel: 4869891.

SETÚBAL

Troia Golf Club, Torralta, Troia. Tel: (065) 44151 or 44236.

COSTA DE PRATA

Vimeiro Golf Club, Praia do Porto Novo, Vimeiro, about 65 km (40 miles) north of Lisbon. Tel: (061) 98157.

NORTHERN PORTUGAL

Miramar Golf Club, Praia de Miramar, Avenida Sacudura Cabral, Valadares, near Oporto. Tel: (02) 7622067.
Oporto Golf Club, Pedreira, Silvada, near Espinho. Tel: (02) 720008.
Vidago Golf Club, Vidago, about two hours from Oporto. Tel: (076) 97106.

ALGARVE

This is a selection from a large number of excellent courses.
Palmares Golf Club, Meia Praia, near Lagos. Tel: (082) 762961 or 762953, fax: (082) 762534.
Penina Golf Club, Penina, near Portimao. Tel: (082) 415415/415500, fax: (082) 415000.

Quinta do Lago Golf Club, Almancil, near Loulé and Faro. Tel: (089) 394270, fax: (089) 394683.
Vale do Lobo Golf Club, Vale de Lobo, near Loulé. Tel: (089) 394145 or 393939.
Vilamoura-1 and Vilamoura-2 Golf Clubs, Vilamoura, near Loulé. Tel: (089) 302977 or 302978.

TENNIS

In Lisbon, the **Marinha Golf Club** and **Lisbon Sports Club**, listed above, have tennis courts. Try also the **Clube Internacional de Ténis** in Compolide (tel: 3882084); the **Clube Ténis de Monsauto** (tel: 3648741); or **Estoril Tennis Club** (tel: 4681675).

In Oporto, the **Miramar Golf Club** has facilities. There are also municipal courts at the **Clube de Tenis do Porto**, Rua Damala Góis (tel: 488506).

In the Algarve, there are courts at the **Quinta do Lago**, **Vale do Lobo**, and **Vilamoura-1** Golf Clubs, and at many hotels. Several towns have their own municipal courts.

WATERSPORTS

There are few rental facilities outside the Algarve. In the Lisbon area there's fun in the sun at Cascais. You'll find surfboards and suchlike on offer at the beaches. For sailing, there's the Cascais Naval Clube. Windsurfers head for the long beaches of the Guincho, further out. For deep sea fishing, check with Turismo. In Oporto, the **Oporto Golf Club** (*see above*) has skindiving facilities. Try the **Leca de Palmeira Beach** (to the north) for sailing.

In the Algarve, all the larger tourist beaches and towns have some facilities. Near Lagos, there are windsurfing and waterskiing facilities at **Luz, São Roque** (Meia Praia) and **Alvor** beaches; the latter two also have sailing facilities. **Praia da Rocha** has sailing, windsurfing and waterskiing facilities; sailing and windsurfing are practiced at **Armacão de Pera**, near Albufeira. **Vilamoura** has extensive watersports facilities, as does **Vale de Lobo**.

SPECTATOR

FOOTBALL

Football dominates Portuguese sports life. From the 10-year-olds playing in the street to the hundreds of professional, semi-pro and amateur teams, to the massive coverage the sport is given on TV and in the papers, football in Portugal is inescapable. The three most important teams in the country are F C Porto, from Oporto (the 1987 European champions), Benfica, and Sporting, both from Lisbon. Every Portuguese, no matter where he's from, is a loyal fan of one of the three.

The football season stretches from September or October to July. Tickets for the big three are difficult to get, as there are many season-ticket holders. In Lisbon, try the ticket kiosk located in Restauradores Square; elsewhere, try the stadiums themselves. Games are usually held on Sunday afternoons.

BULLFIGHTING

Portuguese bullfighting is different from the Spanish. It is considered less violent because the bull is not killed inside the ring (but later outside). Nonetheless, it is not for those with weak stomachs, as the bull is poked and prodded and stabbed until it is quite bloody. Unlike the Spanish, the star Portuguese bullfighters are on horseback; the horses are beautifully bedecked and highly trained. A striking aspect of the Portuguese *corrida* are the teams of *forcados* – eight unpaid local heroes, colourfully dressed in short coats, tight pants, waistband and stockings, who face the bull bare-handed in an exhibition of purest *macho*.

Bullfighting is popular primarily in the Ribatejo (just outside Lisbon) and in Lisbon itself. The season begins in the spring and ends in the fall. In Lisbon, fights are held in the Campo Pequeno bullring. There is also a ring in Cascais. The most famous bullfights, however, are held in Santarém and Vila Franca da Xira, northeast of Lisbon. (Take the train from Santa Apolónia.)

Ribatejana festivals, which are frequent during the summer, almost always feature bullfighting and the freeing of bulls in the streets.

LANGUAGE

GETTING BY

If you speak Portuguese you can read Spanish and understand most speech. There are also slight similarities with written French. Otherwise Portuguese, which has many zzzhh and nasal sounds, is not easy to follow. Many Portuguese speak a second language, and most have the tolerance and courtesy to help resolve any problem or query. At Turismo and in virtually all hotels and many restaurants you'll find the major European languages fluently spoken. Yet learning just a few words and phrases in Portuguese will enhance your visit.

Essentials

Good morning	*Bom dia*
Good afternoon	*Boa tarde*
Good evening	*Boa tarde/Boa noite*

Goodnight	Boa noite
Hello	Ola
Goodbye	Adeus
Please	Faz favor
Thank you	Obrigado (from a man)
	Obrigada (from a woman)
Many thanks	Muito obrigado/a
I don't speak	Não falo portugûes
Portuguese	
I don't	Não compreendo
understand	
Yes/No	Sim/Não

Days of the Week

Sunday	Domingo
Monday	Segunda-feira
Tuesday	Terça-feira
Wednesday	Quarta-feira
Thursday	Quinta-feira
Friday	Seixta-feira
Saturday	Sabado

Numbers

1	Um/Uma	16	Dezasseis
2	Dois/duas	17	Dezassete
3	Três	18	Dezoito
4	Quatro	19	Dezanove
5	Cinco	20	Vinte
6	Seis	30	Trinta
7	Sete	40	Quarenta
8	Oito	50	Cinquenta
9	Nove	60	Sessenta
10	Dez	70	Setenta
11	Onze	80	Oitenta
12	Doze	90	Noventa
13	Treze	100	Cem (Cento)
14	Quatorze	200	Duzentos
15	Quinze	1,000	Mil

Questions

Where is...?	Onde é...?
When...?	Quando...?
How much...?	Quanto custa?
Is there...?	Há...?
Do you have...?	Tem...?
At what time...?	A que horas...?
What time is it?	Que horas são?
Do you have a room?	Tem um quarto livre?

USEFUL ADDRESSES

TOURIST OFFICES

Aveiro: Rua João Mendonça, 8. Tel: (034) 23680, fax: (034) 28326.

Azores: Casa do Relogio – Colónia Aleniã, 9900 Horta, Faical. Tel: (092) 23801, fax: (092) 31496 or Avenida Infante Dom Henrique, 9500 Ponta Delgada, São Miguel. Tel: (096) 25743.

Beja: Rua Capitão João Francisco Sousa, 25. Tel: (084) 23693, fax: (084) 22300.

Braga: Avenida Central, 1. Tel: (053) 22550, fax: (053) 613660.

Bragança: Avenida Golade de Zamora. Tel: (073) 22273, fax: (073) 331913.

Cascais: Arcada do Parque, Tel: (01) 4680113, fax: (01) 4688082.

Castelo Braucco: Alameda da Liberdade. Tel: (072) 21002, fax: (072) 23073.

Coimbra: **Largo da Portagem**: Tel: (039) 23886, fax: (039) 25576.

Elvas: Praça da Republica. Tel: (068) 622236, fax: (068) 629060.

Évora: Praça de Geraldo. Tel: (066) 22671.

Faro: Rua da Misericórdia, 8–12. Tel: (089) 803667, fax: (089) 803673.

Guimarães: Alameda Resistência Fascismo, 83. Tel: (053) 515123, fax: (053) 515134.

Lagos: Praça Marquês de Pombal. Tel: (082) 763031.

Leiria: Jardim Luís de Camões. Tel: (044) 32748.

Lisbon: Praça dos Restauradores. Tel: (01) 3463314 or 3463624.

Madeira: Avenida Arriages, 18. Tel: (091) 29057 or 25658, fax: (091) 32151.

Oporto: Rua Clube Senianos, 25. Tel: (02) 323303, fax: (02) 2084548.

Sebútal: Praça de Quebedo. Tel: (065) 29507.

Tavira: Rua da Galerie (opposite the Misericórdia church). Tel: (081) 22511.

Tomar: Avenida Dr. Candido Madureira. Tel: (049) 313237, fax: (049) 314677.

Viana do Castelo: Rua do Hospital Velho. Tel: (058) 822620 or 24971, fax: (058) 829798.

Viseu: Avenida Gulbenkian. Tel: (032) 422014, fax: (032) 421864.

LISBON

Australia: Avenida da Liberdade, 244–4°. Tel: (01) 523350.
Canada: Edifico MCB, Avenida da Liberdade, 144–3°. Tel: (01) 3474892.
Great Britain: Rua São Domingos, 37. Tel: (01) 3961191.
Ireland: Rua da Imprensa, 1–3°. Tel: (01) 3961569.
United States: Avenida Forças Armadas. Tel: (01) 7266600.

OPORTO

Great Britain: Avenida Boavista, 3072, 4100 Oporto. Tel: (02) 6184789.
United States: Rua Júlio Dinis 826–3°, 4000 Oporto. Tel: (02) 6063094.

FURTHER READING

Although the Portuguese have a long and rich literary tradition, few books have been translated into English; fewer are still in print. The following is a partial list of works available in English.

Baltasar and Blimvada, by José Saramago. Is but one most masterly novel by Portugal's leading (and often controversial) writer.
Brother Luis de Sousa, by Almeida Garrett, an important 19th-century poet and playwright.
Fernando Pessoa. This early 20th-century poet is second only to Camões in the long list of illustrious Portuguese poets. Many of his poems have been translated into English; others were originally written in English. Pessoa wrote under other names including Alberto Caeiro, Ricardo Reis and Alvaro de Campos; not simply changing from pseudonym to pseudonym, but transforming his style with each persona as well.
Mountain Doctor, by Fernando Namora. One of the Portuguese "neo-realists" who tried to capture the ordinary texture of life. Another good neo-realist is Mario Braga, who wrote short stories.
South of Nowhere (*Os Cus de Judas*), by António Lobo Antunes. The author writes psychological novels of great intensity.
The Emigrants and *The Mission*, by Ferreira de Castro. Another modern Portuguese author of interest.

The Lusiads, by Luís de Camões. An epic poem, written in 1572, celebrating the Portuguese Era of Discoveries. Written by Portugal's premier poet and national hero.
The Maias, The Illustrious House of Ramires, The Mandarin and Other Stories, The Relic, and *The Sin of Father Amaro*, by Eça de Queiroz. One of Portugal's best-known and most enjoyable authors. Eça wrote in the latter half of the 19th century.

BOOKS ABOUT PORTUGAL

Again, the selection in English is not wide, and sometimes hard to find. The following is a short compilation of historical, anthropological, and sociological books about Portugal, listed in rough chronological order according to the time periods they cover.

A Portuguese Rural Society, by José Cutileiro. Clarendon Press, 1971. A study of Portuguese village life.
Contemporary Portugal, by Richard Robinson. Allen and Unwin, 1979.
History of Portugal, Vol. I, From Lusitania to Empire, and *Vol. II, From Empire to Corporate State*, by A.H. Oliveira Marques. Columbia University Press, 1976. The best general history of Portugal.
In Search of Modern Portugal, the Revolution and Its Consequences, by Lawrence S. Graham, and Douglas L. Wheeler (eds.). University of Wisconsin Press, 1983.
Portugal's Struggle for Liberty, by Mário Soares. Allen and Unwin, Ltd, 1975. By Portugal's most eminent political figure – a longtime president and a key personality in post-Revolution events.
Portugal, by Charles E. Nowell. Prentice-Hall, 1973. Also, *A History of Portugal*, Van Nostrand Co., 1952.
Portugal, by H.V. Livermore. Also, *A New History of Portugal*. Cambridge University Press, 1976.
Portugal: 50 Years Of Dictatorship, by António de Figueiredo. Penguin, 1975. A general survey by a former political exile. Also, *Portugal and Its Empire: The Truth*. Gollancz, 1961.
The Portuguese Seaborne Empire 1415–1825, by C.R. Boxer. Hutchinson, 1977.
The Portuguese: The Land and Its People, by Marion Kaplan. Penguin, 1992. The first book in years to take a close look at the country, its history, and modern life. Revealing, readable and entertaining.

OTHER INSIGHT GUIDES

Other *Insight Guides* which highlight destinations in this region are:
Insight Guide: Lisbon,
Insight Pocket Guide: Lisbon, and
Insight Pocket Guide: Algarve

ART/PHOTO CREDITS

INDEX